THE Orangeman

OGLE R. GOWAN

THE Orangeman

The Life & Times of Ogle Gowan

DON AKENSON

James Lorimer & Company, Publishers
Toronto 1986

CANADIAN CATALOGUING IN PUBLICATION DATA

Akenson, Donald Harman, 1941-
The Orangeman: the life and times of Ogle Gowan

ISBN 0-88862-963-X

1. Gowan, Ogle Robert, 1803-1876. 2. Orangemen - Canada - Biography. 3. Canada - History - 19th century. 4. Canada - Biography. I.Title.

FC471.G69A64 1986 971.05'092'4 C86-094504-9
F1031.5.G68A64 1986

DESIGN: Brant Cowie/Artplus Ltd.
COVER ILLUSTRATION: Jack McMaster
AUTHOR PHOTO: S. Thompson, *The Reporter*, Gananoque
OGLE GOWAN PHOTO: Public Archives of Canada

James Lorimer & Company, Publishers
Egerton Ryerson Memorial Building
35 Britain Street
Toronto, Ontario M5A 1R7

Printed and bound in Canada by John Deyell Company

5 4 3 2 1 86 87 88 89 90

Dedicated to my father
Donald Nels Akenson

Contents

ACKNOWLEDGEMENTS

I am especially grateful to the John Simon Guggenheim Memorial Foundation for financial support in writing this book. The Virginia Center for the Creative Arts, the Corporation of Yaddo, the Tyrone Guthrie Centre, Annaghmakerrig, County Monaghan, and the Australian National University provided facilities and an encouraging environment when it was most needed. The Social Sciences and Humanities Research Council for Canada, and the Advisory Research Committee of Queen's University generously provided funds for research.

ALSO BY DONALD HARMAN AKENSON

HISTORY
Being Had: Historians, Evidence, and the Irish in North America
The Irish in Ontario: A Study in Rural History
A Protestant in Purgatory: Richard Whately, Archbishop of Dublin
Between Two Revolutions: Islandmagee, Co., Antrim, 1798-1920
Local Poets and Social History: James Orr, Bard of Ballycarry, with W.H. Crawford
A Mirror to Kathleen's Face: Education in Independent Ireland, 1922-1960
The United States and Ireland
Education and Enmity: The Control of Schooling in Northern Ireland, 1920-1950
The Church of Ireland: Ecclesiastical Reform and Revolution, 1800-1885
The Irish Education Experiment: The National System of Education in the Nineteenth Century

FICTION:
Brotherhood Week in Belfast
The Lazar House Notebooks

Preface

Roland Barthes once wrote that "the historian's tactic of writing only assertive statements, rather than dealing with what did not happen or what might have happened, is akin to the repressive stance of psychotic or schizophrenic discourse." I think that what he meant was (among other things) that even though one does not know everything about an historical person or event, one still has the right to speculate sensibly about things, and, if possible, have a little fun along the way.

Ogle R. Gowan first crossed my path when I was working on a book called *The Irish in Ontario: A Study in Rural History* (1984). Almost single-handedly, he broke the Family Compact in eastern Ontario and he was fascinating to watch. In many ways he behaved like a thug, and at times he had the cultural predilections of a Goth, but that was refreshing: amidst all the smugness of the United Empire Loyalist world, it was interesting to encounter a *mensch*. Of course I had encountered the Gowan family in the Old World. They were one of those Anglo-Irish families whose war with the Catholics was, literally, to the knife. In their Canadian incarnation, the Gowans were remarkably upwardly-mobile, counting in their clan Sir James Gowan, the great law-giver of the nineteenth century, Howard Ferguson, Tory premier of Ontario, and Emily Gowan Ferguson Murphy, Canadian feminist pioneer.

The family's Canadian founder, Ogle R. Gowan, hobnobbed with John A. Macdonald in the days before Macdonald became a big time operator, went head-to-head with William Lyon Mackenzie, pounded on the desk of Egerton Ryerson, and was a longtime object of the hatred of George Brown of the *Globe*. A fascinating man, but Ogle R. Gowan remains chiefly an offstage persona, a figure who pops in and out of numerous stories, but never is given the spotlight. He certainly deserves a full conventional biography, but he never will have one: he left too few papers to make that possible. He is the kind of high-risk subject that historians usually avoid and, as Barthes so shrewdly realized, we thereby impair the range and richness of our discipline. I have tried to make everything in this fictionalized biography consistent with the known facts, but most of the dialogue, several of the settings, and some of the interstitial events are fiction. My historical sources are discussed in the Afterword.

Unlike his notable descendants, Ogle R. Gowan was not respectable, desperately though he wished to be. But socially marginal though he was, he stood four-square behind the constitutional and governmental forms that were quintessentially English-Canadian. At his apogee he had an enormous influence. He planted the seeds of the National Policy with John A. Macdonald, was way ahead of his time on Confederation, and, as much by accident as by design, helped lay the foundation for the conservative coalition of interests that has so long endured in Canadian politics. He used his influence to inculcate the loyalism, constitutionalism, and deference to state authority that is the hallmark of the modern Canadian polity. Gowan illustrates the unhappy fact that the origin of state power in this country is not found only in high philosophic notions, such as justice and natural law, but in the successful attempt of one group of Canadians to shaft another.

The life of Ogle Gowan also reminds us that what passes for the history of English Canada in the nineteenth century is not primarily Canadian, but instead is necessarily the chronicle of the antics of parvenu foreigners and their offspring. Gowan calls attention to the fact that the Irish — not the Scots, not the English — were the dominant group in English-speaking central Canada in the three or four decades before Confederation.

Hence, this book is also about the Irish in central Canada, about the immigrant experience in a wider sense; and, perforce, about the sectarianism that was such a powerful force in nineteenth-century Canadian life. That sectarianism was one of the items of cultural baggage that migrants from the British Isles brought to North

America, and central Canadian religious tensions (even those of the present day, as, for example, the argument about funding of separate schools), can only be understood if one recognizes that they are not indigenous to these shores, but are cultural transplants from the Old World. Thus, one must recognize the necessity of rooting the story of any immigrant in a full examination of his experience in the Old World.

D.H.A.
1 May 1986

BOOK I

OLD WORLD INHERITANCE

CHAPTER 1

Rumours of War, 1798

THE MOST important event in the life of Ogle Robert Gowan happened five years before he was born: the 1798 Rising.

The rising fused in a single crucible every major Irish problem — landholding, religion, intranicine terror, state-legitimated violence, loyalty, treason, law, and constitutionalism — into an amalgam whose character, like some adamantine compound, forever defies separation or even rational analysis. The history of modern Ireland in many ways is a footnote to 1798, for the Rising and the governmental response to it precluded permanently any chance of pluralism within Ireland, no matter how the society was rearranged, partitioned, or gerrymandered. Ireland, though famous for lawlessness, actually became the most law-ridden society in the British Empire. After 1798, the solution to every Irish problem was found in the courts, the police, and the legislature, and the only real difference between Irish rebels and Irish counter-revolutionaries was on the question of who would control the courts, and police, and the legislature. When they poured into Canada, the Irish, Protestant and Catholic alike, brought with them a sense of the way the social and political game was played that was realistic, hard, and efficiently self-serving. Whatever else they were, they were not fools.

Monday evening, 2 April 1798. "Mount Nebo," County Wexford.

Ogle's father, John Hunter Gowan, was great company if one liked hard riding, recreational violence, heavy drinking, and rough fornication. He was engaged in the last-named activity when he was interrupted and sent into a black temper. The senior Gowan was sixty-one years old and was living disproof of the notion that Natural Law governs human beings: a lifetime of hard living had left him as vigorous, aggressive, and vain as a twenty-five-year-old. At the moment when his groom began pounding on his chamber door, he was busy rutting with Margaret Hogan, a woman less than half his age, ostensibly a governess for his children. Gowan's wife (*née* Frances Norton of Ballinacoola), had died six years previously, worn out, as Hunter himself expressed it, like an old ewe from too many birthings. She had served as dam for sixteen of Gowan's children, most of whom had lived, and she had passed away, not from any specific disease, but from overuse, and in that respect was far from unique among Irish women of her era. While he pumped in and out of Margaret Hogan, Gowan kept one hand on his member, and endeavoured to keep the ill-fitting condom, made from a sheep's intestine, from slipping off. He had quite enough goddamchildren, he often said, and, anyway, Margaret Hogan was not the sort who should have his progeny: she was a local girl from nearby Hollyfort. Protestant to be sure, but from a barely-respectable family of small tenant farmers.

The groom knocked several times before Gowan heard. Then he called over his shoulder, "Away, damn you, I am busy."

Something was said outside, but the thick doors made the words indistinct. Then a piece of deckled paper was slipped under the door. Folded into fours, once in the room it sprung open, as if the paper itself understood the importance of its message.

John Hunter Gowan unceremoniously removed himself from Margaret Hogan, leaving her to lower her several petticoats and skirt, and going over to the fire he flung the bit of sheep's intestine into it, where it made a crackling noise. He read the note quickly and then crumbled it into a ball and flung it on the floor. "By Jesus Christ, if those villains are having a party without me, I will have a party for them, markmywords." Margaret Hogan greeted this enigmatic statement with a puzzled look, but she was too familiar with the Gowan temper to risk asking what this was all about.

The message came from one Hawtrey White and, strangely, it

concerned a dinner party. At that very moment in the county town, Wexford, some twenty English miles from Mount Nebo, a group of people Gowan disliked socially and distrusted politically, was gathered. Lady Colclough, and her husband, a Roman Catholic of deep roots in County Wexford, were using the visit of their Protestant near-relatives — the Barringtons — as an excuse to assemble some very rum gentry. The visit of Sir Jonah and Lady Barrington was a major occurrence, for Sir Jonah was a leading Dublin lawyer and a member of the Irish House of Commons, and was tipped to be made an Admiralty judge in the near future. John Hunter Gowan thought that Barrington was a canting fool, and that he would sell his soul for a ha'porth chance at a peerage. He thought even less of the other guests. One Beauchamp Harvey, a fine Protestant gentleman, was so lacking in spine that he would make a jellyfish seem resolute. Another name, that of the septuagenarian, Cornelius Grogan, made Gowan bristle: he was one of the wealthiest landholders in County Wexford, had been high sheriff for the county and an MP for Enniscorthy, County Wexford, and several times had cut Gowan in public. For only one of the guests, a Captain Matthew Keogh, did Gowan have grudging respect. There were two other names on the list, a man named Hatton and a Dublin lawyer whom Gowan did not know.

The note that Gowan received from Hawtrey White, of Peppard's Castle, was identical to ones sent to two other gentlemen, James Boyd and Archibald Hamilton Jacob. What the four men — Gowan, Boyd, White, and Jacob — had in common was that each was a leaseholder of a medium-sized estate (100 to 500 acres) and each was a magistrate of the county. Not the only magistrates, to be sure, but they were the serious trustworthy ones, the ones who could be depended upon to uphold the Constitution against enemies from abroad or from within. The four shared a bond, that of being what Gowan called True Blue. White's note summoned them to meet with him at once, to discuss an impending danger to Law and the Constitution.

John Hunter Gowan read the note and, inconvenient though it was to his personal enjoyment, he immediately dressed and set out for White's estate. His groom now had a horse ready, a large white gelding with a black diamond on its forehead. Before mounting, Gowan took a brief inventory of his estate. Mount Nebo was not the largest or finest estate in the county, but he was proud of it.

The house itself was a full two stories, a nicely proportioned neo-classical structure, with unusually large windows. The house sat in a forest that Gowan's father had begun and to which he himself had added. Most of the land was too hilly to be of much use, except as rough pasture, but the house sat on a considerable elevation, so that, fortress-like, it surveyed the surrounding neighbourhood. Gowan rode out the main avenue and proceeded at an easy trot.

In summoning his trusted fellow-magistrates, Hawtrey White was not being alarmist. His suspicions were shrewd and, indeed, at the very time Gowan and the others were assembling, the dinner party at Lady Colclough's was passing from the political to the treasonous. Against the objections of Sir Jonah Barrington, the male members of the company, one by one, affirmed that if a Rising did begin, they would be on the side of the people against the government. There was much earnest talk of the virtue of the French Revolution and of the desirability of emulating it, while avoiding its worst vices. None of those present accepted Sir Jonah's view that if a real rising came, the peasantry were not apt to accept the gentry as their leaders.

Sir Jonah was much upset by being in the company of absolute, if unavowed, conspirators, and recognized something that the Protestant small gentry in the countryside already knew: that a social explosion was much nearer than the government expected. He pondered for a time walking out of the dinner party altogether, but was afraid of being thought a prig. Instead, he tried the ploy of laughing at the subject, in the belief that ridicule will cut deeper than pomposity. To Captain Keogh, he said, "Now, my dear fellow, it is quite clear that you and I in this famous rebellion shall be on different sides of the question; and of course one or the other of us must necessarily be hanged at or before its termination — I upon a lamp-iron in Dublin, or you on the bridge of Wexford. Now we'll make a bargain — if we beat you, upon my honour, I'll do all I can to save your neck; and if your folks beat us, you'll save me from the honour of the lamp-iron!" Sir Jonah and Captain Keogh shook hands on the bargain and this created much amusement.

While this merriment was going on, John Hunter Gowan rode through the night to meet his fellow-magistrates. He thought blackly of two names that were on White's list, the man Hatton and the damned Colcloughs. The Hattons were distant relations of his and one of the Colcloughs was sniffing around one of his own daughters. The name of William Hatton on the list sparked off particularly bad family memories. In the middle of the eighteenth century, John Hunter Gowan's father had married the daughter of the rector of the nearby parish of Gorey, the Reverend William Hatton. This Miss Hatton was the niece of Colonel Hatton, MP for County of Wexford, and the family was very old, very well-connected (they were related by marriage with the Aran and the Abercorn dynasties) and very rich. Miss Hatton brought with her the estate of "Raheencullen," which was later renamed Mount Nebo, and it was this gift that made the Gowans real gentry. The trouble was that the Hattons also were people of long memory, and William Hatton never lost an opportunity of scoring publicly by reminding people of the Hatton family's generosity to their poorer kin.

And the other name, the Colcloughs! Like a number of the leading families in Wexford, they had straddled the Protestant-Catholic line during the Penal Era of the eighteenth century and thus largely had kept their lands intact. How Protestant they really were was open to question; the Colcloughs were intermarried with the Catholic clan that to John Hunter Gowan's loyalist nose was the most noxious, the Byrnes of Wexford, and this family linkage may have accounted for the Colcloughs becoming involved in radical politics. From the Byrnes family, especially the great raconteur Miles, came stories that were retold by the Colcloughs more than anyone else, tales that belittled John Hunter Gowan. These tales held the Gowans up to ridicule because they were *parvenu*, which was about half true. John Hunter Gowan's father had come to County Wexford in 1725, a lawyer, not a landed gentleman, and had acquired land largely through marriage. Still, by 1798, the family had been there for nearly three-quarters of a century, a long enough time, except by the standards of the old Wexford gentry who invariably claimed descent from the Dál Cais of the tenth century, or earlier. More wounding was the tale, most hurtful when told by a Colclough or a Byrne for its being true, that, while a young buck, John Hunter Gowan had been horsewhipped by the old Catholic aristocrat Garret Byrne after an argument about hounds and hunting. There had been a legal case about this which Gowan had won in court, but lost in the countryside.

But the greatest insult to the Gowans that the Colcloughs, especially the Catholic Colcloughs, spread, concerned John Hunter Gowan's name. Except on legal documents, he was known as Hunter Gowan (a usage that we shall now adopt), and he was proud of the name. It came from a great-grandfather, a John Hunter of County Tipperary, who had been genteel, rich, and without male heirs so that his daughter, then a Miss Hunter, had married Hunter Gowan's grandfather and made it unlikely that the Gowans, if not yet gentry, would ever again be bog-Irish. Now the genius of Hunter Gowan's detractors was that they took the old family name of Hunter and adopted a false etymology for it: that in not-long-gone penal times, Gowan had been a "priest Hunter" — one who turned in Catholic priests to the government for the bounty on their heads — and that this was how he acquired his name and his family fortune. The Byrnes and the Colcloughs noised this story abroad and it became accepted as fact. More than anything else, this slander infuriated Hunter Gowan. He had only to hear a whisper of "Preesht Hunter" from some unidentified cottier on market day, and he would ride his fine white gelding into the nearest group of Popish peasantry, laying about him with his riding crop.

Remembering these various insults to his family and to his good name, Hunter Gowan was in a murderous frame of mind by the time he arrived at the estate of Hawtrey White and was in little mood for polite conversation. The four hard men met behind closed doors for only five minutes. The only distinguishable sentence that was heard by the eavesdropping servants was uttered by Hunter Gowan as he threw open the door to leave. "It's agreed, then, gentlemen — we have been patient long enough. From henceforth we must be serious. We must enforce the Law."

What he meant by that, all County Wexford was soon to learn.

On the surface, it seems strange that this was happening in County Wexford. Even more strange was the fact that the '98 Rising was to be worse there than any other place in Ireland.

Certainly this was not because Wexford was poor. It was one of the richest of Irish counties and the peasantry were relatively well off. Poor, yes, but not starving. There were said to be fewer estates managed by absentee landlords in Wexford than in most counties, so that was not the problem. Nor was it that the United Irishmen, with their French and Painite ideas, were strong. They were weak in Wexford. Neither was it because of the residual effects of the iniquitous anti-Catholic penal laws of the earlier eighteenth century. These had affected the whole country, and had not fallen any harder on the Catholics of Wexford than on those of any other county.

One reason for this unique situation was barley. Wexford had a singular trade in barley growing and in barley malting. There were nearly 1,700 licenced malt houses in Wexford in 1790, most of them small establishments, and thousands of persons were busy growing barley. This was a cash-crop, not a subsistence measure, and it meant that even very small Wexford farmers had a chance of making a cash income, no small thing in an era when most Irish small farmers saw hardly a shilling from one month to another. Up to July 1797, barley prices were high, but then they began to fall and they fell drastically for the next two years. Worse yet, in 1797, the Irish House of Commons, in an attempt to pay for some of the expenses engendered by the war with France, imposed a heavy malt duty. The results were disastrous: the areas where the soil was most suitable for barley growing was virtually coterminous with the areas that were proclaimed by the government under the Insurrection Act as being most seditious.

More than that, though, Wexford was socially pre-ordained for violence, especially in the northern part of the county, along the County Wicklow border. This was a cultural frontier. It comprised the most successful Protestant settlement in Ireland, outside of the Province of Ulster. The Protestant proportion of the population (almost entirely Anglican), was 15 to 20 percent in many parishes, and as high as 40 percent in the northern parishes; the same held true just over the border in County Wicklow. In other words, this was the only place outside of Ulster where the sides were evenly enough balanced to permit an honest-to-God civil war. Everywhere else in southern Ireland, a rising would be essentially a matter of Catholics against governmental troops. Here, it would be a matter of neighbour against neighbour.

Throughout Irish society, Protestants and Catholics were, metaphorically at least, at daggers' drawn. That most of the Irish people had refused to accept the Protestant Reformation, while most of the populace of England and Scotland had embraced it, is well known. These choices had more than merely religious import in the sixteenth, seventeenth, and eighteenth centuries, when the

English and Scottish wars were, in part, religious. Therefore, for reasons of state policy, the potentially-treasonous Irish Catholics had to be prevented from making alliances with the Continental Catholic powers — or so it seemed to the London government. Given this perspective, the introduction of large numbers of English and Scottish settlers into Ireland was a form of official policy aimed at controlling a dangerous neighbour. And these settlers, during the eighteenth century, in turn used instruments of government to improve their own position by introducing a "Penal Code" that inhibited the practice of the Roman Catholic religion and downgraded the ecomonic postiion of Catholic landowners and others of substance. That the Catholics should hate the Protestants therefore is understandable. What is less obvious, is the combination of fear and hatred that the Protestants — always a minority amongst a hostile majority — felt toward the "Papists." Although there were persons of civility and, frequently, of generosity, on both sides, there was always the chance of an upboiling of mutual hatred so intense that it would leave Irish society scorched, as if by the flash-fires that inevitably accompany a volcanic eruption.

The explosive social situation was exacerbated by the fact that in Wexford the Roman Catholic gentry had done remarkably well in holding their social and economic position, despite the pressure of the Penal Code. The Byrnes, the Catholic Colcloughs, and many other gentry families had not buckled. There was intense social rivalry between Catholic and Protestant gentry. The Byrnes family, who took great pride in their horse-whipping of Hunter Gowan, had their seat only two miles from Gowan's. Certainly, when trouble came, enemies knew where to find each other.

Wednesday, 4 April, 1798. The Village of Gorey, two-and-a-half miles east of Mount Nebo.

The nightime meeting, two days previously, of Hunter Gowan and his fellow-magistrates was bearing fruit. They had decided to take up the practice of law, their way. Nothing that Hunter now did had much to do with a court of law, but everything was legal.

Mounted on his large white gelding, he was speaking to thirty-five assembled members of the "Wingfield Yeomanry," of which the Dublin Castle authorities had made him captain. He had raised the corps himself and every one of the lads was Protestant, true and trustworthy, and almost all were members of a semi-secret

Protestant society, of which Gowan was the local master.

"... and so my good fellows, it is up to us, the legally-constituted guardians of the county, to protect the Crown and the Constitution in this the time of need." Hunter Gowan, dressed in an old-fashioned frock coat, tight trousers, and a top hat, looked anything but military. Rather, he looked like an experienced hunt jockey impatient to be off. He wore high leather boots with spurs screwed into the heel, and a black arm-band on his right coat sleeve.

"Truth to you! Hunter," one of the assembly hollered. The men who ranged around Hunter Gowan had each dismounted and held their horses to hand. Their ages ranged from fifteen to mid-fifties, and their dress ran from the clean frock coats of the few upper gentry, down to the unravelled waistcoats that the sons of small tenant farmers wore under heavy morning coats (undoubtedly purchased second-hand in Dublin). Several of the horses were obviously double-purpose beasts, used both as draught animals and for the occasional ride. The men all had weather-beaten faces, and strong, large hands, and each wore a black armband upon his sleeve.

Militarily unimpressive as the Wingfield Yeomanry appeared, the Dublin government had little choice but to trust various yeomanry units: there were no more than 600 regular army or militia men in all of Wexford. As far as Dublin Castle was concerned, if there was trouble in Wexford it would have to be handled by Protestant locals. So, making the best of a bad situation, the authorities had accepted the "yeomanry" and thus legalized their inevitable activities. Although there were several other yeoman units in County Wexford and in the south of neighbouring County Wicklow, the Wingfield Yeomanry was special: As a Dublin Castle investigator, one Major Joseph Hardy, had only recently noted, too many of the yeomanry corps were full of Catholics and thus corrupted, and many of the magistrates who were set in charge of the units were weak. Not Hunter Gown. So trustworthy was he that Major Hardy recommended giving him a rare, special commission that would allow him jurisdiction on both sides of the Wexford-Wicklow border.

"... Our first purpose, then, is to bring to justice as many of the Popish blacksmiths, ferriers, and metalworkers as possible. Then let those Croppy devils try to find a pike!" Hunter Gowan was finishing his address to his yeomanry. "Mount up then, lads, and we'll find that villain Haydon."

The troop mounted up and disappeared out of Gorey to the east. They left a whirl of dust behind, which was unusual, but this year in the south of Ireland was already one of the driest in living memory. Even a single rider would leave behind him a small trail of airborne grit. In order to allow the small farmers, mounted on their draught horses, to keep pace, Hunter Gowan led the way at a slow trot. They were headed towards a crossroads near the estate of Squire Ram, one of the leading Protestant landowners. At the crossroads was the cottage and blacksmithing establishment of James Haydon, a tall, massively muscled Catholic. He had shown scant deference to Squire Ram. In consequence, that gentleman had mentioned to Hunter Gowan that should his yeomanry ever need exercising, a chase after Haydon would be well worth their time. Whatever the yeomanry did would be legal, because Haydon lived in one of the sixteen parishes of County Wexford that had been proclaimed under the Insurrection Act in November 1797.

As they approached Haydon's corner, Hunter Gowan turned to his second-in-command, and said, "I will wager a shilling to a pound, that the cur has run."

"I would too, if I saw this cloud approaching!" his lieutenant replied, motioning over his shoulder towards the dust that swirled with the corps towards the smithery.

But James Haydon had not run. He met the approaching troop standing full in the middle of the road, his massive forearms folded across against his chest. He wore a white shirt, soaked with sweat, sleeves rolled up above the elbow. A long leather apron was round his waist. Haydon said nothing, but stared Hunter Gowan directly in the face, an insolence that no gentleman would accept. Haydon's hair was very short.

"You are James Hadyon?" Gowan did not get off his horse.

A nod was the only reply.

"And you crop your hair short, I see. Is that to show your sympathy for the Jacobin murderers from France?"

This time Gowan received no reply at all.

"And, you make pike heads and reshape scythe blades to arm your Popish friends to commit treason with." It was not a question, but it elicited a reply.

"No, sir, I do not and I would not." As he said this the blacksmith for a moment took his eyes off Hunter Gowan's face; he had caught the motion of his wife coming out of the doorway of the dwelling that abutted his work smithy.

Hunter Gowan caught the smith's look and turned to see Mrs. Haydon. With excessive gentility, but no conscious sense of parody, he turned his beast toward her and swept off his hat in a broad arc. He inclined his head and said, "At your service, madame." Hunter Gowan thought of himself as a man of the world and he always had an eye for women.

"No, sir, I do not," the blacksmith repeated emphatically. Manifestly, he wanted Gowan's attention anywhere but on his wife.

"We shall see about that," Gowan replied and immediately ordered his men to dismount. Six of them were sent to search the smithy. These six had come armed with long staves that had saw-toothed blades attached, for cutting from below into the thatch of store houses or dwellings in search of hidden weapons. These implements were of Hunter Gowan's own design. They were remarkably effective in uncovering secreted weaponry, although their use inevitably left the dwellings of even the most innocent of persons in need of immediate thatching.

Soon the screech of metal upon metal told everyone that the serried blades had encountered something. "Captain, come and see this!" an excited young yeoman called, and Gowan dismounted and hurried into the smithy. There the searchers were busily bringing down the entire thatch; they had already found a half dozen pike-heads and a homemade broad sword. Gowan smiled happily, just as he did when, in the heel of a fox hunt, his hounds surrounded their quarry. Just then, the loading rod of a musket tumbled down, and in a moment an entire gun followed. Gowan was delighted to find such a horde, and surprised that any smith would be so stupid as to hide weaponry on his own premises. He picked up one of the pike-heads and walked outside to where the smith now was being held, hands tied behind his back. Shifting the pike-head from one hand to the other, Gowan examined the workmanship as he approached the smith. "Ah, James Haydon, I see that you are not much of a craftsman. These edges, mark you, are rough and they will never hold a cutting edge. It seems to me, Haydon, that you stinted on your fire. More heat, man, more heat is what they need!"

Haydon immediately understood what Gowan was driving at, and for the first time he looked frightened.

"Yes, MORE HEAT!" Gowan repeated, and, as an order to his men, "We must purify this smithery with fire!" Immediately his lieutenant went inside the building and uncovered the coals of fire that were perpetually banked in such a place. It was the work of a moment to gather up enough of the fallen thatch to make a keen blaze. Soon smoke poured out of the door and from the central smoke-hole in the roof. Shortly thereafter the whole roof took fire.

Inevitably, the smith's dwelling would burn as well, for it shared a common gable wall with the smithery, and the blacksmith's wife began alternately crying hysterically and calling down curses upon the Wingfield Yeomanry. "You are called the Black Mob," she spat out in one of her more coherent moments, "but it's not because of the colour ye wear. It's because of your hearts!"

Hunter Gowan found agitated women attractive and was meditating putting her shudderings to personal use, when an enthusiastic young yeoman approached him. This young man, no more than nineteen years of age, and, despite his low rank, obviously was permitted direct access to the captain.

"What should be the disposition of the two prisoners?" the young man asked. His speech had the formality of a real idealist, of someone who had thought a lot about the cause in which he was engaged. The query brought Hunter up short. He looked first at the smith's wife, whom he had just been rogering in his mind, and second, at the smith, who now was shivering uncontrollably. The smith, Gowan had decided just a moment ago, was to be purified by roasting in his own smithery. The innocence of the young man's query saved the smith's life and the wife's honour. Hunter Gowan abandoned his personal inclinations and gave the young man a most pompous lecture on gentlemanly behaviour and the law.

"The female person shall be let go. We are, after all, gentlemen. Four of my troopers shall escort her to the home of Squire Ram, where doubtless she will be given all the firm but generous treatment one expects from our local magistrate." The young yeoman seemed to believe this.

"And . . . ?"

"And the smith shall be tried this evening before a court composed of myself, as magistrate, and three of my more serious fellow justices of the peace. As you know, my good man, under the Insurrection Act, three or more magistrates may sentence a villain to transportation for life in these circumstances."

Thus, Hunter Gowan had occasion that evening to meet once again with his fellow True Blue magistrates, Messrs. White, Boyd, and Jacob. Present as secretary for the proceedings was the keen young yeoman. The procedure took surprisingly long, about an hour and a half, as points of procedures were meticulously followed. That, after all, was the Law. In the end, James Haydon was found guilty, was sent under guard the next morning to a prison ship in Dublin harbour, and by mid-April had seen the last of his wife, his friends, and of Ireland.

The keen nineteen-year-old yeoman learned a great deal from these proceedings, as he knew that Law was everything. He was Henry Hatton Gowan, a relative of his commander, John Hunter Gowan.

Saturday evening. 28 April, 1798. The dining room, Mount Nebo.

The fire was burning, and a set of candles flickered on a sideboard. Alone in the room, Hunter Gowan sat in a leather chair that he kept near the fire, a set of three silver objects at hand.

These items helped to affirm his belief that hard riding, raw courage, and severe punishments would submerge all social unrest, for they had been awarded to him at an earlier time, when a clandestine group had terrorized the countryside. That was more than a score of years ago and the group was the so-called Catholic "Whiteboys." The first Whiteboys had begun their nocturnal depredations as long ago as the autumn of 1751. Depending on one's place in the social scale they either were Catholic agrarian rebels or local criminals. In Counties Wexford, Waterford, Tipperary, Kilkenny, Carlow, and Kildare and the Queen's County, they burned the cottages of Catholic tenants whom they called "grabbers," that is, those who had outbid them for a small piece of land; they used wool-cards — small paddles with nails through them for the straightening out of wool before weaving it into yarn — to "card" the naked skin of men who tried to collect the tithes on potatoes payable to the Established Church; they burned the storehouses of several Catholic priests who were considered grasping landholders; they slashed the houghs, and cut the udders of the cows of dairymen who tried to displace potato farmers so that the land could be grazed by cows. This went on, sporadically, and at widely separated places in the south of Ireland, from 1761 until 1776 and it sputtered onwards in County Wexford for nearly a decade after that, sometimes under the name "Whiteboys," sometimes as "Carders," or under a half dozen other gang names. As a landlord, Hunter was naturally against them.

He well remembered that in the summer of 1775 the Wexford gentry had established a number of volunteer companies to fight Whiteboyism. They put together an armed force of 4,000 men and introduced a policy of publicly executing all Whiteboys, sometimes at well-advertized hangings (10,000 persons were reported to have attended one such event in a County Wexford field), and other times at "instant executions," that is, hanging within a few minutes of the Whiteboys' conviction by a grand jury. The Whiteboy bands often were of considerable size, sometimes several hundred, so these public entertainments were hard won. In this business, Hunter Gowan was magnificent, chasing down thieves and murderers, as he regarded them, with the relish of a born huntsman. And since he sat on the grand jury for the County of Wexford, he had the satisfaction of voting for the hanging of several villains. Gowan kept hunting the vestiges of the Whiteboys well into the middle 1780s, when they finally disappeared.

Hunter Gowan liked to brag that for his services he was offered a knighthood by the Duke of Rutland, Lord Lieutenant of Ireland, in the mid-1780s and that he had turned it down. This offer was never actually made, but Hunter's vainglorying was a foreshadow of his son Ogle's penchant for bestowing imaginary glories upon himself.

Fundamentally, however, Hunter Gown was a man of very concrete mind, so that as he sat by his fireside he thought of his past heroism, not as part of a social tragedy, or even as part of a small domestic war, but as something that had brought him these three trophies that he picked up and held, one after the other, so as to catch the firelight in their polished surfaces. These items were a silver coffee urn and two matching silver cups that had been presented to him by a deputation of the region's leading men: the Marquis of Ely, the Earl of Arran, the Right Honourable George Ogle, MP, and Henry Hatton, MP. The gift, valued at 150 guineas, was inscribed:

Presented
at
Spring Assizes, 1785
to
John Hunter Gowan
by
the Grand Jury
and several
Noblemen and Gentlemen
of the
County of Wexford

To be able to touch these trophies, to read the inscription, to watch the firelight shimmer off the handwrought artifacts, gave Hunter Gowan positive and concrete evidence that his method of enforcing the Law and protecting the Constitution worked.

Hunter Gowan had another prize that he often examined. This he kept locked in a small strong-box. It was private and vaguely magical, although Hunter would have scoffed at the idea of his being superstitious. It was a piece of parchment adorned with ribbons and seals:

No. Four hundred and six,
February tenth 1798,
By virtue of this Authority,
Our well beloved Brother Orangeman,
John Hunter Gowan, Esquire,
of Mount Nebo,
in the County of Wexford,
and District of Gorey,
is permitted to hold a Lodge,
or Brotherly Society,
to consist of true Orangemen,
and to act as Master,
and perform the requisites thereof,
Given under our Seal
Thos. Verner, Grand Master,
J.C. Beresford, G. Sy.
Wolsey Atkinson, G. Secy., Armagh.

If the engraved urn and cups are the key to one half of Gowan's world view, the Orange warrant unlocks the other.

Hunter Gowan was one of the elect. It was he who, like one of our Lord's apostles, spread the Orange gospel through County Wexford. Orangeism, which had first crystalized in County Armagh in 1795, was the natural outgrowth of a sectarian-split society. The spectre of a Catholic rising long had haunted the Protestants and now the fires of the French Revolution made them fear more than ever a Papist revolutionary conspiracy. Their new Orange alliance yielded a comforting mixture of non-denominational Protestant beliefs, veneration for the Constitution, and fear of the Roman Catholics: an addictive amalgam of high sentiment and low hatred. Hunter Gowan founded the first lodge in County Wexford, and, in fact, the Wingfield Yeomanry was his lodge in a different guise.

For a man with little taste for abstract thought, the Orange Order was perfect. It gave Hunter Gowan a ready-made explanation of the way the world worked, a justification for his own past actions, and a prescription for future behaviour. The Order's purpose was to protect the Crown, the Constitution, and the Protestant faith. Its "Orange" reference, of course, was to the late king of England and Ireland, King William of Orange, who displaced the Catholic James Stuart with a Protestant monarchy. Whatever had been done in the past to protect that glorious and immortal constitutional arrangement was morally justified. And in excluding papishes, in revealing the Catholics as rebels, traitors, and sons of Beleel, the Orange system gave a firm moral base to the front-line warriors of 1798.

When, on March 8, 1798, nearly a month before the capture of the blacksmith Haydon, various important Orangemen met in Dublin, Hunter Gowan was there. The purpose of the meeting was the "organizing of the Orange Men of Ireland and rendering them more effective in support of their King and Constitution" and a "Grand Lodge" was set up to keep the local lodges throughout the country in touch with each other. A system of districts was created and the structure became one massive Protestant pyramid. And, exactly a month later, Hunter Gowan was back in Dublin, taking part in the first formal meeting of the Grand Lodge. Near him sat the marquis of Drogheda, the Earl of Annesley, and the Earl of Athlone, several ranking militia officers, a handful of MPs, including his increasingly good friend George Ogle, long-time MP for Wexford, and now for Dublin. George Ogle was now organizing his own Orange Lodge-cum-Yeomanry unit in County Wexford.

But behind all the organizational matters, the contracts with gentry and aristocracy, the feeling of being part of something national, the thing that attracted Hunter Gowan most about Orangeism was the combination of righteousness and of mystery.

That is why he now went upstairs and returned with a metal strong-box. It was only yesterday, April 27, that the full force of martial law had fallen on County Wexford and Hunter knew that soon he would have to take to the field with his Wingfield Yeomanry, his Orange Lodge. He was engaged in his equivalent of spiritual preparation for the task at hand.

From the strong-box he took three objects: the warrant for his lodge, a Bible, and a piece of foolscap folded to about the size of his hand. Gowan set the warrant carefully aside and took up the Bible and read, for perhaps the twentieth time since becoming an Orangeman, the sixth and seventh chapters of the Book of Judges. He knew parts of it by heart, especially the twenty-fourth verse. This chapter has to do with Gideon, the literal meaning of which is taken to be "the cutting off of iniquity from the people," and an important phrase is JEHOVAH-SHALOM, "The Lord send peace." From this was derived the first pass-ritual of the Orange Order: *THE LORD SEND PEACE!*

Saturday, 19 May, 1798.

On this day two signal events occurred in Dublin.

Daniel O'Connell was called to the Irish bar. This was little noticed at the time, but O'Connell eventually was to create the modern Irish Catholic nation. One consequence of his eventual success was that one of Hunter Gowan's sons, Ogle R. Gowan, emigrated to Canada.

On the same day, Lord Edward Fitzgerald, the only nationally-known figure amongst the United Irishmen still at large, was arrested. The Society of United Irishmen, like the Orange Order, had begun in the north of Ireland in the 1790s and in ideology it may be considered as the reverse image of the Orange movement. The United men preached a slightly watered down Irish version of the Jacobins' Liberty, Equality, and Fraternity. The Orange movement stood for Order, Hierarchy, and Ascendancy. Both were secret, or semi-secret in their activities.

The most important contribution to the impending Rising of both the United Irishmen and the Orangemen was their mutual existence. Each gave the *other* side something to fear. May 1798 was a month of expanding mythologies, as Protestants and Catholics each developed self-terrifying beliefs about what the other side was doing. 1798 was the year of insecurity for everyone in County Wexford, and May the month of paranoia.

Hunter Gowan and his Black Mob, Hawtrey White and his "Blazers," the "Camolin Cavalry" and other Protestant groups, spent the month enforcing the Law. They did this by flogging persons suspected of being United Irishmen, in the hope that they would inform on their fellows, and in burning the houses of suspected rebels. During the first three weeks of the month they stayed just barely within their legal powers in that they did not kill anybody outright. By accident, rather than by calculation, these law-keepers raised the terror-level of their activities exponentially, by making them random. They were not full-time soldiers. Often a troop would take three or four days off, to allow its members to return home to take care of their own farms, and then would form up again. The Catholic peasantry took to calling all the yeomanry "Orangemen," and many believed that all the Protestants were in a secret Orange league. The myth grew.

Significantly, the counter-revolutionaries were themselves being frightened by a mythology. The loyalists kept hearing not only about the plans of the United Irishmen (Dublin Castle had so many informers on its payroll that an entire set of clerks was required just to collate reports), but also stranger and more unsettling reports that came, not from earth, but from heaven. The Catholic peasantry circulated a bizarre, but comprehensible millenarian literature. In tattered pamphlets and by word of mouth, the utterings of a score of self-decreed prophets were spread throughout Wexford. One of these, originating in Ulster three years previously, had a particular local relevance, for it proclaimed that "the Black Militia" (taken to mean Orangemen generally, and, locally, Hunter Gowan's Black Mob in particular) were bent on the extermination of the entire Catholic population. This prophecy was ascribed to the sixth-century Irish saint, Colum Cille, and is yet another evidence that, in Ireland, even the most distant history is alive.

CHAPTER 2

The Great Rising, 1798

Monday, 21 May, 1798. Gorey, two and one-half miles east of Mount Nebo.

It is two days since the arrest of Lord Edward Fitzgerald, and the countryside has yet to learn of that event. County Wexford, however hears of Hunter Gowan.

Hunter Gowan's actions on this day made him a local legend. He and his Black Mob were out "foraging and campaigning" as he called it. The foraging consisted of sweeping in upon any Catholic small farmer who had a decent horse, pretending to interrogate him as a United suspect, and then letting the swithering fellow go, after one of the Orange yeomanry had traded his old horse for the farmer's better one. No farmer dared protest, and by mid-day Gowan's men were looking considerably smarter than when they had started out.

During the afternoon, Hunter and his men stopped their foraging and began to seriously run down suspected United Irishmen. They flogged a couple of peasants early in the afternoon, to no avail. From a mud cabin they ferreted out a man whom they particularly wanted, for he was the kind of Catholic peasant they could least comprehend and therefore found most dangerous: a man who, though miserably poor, carried great weight in the community, even amongst his social betters. The suspect was unusually tall, somewhat over six feet, with heavy black hair and clear features. He showed no outward fear as he was brought towards Gowan by two of the yeomanry. Even when Gowan ordered him to be stripped to the waist, he remained stoic.

Then an idea occurred to Gowan: they were wasting their time beating this basilisk-like Papist. He turned to his lieutenant and ordered, "Let us elevate these proceedings, shall we?"

The lieutenant looked puzzled.

"I mean, let us elevate one of his miserable offspring and see if that loosens his tongue." Captain Gowan was referring to the increasingly popular practice among the yeomanry of "half-hanging," that is, of hoisting a suspect off the ground by a rope tied around his neck. The purpose, unlike that of a public execution by hanging, was not to snap the neck, but to choke the victim for a while and then revive him. Occasionally, miscalculations occurred, and the subject died.

"Sergent, bring yonder lad over here!" ordered the lieutenant, "and prepare a rope." The boy in question was twelve or thirteen, already growing tall and sturdy, a four-fifths sized simulacrum of his father, who looked on, and now began to struggle with the two troopers holding him. They maintained a firm grip and another trooper tied a large slip-knot, passed it around the youth's head before passing the rope up to the lieutenant. The trick was for the lieutenant to take up as much slack as possible and then, with the lad positioned close behind the horse, to trot briskly forward a few steps, thus tightening the rope smartly.

The arrangements were almost completed when the suspect's fear for his son gave him a surge of immense strength. He broke away from his captors, and rushed at the lieutenant, bellowing like an enraged bull. He tore the rope from the lieutenant's hand, but in doing this he received a kick in the face from the officer's spurred boot. That gave one of the troopers from whom he had just escaped the opportunity to catch him broadside with a sword. The trooper gave him a deep thrust into the stomach, pulled out the weapon and, as the man staggered, gave a victory wave with his weapon. The victim raised his hand as the sword flashed in a circle over him and it just caught him, severing his index finger cleanly. Moments later he died.

This was enough of a day's work for the Black Mob, and Hunter Gowan ordered the men to remount and march back to Gorey. He left the young lad, the rope still around his neck, staring immobilized, as he and his men disappeared.

Captain Gowan, knowing full well the importance of physical symbols, rode into the village of Gorey at the head of his yeomanry. His sword was held in ceremonial position, upright in his right hand. Spiked atop the sword was the dead peasant's finger.

Gowan and his officers retired to a public house and there they ordered a celebratory punch. It came in a large four-handled bowl that they passed around like some outsized communion chalice. To stir the punch they used the amputated digit.

Tuesday, 22 May, 1798. Camolin, five miles from Mount Nebo.

Word was spreading quickly about the exploits of a new group of yeomanry, recently taken to the field, the "True Blues" or alternately "Ogle's Blues" named after George Ogle, formerly MP for County Wexford, at present MP for Dublin, and now a pioneer Orangeman in Wexford. They did so well in rounding up suspects that the gaol at Camolin was full and twenty-one blacksmiths, suspected United men, had to be marched off to prison in Dublin.

Wednesday, 23 May, 1798.

In the Province of Leinster, in several towns surrounding Dublin the long-awaited United Irish Rising began, not smoothly, not, really, successfully, but at least it had started. For the moment, this Rising had nothing to do with County Wexford, for the events in Leinster were like the flash of light emanating from the explosion of some, as yet unknown nebulae: the event had happened, but the news had not yet travelled to our own sphere. On May 24, some of the militia and yeomanry learned of the events. Only late next day did a few of the United Irish leaders in Wexford hear of the Leinster Rising and not until the 26th was the news generally known.

Thursday afternoon, 24 May, 1798. Near the "Grove Bridge," three-quarters of a mile from Mount Nebo, and a mile from Moneyseed.

Here, in reaction to the news of the Leinster Rising, the Wingfield Yeomanry under Hunter Gowan committed (1) either their first out-and-out murders, or (2) scored their first direct and unreserved hits on an enemy who, having declared war, now could legitimately be fought without quarter. It is all a matter of perspective.

The first of the trophy heads taken, as it were, by the Wingfield hunt was one Garrett Fennell, who had just retutrned to Ireland from England. A local man, he was a spallpeen — that is, a migrant labourer — and he was planning on remaining with his family until leaving for Scotland in the late summer, to do harvest work. the United Irishmen he knew very little, but he had been abroad and had no one to vouch for him, so he awakened Hunter Gowan's suspicions that he was a mendicant United Irish organizer. Gowan, relying, as usual, on the Law, knew that spies could be executed without benefit of trial if they were caught in the field, so he had a rope tied around each of Fennell's wrists and then had him bound facing a tree, his arms spread wide, the two ends of the rope being knotted together on the opposite side of the tree. Captain Gowan ordered fifteen of his men to stand down with their firearms. He drew a line with the heel of his boot thirty-five feet from Fennell's exposed back, and announced, "There, lads, time for target practice," and at a command, each of the yeomen lodged the contents of his weapon into Fennell's body.

The lust for blood being up, Gowan sent his troops nearby to the house of a reputed United man, one James D'Arcy, a man Gowan had been keeping his eye on for weeks, but on whom he could find no evidence. D'Arcy, the father of five children, was simply told to stand against his cottage wall and was shot. This time, Hunter Gowan made no pretense of invoking Law, save to note that all United Men were traitors and therefore fair game.

The bodies of Fennell and D'Arcy were waked in the Catholic chapel of Moneyseed which, a few days later, was burned.

Friday, 25 May, 1798. Along the Wexford-Wicklow border, all is hysteria.

Mount Nebo was effectively the epicentre, the point around which all forces radiated. This does not mean that Hunter Gowan or his yeomanry caused the Wexford Rising. But just as any major earthquake will have a single appropriate reference point, so social earthquakes have their central assessment point also, and, for the '98 in Wexford, Mount Nebo is it.

It is also providential that the area from which the Canadian

Orange Order (Canada's largest-ever ethnic Society) stemmed, also happened to be one of those points in Ireland for which we have accurate and graphic information.

Saturday, 26 May, 1798, early evening, Boulavogue, nine miles southeast of Mount Nebo.

At six o'clock, Father John Murphy, priest at Boulavogue, began his brief military career. (It lasted until June 26.) He had signal fires lighted on a hilltop near his own house and soon several hundred people joined him. He was going to war.

Father John's first taste of glory occurred soon after his men assembled, just before the setting of a late summer sun. A cloud of dust was seen on the horizon, indicating the approach of horsemen. These turned out to be a party of the much-hated Camolin yeomanry. Father John had his men, small farmers and labourers, armed with pikes, form a simple road block. That was a bigger job than it sounds, as he was asking the peasants to stand firm against a group of yeomen whom they held in terror. The band of yeomen rode up, stopped, and their leader began haranguing the peasantry, telling them to throw down their arms. The yeomen were answered by a flurry of bullets and stones. The pikemen advanced and impaled several of the luckless yeomen. The remainder escaped to raise the alarm.

Even as this was happening, men (and a surprising number of women), were flowing to Father John. Before midnight, he had 500 followers and the numbers grew several fold during the night and the next day. As they came to join him, the recruits made a visible trail in the dark sky: from eleven o'clock on Saturday night until daybreak on Sunday, the light from scores of fires could be seen, blazing up, flickering down, then rearing upwards again as the flames again found something combustible to destroy. These fires were Protestant houses which Father John's recruits burnt on their way to war.

Monday, 28 May — Thursday, 31 May, 1798. Gorey, two-and-one-half miles east of Mount Nebo.

To anyone in Hunter Gowan's position, the future had to look grim. On the previous day, Whitsuntide, a detachment of the Cork

Militia, as well as some local yeomen, had been almost completely destroyed by Father John's rebels, now grown to four or five thousand strong, at Oulart Hill, ten miles south of Mount Nebo. Another army, it was learned, was being formed under Father Michael Murphy of Ballycanew, and this group was now joining up with Father John's insurgents. "Camolin Park," only four miles south of Mount Nebo, and the seat of the Earl of Mount Norris, one of the most liberal of Protestant landlords, was burned by rebels.

Hunter Gowan saw this, and he saw more in his immediate vicinity. Most unsettling of all was the sudden abandonment by loyalist forces of his own small Protestant garrison village of Gorey. This occurred so fast that he could not do anything about it. Gowan only learned about the abandonment of the town around ten o'clock on the morning of May 28. He was at Mount Nebo and had only a handful of his yeomen with him. Most of them had been granted permission to see to the safety of their families. (Gowan, no fool, realized that had he not granted permission, the men would have gone off anyway.)

At mid-morning, Gowan noticed a cloud of dust to the east, and thinking it might be a rebel band, went out to reconnoitre. What he discovered was upwards of 2,000 loyalist civilians, leaving Gorey on their way to the fortified garrison of Arklow, ten miles north in County Wicklow. The order to abandon Gorey, a small one-street village that offered no possibility of successful defence, had been given by one of the government's professional soldiers, when he heard of Father John's victory over the Crown forces at Oulart Hill. The soldiers, most particularly about thirty men of the North Cork Militia, were the first to leave. Behind them, the road was filled with a frightened Protestant crowd, consisting chiefly of wagons and horse-carts, loaded with women and children, accompanied by a multitude of terrified walkers, many of them women with infants bundled on their backs. Because the weather was so very hot and dry, the people proceeded in a long cloud of dust, all but the leaders being choked by road grit.

Gorey, when Hunter Gowan reached it, was uniquely silent. Gowan and his handful of men dismounted at the top of the town and walked slowly down the single street, looking carefully into each small alley that ran off the main road. Going by one alley, they set off the howling of a pack of hounds that had been locked in a storehouse by one of the fleeing loyalists. Then, in a small *cul-de-sac*, they came across the bodies of six men who, though unarmed, had been taken prisoner that morning by the North Cork militia, and afterwards shot and left for dead in the sudden retreat. One still had a vestige of life and, though unable to utter a word, raised a fist in a last defiant gesture before slumping sideways in death. In the middle of the town the slowly walking yeomanry flushed out a Catholic woman, known locally as Generous Nell, and she burst forth like a capering partridge: frantic with joy at the flight of her Protestant enemies she fluttered in front of the solemn yeomanry, raising her skirts lasciviously, and then turning to show them her bare arse. Hunter Gowan was too preoccupied with the seriousness of the situation to pay her any heed nor did his men.

When they reached the bottom of the small town, Gowan turned sharply on his heel and smacked his open palm with his riding crop. To no one in particular, but to the world in general, he announced his resolve. "By Christ, I shall not play the Protestant hare to the Papish hounds!"

He sent each of his few men to summon the rest of his Wingfield Yeomanry, leaving him alone to occupy the town. Here he had a great measure of good luck: Father John had decided to let Gorey alone for the moment, and was instead marching towards Enniscorthy. Soon, people began filtering back into the village. The first to come were what loyalists called the "better sort of Romanists," that is, the Catholic *bourgeoisie*, who came out of the fields and hedges to protect their own property and keep an eye out for looters. Soon, some members of the Tinnahely Yeomanry, who were detached from their main unit, appeared and Gowan set them to picket duty. By the next day, Tuesday, May 29, Gowan had the full company of his own Black Mob with him, and loyalist civilians began returning. And the next day, the North Cork militia and some members of the Antrim militia came to Gorey.

At best, in almost single-handedly occupying Gorey, Captain Hunter Gowan had prevented a defeat. He had won no victory. But undeniably he had laid to rest any suggestion that he was a coward. The man was hard, yes; cruel, certainly; but, undeniably, he was brave. Raw courage and hard behaviour was a family trait.

Wednesday, 30 May — Thursday, 21 June, 1798. The town of Wexford.

For certain people who, unlike Hunter Gowan, had good manners — in particular the guests at Lady Colclough's dinner party of April 2 — events were moving in ironic arabesques. First,

Beauchamp Bagenal Harvey of "Bargy Castle," was arrested by Crown authorities just before midnight on May 26. The arresting magistrate was James Boyd, colleague of Hunter Gowan. John Henry Colclough also ended up in jail. On the other side of the town of Wexford lived Captain Matthew Keogh, another of the guests at that ill-starred dinner party. He learned of the lodgement of his friends, but had the good sense to keep quiet.

Then came the twisting of Fate's loop. On May 13, Wexford town was abandoned by the government forces and one of the insurgent armies, roughly 15,000 strong, took the place, and held it until June 21.

Captain Matthew Keogh (who came by his military rank legitimately; he had been a captain-lieutenant in the army and was a half-pay officer) was made the "Military Governor" of Wexford. John Henry Colclough, released from Wexford gaol, was made a rebel colonel and Beauchamp Bagenal Harvey was appointed, by popular demand, commander-in-chief. This was more than Harvey ever had wanted, for he had been a drawing-room rebel, not a real one. Still, better to lead the crowd than be trampled by it, and he adapted to his new rank by adding to his everyday wear a set of silver epaulets.

Cornelius Grogan, seventy years old and suffering from gout on the day of Lady Colclough's dinner party, was a little older and a lot more gout-ridden eight weeks later, when a band of several hundred rebels approached his country residence, "Johnstown Castle," and forced him to come with them to Wexford town. There he was given a minor position of authority on the Committee of Public Safety that Matthew Keogh headed.

The drawing-room radicals, Keogh, Harvey, Colclough, and Grogan were experiencing the most terrifying of all human nightmares: their ill-framed dreams were coming true.

Tuesday, 5 June, early evening. Mount Nebo.

Atop his large white gelding, Hunter Gowan surveyed the smoking ruins of his house. He had not moved for several minutes, and the squad of yeomanry he had with him kept quiet. For the first time in his life, Gowan was losing heart. Was fighting the Papishes really worth the cost?

The week just past had left Gowan feeling disoriented and

wondering if perhaps he was getting too old for this sort of life. On the previous Friday, he and his Wingfield Yeomanry had saddled up alongside his good friend, Hawtrey White and the Ballaghkeen Blazers, the Camolin Cavalry, the Gorey Volunteers, and seventy-two professional infantrymen. Together, they had marched from Gorey to attack a division of the rebel army under Father Michael Murphy of Ballycanew (not to be confused with Father John Murphy of Boulavogue). The whole Protestant force consisted of only 392 men. The rebels were several times that number, but the smaller force carried the day, leaving 150 rebels dead and capturing horses, guns, pikes, and provisions. Things were going well, and this seemed to be confirmed when in two days 1,500 professional troops arrived to defend Gorey, bringing with them five pieces of field artillery.

But the victory at Ballycanew and the reinforcement by fresh troops merely succeeded in calling the attention of the rebel chiefs to the inconvenient situation at Gorey. One part of the rebel army, numbering roughly 20,000, was nearby. A large portion of them was sent to capture Gorey, and their numbers, when combined with extraordinary incompetence on the part of the colonel of a British fencible unit, left wee Gorey in rebel hands. Gorey! Gorey the Protestant jewel, that Hunter Gowan had believed saved just a few days previously. God, it made a man want to cry!

The next morning, Tuesday, June 5, the rebels sent out demolition parties, charged with burning the house of "that monster Hunter Gowan" (the words are those of Miles Byrne, Gowan's near-neighbour and *bête noir*). The houses of the two Ram families, the leading Protestants in the area, were also special targets, and they too blazed.

Thus, for more than an hour, Hunter Gowan watched the ruins of Mount Nebo smoulder, his men shifting uneasily behind him. Finally, he dismounted and in his heavy leather cavalry boots, strode into the embers, giving no indication that he felt the residual heat, much less any pain. He was looking for something specific, and used the back edge of his sword to push aside pieces of debris. He found his now-blackened strong-box quickly and pried the hasp open with his blade. As he had feared, his beloved Orange Warrant had been totally charred by the heat. Hell roast the bastards for that sacrilege! He moved next to where the sideboard had been, but could not find the urn or the two silver coffee cups he had won by his Whiteboy hunting. After poking savagely for ten minutes, Gowan gave up, concluding that the God-be-damned rebels had looted the house before setting fire to it. He stepped angrily back towards his horse, but in so doing twisted an ankle by slipping into what had been a disused window well. His instinctive oath was cut short when he caught sight of the beloved urn, which, miraculously had been tumbled into the well by the random force of explosion. The two cups from the set were nearby, blackened but intact, "Presented . . . by the Grand Jury and several of the Noblemen and Gentlemen . . . ," the words were still there, clear, and Gowan ran his fingers over the engraving, once again letting tactile sensations and concrete objects overcome the debilitating dangers of too damn much reflection. Yes, tired though he was, he would fight on.

Tuesday, 5 June, 1798. Scullabogue, the estate of Captain King, twelve miles west of Wexford, five miles east of Ross, twenty miles south of Mount Nebo.

In losing his house, Hunter Gowan lost nothing that he could not afford, for the only irreparable loss is that of life, as many of his Protestant co-patriots had discovered earlier on that same day. They were all non-combatants. Also on that day, the insurgents had suffered their first serious defeat, in an epic battle at Ross, and this had proved disastrous for more than 200 prisoners being held in a barn on Captain King's recently abandoned estate. All of them were mercilessly destroyed.

The massacre at Scullabogue was not an isolated event, any more than in the weeks before the Rising one of the Croppy-hunting raids of Hunter Gowan was a singular occurrence. The Scullabogue atrocity, like the loyalist coercion, was part of a continuing pattern and in it one sees with especial clarity some of the rebarbarative characteristics of the Rising. For example, the Scullabogue barbarism highlights the peculiar position of women in the '98 Rising. They accompanied the men in large numbers, but they were more than just the usual camp followers. They were engines of hatred. They did cooking, a few semi-military tasks (moulding bullets and the like), and they coupled with the men in the fields and hedgerows. In the unusually dry warm early summer of 1798, the fields surrounding the rebel hilltops were one large bagnio. These rebel country women were particularly acquisitive and they stripped dead bodies, wounded soldiers, and even ambulant prisoners with dexterity and avidity. At Scullabogue, the first thirty-seven loyalist prisoners to die were taken out from the barn that served as a gaol, and shot in groups on the estate's lawn. The moment the shots were fired at each lot of ill-fated Protestants, the women jumped toward them. They stripped the valuables from the still-bleeding bodies with the delicate flying fingers of born lacemakers.

The next step in the Scullabogue atrocity also reflected a general phenomenon: the existence amongst the insurgents of a high propensity for recreational cruelty. Shooting of prisoners was relatively tame, and some of the rebels preferred instead the entertainment of a good Protestant roast. Still in the barn were 184 men, women, and children, entire families, couples, lone children, arrested for some reason or other. A fire was set, and these people all crowded together, began shrieking and alternately begging for mercy as the flames came in upon them. In their terror, they trampled each other and many suffocated; others given strength by their fright, almost pushed open the rear door of the barn and there was great amusement as the guards hacked away the fingers and hands that thrust around the door edge. It was a carnival of blood. One two-year-old child managed to creep out under the door, but he was noticed and skewered with a pike. Horrific as this event was in its barbarity, it was repeated on a smaller scale in hundreds and hundreds of individual cases during the brief Wexford war. Non-combatants, men, women, and children were the victims.

An apposite symbol of the kind of mind that could produce a Scullabogue, was the poor wretch found wandering aimlessly after the insurgents had abandoned the estate. This loyalist had survived because he had been made a rebel plaything, and they had not finished with him when they were ordered to move out. When found days later by sympathic neighbours he was sitting on the ground, a blanket around him; his eyes were picked out of their sockets, his tongue cut off, and his head and body covered with ulcers from pikings and beatings. Yet, he lived.

6 June — 21 June, 1798.

The people on both sides suffered intensely for another month, and then, with the rebellion broken, some of the insurgents took to the hills and the government took to selective vengeance. During this month, there were massive battles, the most important being the defeat of the rebels on June 9 at Arklow (this blocked the insurgent path to Dublin), and that of Vinegar Hill, near Enniscorthy, on June 21, where the rebels were beaten, although not wholly vanquished.

At Arklow, County Wicklow, Hunter Gowan and his yeomanry made easy pickings of one band of insurgents, who tried to enter the town by way of the River Avoca. The white gelding on which he had soldiered so far was shot from under him and the middle finger of his own left hand was shot away. By now he was suffering from battle-fatigue, and he accepted these twin events in a manner more bemused than angry. "Well, today I lost the finest horse I ever owned," he told a militia captain from the north of Ireland whom he later met in a public house. "Almost my best friend that horse." He lifted his left hand, now missing the middle finger. "And then, if that weren't enough, I had to go and lose my whore's best friend." He seemed genuinely perplexed by fate's strange dealings.

If Gowan, through battle-fatigue, had become a benumbed observer of Wexford's painful ironies, there were other observers who were not yet so emotionally cauterized. One of these was a Roman Catholic priest who was to have a great influence in Canada, the Reverend Alexander Macdonnell. He was a quiet man who, though only in his mid-thirties, projected the kind of icy dignity usually only possessed by venerable prelates. He spoke slowly, and always in the literary tongue of Edinburgh. His diction was perfect, his pronunciation clear, but he spoke as one who has learned a foreign tongue through laborious effort. Macdonnell upset all the equations upon which the lives of men like Hunter Gowan were based, namely that to be Catholic was to be politically treasonous. Macdonnell's loyalism was above reproach. Born in the Highlands of Scotland, near Loch Ness, he had been educated for the priesthood in France and Spain and then sent to be a missionary in one of the bleakest and poorest parts of the Highlands. His reaction to the poverty that surrounded him was to find employment for upwards of 600 of his parishioners in Glasgow.

When in 1793 the war with France broke out, he offered the government an entire corps of his unemployed Highlanders. These troops under their chief, Macdonnell of Glengarry, were Gaelic-speaking, intensely Catholic, and thoroughly loyal. Father Macdonnell himself received a commission as chaplain and, thus found himself with the Glengarry fencibles, in the midst of the flames of County Wexford; his was a force of loyalist Catholics whose task was to put down disloyal members of their church.

After the incomplete victory of the government troops at Vinegar Hill, the war wound down in vile spasms, each side settling old debts and establishing the basis for future vendettas. There had been intense fighting for Enniscorthy itself, and, after defeat of the insurgents, a set of governmental atrocities took place, the most notable being the burning of the rebel's hospital, with the patients still inside. Soon thereafter, the insurgents abandoned Wexford town and it was found that during their period of occupation (May 30-June 21) the rebels had been remarkably savage. Nearly 500 men, women, and children, virtually all of them Protestants, had been murdered, mostly in forms of sadistic theatre: show-killings, sequential woundings, and such bits of drollery as having four men pike a victim aloft on their upraised weapons, and then toss him about like Chinese acrobats twirling plates on the top of long bamboo sticks.

For many, the most accurate symbol of the Rising was a bizarre and zombie-like figure, the massive Lieutenant Heppenstall, the "Walking Gallows." For his era he was tall, six feet two inches, and very strong and broad. He could lift a ton, it was said, but he was muscle-bound and, like some great ox, could not leap a rivulet. For a time he went about Wexford and the midlands of Ireland, hanging on his own back persons whose faces looked to be those of rebels. His method was effective: simply taking a rope, or even his own silk cravat in hand, he wrapped it round his suspect's throat, turned around, bent over and hoisted the victim aloft, where, after some plunging and kicking, he died.

Under martial law, Heppenstall's work was legal. Indeed, Law was the Catholics' great enemy now, and the hissop with which the extreme Protestants could scourge them. The law of treason was operative, but it was woefully inappropriate for meting out justice after a massive rebellion, particularly a revolt that was as much, or more, a sectarian feud than a direct attempt at revolution, in which many, perhaps most, Catholic participants had been swept by fear, either of Protestants or of Catholic zealots. Even Hunter Gowan had a brush with martial law, for he was arrested on charges of murder and robbery, but, not surprisingly, these were dropped: the Law, at the conclusion of a war exists to punish the losers, not the victors.

Hunter Gowan, meanwhile, was gazing with much satisfaction at a sight which was, to him, the vindication of Law and the summation of the Rising. On the left corner of the courthouse was the head of Captain Matthew Keogh, the former rebel governor of Wexford. He had been hanged on the town bridge and his body dropped into the river, but not before his head had been severed and placed on a spike at the courthouse. On a spike near Keogh's, was the head of Cornelius Grogan, an old fool in Hunter Gowan's eyes and now, by dint of a lot of bad luck, quite incapable of further follies. In his life Grogan had made many bad judgments, of which the last was not the least, but at least it was the last.

Interesting sights, but the best ornaments to the judicial building were two other heads shoved on spikes on the other side of the central entrance: those of John Henry Colclough and of Beauchamp Bagenal Harvey. These men had both returned home after the rebels were broken at Vinegar Hill on June 21, and had then tried to escape punishment in a manner as inept as their earlier revolutionary deeds. They fled to one of the Saltee Islands, off the Wexford coast, there to hide until martial law ran out, or they were lifted for foreign parts. They intended to hide in a cave for quite a time, so for their comfort they took a feather bed, a keg of whiskey, fresh water, pickled pork, a live sheep, the family plate, and Colclough's lady wife. They were surprised to learn that their flight had not gone undetected. Nothing in this life gave Hunter Gowan such satisfaction as seeing those two heads, paticularly that of the hated Colclough, and he was only sorry that the ornaments were hung high above public touch, or he would have had some final words to say into the fly-encrusted eye of that Romish cur who once had dared to look down on such as a Gowan.

As for the mortal remains of poor, unlucky old Cornelius Grogan, his body was dumped into the sea. It was later washed ashore and buried at Rathaspick churchyard. Still later, an old family servant by the name of Devereux managed to recover the emaciated head of the late gentleman. Grogan's body was dug up, and it and his head were reinterred. After 1798, the chance of joining Irish Protestants and Irish Catholics together in a supportive, living relationship was as small as the chance of bringing to life the reunited body and head of Cornelius Grogan.

CHAPTER 3

Learning the Language of Life 1803-1823

SIXTEEN HOURS of screaming, sobbing, and intermittent palpable silence made it wrenchingly clear to the family and the servants that Margaret Hogan, the kept woman of Hunter Gowan, was having a difficult time in childbirth. It was near dawn, on Wednesday, July 13, 1803. Miss Hogan, who sometimes affected the name Gowan, was encouched on a large mattress of straw, covered with coarse yellow linen, and this rude covering was drenched with perspiration. The servants were experienced in these matters, for Hunter Gowan had already fathered seventeen children. Margaret Hogan did not have the luxury of giving birth in the four-poster bed that had belonged to the real Mrs. Gowan, for that had gone up in the '98 fire, but she was provided with a useful set of ropes. These were hung from a hook above the bed, and when she strained in labour they gave the delivering mother a bit of leverage. There was no mystery about birth in this Anglo-Irish household. During the extended labour several members of the family, as well as female servants, passed through the birthing room at intervals, and now and then Hunter Gowan poked his head into the room. He checked on things, just as he would a good mare in foal.

Mount Nebo had never recovered from the '98 Rising, but its occupants seemed oblivious to its decline. After the house was burned by rebels, Hunter Gowan moved his family into a set of out-buildings that previously had been a combined granary and stables, and there he carried on as if ensconsed in one of the county's manor houses. Then he built a very simple two-storey structure, abutting at right angles the old out-offices, so that someone approaching the new dwelling from the front would not immediately notice that most of the household's living space was in the converted agricultural offices, jutting to the rear. Thus, it was in a converted set of horse-boxes, that Margaret Hogan gave birth to Ogle Robert Gowan.

The birth was tearingly hard, noisy and messy; and nearly fatal. Such comforts as hot water and towels were not considered necessary to childbirth. The crone attending Margaret was no midwife — they were then unknown in the area — but she had seen enough of the Gowan family's parturitions to know what was right and what was not. This was Margaret Hogan's second child: the first had been William Gowan, born in June 1800. By rights, the birth should have been fairly easy. The old woman, though, recognized that something was wrong. It was not Margaret's cries, nor even the length of labour that was unusual: before the development of modern intervention techniques, births frequently required two days of near-killing labour. What was wrong was that Miss Hogan was dilating as if she were about to deliver but nothing happened. She was in hideous distress and attempted to thrash about, but when she did this the old woman summoned two of the female members of the household who pinned her arms to the mattress so that she could not injure herself. In the pauses between Miss Hogan's fruitless seizures, the crone searched her memory for a remedy. Nothing came to mind, and at last, in despair, she determined, "Och, girls, let nature take its course. If she wants to thrash, so be it." They moved hesitatingly away, and were pushed towards the door by the old one who did not want them to see what promised to be a tragedy.

Margaret Hogan, taken again with labour, now rolled about unconstrainedly and finally went right off the mattress. She hit the rough deal floor face-down. "Dear Christ, that will kill her," the old one murmured and, pityingly, "Dear God . . . !" as a rush of maternal waters came forth. Then, suddenly relieved, "Och, so that's the trouble," as a foot poked out of the poor mother. "The wee bastard is in backwards." Quickly the crone left the room and returned with a groom and a stable boy. They righted Margaret and lifted her onto the mattress. The old woman worked quickly, for once a breech-birth starts the umbilical cord rips, and the child will either be dead or permanently brain-damaged unless its lungs soon fill with air. Her long, dirty nails gave the old woman a purchase on one slippery, membrane-covered leg, and she reached inside the mother, caught the other leg and, in concert with Miss Hogan's agonized straining, the crone pulled.

The chances of a mother's surviving a breech-birth in those days was well under fifty-fifty, but somehow Margaret lived. Many women in such circumstances literally had their insides ripped out, but she suffered no permanent ill-effects. Indeed, she eventually bore two more Gowan children.

Ogle Robert Gowan thus came into the world as he was destined to spend his time in it: stridently, and with an assertion of his identity that caused as much pain as it did joy.

Surely one might guess that the offspring of such a strong character as Hunter Gowan would himself have a robust personality. Not necessarily. Often strong fathers come down so hard on their sons that the children, far from being assertive, become passive, quiescent, and cowardly. There was nothing automatic about Ogle Gowan's developing a world-class Will.

The development of his personality stemmed from singular circumstances. Among these was Hunter Gowan's extraordinarily disorderly habits. He could not take the time to be sure the farm labourers cut back a hedge properly, much less carefully scrutinize the upbringing of bastard children. Thus, paradoxically, his children were left free to imitate him; that is, to be wilful, bloody-minded, vulgar, courageous, impulsive, self-seeking, and inventive. Equally important was Ogle's being caught in a complex set of binds from which he could escape only by continual and unremitting self-assertion.

The first of these binds was formed by a particularly strong Irish mind-set. Almost everyone thought genealogically, and the Gowans were no exception. The family proudly traced its alleged ancestry to the year 165 A.D. and to the semi-mythical Conn of the Hundred Battles. The name Gowan (meaning "smith" or "armourer") had several variants: O'Gowan, MacGowan, Gobhain, Mac-an-Ghobhain. The Wexford Gowans believed that their people had been driven by the English into County Donegal, soon after the Norman conquest of Ireland, and only later did one branch of the family find its way back to Leinster. The earliest firm record they had was of one Maurice MacGowan (born 1514), who was said to have been the first Protestant in the family line. Roughly a century later, one Philip Gowan dropped the "mac" prefix from his name. The family flourished, keeping itself as much Protestant and as little Celtic as possible. As young Ogle Gowan grew up, this tradition was a natural part of his education and, in later life, he produced more than one genealogical tree for himself.

It was certainly a rich heritage, but it equally posed a threat to Ogle. In a society that thinks genealogically, being of an illegitimate line handicaps one terribly. One must either accept a low rung on the social ladder or, through ability and self-assertion, overcome the gross limitations of one's birth.

There were literally two tribes in Hunter Gowan's house, the one consisting of first-born, legitimate children, who expected by custom and by law to inherit the family lands and goods, and the second smaller one, of late-born illegitimate children, who had a right to nothing and either had to charm their way into the sunshine of paternal charity or, through guile, to steal the birthright of the other.

Of the sixteen children born to Hunter Gowan's wife between 1771 and 1791, four died young. That left twelve legitimate offspring, whose interests were pitted against the three surviving children of the four borne by his mistress, Margaret Hogan. Moreover, the birth of Margaret's first child was separated by nine years from the last of the legitimate line, her four, one of whom died young, coming in rapid succession between 1800 and 1805.

Despite their illegitimacy, as they grew up Ogle and his older bastard-brother William had three things going for them: most of the legitimate tribe was female, and thus not primary heirs; Ogle and William's own mother was alive and still attractive to their ever-vigorous father; and they themselves were young and less apt to vex him than were the other sons who, as adults, had a quarrelsome bent. Early on, William took to being particularly helpful to old Hunter Gowan, and was a great aid in managing the family estates. Ogle found other ways to make his mark.

The obstacles still remained formidable for the young bastards. Granted, Hunter Gowan allowed his illegitimate children to live at Mount Nebo in the same house with his legitimate offspring: they all received the same schooling and dined together *en famille*. But everyone knew who was whom; and whenever guests were present for dinner, only the legitimate children were permitted at table.

The year of Gowan's birth, 1803, is an important one in the genealogy of Irish nationalism, and another of the binds faced by young Ogle. That year's signal event was the abortive rising of July 23, instigated by Robert Emmet. Emmet had been a United Irishman in 1798, but the evidence is scant about what he actually did. He was not arrested and it appears that no government informer ever had news of him. After the '98 Rising failed, Emmet and his associates tried to pick up the strands of the United Irish organization. He slipped off to France for a time and, as usually was the case, the French gave him plenty of encouragement and little else. Upon his return, Emmet set about rebuilding a national revolutionary network. They were successful chiefly in the Dublin area. In point of fact, his entire secret organization was honeycombed with government informers.

Robert Emmet was that rare breed, the Irish Protestant who identified with the cause of Irish Catholic nationalism. This was one way to resolve the cultural bind that confronted every Irish Protestant outside of the province of Ulster: how to relate to the Irish Catholics who, though generally disparaged, nevertheless were an overwhelming majority of the local population.

This bind pinched doubly tight for Ogle Gowan, because of an unspoken, but real, analogy: namely that Ogle Robert Gowan, disadvantaged as an illegitimate child, was, to the legitimate offspring of his father, what the disadvantaged Roman Catholics generally were to the Irish Protestants. His marginal position in his own family and in polite society meant that Ogle was closer in status to the Catholics than were most of the Ascendancy class. As he grew up, Ogle, caught in the middle, had two choices. Either to identify, as Robert Emmet had, with the Catholics and assert his personal integrity by repudiating his father's Orange heritage, or embrace hyper-Protestantism with such vigour that he would never be associated with *them,* the despised Papishes. No middle course would do.

Here his patrimony was decisive. Hunter Gowan had found a

godfather for his newest bastard whose character was to be a determining factor: the Right Honourable George Ogle, former Colonel in the Wexford Volunteers, sometime MP for County Wexford and for Dublin, pioneer Orangeman in Wexford, yeomanry officer and organizer of Ogle's True Blues in 1798, a unit that he equipped at his own expense. George Ogle, for whom young Ogle Gowan was named, was a man of culture as well as worldly importance. He had done translations from Petrarch, Chaucer, and Boccaccio, and had even turned his hand to (truly awful) poetry. George Ogle was a fervid Orangeman and from 1801 to 1814 inclusive, was Grand Master of all of the Orangemen in Ireland. He had a direct and strong impact on young Ogle's developing character and had been instrumental in persuading Hunter Gowan to keep on an excellent tutor for his by-blows, once his services were no longer needed for the legitimate offspring. In his mid-twenties, Ogle described his godfather as "one of the most respectable gentlemen, the most enlightened scholar, the most accomplished statesman and the most uncompromising Protestant that this country ever could boast of." Strong emotional identification with such a namesake guaranteed that when young Ogle Gowan, self-assertive to a fault, began to put himself forward in life, it would be in the guise of an educated gentleman and a hyper-Protestant.

By his late teens and early twenties Ogle was writing Orange addresses and Protestant pamphlets in strong flowing prose, an admixture of the Ciceronian style, that was affected by most writers of English of his time, with a crisp, aggressive argumentation that was much less common. He had been taught to avoid solecisms, to eschew ambiguity, and to use strong verbs and memorable metaphors, and his writings are unusual for being grammatical. Ogle Gowan eventually became a man with many voices — ranging from the scholarly, to the gentrified, to the demotic — and he could slip from one to another the way a multi-lingual person switches from one language to another, to suit the propensities of his audiences.

In bits and pieces, Ogle Gowan picked up the education of a gentleman, but there was one short period in his youth when he nearly was deposited in the detritus of trade. Only his self-assertive spirit saved him. This occurred in 1815 when Ogle was twelve years old. Mr. Dairs, his tutor, had to be discharged because he had turned his sexual attentions to some of Mount Nebo's ovine livestock, and people in the neighbourhood were beginning to talk.

Hunter Gowan took this opportunity to "put the bastard cub into the way of earning a livelihood," and decided to have Ogle apprenticed to a respectable tradesman. A brother of Hunter's (that is, an uncle of Ogle), lived in Gorey. There he kept a shop that produced custom-made saddles and riding boots for the gentry. He was a soft-spoken man, quite unlike Hunter, and got along well with all sorts, Protestant and Catholic alike. He had few pretensions to gentility himself: he was in trade and not ashamed of it. Ogle was placed in this man's shop, with the thought that he would first learn the basic techniques of saddlery and of boot construction, and then worm into the retail side of the business and, eventually, into a full partnership. Ogle was sent to live in Gorey.

The arrangement lasted less than a year, for although Ogle was not adverse to hard work with his hands, he could not abide the obsequious positions he had to assume towards customers. He was taught to stand expectantly while his uncle measured someone for boots or had them arrange themselves on the saddler's dummy, and Ogle had to run-and-fetch for anything required. And, at visit's end, he was taught to bow each client out the shop's door. The arrogance of the customers was scalding to young Ogle, himself an aspirant to gentility. The Protestants looked right through him, as if he did not exist, and the Papishes, devil take them, the Byrnes and their like, made a special point of giving him a ha'penny for his services.

Ogle, though only twelve, saw the future with clarity. If he stayed in the shop he could expect a life of bowing deferentially, of pulling off the dirty boots of his betters, and of making large portable cushions for their fat arses. No! Ogle would not wear such a future and in an act of heroic defiance he marched back to Mount Nebo, asked for an interview with his father, and told him that he would not continue as a bootjack to Papists.

Hunter Gowan, himself nearly fearless, appreciated courage in others, and decided that, by God, the lad had the spine of a gentleman and deserved to have his education completed. Soon thereafter, he engaged another tutor, one James McConnell, who was a well-known classical and mathematical scholar and the proper education of the illegitimate Gowan children was resumed.

Later in life, Ogle was deeply shamed when enemies threw up his past as a former "cobbler's apprentice," but the time in trade was not a dead loss. While in the shop he had learned yet another language, the tongue of the subservient, the wheedling, the obsequious. It, also, would stand him in good stead.

On June 4, 1818, when he was not quite fifteen, Ogle was inducted into yet another language, the arcana of Orangeism. That was a very young age, for most new initiates were in their twenties, but Ogle was special. Both his father and his godfather were great Orangemen and, in a way, his Orange initiation stood as a rite-of-passage, marking his transition from childhood to manhood. The form of Orangeism into which Ogle was initiated was conducted on what nineteenth-century Orangemen called "the old system." It was a fairly crude ritual, quite openly anti-Catholic; later, under pressure of public exposure, the initiation was cleaned up and the anti-Catholicism made less overt.

Ogle stood before one Ralph Stone, Master of Lodge No. 1157. Surrounding him was a hollow square, turned inward, of red-faced farmers and the odd gentleman, most of whom wore an orange apron or sash. The initiation service began with a long prayer, read in a monotone by a clergyman of the Established Church. The intended solemnity of the occasion was somewhat undercut by its venue: it was taking place in a public house, owned by a Miss Rickerby, in the town of Carnew, County Wicklow, about three-and-a-half miles west of Mount Nebo. The centerpiece of the initiation ritual was based on the tenth verse of the seventeenth chapter of the Book of Numbers: "And the Lord said unto Moses, bring Aaron's Rod again before the Testimony, to be kept for a token against the Rebels."

In Ogle's hand was placed a crudely-carved oaken rod, no more than eighteen inches long. He was instructed to hold it over a simple wooden box (representing the Tabernacle of the Chosen People) while he took a series of oaths, affirming his loyalty to Protestantism, the Crown, and Orangeism. When the oaths were done, the Anglican clergyman again invoked the Deity for quite a long time, while the impatient farmers, unused to such inactivity, shuffled their feet. Then the lodge steward cracked open supplies for the toasts. Glasses were raised to the Crown, the Protestant succession, the new "Marksman" and, as the trappings of formality were dissolved by drink, several traditional Protestant toasts, such as:

Here's health to old Ireland,
The King and the Church.
May all plotting contrivers,
Be left in the lurch.

When Ogle himself lurched home late that night, he was a fully accredited defender of King and Church and thus, an adult.

The few secret words and recognition-signs that Ogle learned were really not very important. In fact, when, as occurred every few years, some Catholic enemy of the Order discovered and published its little secrets, the public yawned. What did have power, however, was an Orange sub-code, a set of rhetorical conventions that were used in public, and which had great power over people who were predisposed to certain shared Protestant values. These included a resonant vocabulary of affirmation — Crown, Constitution, Loyalty, Law — and one of denunciation: Rebellion, Foreign Ecclesiastics, Babylon, and Rome. In Orange oratory (and Gowan became one of Orangeism's most effective orators), there was a set of rhythms and a periodicity of repetition of these key words that immeasurably influenced its intended audience, while leaving outsiders puzzled as to why the believers found it so compelling.

All the time that Ogle Gowan was mastering the various voices that he used throughout his frenetic career — the learned, the gentlemanly, the loyalist, and the obsequious modes — he was simultaneously acquiring the demotic. He learned how to talk the language of the everyday farmer, how to exchange Billingsgate with rough country critics, how to frame a memorable insult, and how to engage in friendly bantering gossip with almost anyone. And he also mastered the skills of telling a dirty joke and talking his way into the skirts of attractive women.

Orange Lodge No. 1157 was a perfect vehicle for Ogle's vernacular education, for it was full of small farmers. There he learned to talk with people whose minds were full of the weather, crops, horses; big-handed strong-willed men, who read the Bible and used it as a source of information as if it were an encyclopedia. (One recalls the tale of the Wexford Orangeman who, when taxed by a Catholic neighbour about who William III of Orange actually was, replied, "Away and read your Bible, man!")

It is easy to forget that despite the phrase "Protestant Ascendancy" there were large numbers of Irish Protestants who were small farmers on the borderline of poverty, and who were perceived by contemporaries as being well off only by virtue of their being compared to the poorest Catholics. The men Gowan came to know in the Carnew Lodge were the sort of people who migrated to Upper Canada in large numbers. In the Old Country they were people of small, one-and-a-half storey houses, two horses, a cow, two acres of potato land, three of grain, five of rough pasture, and a lot of kids.

Ogle's coming to understand the mind of the Protestant small farmer of Wexford yielded words and techniques that could be used to manage any Protestant small farmer, whether from Ulster, Leinster, Munster or Connaught. These people ate potatoes for at least two meals a day, drank quart after quart of filthy black tea, were sometimes drunken and perpetually superstitious. They were not very much different in these regards from those Roman Catholics who held the same amount of land.

This is precisely why the Protestant small farmers spent so much of their social chatter in delineating just how different they were from the Papishes: when one so closely resembles one's enemies, one has to wear a lot of war paint. Thus, as the whiskey punch went round and the clay pipes were smoked in the social hours after Lodge meeting formally adjourned, Ogle heard hundreds of stories whose single recurrent theme was: how different we are from those ignorant Roman Catholics. The lodge brothers told derisory stories about Catholics who believed in white magic, especially in unseen forces such as fairies and earthbound angels; they laughed at Popish farmers who would plant their land only after being told by a fortune-teller that the denizens of the spirit world found it propitious; they found amusing the Catholics' recourse to quack healers who removed warts by sticking gooseberries on thorn bushes, and who tried to cure headaches by having the patients stand on their heads.

The litany of Catholic follies were not calumnies. The reports were true. But they had their counterparts in the beliefs of the Protestant small farmers. The real difference was that the Protestants were ashamed of their own magical and superstitious beliefs and the Catholics were not. Rationalists in public, believers in magic in private, the Protestant small farmers could be easily manipulated by anyone who had a knowledge of their secret world.

Where Protestant small farmers differed from their Catholic counterparts was not in how they thought the world worked, but in what they thought specific events meant. The story of "Captain Grant," a famous social bandit in the Wexford-Kilkenny-Queen's Counties is an example. He actually existed and was very successful, there is no doubt about that, but there agreement ends. In Catholic folklore he had the combined attributes of Robin Hood and of that later hero, the Scarlet Pimpernel. In Protestant folklore, he was a terror and a bullying coward. The signal point is that Catholics remembered his heroic crimes, while Protestants memorialized his capture. The story of his apprehension, endlessly retold by locals, involved Henry Hatton Gowan, Ogle's uncle, who as a young lad had served under Hunter Gowan in the Black Mob. Eighteen years later, in 1816, Henry Gowan made himself into a local legend by capturing this man Grant, the last of the wild Irish rebels, the only man of '98 who had declined an offer of amnesty and who continued to lead a band of marauders.

"A great man for the pluck was Henry Gowan," was the way an Orangeman would bring up the tale. "He knew the Captain and his rebel band were in Killoughrim Wood. They planned to use that as a temporary hidey-hole 'till the yeomanry on their tail gave up the hunt and went home."

Ogle, sitting with his lodge brothers after the formal meeting was ended, would nod; he had heard the story three-score times, but nevertheless wanted the story-teller to go on. "Now, the number of soliders wasn't great — no more than fifteen, and they were under Captain Dawson. The bandit Grant must have had twenty followers with him, though some weren't worth the piss from a dead donkey. Anyroad, the resident magistrate in the area and a great man for putting down rebels — was Mr. Henry Hatton Gowan."

"My uncle," Ogle would note at this point.

"The very man." The story-teller would acknowledge this comment as if it were news. "And didn't the yeomen come upon the bold Captain Grant and his men by accident? That Killoughrim Wood is dense as rain on a November night, and didn't they just fall upon the villains? Och, and the bold Captain put a gun to his shoulder and tried to blow the head off Mr. Gowan, the decent man, but only hit him in the shoulder. And didn't Mr. Gowan not fall, but like a man with the wrath of God in him run forward and seize the rebel chieftain by the leg? And didn't he hold on like grim death? And didn't all the other rebels run away except those that were captured?! And wasn't the bold Captain Grant's capture a good thing? Praise God that he and his filthy men were executed for their murders and all their other offenses!"

With this Ogle would agree heartily.

"... And, so, the lady loosened her *corset* and the bishop *stayed* all night!" Ogle Gowan, as a recognized adult, was telling his first dirty joke to his Orange Lodge brothers. He looked anxiously into the encircling smoke and to his relief his *confrères* began to laugh heartily at the low pun. It was a joke he had heard his father tell a visitor, so he knew it was good.

This was one of the last rituals of manhood: learning to talk about sex in the rough way that males in the western world have developed to cover their uneasiness.

A lodge brother followed Ogle with a long story about a stranger enquiring at a farmstead exactly where he was. "You're near Moneyseed," the householder replied, and then, to prevent being asked for alms or for hospitality, continued, " . . . where men are men and the sheep are uneasy!" Everyone roared, though they had heard the story a dozen times before. This is grand, Ogle thought, being a man and talking like one.

The language of male sexual bravado that Ogle learned from his father and other adults, such as his lodge brothers, was a mixture of braggadocio and low humour.

Sometimes this vein of humour has run as an underground stream (particularly when religious authorities have gone on anti-sex campaigns), and at other times it has been quite openly enjoyed in male company. Only very rarely have women been admitted to the Rabelasian conversations, for that, potentially, is disastrous, as men would discover that women have jokes of their own. A lot of the sexual stories had an anti-Catholic element. Some of this was ill-informed (such as the traditional speculations about nuns and priests), but a lot was dead accurate. For instance, despite strong sanctions against pre-marital sex, and against illegitimacy among the Roman Catholic peasantry, their behaviour was often salacious, much to the distress of their priests. The local Protestants loved to repeat tales of the games frequently played at Catholic wakes. One local favourite was a game called "Making the Ship," where individuals of the two sexes alternately formed parts of the vessel — laying the keel, forming the stem and the stern, erecting a mast, which always was done by a female with unmistakably obscene gestures — until there was a pile of warm bodies pressing into each other on the cabin floor. Another game, called "Frimsy-Framsy" involved everyone, save the elderly, pairing off into couples. Then a stool was placed in the middle of the floor, and the master of the game called the name of a couple. The man of that couple sat on the stool and called his sweetheart, or any other female he fancied, and she came forward and they exchanged kisses. Then she sat on the stool and called *her* sweetheart, or anyone else she thought attractive. "Frimsy-framsy, who's your fancy?" was the chant while the game was played, and two hours or so of kissing led to more robust courting. There were other wake games, wherein women put on men's clothes and acted out both parts of a sexual encounter and, in one rare old game called 'Drawing the Ship out of the Mud," men, and sometimes women, actually emerged stark naked.

Such activities gave the Catholic priesthood nightmares and were successfully repressed only after the Great Famine. In telling these tales, the local Protestant men had the benefit of feeling morally superior to their enemies, while getting turned on. Not a few children were conceived after some Protestant farmer had spent two or three hours drinking whiskey punch and listening to such talk.

Only rarely were the jokes told around the lodge punch bowl funny. This is not simply because styles in humour change. It is because a really funny dirty joke is a rare phenomenon and should be treasured, like a natural black pearl. Yet, it was bad jokes, flip, callous, and pointless as they often were, that helped to teach Ogle Gowan what his attitude towards sex should be.

Equally important, his father set an example, quite an extraordinary one. Hunter Gowan was notoriously randy and not very good at taking contraceptive precautions. For a time, after his wife's death, he attempted to disclipline himself when he began taking the jumps with Miss Margaret Hogan. But after two "mistakes," which had resulted in the births of William and Ogle, he gave up. By this time, he was in his late sixties, so he thanked God for his fine constitution and let Miss Hogan "breed," as he put it. Her fourth pregnancy, in 1805, left her temporarily incapable of further child-bearing, but she still was sexually receptive, and everyone at Mount Nebo knew full well that the old master remained devoted to his favourite form of steeple-chase riding.

Possibly young Ogle might have become sexually active in a way that was not personally disastrous, such as visiting the village slut in Gorey, but unfortunately Mount Nebo itself had too many temptations. It was a tinder-box, and he was a lad given to playing with flints. The children of Hunter Gowan's first family were a good deal older than those of the second, illegitimate clan. Several of the older daughters had married, given birth to children, and either lived in the vicinity of Mount Nebo, or at least visited the estate frequently. They brought with them daughters, near to Ogle's age, and these children grew up playing, first, innocent childhood games and later, in the plantation woods or behind-the-curtains, the more titillating games of early adolescence. Anglo-Irish children of that era were permitted unsupervised freedom to a degree that the Victorian English would have found heart-stopping, and Mount Nebo, even by Anglo-Irish standards, was unregulated.

Among the half-nieces with whom Ogle played was Frances Ann Colclough Turner. She was a grandaughter of Hunter Gowan, by way of his legitimate daughter Jane Amelia, who had married one Edward Haycock Colclough Turner, Esq., of the Protestant side of that very good local family. (Confusingly, Jane Amelia usually called herself "Mrs. Colclough.") The couple had a son and a daughter, and it was with the daughter (who usually was referred to as "Frances Colclough") that Ogle playfully wrestled in Mount Nebo's woods, and from whom he learned the parts of the female body in detail. And whom, he discovered to his horror, he had made pregnant. Ogle was only nineteen years old at the time.

CHAPTER 4

Folds in Fortune, 1823-1824

OGLE AND Frances were married on 20 August 1823. As befitted an aged *roué*, Hunter Gowan did not rage at Ogle when told of the requisite marriage. In fact he himself had been required to marry his own wife in similar circumstances. He granted permission for the young couple to live in Mount Nebo if they so wished, but he also made clear that this was to be a temporary arrangement. When the estate passed to Thomas, the chief heir and particular enemy of Ogle, they would have to leave. Save for a modest legacy, they would be on their own.

Ogle's relationship to Frances was like that of Hunter Gowan to the two women who bore his children — and, like that of the Anglo-Irish small-gentry of the era in general. He felt moments of passion towards his wife, but, mostly she was an accessory, not a partner. Women, like other pieces of property acquired by the gentry, helped raise a man's social status, but, as Ogle often reflected, they could be damned expensive.

Frances, for her part, viewed Ogle as someone special. When she looked at him, she saw energy. He was not a big man, five feet nine inches or so, but he had a large chest and the aggressive look of a pug bull. People took notice of him. He had an unsettling way of going from apparent repose to quick-paced, almost frenetic action, and then, just as quickly, back into silent watchfulness. When he talked, he was animated, moving his arms about and frequently pushing his ginger hair back from his forehead. At such moments, he was like a large boy-child, and she loved him for it.

During September and October 1823, Ogle and Frances celebrated their marriage by taking what today would be called a honeymoon. Unlike the European tour often enjoyed by real Anglo-Irish gentry after marriage, their small tour never got more than fifty miles from Mount Nebo. Yet, it opened Ogle's mind to new worlds. The new Mrs. Gowan (in addition to being Ogle's half-niece) was, through her father's line, descended from the Colcloughs — that family whose Catholic members so bitterly vexed Hunter Gowan. Their ancestry, however, was impeccable and the Protestant side of the family, therefore, was highly acceptable. Frances Gowan was pleased to trace her descent to the Colcloughs of Tintem Abbey in County Wexford. In the seventeenth century a Colclough had married a daughter of Adam Loftus, Lord Chancellor of Ireland. Somewhat later, the family had owned Duffrey Hall in County Wexford, and it was this now-vestigial attachment that led the young couple to an area known as "The Duffrey," as the first destination on their tour. This Duffrey (variation: Duffry) was a woods that in mediaeval times had stretched from Mount Leinster to the river valley at Enniscorthy, County Wexford. "Duffrey" was from the Irish "Duibhtire," meaning dark territory, or black place, and was so named because the woods once were extensive and nearly impenetrable. The forest now was reduced, but still romantic, although neither Ogle nor his bride was sufficiently up on contemporary aesthetic fashions to use that word. They took long walks in the darkened vale, talked for hours about Ogle's future career, and several times they made love in the woods. The first time, Frances said that she felt that someone was watching. Later, she said that she hoped someone was.

The Duffrey was not just an enclosed forest world, but was a social universe as well. People from within a five-mile radius of the woods talked of being from The Duffrey, and this social world had a verdant culture of its own. (This is well described in the fiction of Patrick Kennedy who lived there at this time.) That society had its own *demi-monde* in the town of Enniscorthy, one of whose entrances was known as the Duffrey Gate. There was at that time in Enniscorthy an iron-monger by the name of Ellis, whose wife was a fortune-teller. They were Protestants of Palatine lineage, and for a time had been in the linen trade. Mrs. Ellis was given to reading tea-leaves and to referring to herself darkly as a "spae-wife" or diviner. Publicly, Ogle always had dismissed the freets of the fortune-tellers as ignorant superstitions, while wondering secretly if there really might not be something in them. When his new bride suggested that they see Mrs. Ellis, he offered only token opposition. "It will not do you any harm, Ogle," Frances suggested archly, patting him on the hand in the manner used by nannies to reassure their reluctant charges. "Besides, dear husband, I need to know your future as, should it be very grand, I shall be obliged to purchase suitable dresses and bonnets."

Thus, Ogle and Frances entered the Ellis ironmongery. The young couple looked out of place, for they were wildly overdressed in what they took to be fashionable afternoon wear. They had stayed the night at an inn in Enniscorthy and spent the day perambulating the town, letting the locals have a look at them. Young marrieds, indeed. Frances wore a one-piece dress with a billowing skirt that hid her pregnancy, a bodice decorated with false pearls and a set of massive *gigot* sleeves, one of which caught on the door latch as they entered the unlit ironmonger's shop. Ogle was in a high-collared "promenade coat," dark blue, with tight trousers that were strapped down over his boots in cavalry fashion. Anyone familiar with Hunter Gowan's family could have suggested that the outfit looked suspiciously like one owned by Ogle's half-brother John, who had been a cavalry officer in Egypt and at Waterloo, and had died in 1819 after a fall from his horse. Despite their costume, they were an undeniably handsome couple. Frances had a pneumatic beauty, not yet running to blowsiness and Ogle, ginger-haired and slightly swaggering, had the compelling energy of a banty rooster.

Mrs. Ellis, the spae-wife, immediately recognized Frances, whose family was well known in the town, and unctuously asked, "Is it about an item for metal work or domestic use that you are calling for today, Mrs. Gowan?" Shrewdly, she used the girl's married name. "Or would you like to take a cup of tea and discuss the future?" She nodded towards Ogle. "I belive that your fine husband is as much interested in the future as are you, dear lady."

Ogle, momentarily embarrassed, nodded to confirm his own interest, and then, recovering his confidence, boomed out, "Of course, madame. Every person wishes to know the future. The question, madame, is whether or not you are capable of fortelling it accurately." He crossed his arms in front of his chest, like bare-knuckle boxers did when posing for engravings.

"The future will be what I shall see, and I shall see what it shall be," Mrs. Ellis turned on her heel and motioned the young people to follow her into her viewing parlour, a small room off the main shop. There, without uttering a word, she seated her clients and turned to make preparations. Frances started to say something, but the diviner turned and silenced her with an imperious glare. She wetted a pot that was seemingly half-full of tea leaves, with boiling water and, after a silent five-minute wait, poured out two cups of coal-black tea. She placed them before Ogle and Frances and finally broke her silence. "Drink them if you have a mind to," she said and went back to her preparations. She decanted the remainder of the tea into a white porcelain jug and then, with a long, thin spoon, dipped out some of the leaves and put them onto a large saucer, about six inches in diameter. To these she added a little cold water, just enough to make the tea leaves half-float. She gently rotated the saucer so that the leaves moved about and then tipped out the water, being careful to leave the pattern of the leaves undisturbed. "Come close," she hissed and when the young Gowans did so, took each of them by a wrist. Ogle found her touch repulsive, but did not flinch.

"I see a Trinity of things for you, dear children."

"A Trinity?" Frances had been to fortune-tellers before, and knew that the proper form of response was that of a litany.

"A Trinity, yes. The first item in it is Great Position."

"Great Position? Shall we have that?" Frances inquired. Ogle leaned forward.

"The leaves say you shall be near it. Whether you shall have it — and whether you shall keep it long if you do have — the leaves do not say." Clearly the Gowans wanted to know more, but the diviner was unmoved. She looked intently into the saucer and said in an enigmatic monotone, "Trying Times."

"Trying Times? Are we to have them? — How so?" Frances was somewhat anxious.

"The leaves again are silent. You may pass through well or you may not."

Ogle leaned back from the table and breathed out heavily. He was confident that he could handle any trial.

"Silver. The third part of your Trinity is Silver."

Ogle joined the litany. "Is it silver you want?" he asked the spae-wife.

"No, fool, no. You will pay me later. The Silver is for you. It is in your future."

Ogle smiled, for silver had been on his mind.

Silver. Ogle needed it badly. He and Frances had returned to Mount Nebo and settled into a room on the east side of the house. As the autumn days drew in, Frances sat in the drawing room, did needlepoint, talked with her mother who made increasingly frequent visits, and grew daily more pregnant. Ogle made several trips to Dublin to scout for ways of earning a living. When back at Mount Nebo, he moved busily about the estate, but actually there was little for him to do as his elder, illegitimate brother William did most of the management. Ogle had little money in his pocket and he soon would have another dependent. Hunter Gowan, after a long and roisterous life, was ailing. His vigour was daily diminishing: he was completely white-haired, was losing weight and certainly he would die within the year. To his illegitimate children, Hunter made it clear that they would be remembered in his will, but that the lands would go to the legitimate line. However, anything Ogle could expect from his father's last will and testament was in the indefinite future; he needed money now.

But in Ogle's mind silver was not just money, it was a symbol, something a gentleman required, like a proper escutcheon. Still very young and easy to goad, Ogle was baited by the legitimate offspring of Hunter Gowan who, with increasing frequency, called in at Mount Nebo, ostensibly to enquire about their father's health, but actually to gauge his nearness to death. Just the odd word, the oblique jibe from one of them, and Frances had to spend the rest of the day calming down her spouse. The nastiest of the lot was Thomas Gowan who, since the death in 1819 of John Gowan, was the oldest male heir in the legitimate line. He took to calling in on Frances and, ostensibly with great courtesy, giving her each time a shiny new shilling, "to put aside for the baby." Frances would nod acceptance and then Thomas would add, "After all, he won't see much silver in his lifetime." Sometimes, when he was being especially unkind, Thomas would leave by way of the dining room and while passing the sideboard would give the coin a casual flip, so that it hit the ornate silver urn that the Wexford grand jury had given Hunter Gowan, and dribbled off to the floor. Frances would wait until Thomas was out of sight and then would go down on her hands and knees and search for the shilling. When Ogle heard of this he said nothing, but the large vein on his forehead stood out and pulsed noticeably.

Hating his half-brother Thomas, worried about his own financial situation, embittered by the knowledge that his illegitimacy would cost him most of what he believed was his rightful share of the family fortune, Ogle sat up nights. Frequently, in the dark hours after midnight, he came down to the drawing room. He brooded and, increasingly, tied together silver, his own perilous financial condition, the probability that he would receive little or nothing from his father's estate, and the injustice that would be. Thus, one such night in late November he entered the dining room and rummaged through the old sideboard where his father kept artifacts of value.

He removed one of the two silver cups that the Wexford grand jury had given to Hunter Gowan in 1785 for fighting Whiteboys. "This, by God is *mine*" he said aloud and stuffed the object into his coat pocket. The cup, Ogle instinctively understood, was more than merely a piece of precious metal. It was the family's social and ideological patrimony, for it indicated recognition by the Gowan's social superiors that they were valued lieutenants in the fight against the enemies of Law, Protestantism, and the Constitution. However unconsciously, in making this symbolic appropriation of part of the family inheritance, Ogle acted with strict fairness: he did not take the other cup or the ornate urn. One cup, his share, would do.

Thomas Gowan was the first person to notice that the cup was missing and he made a shrewd and instinctive guess about what had happened. He sought out Ogle and, finding him behind the stables, told him that the cup was missing. Like many a sibling, he knew when a lie was being told: Ogle strenuously and vociferously denied having stolen the cup ("But who said it was stolen?" Thomas replied). Thomas went to a magistrate and swore out a warrant against Ogle for felony theft which could be done on the say-so of any substantial gentleman without the necessity of any direct proof of theft. Thomas calculated that the grand jury investigation that would follow would be too much for Ogle to brazen his way through, and that he would be discredited permanently in Hunter Gowan's eyes. In proceeding this way, Thomas was acting in a fashion similar to the way he would later move to protect his larger inheritance; he used the full force of the law to enforce the claims of the legitimate line against those of the bastard sept. The case was held over for the spring assize; the Gowan family's many enemies awaited the case with anticipation.

The assize was held in a large country inn at Coolgranny. The Irish "grand jury system" of this era was not just a system of justice (or frequently injustice), but an amalgam of legal and administrative activities, run by the social *élite* of the county. For anyone pretending to gentility, a grand jury session would be the most embarrassing place to air the family's dirty linen.

Over the winter, Hunter Gowan became an ever-frailer, ever-paler replica of himself. Overtaken with lassitude and a tiredness-unto-dying, he did nothing about Thomas's charges against Ogle, except to hope that the matter would pass over. The cup was still missing and although Hunter agreed that Ogle certainly must have taken it, the case was merely circumstantial. To the old man, the problem of the theft by Ogle was less important than Thomas's bringing the family name to obloquy. Hunter, like his warring sons, recognized that the real value of the cup was not in its precious metal. It was the engraving on its accompanying ornate urn, the thanks of the country's aristocracy and gentry, that made it truly valuable. And Hunter Gowan realized that anything which made his family look ridiculous in public would cancel that valuable inscription, just as surely as a vandal's hammer would shatter a piece of cast-iron statuary.

When several talks with Thomas failed to convince him to withdraw the felony theft charge, Hunter finally animated himself and moved decisively. He did this the only way he could in his failing state: by working himself into a temper and using that black energy to propel him on a cold mid-March day to the inn at Coolgranny where the trial was scheduled. When the high sheriff called the case, he shuffled forward and asked leave to discuss the case with the jurors in camera. This was granted, and the courtroom was cleared of spectators, save for members of the Gowan family. In a truckling voice that Hunter hated himself for using, he touched briefly on the problem of raising so many chldren, the absence of direct evidence against Ogle, the inevitability of domestic dispute within any family, and the fact — damnation, he hated himself for this — that he would soon leave this vale, and would not leave in peace if the family name was blotted by a felony conviction.

The two warring men, Thomas and Ogle, listened to their father's pleading. They sat in opposite rear corners of the courtroom, like two fighting cocks being kept apart until the main event. Thomas, tall, and dressed in gray breeches, a white stock shirt and morning coat, looked the embodiment of responsibility. As he listened to his father, he stared straight ahead. Despite his resolve at composure, he felt himself flushing red as the old man pleaded Ogle's acquittal. In contrast to Thomas, Ogle wore plummage — a bright waistcoat that clashed with his ginger hair. Whereas Thomas had a certain insouciant grace, Ogle was a coiled spring, compact, the compressed energy within him palpable. Ogle listened to his father's plea with direct and fierce concentration. The old man is doing well, he thought: I may still get by this embarassment after all.

"Therefore, gentlemen, my eldest son and chief heir, Thomas, is willing to withdraw the charge." This conclusion to Hunter Gowan's plea came as a surprise to everyone, including Thomas, who seemed about to contradict his father when Hunter added, ominously, that should this not be the case, Thomas no longer was an heir.

Sullenly, Thomas nodded assent: the charge could be dropped.

Ogle, standing in the corner opposite Thomas, permitted himself a small smile. And so the high sheriff formally requested of his fellow-landowners that the case be withdrawn. They each indicated agreement and there the matter died.

Hunter Gowan did not speak to any of his children. The rage that had propelled him to the assize had been stoked further by the humiliating ordeal he had had to undergo, and he could not look at his sons without feeling homicidal. Directly upon leaving the courtroom he ordered his groom to take him to visit a favourite nephew who lived in Enniscorthy and there he stayed for some days, coughing, spitting blood, and denouncing as damned-fooldungeaters his entire battalion of heirs.

The silver cup reappeared at Mount Nebo. Nobody asked how.

Hunter Gowan died on May 25, 1825, but not before cancelling a last will and testament that he had written sometime in the previous winter and replacing it with one dated twenty-one days before his death. The pelf was divided as follows:

Illegitimate children

1. William, eldest illegitimate son. £100/year in perpetuity to William and his heirs, chargeable on Ashwood estate.
2. Ogle, £200/year.
3. Margaret, £200/year.

Legitimate children

1. Thomas, eldest living son: Mount Nebo estate and lands of Hollyfort, leased from Viscount Powerscourt.
2. George, second eldest son, £500/year.
3. Hunter, third son, £550/year.
4. Anne, eldest surviving daughter, £500/year.
5. Frances, daughter, £500/year.
6. Jane, daughter, £500/year. (Ogle's mother-in-law.)
7. Isma (var: Ismay) daughter, £500/year.
8. Harriet, daughter, £550/year.
9. Charlotte, daughter, £499/year.
10. Mary, daughter, £400/year.
11. Catherine, daughter, £200/year.
12. Elizabeth, daughter, £20/year.

GRANDCHILDREN

1. Frances (Ogle's wife), £100/year.
2. John Beacon, £20/year.
3. John Gowan, £50/year.

Like every document, Hunter's will had a hidden text. No provision was made for Margaret Hogan, longtime concubine. William Gowan, the eldest illegitimate child, was slated to do better than it might at first appear. Unlike the other lands held by Hunter Gowan, the Ashwood estate was a freehold: Mount Nebo and Hollyfort were leased. Hence, William's being provided for from a freehold estate was the most secure form of protection possible, and moreover, his bequest was to his heirs forever, while the other bequests were only for the lifetime of the recipient. Substantively, the will would survive two court cases, but with somewhat drastic consequences for William and Ogle.

In an unusually sensitive gesture, Hunter Gowan divided the silver pieces that had been presented by the Wexford Grand Jury in 1785: one cup and the silver urn went to Thomas, the senior male in the legitimate line and the other cup to William, the senior of the bastard line. If not equal, the two lines each were his own spawn, and he wanted each recognized as such.

After he made this will, Hunter Gowan, sickly and no longer able to move about, came under pressure from the legitimate side of the family and their friends to reduce the value of the award to the bastard, William. Hunter made two codicils, the most important of which reduced the annual amount paid to William to £50. Still, this amount was in perpetuity and William was named as one of the three executors of the will. He was to share the management of Ashwood with the other two executors, the Reverend Mr. Medlicott, a clergyman of the Established Church, and Robert Hopkins, a local shop-keeper and attorney-at-law, and spouse of Mary Gowan, one of Hunter's daughters.

Considering that Ogle had begun the year 1824 with the threat of a felony conviction hanging over him and the possibility of consequently being cut out of Hunter Gowan's will, he had done well. Manifestly, his father had forgiven him. He and his wife Frances had the promise of £300 a year between them — provided, of course, that Hunter Gowan's estate would bear all the charges assigned to it.

Frances Gowan had never seen Ogle so happy. He had been vexed for a long time about the last will and testament — "how will it all turn out?" he had asked over and over — and now he was immensely relieved, not just about receiving the money, but that the will had been probated so easily.

For the first time, the young couple had financial security. They decided to move to Dublin, where Ogle could capitalize on both his abilities and his good fortune.

CHAPTER 5

Trials of a Young Married Man, 1824-1826

THE DUBLIN to which Ogle and Frances moved from Mount Nebo was a tired whore of a city. Since January 1, 1801, when the Act of Union of Great Britain and Ireland became effective, Dublin had ceased to be a capital city, and its pock-marked countenance had become more obviously disfigured each year. In a richly symbolic gesture, the old Irish parliament building was sold to the Bank of Ireland; part of the agreement was a requirement that the bank alter the building to obscure the structure's former purpose. No one wanted to be reminded of former glories. Once the Irish parliament was gone, the great families sold their houses, for the big-stakes power-game now was played in London. For a time, dowagers kept up the houses, but one by one they died and the better-off merchants and professional men snapped up the domiciles on the cheap and ran them with reduced staff. Of course, just as there was a residual, if constantly shrinking, treasury of fine eighteenth-century architecture, so there was a vestigial governing class, astronomically rich in comparison to the wretched poor. But behind the façades of many of the handsome Georgian houses were found temporary walls and hastily thrown-up partitions, which cut these once-fine houses into boarding accommodation or into flats. An "enormous acreage" of Dublin's Georgian buildings was let to boarders. These accommodations ranged in quality from small, single rooms, shared by several labouring men, to self-enclosed flats, quite adequate for a family.

In one such Dublin flat, Ogle Gowan installed his wife and new son. The address, No. 3, Parnell Square, was well chosen. Located at the top of Sackville Street near the Rotunda, Parnell Square had been very fashionable in the days before the Union. Indeed, in 1792, one observer discovered that no fewer than ten members of the Irish House of Lords, twelve MPs, and two Lords Spiritual had residences there. Now, with the Irish parliament gone, the square was no longer exclusive, but for a reasonable rent it offered an address that had a thin patina of aristocracy.

In Dublin, more than any other place in Ireland, the movement of two major forces was apparent: the Catholics were becoming more aggrieved, increasingly aggressive, and were rising socially, while the Protestants were aggrieved, defensive, and declining. As with massive geological plates shifting on the earth's surface, these forces crushed anyone caught between them. Looming over this entire tectonic display, like a figure from the Apocalypse of St. John, was Daniel O'Connell. Even in the mid-1820s, Ogle could see clearly that an Irish-Catholic nation was being formed by O'Connell, one that would not be denied power, and one that had no room for the Gowans of this world. Daniel O'Connell's campaign for Catholic Emancipation (that is, for the right of Roman Catholics to sit in Parliament) was not merely political. It was nationally epochal; he taught Irish Catholics to organize, to look to each other for support, and, most important, to hold their heads up.

Frightening to Protestants, this certainly was, particularly those with any sense of the long-range future. But, in the short-run, anyone who promised to help Dublin's embattled Protestants fight back would find work.

From the time he was eighteen onwards, Ogle had gone often up to Dublin to scout opportunities and pick up work. Journalism seemed most promising, being, if not genteel, at least not trade, and it suited his talents. He did the odd piece for various Protestant papers, but nothing developed. At first these Dublin forays were good entertainment for him, even if he did not turn up professional opportunities, but after Ogle learned that Frances was pregnant, he began seriously looking for work.

That is why one evening he slowly opened a door at the back

of one of the Rotunda assembly rooms and slipped sideways through the aperture. He was ill at ease but determined not to show it. At the front of the room, lecturing with extravagant gestures, was Sir Harcourt Lees, Anglican clergyman, baronet, pamphleteer, and Protestant champion.

Lees was in full flight before an audience composed, equally, of Anglican clergy, Anglo-Irish ladies, and keen evangelical laymen. He was reading large portions of a letter he had written to "JKL," James Doyle, Roman Catholic bishop of Kildare and Leighlin, and author of a noted series of published letters in favour of Catholic Emancipation. "So, JKL, you are in an awkward kind of dilemma in which I have entangled you, my old boy, in my last letter, with a basketful of your general councils on the top of you and before I have done if I don't smother you like a Buck Rabbit in Onion on your own vegetables (for, it is by the historical declarations of Romish authorities, I will annihilate you), you may say I am not a better scholar or more proficient reasoner than your Right Hon. allies, Mr. George Canning and Mr. Marshal Rock . . . . "

The reading was interrupted by applause which Sir Harcourt graciously acknowledged by bowing deeply at the waist; he took a large linen handkerchief from the tail of his cutaway to mop his brow, wet with the noble exertion of his oratory. Although he could not grasp the argument being made, Ogle joined in the applause as he moved quietly to a seat at the rear of the assembly room.

Lees continued, now in a historical vein. "When I consider the Cabinet proceedings of the reign of Charles I and compare them with the ministerial intrigues of the present day, I cannot refrain from expressing an ardent wish that the Prelates of the Established Church in Ireland would at length come forward with a strong protest against extending political power even to my tolerant and excellent JKL — which, if it is granted, will inevitably consummate Romanist religious ascendancy."

"Hear, hear," called the evangelical laymen and a few of the Anglican clergy.

"I hold up to those prelates of our church the Remonstrance made in the reign of Charles I, by the archbishop of Armagh and other prelates, when incipient rebellion was in progress — as it is at this hour in Ireland. That Remonstrance states that to grant the papists a TOLERATION . . . is a great sin — a sin! — and so it is also a matter of most dangerous consequence — the consideration of which we submit to the wise and judicious, beseeching the God of Truth to make them who are in authority zealous of God's glory, and of the advancement of true religion, zealous, resolute, and courageous against all Popery, Superstition, and Idolatry!" Lees thundered out the last phrase and brought forth universal applause; even the more reserved of the Anglo-Irish ladies joined in. Ogle Gowan was listening with fascination. He had come to measure the man and to importune him for employment, but was being swept up in the rhetoric, a flow of words whose unspoken, fundamental assumptions fit perfectly with his own beliefs.

The man whom Ogle was beginning to admire, Sir Harcourt Lees, was an extravagant figure, but not a fool. He was approaching fifty, a striking man, tall, modishly dressed, with a strange stork-like way of moving. When he walked he habitually kept both hands clasped behind his back and took inordinately long steps. In his speech-making, he frequently bowed at the waist, deeply and jerkily, to acknowledge his audience's approbation. Anglican clergymen of the period were allowed considerable latitude in their garb, but most of them affected sombre black in their habiliment. Not Lees. This day he was in a blue, long-tailed cutaway dress coat, with gilt buttons, a velvet collar, and under the coat a fancy-patterned fine cambric cravat. Sir Harcourt had been educated at Trinity College, Cambridge and had taken Holy Orders. For a time, he held preferments in Ireland, but resigned them in 1806 and lived on his private income. He married, had four sons and a daughter. In 1819 he came alive politically and began writing a series of anti-Catholic pamphlets that were generously described as "distinguished by extreme animation of style."

"I ask of you, respected ladies and gentlemen, what does this Kingdom of Ireland, once so virtuous and devout, require?" This was a rhetorical question and Sir Harcourt took a moment to answer it.

To his surprise, a young man at the rear of the room stood up and said something. "With great respect, reverend sir," said Ogle Gowan, bowing his head to Sir Harcourt, "it requires an *Antidote*!" Ogle Gowan sat down quickly, amidst laughter and a smattering of applause. "Well said, young man," commented one of the evangelicals.

Ogle was referring, in the first instance to Sir Harcourt's initial foray into anti-Catholicism, of 1819, *The Antidote or Nouvelles à la Main. Recommended to the serious attention of the Right Hon. W.C. Plunket and other advocates of unrestricted civil and religious liberty.*

And, Ogle also was referring to a weekly newspaper that had begun to appear late in 1822, *The Antidote, or, Protestant Guardian*. Sir Harcourt was the *eminence gris* behind this weekly publication, and most issues of the paper included a long excerpt from one of his several pamphlets.

Sir Harcourt took Ogle's interruption in good spirit and, after a brief apostrophe on the value of that particular newspaper to Protestant interests, concluded his address with a peroration that incredibly tied together the threat of Catholic Emancipation with the spread of Jacobinical principals, and the atheistic and regicidal French revolution.

After the evening's program was completed, Ogle, having successfully called himself to Sir Harcourt's attention, waited patiently as the Anglo-Irish ladies twittered attendance on the baronet. When their ranks finally thinned, Ogle moved forward and at last was able to present himself to Lees. He did this as Ogle Gowan, son of Captain Hunter Gowan of Mount Nebo, County Wexford, and godchild of the late George Ogle, MP. In this social setting, he could not ask directly for employment, but he expressed unbounded admiration for Sir Harcourt's work, and stressed his own enthusiastic desire to contribute to the cause. The baronet, sharp of eye, despite his own apparent foppery, recognized immediately that this was an encoded application for employment. The young man seemed able enough, so he suggested that Ogle draft a few pieces for *The Antidote*, and that when these were done he should take them directly to one of the paper's printers, George Perkins Bull, who would look them over and insert them in the appropriate place.

Ogle, it turned out, was a natural for *The Antidote*. He was an undeviating Protestant loyalist, who wrote both quickly and well and, in line with the prevailing journalistic practice of the time, he had few scruples about borrowing items previously published elsewhere. He contributed to *The Antidote* off and on for a while, then, after several months, began to work for it full time. The paper had an administrative structure that was passing mysterious. Various members of a Dublin printing family, the Bulls, (most notably George Perkins Bull, when he was not in prison, and his brother, William,) were involved both as printers and as nominal proprietors. Getting along with the Bull brothers was the hardest part of Ogle's job: one moment they were matey, the next truculent, and their attitudes swung from wildly energetic, when dealing with strongly anti-Catholic items, to lethargic in matters of day-to-day chores.

Sir Harcourt Lees had a *sub rosa* connection, as financial godfather and *de facto*-publisher. For a time, William Gowan had a business association with the paper, collecting overdue accounts in the north of Ireland, and acting as its subscription agent in the Wexford-Wicklow region.

In the first week of July 1824, Ogle, using the promise of a legacy under Hunter Gowan's last will and testament as collateral, took a big step: he assumed full proprietorship and editorship of *The Antidote*. This effectively demoted the Bull brothers, who had been nominal proprietors, and William Bull quit. George Perkins Bull sullenly agreed to stay on as printer. Ogle moved the paper's offices from 3 Redmond's Hill (near Aungier St.) to No. 1 Suffolk Street, just a block off College Green. Not bad: twenty-one years old and a newspaper publisher.

"By the stars, young Gowan, you write with bottom!" Sir Harcourt Lees was reading the draft of a long pamphlet Ogle was writing, and his use of a hunting phrase was apposite, for Ogle jumped logical obstacles with the *sang-froid* of a good rider clearing a high hedge. The draft in question was in the form of a long letter — seventy-three foolscap pages — to Lord Wellesley, and it may be fairly taken as an example of Ogle's Protestant apologetics. His draft, entitled "The State of Things," started formally and respectfully:

> To His Excellency, the Most Noble, Richard Marquis of Wellesley, Lord Lieutenant and General Governor of Ireland. My Lord Marquis,
>
> Permit me to lay before your Excellency what, in my opinion, appears to be the real state of affairs of this happy country, over which your Lordship has the distinguished and merited honor to be placed as vice King.

("Through no fault of ours, the loyal Protestant people," snorted Sir Harcourt, who was reading the pamphlet aloud.)

> It is one of the Glories of our unrivalled Constitution

("Good lad, Gowan, always refer to the Constitution early.")

> that the most humble is privileged to state to his Majesty or his representative, the expression of their feelings, and it is a still greater glory that the expression of such feelings are seldom unattended to, provided they fail not in due respect.

That provoked Sir Harcourt to laughter. ("Seldom unattended to, indeed!")

He and Ogle were on the second floor of the office that Gowan kept in Suffolk Street. The Bull brothers' printing equipment was on the ground storey below. The building was brick, narrow, of no architectural distinction, and Ogle's office had only a single window, a tall, narrow rectangle of light, cut into eight small panes.

> Conciliation is a game long played by your excellency and most probably reflects great honour upon your character, for the conscientious motives that influence your Excellency's conduct.

But a little later Ogle added, waspishly,

> My Lord, the expanded genius of your enlightened mind must have long since exhibited to your view that would be the effects of this visionary scheme, judiciously termed conciliation. Your Excellency must have seen that with it, the splendid fabric of distorted fancy was erecting — ideal grievances gathered and egregious and treasonable publications inundating our streets — the madmind harangues of infuriated fanatics bellowing in our ears — conciliatory merit bestowed in profusion on the whining inconsistencies of mock patriots — darkness superceding light — the mists of delusion and error enveloping the sun of truth and reality — and reason (the noblest faculty of man) degraded and enthralled!

Sir Harcourt was enjoying this so much that Ogle thought the worthy baronet might fling open the window and read the lapidary prose to passersby on the street below. Sir Harcourt, though, was momentarily out of breath from his stentorian proclamation of Ogle's gospel. He paused, flipped a few pages and, coming across another passage that he liked, he held the foolscap before him in his right hand, his left hand clasping the satin lapel of his own frock coat: the traditional pose of the Irish parliamentary orator. For a time, he read Ogle's work in a steady voice, assuming the tone of a rational man trying to show a worthy opponent the error of his way:

> My Lord, it is not now denied by any party that the influence of the Roman Catholic Clergy over the minds of the laity of that persuasion is ironhanded. So far, my Lord, from its being denied, the Clergy have boasted of it . . . and their advocates both in and out of Parliament have glorified in their possessing such influence. Well, then, my Lord, we take it that such influence does exist.

Sir Harcourt gradually was carried away again by the prose. His voice rose and he gesticulated widely with his left hand.

> Then, my Lord, it cannot be denied that a foreign potentate possesses not an equal, but a greater influence over the minds of the clergy of the persuasion, who are *unconditionally sworn and sworn and sworn again* to obey him!!

For a moment the thought of Popish perfidy made Sir Harcourt sputter. He returned to the text:

> Here we have a foreign potentate commanding the Bishops, the Bishops commanding the Priests, and the Priests commanding the Laity, so that at any perilous and eventual period, a foreign Court may think proper to do so, it can command a general and simultaneous rising of near six millions of people in this small island!!!

"My god, that's strong medicine, young Gowan, first-rate stuff. The Papishes are the greatest threat to the Constitution, Crown, Law and Order — that fact we cannot ever let our countrymen forget!"

Ogle, very pleased, acknowledged the compliment and took the liberty of calling Sir Harcourt's attention to what he believed was the best part of the pamphlet and this the baronet read with avidity:

> Do not the Roman Catholics, my Lord, enjoy the most perfect toleration of their religion? The fullest security of their Property? The most complete personal Liberty? The utmost spiritual and temporal blessings, and much More?
>
> They do.
>
> Then let them be content . . . and by no means, My Lord, either now or ever after attempt an interference in the government of this Kingdom, as such interference would be incompatible with *The Protestant Ascendancy* which every good Protestant should resolve with his life and fortune to maintain. And, further, my Lord, to prevent all skeptical cavilling or doubts remaining as to the extent and meaning of The Protestant Ascendancy, it is as follows:
>
> A Protestant King,
> A Protestant Parliament,
> A Protestant Hierarchy, Protestant Electors and Government,
> The Army and Revenue, through all their branches and details Protestant.
>
> This, my Lord, is *The Protestant Ascendancy!!*

Under Sir Harcourt Lees's tutelage, young Ogle Gowan successfully put together his own private syndicate of Protestant apologetics. He edited *The Antidote,* served various proselytizing societies, and wrote tracts and pamphlets. The character of his religious writings can easily be inferred from their titles: *Catholic Relics, The King's Vision, The Pope's Bull, The Primate's Answer,* and *The Real Truth-Teller.* Certainly there was a market for his work: the Religious Tract and Book Society for Ireland distributed 2.7 million pieces of religious literature in a six-year period, and it was only one of several such groups. In being a professional Protestant, Ogle was into a potentially very lucrative business.

In the fabric that was Ogle's emerging vocation, the various strands of Protestant apologetics — his paper, the pamphlets, his functionary roles in various societies — formed the woof. But the warp was provided by the sturdy threads of Orangeism. The Orange society was Ogle's real source of strength, for it gave him social contacts, a personal ideology, and hope of a career serving the Order. The Society in the late 1810s and early 1820s was in decline. As the threat of a foreign (and, presumably Catholic) invasion or revolution died down after the Napoleonic Wars, lassitude overcame the membership. At the same time, many of the original stalwarts of the Order either stepped down from office or died. A new generation of leaders grew up, many without real authority over the scattered country lodges. Hence, various unauthorized lodges and new "orders" sprouted, and the new authorities tried to suppress the variants by introducing a new set of rules. This was only partially successful and, by mid-1821, the Order was at a low ebb.

Ogle saw an opportunity here and manoeuvred brilliantly: he calculated that the Order well might revive if the threat of O'Connell and his Popish hordes became greater and thus he began working himself ever closer to the centre of Orange power. First he managed to have himself made master of a lodge in Shillelagh, County Wicklow, thus giving him membership in the Grand Lodge of that county. Young though he was, he inspired respect from the worshipful members. The men of Shillelagh Loyal Orange Lodge No. 1666 on July 12, 1822 apostrophized Ogle, who had been away in Dublin seeking a career:

> We . . . avail ourselves of the opportunity which your visit to this part of the Country affords, to renew to you those sentiments of affectionate esteem, which we have on former occasions expressed, particularly during the period we were favoured with your presence as *Master* of our loyal and respectable Society . . . .
>
> Rejoicing to see you once more amongst us, we are certain we cannot offer any tribute more grateful to your feelings than the pleasing proof that your exertions in arousing the Protestant spirit of the country have not been in vain and that you will this day meet many persons, who heretofore opposed your Constitutional exertions, now coming forward to offer the voluntary tribute due to integrity of heart and purity of intention.

Young Ogle replied smoothly. The unctuousness of his words hid the excitement he felt at being recognized as the spokesman for these rough men. He envisaged leading them not only as their

Lodge Master but, someday, as their member of Parliament. For the moment, however, humility was the right note:

> The warm expression of your attachment . . . I receive with the *pride* and *spirit* of an Orangeman. Be assured I shall endeavour, while God spares me life and intelligence, to merit a continuance of your approbation, by a strict adherence, as well as from Inclination as from Duty, to the good old cause, the establishment of which we this day assemble to commemorate . . . .
>
> Feeling as I do, the necessity of preserving a *community of feeling* amongst Protestants of all denominations, and viewing our religious and loyal Society as the mainstay of the British connexion, I need scarcely say, how much it shall be my endeavour to uphold the house and maintain the glory of the Orangemen of Ireland.

Ogle used his mastership of the Shillelagh Lodge to advantage. He quickly made himself useful to the members of the Grand Lodge of Wicklow and by the spring of 1824 he was "grand secretary" of that county's grand lodge. He was well on his way to working out a formula that he used for the rest of his life — to serve the Order's ends — and thus make the Order serve his own ambitions.

"Above all, the Orange Order must be respectable." That was an opinion young Ogle was willing to share with anyone, but in this case his audience in his flat at No. 3 Parnell Square consisted only of his wife Frances, his half-uncle, Henry Hatton Gowan, and his nephew, the nine-year-old James Gowan, up from the country for a taste of Dublin life. "That is why," Ogle continued, "I am in complete agreement with our Law Committee that the twelfth of July festivities should be cancelled this year." Uncle Henry and little James Gowan were among Ogle and Frances's first guests in Dublin. They were an easy pair to entertain: Henry, captor of the famous Captain Grant, was a vigorous man, interested in everything and anything, and young James got on famously with Frances, whom he was permitted to call "Fanny." Ogle and Frances's flat, like most Georgian buildings in Dublin, was a trifle shabby; some of the ornate plasterwork was crumbling and one of the windowpanes was cracked. Still, the young married couple made a good effort at being genteel. They had a dark walnut sideboard with a leaded crystal decanter, several decent goblets, and an oriental runner in the space they called "the drawing room."

"But there is treason in the ranks. Take those scoundrels, George Atkinson, William McCullagh, and John Atkinson — and I wish someone, perhaps the devil — would take them: they actively planned to disgrace the Order. Loyal brothers they said, and then what do they do?" Ogle was on to one of his crotchets, the ignominious deeds of some Orange brothers in 1822: at a perform ance of *She Stoops to Conquer* the Lord Lieutenant, the Marquis of Wellesley, was hissed and had things thrown at him by Orangemen. Henry Hatton Gowan always found his nephew engaging, and now he nodded encouragingly.

Ogle continued. "Yes, I have it on excellent authority that those three Brothers plotted one of the most formidable and deep-laid conspiracies we have on record; the ultimate design of which was to disgrace and finally to dissolve the Orange Society in Ireland."

"Really? How so . . . "

"They were in constant communication with the Right Honourable — right honourable indeed! — William Conyngham Plunket, that arch-enemy of the Constitution and of our Order. And they organized the riot that in 1822 so embarrassed our Order. Of course Wellesley is a fool and a blackguard, but one does not throw rubbish at the Monarch's viceroy! These men collected money, gave instructions, and circulated admission tickets free!! And they were in constant communication with Plunket who paid their expenses."

"Rascals, to be sure." Henry Hatton Gowan was less indignant than Ogle would have liked, but clearly interested. Little James looked on and, as Ogle grew more animated, became slightly frightened. He snuggled up closely to his Aunt Fanny who was soft, warm, and smelled nice.

"And were it not for the law of slander, which, alas, punishes even a truth-sayer, I should take it upon myself to say that these men were rewarded either by hard cash or by permanent positions in the police and revenue departments. What do you think of that — a government conspiracy to tarnish our Order!"

Ogle's paranoia about the government was not without reason. On July 18, 1823, the United Kingdom Parliament had passed an act making unlawful most associations bound by oaths, and this included the Order. So keen were the Order's leaders on keeping themselves legal and respectable that the Grand Lodge immediately issued orders against the administering of oaths by local lodges. Instead, they had each new member produce evidence that at some time he had taken the (perfectly legal) oath of supremacy, or the oath of allegiance to the Crown.

"And that is why," Ogle concluded, "I shall bring that traitor McCullagh to heel. The two Atkinsons are beyond reach now, for they have left the Order, but McCullagh is still a grand lodge officer. And, worse, sits on our finance committee. Yes, I shall nail his hide to the drying board yet!"

Ogle waited and then, the moment right, pounced cheetah-like. William McCullagh, whom he believed to be a traitor to the Orange cause, was one of a "Committee of Six" who oversaw the day-to-day business of the Grand Lodge of Ireland. Gowan saw them as a "cabalistic junta" made up of "chums and *élèves*." Ogle, having been well-schooled by his tutor in basic ciphering, knew that the sums in the Order's account books did not add up. They got away with this, only because the six men on the finance committee were the same persons who examined the half-yearly accounts and, not surprisingly, always found them acceptable. Like most successful petty thieves, the men with their hands in the till became greedy. Ogle was particularly outraged that on February 4, 1824, the Committee of Six had met and "after most serious consideration," recommended that the Grand Lodge form a "house" in Dublin "to be conducted upon similar principles with those of other public establishments in this city." On those principles! Ogle thought sarcastically, means that they will be charging our Brothers for short measure on their drink and putting half the proceeds into their own pockets.

It was on Monday, August 2, 1824, that Ogle made his move. He previously had canvassed some brothers of the Grand Lodge, and a few had promised to support him in a vote, but no one was willing to speak out in debate. His chosen moment was a regular meeting of the Grand Lodge of Ireland. Ogle was fortunate that General Saunders was in the chair, for he was past grand master of County Wicklow and was favourably disposed to Gowan. Ogle stood up and, slowly at first and then with gathering speed, went through the sins of the Committee of Six, pointing out the accounts that did not add up, the absence of any external scrutiny of the books, the monopoly of important decisions by the cabal, the danger to the Order's respectability if a public house were set up by this junta, and more. Ogle recited this litany of malfeasance with four of the members of the Committee of Six present (to Ogle's regret, William McCullagh was one of the two men absent). These were men of substance within the Order and he was taking a terrible risk in moving:

> Resolved — That as some bretheren of the Grand Lodge, particularly those residing in the country, entertain sentiments of suspicion and distrust as to the regular and legitimate expenditures of the funds of this Society . . . that therefore it is highly expedient to adjourn this meeting for a month.

His plan, clearly, was to swamp the next meeting with country delegates, but if his resolution lost, he was as good as out of the Order himself. Naturally, the Committee of Six members argued vehemently against the motion and pointed out the dangers of listening to the yappings of a young pup, one barely past the age of majority. Nobody seemed in favour of Ogle's motion, and even Sir Harcourt Lees, though favouring Gowan's views, was silent.

Yet, when the decision came, Ogle won — by a single vote. He had broken the cabal, for, inevitably, when the country members came up to Dublin in a month's time, they would throw out the Committee of Six.

Ogle's courage paid off: in more ways than one. On September 13 at a massive grand lodge meeting his enemies, including the hated William McCullagh, were "everlastingly expelled" from the Society. At the same time, the Society reorganized itself nationally (doing so by the unusual tactic of dissolving and then re-creating itself in the course of a single day) and elected new national officers. Ogle Robert Gowan was named acting grand secretary of the Grand Lodge of Ireland and his mentor, Sir Harcourt Lees, one of the assistant grand chaplains.

Equally important, the Grand Lodge resolved to adopt *The Antidote* as their official organ. Recognizing the financial benefit such patronage implied, Ogle rushed off to buy new, more elegant typefaces.

"The tapestry of my life is developing wonderfully," Ogle reflected to Frances one evening. She was pleased, for existence in the flat was confining. She was willing to be a dutiful wife, but she preferred living in the country and looked forward to having a small, but tasteful country house and a household staff.

But it was then that the threads in Ogle tapestry began to unravel. The first one snapped on 18 March 1825, and that was the single most unsettling day Ogle had yet experienced; far worse than finding out that Frances was premaritally pregnant, and even worse than being served with a felony writ by the Wexford assizes.

That day, Ogle and Sir Harcourt Lees walked away from a meeting of the Grand Orange Lodge of Ireland for the last time. They went out the door with their heads down and, for once, Sir Harcourt was silent. The Grand Lodge had just dissolved itself, permanently it seemed. Only a few short months after becoming a national functionary, Ogle saw the Order disappear as a national institution.

It was an event from which he had tried to hide, but to do so was as difficult as hiding from the effect of a volcanic eruption. The great force presently unleashed was Daniel O'Connell's New Catholic Association. It side-stepped the legislation against oath-bound societies and enrolled literally millions of Catholics in a society whose members pledged themselves (but not by oath), to obtain the right for Catholics to sit in Parliament, and, ultimately, to open the way for Catholics to acquire real power over government. In a quixotic attempt to control this New Catholic Association, Henry Goulbourn, the Chief Secretary for Ireland, gave notice in early February 1825 that he would bring in a bill to prohibit all political societies in Ireland that had a duration of more than fourteen days.

Anyone who paid the slightest attention to Irish events knew that this spelled doom for the Orange Order, because the administration's long-standing "impartiality" policy meant that there would have to be a Protestant sacrifice to balance the Catholic one. Ogle, whistling as he approached the Order's graveyard, told his *Antidote* readers on February 12, 1825, that "some people have absurdly imagined that the proposed bill will have the effect of extinguishing ALL associations whatever, and that Orangeism, in particular, will be levelled to the dust by it, but we have no hesitation in pronouncing such an opinion to be quite erroneous." Two weeks later Ogle printed, without comment, Goulbourn's bill: Orangeism would be banned. Ironically, Goulbourn's legislation yielded one of the few instances of the Order and the Catholic Association agreeing on anything: O'Connell went to London to lobby against the bill and so did prominent Orangemen. Neither effort had any effect and on March 9 the measure received the royal assent. On March 19, 1825, the Orange Order and the Catholic Association, tied together to the bitter end, each dissolved itself.

As Ogle and Sir Harcourt walked out into Dawson Street after that last meeting, they had the melancholy satisfaction of knowing that they had been loyal to the very end. In fact, before dissolving, the Grand Lodge had sent a message to the Brethren throughout Ireland, an address tinged more with the language of sadness than of embitterment, asking them to keep the faith in the Constitution and in the Principles of the Order, even if that body formally had ceased to exist. Virtually the last thing the Grand Lodge did was to thank its officers, and especially Brother Gowan, for drawing up the final address to the Brethren. Ogle had stayed at his post to the end.

The late afternoon air was damp and Sir Harocurt and Ogle were chilled, but neither suggested going to an inn or tavern. They walked, coat-fronts held tightly to their chests, towards St. Stephen's Green and silent, driven, they walked around the paling-protected square two, three, four times. Sir Harcourt pointedly did not doff his hat to the statue of King George II: at last they went towards the Suffolk Street office of *The Antidote*, where Sir Harcourt left Ogle with a sentence that, for him, was singularly to the point.

"Young Gowan, we must do *something*."

However strong his constitutional and loyalist ideals, Ogle's first action was characteristically practical. The *Antidote* of March 19, 1825 carried this notice: "After this day, no Paper leaves our Office which is not paid for in advance; this rule extends to every person without exception, who may be in arrears to our establishment, and this notification is final and conclusive." Ogle had immediately recognized that, with no Orange Order to act as patron to his paper, he would have to collect accounts assiduously if he wanted to stay in business.

Gowan's next piece of self-protection was to put himself in

contact with the main functionary of the Grand Orange Lodge of England. The English lodge was not affected by the legislation banning the Irish lodges. Formed in 1808, the English Order differed from the Irish in being formally organized as a benevolent society, that is, as a philanthropic and mutual insurance society. It was not an oath-bound or political agency, although in practice its members strongly supported Protestant causes. Centred in Manchester, it was financed by new money from the rising industrial *élite*: not gentry, but respectable.

Ogle had always been good at attracting patrons and even before he had come to know Sir Harcourt Lees, he had cultivated a respectful friendship with Eustace Chetwoode, the secretary and main permanent officer of the English lodges. So, Ogle's first-born was named Nassau Chetwoode (variation: Chetwood) Gowan, and his second, Harcourt Potter Gowan.

With no difficulty, therefore, on December 1, 1825, Ogle was made a member of the "Britannic Institution," and was given the right to confer membership upon others. For the moment, Gowan did not exercise his authority to create lodges under the English Order.

In establishing this English link, Ogle was simply hedging his bets, making certain that he had some kind of Orange connection in his life. But Sir Harcourt Lees's question to him was this: "Why, young Gowan, why join the English Order, when you and I might instead guard the sacred flame of Irish Orangeism by ourselves founding a new Order in Ireland?"

Ogle recognized immediately where a path of opportunity lay and even while making application to join the English Order, he worked closely with Sir Harcourt on the Orange resurrection project. Their joint view was that the old Irish Order had been abolished because it was perceived as dangerous by government officials. Sir Harcourt stated that their new Order should be so respectable that a dowager duchess could sift its membership without soiling her white gloves. And respectable it certainly was. The "Benevolent and Religious Orange Institution," founded on December 13, 1825, had as president and vice-president (that is, as front-men), respectively the Earl of Aldborough and Viscount Montmorris. Ogle and Sir Harcourt, of course, were the working forces. The society's patron was the Duke of Gordon and Sir Harcourt assumed the title of "vice-patron," with an address of

"Blackrock and Essexford." Ogle, as secretary of the new Institution claimed a new address, "Annesley Lodge, and *Antidote* office."

The new Orange Institution was polite to the point of being delicate. "The intention of the Society," its rules stated, "is to protect and educate (in the principles of the Protestant religion) destitute and deserted orphans and to print and circulate such publications as tend to inculcate the principles of the Protestant religion." And, to make certain that government officials recognized that this was solely a benevolent and philanthropic religious body, the rules clearly stated that, "the society shall never be connected with any object merely political." In joining this society, the noble patrons of the effort subscribed £10 and young Ogle, emphasizing his own gentility, subscribed £5.

Wonderfully respectable, clearly benevolent, this new less contumacious form of Orangeism can only have pleased the government. The trouble was that old-time Orangemen were not pleased. The Wexford hunting men, who remembered their fathers' chasing Croppies like foxes, compared the new institution to a three-legged gelding; the red-faced country gentry of west Munster said the new Order was of no more use than a fifth teat on a cow; and Protestant small farmers, in the mixed districts of Armagh, Tyrone, and Fermanagh stuck to their old lodges, illegal though those now were. In the Presbyterian communities of Antrim and Down, the old adherents turned away when canvassed for membership. The former leading names of the Orange movement, Verner, Blacker, Archdall, gave no support. Therefore, Ogle and Sir Harcourt were each forced to go on missionary tours, beating the provinces for members.

On these tours, Ogle had two separate routines, one styled for the south of Ireland, the other for the north. In the south, he would call on the leading gentlemen in each locale and he would, alternately, act the clear-eyed idealist and the name-dropper. Despite his being at daggers-drawn with his legitimate sisters and brothers, he would use their names without hesitation: Anne was married to a barrister-at-law; Elizabeth had first married a major in the royal artillery, but, poor dear, had been widowed, and was now the wife of a respectable Dublin attorney. Catherine, first married to a Sligo gentleman and also widowed had, as her second husband the Honourable John Fleming, third son and heir of Christopher, Lord Slane. A fine and noble man, Ogle was proud to say. Even Ogle's late brother, John, was put to use. With apparent sadness, he dropped the information that John had served at Waterloo and died, unmarried, a brave and solitary man to the very end.

This sort of line went down well with the Ascendancy gentry, and he frequently gained their adhesion to the institution in the south. But in the north it did not work, and Gowan, ever adaptable, quickly learned how different were the rules of northern life. Ogle found that in the north there were thousands and thousands of poor Protestant families, and the men who headed them thought differently from the southern Irish poor. In north-central Ireland — especially in County Armagh, where the Orange Order had been founded in 1797 — most of the Protestants were of English descent, Anglican by religion, and small farmers by occupation. Farther north, in Antrim and Down, the descendants of lowland Scots predominated. They were Presbyterian by religion and also mostly small farmers, who had no pretentions to gentility. Although they usually followed the political and social leadership of the local aristocracy and gentry, they did so with a cranky individuality that scared their betters. The upper classes in the north always had a background fear that unless they kept their Protestant tenants happy, some day these people would unite with their Roman Catholic counterparts and dismantle the whole social order. Gowan soon learned that to talk to these tough small farmers of the latest turf news, or of Lord Wellesley's foppishness, or of his own family connections, was no use at all. If they marched, it was to their own drummer, or not at all.

Ogle had no luck in recruiting such people to the Benevolent Orange Order, and, indeed, he hardly tried. But he did learn a lot about people and to great eventual effect — in the 1830s, many of the Irish migrants to Upper Canada were people from the small farms of this hard northern world.

Late in 1825 another part of Ogle's life threatened to come unravelled. As Hunter Gowan had become ever-frailer during the winter of 1823-1824, the heirs had closed in, each a jackal wanting its share of the prize and, inevitably, some of the heirs were dissatisfied with their portion. But there was more to the matter than that: William Gowan, the eldest illegitimate male, claimed to possess a deed to the Ashwood Estate that was executed by Hunter Gowan, and which took precedence over Hunter's last will and testament. So, when on October 14, 1824, Robert and Mary Hopkins (*née* Gowan) filed a suit in Chancery against all of the other Gowan heirs and seeking to gain possession of the Ashwood property, they were engaged in a complex double manoeuvre, designed not only to discredit the alleged deed to Ashwood but to force William out of the premises. Technically, for Chancery to consider the matter, they had to file a suit against the whole will and all the other heirs, but as the case developed it became clear that this was another repetition of the fundamental Gowan family war, the legitimate versus the illegitimate.

The Irish High Court of Chancery sent to County Wexford a one-man commission in the person of Stevens Goff. His task was to examine, under oath, people who were familiar with Hunter Gowan's last days and, eventually, to allow the High Court of Chancery to decide if further legal action were required. Then, as now, the ways of Chancery were not swift and Commissioner Goff plodded forward, day-by-day, throughout December 1825 and January 1826. The pace was slow, but the investigation was wonderfully revealing, and as the context of Hunter Gowan's will and the codicils of May 1824 became clear, the family's brutishness towards the old man was revealed, and the fact that there had been some skulduggery with the title to the Ashwood estate easily was inferred.

The depositions were taken in the only decent inn in Gorey, one belonging to the agriculturally eponymous Richard Furlong. Commissioner Goff sat at a long deal table that was placed, as near as was safe, to the large hearth. A scribner sat at the end of the table, taking notes that he later turned into a fair-copy transcript. In December, the weather was either grey, raining, or, occasionally, snowing, and nobody enjoyed having to travel to Gorey to testify. The procedure was formal, but there was no cross-examination and Commissioner Goff frequently interrupted deliberations to permit the landlord's wife to use the hearth for domestic purposes. Spectators were permitted, but no lawyers were involved, except Robert Hopkins, who attended all of the sessions to protect his own and his wife's interests.

The first witness of consequence was the only one who, during the course of the hearings, arrived in a coach: the Right Honourable James George, Earl of Courtown. He was sixty years old, corpulent, and not terribly bright.

"Did you, my Lord, know well the late Hunter Gowan?" This

was the standard query with which Commissioner Goff greeted each deponent.

He did know him indeed and a fine gentleman was the late Hunter Gowan.

"To your knowledge, did Hunter Gowan ever complain on any occasion of misconduct, ill-treatment, or violence shown to him by his eldest son Thomas Gowan or any of his other children?" This was another of the commissioner's standard interrogatories.

The Earl, after asking for a clarification of what "to your knowledge," meant in law, said no, he had not heard of that.

"Never?"

Well, the Earl recalled that, damnme yes, he did now remember one rumour of ill-treatment of old Hunter by his legitimate children.

"Of what sort?"

His lordship could not remember exactly; just that they were abusing the old man in some way. He was not sure if it was verbal or physical.

The commissioner changed tacks. "Did you ever hear of frequent disputes amounting to actual violence between the legitimate children on one side and the late Hunter Gowan and his illegitimate children, William Gowan and Ogle Robert Gowan, on the other?"

Yes, his lordship had.

"And did you form an opinion as to whether or not those reports were accurate?"

No, the Earl had not. He had no opinion.

"Concerning, now, William Gowan: do you know if he were attentive and especially dutiful to his late father?"

His lordship replied that he had no direct information and, therefore, no belief, but that he had heard that William was a great favourite with the late Hunter Gowan. Growing visibly impatient, he then asked how long the questioning would continue, as he had a steward to interview about arrears in rents.

Commissioner Goff still had some queries. "When was the last time you saw the late Hunter Gowan?"

The Earl explained that it was in March 1824 and that he had gone to Mount Nebo at the request of the legitimate children. There had been a falling out over the winter between them and their father, and he wished to effect a reconciliation.

"Was this achieved?"

Alas, no. The most that could be gained was a declaration from Hunter Gowan that his forgiveness should depend on future good behaviour, especially that of his son Thomas, the senior heir.

"Was there any talk of a will?"

Yes, the Earl recalled. Hunter had said that he had made a will, but that he would alter it when the time was appropriate.

"Does this mean that Hunter Gowan was cutting off his legitimate children from their inheritance?" The Commissioner now was near the heart of the matter.

According to the Earl of Courtown, the answer was no, for Hunter had said to him that he would not alienate his landed property from his legitimate spawn. Perhaps, suggested the Earl, he meant only to cut back the monetary provision for his legitimate children. One never knew.

"And, finally, did Hunter Gowan admit that he had executed a deed or instrument conveying part of his property to his bastard son, Ogle Gowan?"

Hunter Gowan had absolutely denied doing so.

"And, with your lordship's indulgence, one more question: to your knowledge did the legitimate children of Hunter threaten the life of Hunter Gowan and of Ogle Robert Gowan, in the belief that the late Mr. Gowan had executed a deed in Ogle's favour?

No, his lordship had no knowledge of this ever having occurred. His lordship was pleased to step down and proceed about his business.

In dealing with other witnesses, Commissoner Goff used the same mixture of standard interrogatories and spontaneous follow-up questions that he had employed in taking the Earl of Courtown's evidence. Although this was not a very imaginative format, it yielded some surprising results. For instance, one friend of the late Hunter Gowan, a gentleman named George Smith, swore to having known him for thirty-four years or more. When asked about disagreements in the Gowan household he reported, "Yes, disagreements indeed, from post to pillar," He waved a hand expansively and explained. "The worst was about the month of December 1823. Then Hunter complained to me that Thomas Gowan had brought the law into the house to take Ogle Gowan, his half-brother, to gaol. It was about the stealing of a silver cup. Hunter was very disturbed. Furious. He could not speak the name of Thomas without adding a curse."

When asked about possible mistreatment of Hunter by his legitimate children, the same witness replied, "Many years ago now, I don't mind how many, the late gentlemen told me in all confidence that they behaved ill towards him."

Why was this: he was asked.

"On account of the children of the late Frances Gowan — I mean the legitimate children — believing that their father now was acting badly. He was keeping in his house against their wishes Miss Margaret Hogan. A slut they said. They claimed also that Miss Hogan mistreated them."

Had he formed any opinion of the justice of this complaint?"

"No, for she went away after that."

This information surprised Commissioner Goff and even his clerk, a keen little chap by the name of Morrisey, looked up with interest. Goff wanted to be sure of this point and asked, did the witness mean that Miss Hogan, the mother of the illegitimate children William and Ogle Gowan had disappeared?

"Yes, indeed. Hunter Gowan had her sent away. He found that she was pregnant by another man!"

Immediate silence. The landlord's wife, who had been about to enter the room to tend the fire, froze in the doorway. Robert Hopkins, chief litigant, smiled. Commissioner Goff cleared his throat and resumed questioning. For half an hour he asked George Smith, Esq. his standard interrogatories and Smith swore to three revealing facts: that some years ago Hunter Gowan had got into a scuffle with his son George, while trying to throw George out of the house; that Margaret Hogan had tried to induce Hunter Gowan to sell some of his land, and to use the money to benefit her and her illegitimate children; and that right up until his death, Hunter had complained about his legitimate children having abused him verbally, chiefly for his permitting Margaret Hogan in the house.

Unlike a trial, the intention of this hearing was to collect as much hearsay as possible, and, among other things, that material tells us a lot about what the local gentry thought of the Gowans. Take, for example, the testimony of John Christopher Beauman, gentleman, of Hyde Park, County Wexford, a man of sixty years of age, who had known Hunter Gowan since he was himself twenty years old. Like Hunter, Beauman was a former magistrate and a strong Protestant. He was also a prodigious snuff-dipper, which habit made his deposition somewhat inefficient.

"Did you ever hear of any violence towards the late Hunter Gowan by any of his children?" That question had been asked by Commissioner Goff so frequently in the course of the case that Morrisey, the scribner, had his own shorthand abbreviation for it.

"Yes, yes indeed." Mr. Beauman took a large pinch of snuff and stuffed it directly up one nostril. "A short time before his death he complained to me of violence against him and ill-treatment. Especially by Thomas Gowan. But Hunter mentioned the other children of his late wife, Frances, as well."

"Is this violence and mistreatment well known in the district?"

"District?" The witness sneezed forcefully. "You mean in County Wexford, around Gorey and the like?"

"Quite."

"It was known, aye it was, I would say that everyone hereabouts, from mud cabin to castle, knew about it. And talked of it. Oh, aye, talked of it a great deal." This information delivered, Mr. Beauman busied himself removing flakes of rough-cut snuff from his clothes, for his sneezing had deposited detritus about his person.

"On a related point, sir, have you ever heard that the late Mr. Gowan and his two illegitimate sons, William and Ogle, had actual violence, almost a faction fight, against the children of the late Mrs. Frances Gowan? The query was awkwardly framed and Commissioner Goff was momentarily embarrassed. He was about to rephrase the question, but the witness nodded to indicate that he understood what was meant.

"Quite certainly, yes. It was well known in the neighbourhood that old Hunter Gowan and his two bastard cubs had come to blows with the others. Quite a man that old Hunter and . . . ."

"Yes, yes," interrupted the commissioner, not wanting to be lost in reverie for the late reprobate. "Do you, sir, believe those stories to be true?"

"No doubt whatsoever. Hunter Gowan told me so himself. True as God."

After asking several standard queries, Commissioner Goff came to a matter that had begun to run through the testimony of several witnesses, like a counter-theme in a chorale. "Have you ever heard, sir, that the late Hunter Gowan had executed a deed of real property to one of his natural children?"

Before answering, Mr. Beauman took another pinch of snuff.

Commissioner Goff momentarily flinched, for he expected another explosion. This did not happen, chiefly because the witness scattered half of the huge pinch onto his waistcoat. The gentleman sat back. "I did hear that, sir, and it caused me great concern. It was so rumoured in the neighbourhood. That bothered me, sir, because as a gentleman, I believe that landed property should never be alienated from the legitimate line."

Goff was about to probe further, but this was unnecessary, for Beauman had something on his mind and a set of duelling pistols aimed at his head would not have stopped him now.

"Thus, I visited Hunter Gowan. It was within two months of his death. He was an old friend and, therefore, sir, I asked him outright. 'Hunter, is it true that you have made over some of your lands to one of Margaret Hogan's children?' "

"What lands did you mean?" Commissioner Goff interrupted and then cursed himself for being impetuous.

"The Ashwood estate, of course, man! Any dunderhead knows that the only lands Hunter Gowan could alienate in perpetuity would be his freehold estate — because that was the only freehold he had. Mount Nebo is held on a lease-for-lives, nothing more."

"My apologies for the interruption, sir. Pray continue."

Mollified, Beauman continued. "Hunter replied to me outright, 'Damnme, but I have never done such a thing and never intend to leave them an acre.' Those were his very words, true as I am sitting here."

That satisfied the Commissioner and he closed the day's proceedings.

Among the subsequent witnesses, one Thomas Attiwell Moore, an Established Church cleric, gave some insight — doubtlessly more than he intended — into the pressures placed on Hunter Gowan in the month of May 1824. At that time, he was lying abed, dying, and then his legitimate children, having heard the rumours that the bastard line was to be well-cared for, brought all their resources into play.

"You are, Mr. Moore, the clergyman of the late Hunter Gowan's parish?"

"No, I am not." The Reverend Mr. Moore was about forty-five years of age, cadaverous, and, having arrived in a heavy downpour, soaking wet. When he shifted about in his chair, water squished from his clothes. "I am not the incumbent of the parish, but was for a time the late Mr. Gowan's minister. In fact, I am a longtime friend of Mr. Thomas Gowan." The landlord's wife kindly interrupted to give a mug of hot punch to the clergyman. "Not too strong, eh madame, I hope, ha ha," suggested Mr. Moore, in an awkward attempt at bonhommie.

"Continue please."

"Oh, yes; I was just about to say that I am very well acquainted, not only with Thomas Gowan, but with two other sons as well, George and Hunter Gowan."

"Might I take it, sir, that you wished to promote their interests?" Commissioner Goff's voice held the touch of a sneer. Like most Chancery lawyers, he viewed clergymen as incompetent rivals in the making of arrangements for a man's passing from this world to the next.

"Well, yes. Quite. Yes, yes." The wraithlike minister was becoming discomfited. He twisted about in his chair. "But by fair means, mind you. Yes, by fair means. And in concern with the principles of True Christianity."

"Of course," Goff agreed dryly and then led the clergyman through several of his standard questions. These yielded little, but then he struck a vein: he learned that on May 3, 1824, the Reverend Mr. Moore had visited the dying Hunter Gowan.

"What was the occasion of your visit?"

"As a friend and as an old parish minister. I was anxious for his salvation."

"Naturally. But thereafter did you speak of things temporal?"

"Well . . . yes. We talked of his leaving his worldly goods and of their proper distribution." The cleric was reluctant to go further.

"Was it your idea or that of the late Mr. Gowan, to talk of his last will and testament?"

"Well . . . . "

"Well?" The Commissioner's voice hardened.

"I really cannot say. Memory escapes me." The Anglican minister was becoming visibly pale.

"Did the children of the late Mr. Gowan — Thomas, Hunter, George, or any of the daughters — ask you to bring up the topic with their father?"

"Sir, I do not remember." He paused. "Honestly." The commissioner gazed at him sternly and this unnerved him. "I do now remember, though, sir, that I had heard that the late Mr. Gowan had drawn up a will some little time previously that was not in favour of his rightful and legitimate children."

Here Commissioner Goff introduced a surprise question. It was one that he had framed after collecting some gossip from the landlord of the inn, a technically unprofessional, but very effective means of proceeding.

"Is it not true, Mr. Moore, that you threatened the late Hunter Gowan with eternal punishment should he die without making a will leaving his property to his legitimate children?"

The Reverend Mr. Moore gasped and trembled visibly. "No, no it is not!" His voice was reedy.

"And is it not true, Mr. Moore, that you refused to administer the sacrament of Holy Communion to the dying man until he had made such a will?"

"No, please, no."

Cannily, Commissioner Goff said nothing for a time and the weight of the silence seemed to crush in on the miserable parson. "I only gave an expression of opinion to his daughter, Mrs. Harriet Quinlan, who was in the house, waiting on her father . . . "

Waiting on his death, thought Goff sourly.

" . . . waiting on her father's needs, that it was inconsistent with her father's professions of repentance to leave the children born in fornication better off than his children born in Holy Wedlock, a state instituted by God himself."

"This was on the third of May?"

"Yes, to the best of my memory."

The Commissioner leaned forward. "And what, reverend sir, would you infer from your having seen the late Hunter Gowan on the third of May, and his having a new last will and testament favouring the children of 'Holy Wedlock,' as you put it, on the fourth of May?"

"That he, Hunter Gowan, had considered his position before Almighty God and had chosen to follow his Holy Ways!" Now that he was on religious matters, the clergyman was becoming more confident. Commissioner Goff looked over at his scribner and rolled his eyes: the legal profession has different standards of cause-and-effect than does the religious.

"Did you, Mr. Moore, have any occasion to return to Mount Nebo after that day?"

"Yes, I came a second time. A week before the poor man's soul went to be with his Maker."

"You and he were alone?"

"Mrs. Harriet Quinlan, his dutiful daughter, was present."

"Did you at that time talk of Mr. Gowan's last will?"

"Indeed. But not at my instigation. Temporal affairs are not the proper concern of a clergyman of the Established Church." The Reverend Mr. Moore was becoming slightly expansive. His clothes had partly dried out and now he was coming to resemble a thin, but pluming, weasel. "Mrs. Quinlan took the opportunity, quite properly, as a dutiful daughter, to mention in her father's presence, his having left in his last will — the one of the fourth of May to which you, sir, have alluded — a sum of £100 a year, in perpetuity, to William."

"You did not, I assume, bring any pressure to bear on the late Mr. Gowan?"

Commissioner Goff's sarcasm was lost on the parson. "I merely observed to Mrs. Quinlan, in Mr. Hunter Gowan's presence, that I hoped that Mr. Gowan had not done so, for though it was his bounden duty to make provision for his illegitimate children, they being the innocent offspring of a Guilty Commerce; yet that it would be inconsistent with those sentiments of repentance which he had solemnly expressed to me . . . "

Repentance. Commissioner Goff wrote that word in his personal notes and then scribbled an additional phrase: dying old man broken by the parson.

" . . . expressed to me to manifest so decided a preference for his children born in fornication, as to leave them better off in the world than those born in Holy Wedlock."

Listening to this, Commissioner Goff began to look as though he wanted to spit something nasty from his mouth, but was precluded by good manners from doing so. Instead, in a soft voice, each word carefully formed, he suggested: "And Mr. Moore, would I be correct in inferring that when one notes that in reducing the value of the inheritance given to his son, William, that he had, as you express it, once again considered his position before Almighty God and chosen to follow further his Holy Ways?" He gave the last two words an ironic emphasis.

"Quite, sir. The Lord works in Mysterious Ways, his Wonders to Reveal."

At that point, Commissioner Goff considered briefly adjourning the hearing for the purpose of refreshing his memory of the law of justifiable homicide. He denied himself that pleasure and pressed on to one last topic. "Were you, reverend sir, present when the last will and testament of Hunter Gowan was first read after his decease?"

"Yes, I was. As a Spiritual Advisor to the family."

"Who was present?"

"Thomas Gowan, George Gowan, Hunter Gowan, William Gowan, Ogle Gowan and, I believe, four of the daughters and one grand-daughter."

"Did anything singular occur at that time?"

"Most unfortunately. Yes. Quite unseemly. The last will and testament and its codicil were read. Manifestly, the late Hunter Gowan had decided to distribute his goods as befitted a Christian Gentleman. The unfortunate instance, however, was that Mr. William Gowan declared that the will was invalid. He claimed that he was entitled to the freehold lands of Ashwood under a deed executed to him by his father."

"This was William Gowan, not Ogle?"

"Correct. And as a Christian Minister, I exhorted William Gowan not to press the matter to litigation but to be content with the provision made for him in the last codicil. I suggested to the misled and bastard-born young man that it was much more than under the circumstance he could possibly have expected."

That ended the Reverend Mr. Moore's testimony. None of the other witnesses that Goff interviewed in his month-long inquiry rivalled the Reverend Mr. Moore in unctuousness. Most merely confirmed that the Gowan *ménage* had been in turmoil.

One last witness, left an etching of old Hunter Gowan as a lion in winter.

That witness was Stephen Redmond, a tailor of the town of Gorey. He had done business with the late Hunter Gowan for twenty years and, in his presence, Mr. Gowan had complained of violence done to him by his son Thomas Gowan. The telling point, though, comes from the tailor's often having made clothes for Hunter Gowan and his family, including William and Ogle.

On various occasions the tailor purchased cloth for suitings from local shops. "I was asked by his honour, the late Hunter Gowan himself, to keep it a secret when I made clothes for either

William or Ogle. He would pay for his sons' clothes, but he wanted it kept a secret."

"When he gave you these directions, did Hunter Gowan ever explain to you for what purposes he wished it kept a secret?"

"No sir, never. But I believe he was afraid."

CHAPTER 6

Family Pride 1826-1829

THE HIGH Court of Chancery took ten months to consider the evidence and in a Lord Chancellor's decision of December 1, 1826, determined that Ashwood would go to the Hopkinses, but that William would receive £50 a year in perpetuity from its revenues. What their Lordship's reasoning was is not known, but the seeming import of the decision was that neither of the two illegitimate brothers, William and Ogle, had acquired any real landed property from their father; yet, at least they walked out of the Chancery inquisition with their names much less besmirched than had those of the legitimate line who, clearly, had been cruel and venal as the Doges in dealing with their dying father.

The Chancery ruling should have put an end to the Gowan family squabbling about their father's will. Except . . . except . . . except that William kept asserting his right of possession to Ashwood by virtue of his having a deed from his father. Despite the Chancery ruling, he could not be dispossessed of the estate — of which he had taken possession — until an assize or higher court met and ruled, not only on the validity of the last will (which Chancery just had done), but on the validity of the alleged deed. So, the Hopkinses sued again, and in this final trial, the last bit of secrecy surrounding the Gowan family was stripped away and the maggot within the kernel became clearly visible.

This final trial took place in the Wexford courthouse on March 14 and 15, 1827, as part of the spring assizes for the County of

Wexford. Not far from the spot where, in 1798, Hunter Gowan had enjoyed viewing the heads of his enemies, his offspring now destroyed the family name.

As conducted, the case deserved no prizes for juridicial elegance — but then few Irish trials of the time did. The Irish bar was full of men of wit and character, for it was one of the few paths up the social ladder for an ambitious young man, Catholic or Protestant. But the bench usually was occupied by political appointees, men inevitably Protestant and almost always Tory, and often as learned in Law as a side of beef. One recalls, for instance, the "cruel buffoon" (as Sean O'Faolain denominates him), Justice Lord Norbury, who was known as the Hanging Judge. His wittiest moment in life came when he sentenced to death a man who had stolen a watch. "Ha ha!" he chortled. "You made a grab at time, but you caught eternity!" The man who conducted the Gowan trial, the Honourable Judge Burton, was not quite so bad a judge, but he was no Solomon and he had the unfortunate habit of making comments about the participants *sotto voce*, so that those near him were treated to a running commentary on the case.

Because of the importance of the case — formally known as Hopkins vs. Gowan — Judge Burton empanelled a special jury, a procedure unusual at assizes where the pre-existent grand jury usually was employed for trial work. The jury comprised twelve men, all Protestants, and there were four counsel for the plaintiff (Robert Hopkins) and four for the defense (William and Ogle Gowan). The lawyers were in gowns and wigs, as was the judge.

Senior Counsel for the plaintiff, Mr. Scott, of the firm Scott, Dixon, Hatchell and Hamilton, stated the case. "This is an action in which Robert Hopkins desires an ejectment from the lands of Ashwood, to which he justly holds title, of William Gowan. This case, my Lord, grew out of an equity case previously tried in Chancery and the Lord Chancellor has directed that Robert Hopkins should be the plaintiff."

Judge Burton nodded. This much he knew already.

Mr. Scott turned to the jurors. "Gentlemen, you are to say whether a certain deed of the fifteenth of March 1824 was duly executed by the said testator, the late Hunter Gowan, or not. That is the sole question. I admit that property is at stake and I also admit that it affects deeply the character of some of the parties concerned in this case. Whatever the difficulties of the case may be, I hear state that . . . " Mr. Scott took a deep breath and whirled balletically in a half circle, looking momentarily at each juror, " . . . I here state that — THAT DEED IS A GROSS AND INFAMOUS FABRICATION AND FORGERY AND THAT THOSE WHO COME FORWARD TO SWEAR TO ITS EXECUTION COMMIT PERJURY WHEN THEY SO SWEAR!!" Counsel now adopted a quieter tone. "I must say that one of the witnesses to be produced on behalf of the plaintiff comes before you with suspicion. He is one of the witnesses to that deed, but has since repented of his conduct and . . . "

"Sounds like a rogue to me," said Judge Barton under his breath.

" . . . And, he insists that now, having seen the light, he cannot swear to his previous falsehood."

Counsellor Scott now summarized the state of the Hunter Gowan family: that there had been two branches, one legitimate, the other formed by an illicit connection after the death of his wife. "Gentlemen, their jealousies and irritations increased till December 1823. At that time Ogle Robert Gowan procured a Mr. Fearn, a respectable attorney in Dublin, to make over a deed to the lands of Ashwood to his brother William. This deed, Mr. Fearn left with one George Perkins Bull, for Ogle Gowan to pick up. Mr. Bull was printer of a paper in Dublin at that period, *The Antidote.* Mr. Bull read the deed and gave it to Mr. Ogle Gowan." Counsellor Scott again paused to look at each jury member; two of them were already asleep. "Next, Mr. Thomas Gowan happened to be in Dublin and he called in on Mr. Bull, with whom he was acquainted, and Mr. Bull told him of the deed and what was contained in it. Mr. Thomas Gowan asked Mr. Bull if he would swear to the truth of this and Mr. Bull agreed, a courageous act as he had business dealings with Ogle Gowan.

"'And now, gentlemen, let me mention one more wonderous scene. Shortly before Hunter Gowan died, the Reverend Mr. Medlicott sat down with the late gentleman to draw up a codicil to the will. Mr. Medlicott asked all family members — they had been attending their father — to leave the room. But one person remained behind, concealed under a blanket on the floor!! The maid servant gave a hint of this to Mr. Medlicott and he told Hunter Gowan, who ordered the person out. The person concealed was either Ogle Gowan or William Gowan: Mr. Medlicott was too scrupulous a person to look — he turned away so as not to see who it was." (At the mention of clerical scruples, Mr. Justice Burton smiled broadly and seemed on the verge of laughter.)

The jury could follow this argument easily enough — William and Ogle Gowan were being depicted as knaves — but they were becoming restive. Mr. Scott recognized the signs: Irish juries expected a bit of entertainment at frequent intervals, and the counsellor hastened to oblige them. "This codicil to the will was drawn on May 22, 1824, and when Ogle and William Gowan heard of it they entered into a conspiracy. They induced a man named Burland to help them. He was a respectable person up to this period, and a permanent sergeant in the Wingfield Yeomanry, the corps that Mr. Gowan had formed. An intimate of the family as well, so his character would give weight to the transaction. The two brothers, Ogle and William, went to Burland and told him that he must endeavour to draw up a will in their favour! They would simply amend a draft will of Hunter Gowan's that they had obtained. As Burland was a good penman, he was induced to engross it. Gentlemen, we will produce the draft of the fabricated will and show several amendments in the handwriting of Ogle Gowan!!!"

Cries of "Aha!" came from the gallery, and Judge Burton banged his gavel several times, which he loved doing. He hoped there would be more outbursts so he could hammer away some more.

Counsellor Scott was pleased with the effect of his revelations. "And, oh yes, gentlemen: these so-called witnesses all belong to what is called an Orange society. The members of this society are pledged to assist each other on all occasions."

Counsellor Scott concluded the case for the plaintiff by introducing into the evidence fourteen documents and letters, written by William and Ogle Gowan to John Burland and to each other. This strongly implied, although did not directly prove, the existence of a conspiracy.

It was nearing five o'clock in the afternoon when Mr. Scott finished his long opening statement, and traditionally, the Wexford assizes adjourned at eight o'clock in the evening. Scott went swiftly through nine witnesses in the three hours that remained to him: each of them cast more dirt upon the names of William and Ogle Gowan.

News spread overnight through County Wexford that the Gowan case was more entertaining than a travelling melodrama, and when the assize opened at nine the next morning the courtroom was crowded almost to the point of suffocation. The entire Gowan tribe was there, both branches, and so were their respective spouses. The Gowan men looked through each other without even a nod; the women glared fiercely at their opposite numbers.

Just after Mr. Justice Burton took the bench, with exquisite timing another person entered the courtroom. He came through the public entrance at the rear, and immediately a path through the crowd opened for him. Half of the spectators seemed to loath him, half to adore. It was Daniel O'Connell, undoubtedly the most successful attorney-at-law in Ireland. He had been down to Ennis, County Clare, and had some time to pass before an engagement in Limerick. O'Connell could always find time for a bit of good entertainment.

Naturally, none of the Gowans were pleased to provide a spectacle for this man and Ogle, the youngest and most short-tempered of the lot, flushed with anger. His discomfiture was the more intense because one of O'Connell's Catholic admirers, with a great flourish, had relinquished to him a seat in court next to Ogle's wife, Frances, who was once again pregnant. Thus, every time Ogle looked over from the principals' bench towards his Rubenesque wife, he encountered the leonine head of O'Connell, massive and utterly confident.

Mr. Justice Burton, though not a admirer of O'Connell, was pleased that the Liberator's entrance had disturbed the court as it gave him a chance to bang his gavel more than usual. He glared with synthetic menace at O'Connell and gavelled happily away. The court clerk permitted himself a rare smile. It was good to see the judge in a buoyant mood.

The day's first witness, John Burland, Orangeman and permanent sergeant in Hunter Gowan's old yeomanry unit, was quickly in deep trouble: he stood in danger of being accused of conspiracy to commit forgery. After hard prodding by the plaintiff's attorney, Burland identified the draft will of Hunter Gowan that he had been given: it had alterations on it in the hand of Ogle Gowan. This was the document he was supposed to copy for William and Ogle Gowan, and this was the job he had funked. Why? "I was afraid that it should be perfected. The two boys were to sign it; they said that the testator could not come as he was confined to bed."

"And where did you next see Ogle Gowan?"

"In Dublin, just before he went to Newgate prison to see my brother-in-law."

Cousellor Scott had a countryman's nose for the importance of a seemingly irrelevant detail, and asked who Burland's brother-in-law was. "Why Mr. George Perkins Bull, of course. The printer. He was printer of *The Antidote* at the time. He is here today, waiting to be called." The jury immediately caught the drift: in Irish courts of the period, proof of familial relationship was virtually as good as direct proof of conspiracy. Burland continued. "Ogle abused me for not producing the new will days earlier, and then asked me to put my name to it as witness."

"Any further information?"

"Yessir. Ogle asked me at the time if the signature on the document — the name was that of his father — was it a good imitation?"

Ogle had attempted a forgery. His attorney was merciless in cross-examining Burland, but the witness stuck to his story and the lawyer was reduced to heavy sarcasm ("Now, Jack, have you any children?" "I have sons." "Sons, it is a pity that, for your breed should be lost instead of its being increased." Laughter in court). When this damaging testimony was done, Frances Gowan stood up to leave the courtroom. She was flushed and needed air. Daniel O'Connell rose courteously from his seat next to her, stepped into the aisle to allow her to pass, and bowed slightly as she did so.

Almost equally damaging was the testimony of George Perkins Bull. Bull's physiognomy resembled that of his namesake, and he had the habit of tossing his head sideways in answer to queries, as if to gore the questioner. He was an assertive, almost belligerent, witness. Clearly he felt that his occupation as a printer was *declassé*, as he twice referred to himself as the son of an "old English soldier, a captain." He had known both Thomas and Ogle Gowan and in the past had played on both sides: he worked with Ogle on *The Antidote*, but had secretly informed Thomas Gowan about Ogle's attempted forgery of December, 1823. In the spring of 1824, Bull had been in Newgate prison, where he had been lodged for being unable to pay the damages for libelling a Catholic priest. Yes, Ogle had visited him to have him witness a will in Hunter Gowan's name and, yes, he often had seen Ogle practice writing his father's signature.

There, effectively, was the Hopkins' case against Ogle and William: they had entered a conspiracy to forge a title deed to

Ashwood and to fabricate a last will and testament.

At this point, Daniel O'Connell created a mild disturbance by leaving the court room. At the door, he stopped, turned around, and the Catholic tradespeople in the audience spontaneously applauded. It was a great day for the local Catholics: they were not only watching the Ascendancy rulers of their past fall about in disgrace; today, they had seen the man who was creating Catholic Ireland's future.

The case for the defence was an attorney's nightmare. Mr. Doherty, senior counsel for William and Ogle, obviously wished that he were somewhere else. "Your lordship, I must commence by saying how much I regret that this part of the case is not to be disposed of by some person more intimately qualified by a competent knowledge of the circumstances than I." He bowed to the bench. "Unhappily, my short time of being acquainted with the case weakens my presentation ('In other words, don't-blame-me if I lose,' Judge Burton paraphrased)..." Learned counsel on the other side has taken hour after hour telling the jury that this is a highly interesting case, that this is an important case, that this is a *most* important case — but why has he taken so long? Why has he taken up so much of the valuable time of our distinguished gentlemen empanelled in this jury? ('Good idea: insult the opposing counsel and flatter the jury,' whispered the judge to his clerk) ... "The issue is very simple, whether the deed drawn up by Ogle Gowan, conveying the lands to Ashwood to William Gowan, takes precedence over the testator's will. If you find that this was not a true deed, you fix a stigma upon the character of Ogle Gowan and inflict disgrace upon this young man." Mr. Doherty here flung out his arms in a good imitation of a man being crucified.

Counsel Doherty had very little ammunition at his disposal, but he made two very shrewd tactical decisions: first, he ignored entirely the charges that Ogle had tried to forge his father's last will and testament — that charge reflected badly on Ogle's character, but was not germane to the issue at hand. And, second, he began pleading special circumstances on behalf of William and Ogle. "Your lordship must not judge of the moral character of this county by what you have heard on the last two days, for it is far from being a fair sample of our character." Counsel lowered his voice and talked slowly, almost repentantly. "I myself once was at Mount Nebo, and I have to this hour a lively sense of the great kindness and attention I there met from the late Mr. Gowan . . . He was bold, active, intelligent, fond of field sports . . . He had all the virtues of a country gentleman and he had also many of the vices mingled with them." (Several of the Gowan tribe began to stir uneasily; some of the jury nodded knowingly) . . . "He had sixteen children, and after he became a widower he took into his house a woman of bad character. It is in consequence of this unfortunate connection that all these evils have followed."

"Hear hear!" someone in the courtroom called out. Ogle and William both flushed crimson.

Doherty was on an unusual defensive tack, but he was no fool. Now he made another seemingly guileless admission. "I will grant that the conduct of the defendants, William and Ogle Gowan, were in many respects not to be justified! I will admit that there was hypocrisy and craftiness enough to disgust anyone of right feeling in their conduct." ('What can this country lawyer be up to?' wondered Judge Burton, loud enough for the jury to hear . . . .) *"But* but! you are to consider that they were bred of that parent, that woman, and that their father also was cunning and artful. I regret that I must speak this way of Hunter Gowan who is now in his grave; but I cannot forget that he taught his children a lesson by his example and that everyone of them practices it!" ('So that's the ploy,' Justice Burton noted, relieved that Doherty was not making a complex legal point).

"But compare the conduct of William and Ogle Gowan with that of the legitimate children. William Gowan always behaved well and did everything to assist his father; but Thomas Gowan was a young man of strong passions, and he and the other legitimate children exerted themselves only to oppose their father's wishes. Look at Thomas Gowan's prosecuting of his brother Ogle, against the wishes and entreaties of his father. And without evidence. Yes, Thomas said 'I will go on, I will prosecute him, that I may show to my father the rascality of his favourite child.' Could you wonder, then, that the deceased, Hunter Gowan, decided to leave his property not to the Doubting Thomas, but to the faithful line — and thence the deed to Ashwood was drawn" ('But of course that deed was a forgery,' noted the judge so loudly that he had to tell his clerk that it was not part of the official record).

And, then having made these arguments for the record, Mr. Doherty showed that he was a very savvy lawyer indeed: he threw the case, but did it in such a way as to keep Ogle and William out of prison. He ignored the virtually irrefutable evidence that the deed to Ashwood was a forgery, but instead admitted to its being invalid on other grounds, "Mr. Gowan began to consider whether or not he had gone further than the strict justice of the case required, in leaving Ashwood to his illegitimate line and therefore extracted a promise that the deed would be destroyed. William and Ogle Gowan broke that promise! I will admit that they violated the promise made to their father relative to the deed! and that they acted most fraudulently on that occasion!! They affected to destroy the deed, but actually contrived to burn only its envelope or cover in the fire. This they did and they will never profit one shilling by it!"

Doherty had much more to say, but that was what counted: he was willing to admit that the deed to Ashwood was inoperative, but *not* because it was a forgery; rather, because a verbal contract to destroy it had been made between Hunter Gowan and his two illegitimate sons.

This was a *de facto* bid for a plea-bargain. The legitimate line would get Ashwood, but the natural sons would not be prosecuted for forgery.

And that is the way the trial eventually ended. It wound down with Ogle and his brother William each being successful witnesses on his own behalf, in that they did not incriminate themselves in any felony. There was some mirth when plaintiff's counsel suggested that Ogle once had been an apprentice shoemaker, and some smirking when it was noted that William Gowan for a time was reduced to living in the house of a shopkeeper in Carnew; the court also heard that the mother of Mrs. Ogle Gowan was also Ogle's half-sister. None of this was germane to the proceedings, but it was nasty, effective, and it soiled.

In charging the jury, Lord Justice Burton gave a summation of the case that strongly implied he would rather live amongst pit vipers than amidst the gentry of County Wexford. He went on for about forty minutes, muddling matters further with each successive sentence, until the foreman of the jury interrupted and said that it did not seem necessary for his lordship to proceed further. Burton, astonished, agreed and the jury retired. Only four minutes later they returned with a verdict: the will of the late Hunter

Gowan was valid and the deed put forward to contest it was invalid.

Though it was now ten o'clock in the evening, the courtroom still was packed. Upon hearing the verdict the spectators broke into cheering and raucous laughter and Lord Justice Burton was permitted the pleasure of banging his gavel several times before pronouncing the case closed.

Ogle had not gotten away with it.

One is forced to wonder why he risked, not only his reputation, but his own, apparently safe, inheritance. Was he simply trying to help his brother, or was he hoping for a more substantial reward if William had been able to hang on to his land? The facts of the case are now so dimmed by the passage of time and the mists of Irish obscurity that the real truth will probably never be known.

Yet, he just might have survived the *débacle* with his reputation tattered, but not totally destroyed, had his life not been crossed by three personal nemeses — George Perkins Bull, George Nicoll, and Daniel O'Connell.

The Wexford assizes were personally humiliating to Ogle, but they were essentially a provincial happening and would not long have been talked about in Dublin, had George Perkins Bull not been involved. The aggrieved Protestant printer, whom Ogle had pushed aside from his nominal proprietorship of *The Antidote*, joined the opposition in the fight over the Ashwood estate, and he was a deadly enemy. Deadly, because, like all printers, he possessed the ability to make an otherwise evanescent bit of gossip immortal. And that is what he did. Soon after the assizes had given its verdict, he set in type a record of the proceedings and this transformed what had been a provincial *imbroglio* into a matter of Dublin merriment. The pamphlet, *Interesting Trial. Hopkins V. Gowan. Wexford Spring Assizes,March,14, 15, 1827 before the Hon. Judge Burton. . . .* was rivetting reading, the kind of thing that made educated Catholics rub their hands with glee, and made the patrons of the Protestant societies that Ogle served turn crimson with embarrassment. No longer could Ogle slide over his own bastardy, for, as the title page of Bull's booklet stated:

> This extraordinary trial lasted two days; the Jury retired at 10:00 and consulted for a few minutes, when they returned with a verdict

for the Plaintiff, thereby establishing the will of the late John Hunter Gowan and invalidated the Deed endeavoured to be set up by his illegitimate children — William and Ogle Gowan.

And, of course, the conspiracy to commit forgery was clearly ascribed to Ogle. Other details, such as his having been briefly an apprentice in the leather trade, served to damage irreparably his claims to gentility of birth. By mid-1827, Ogle was tainted goods: no longer was he of any use as a bright-eyed young gentleman, a man of principle, willing to act as treasurer, secretary, and pamphlet writer for Protestant proselytizing groups.

In public, he kept his head up and threw his chest out and started to walk with even more of a strut than usual, but at home he often sat morosely, wondering why all this had happened, and trying to think of ways to supplement his declining income.

He comforted himself with the thought that he and Sir Harcourt Lees still had their Benevolent and Religious Orange Institution. Then that too started to slide.

In the spring of 1828, the old headquarters of the Orange Order, 18 Dawson Street in Dublin, started to have frequent daytime visitors and often was used for evening meetings. The members of the old Order, frightened by the relentless drive of Daniel O'Connell for Catholic Emancipation, were mooting ways to get around the prohibition of political associations. Their leaders still were concerned with staying legal — an institution that claimed to support the Law and Constitution had little choice — but just barely legal would do. On July 12, 1828, there were Orange marches in the north, illegal, but conducted with the tacit approval of the old Orange leaders. That same day, the corps of guards at Dublin Castle, Protestant to a man, turned out with Orange lillies on their uniforms. These were immediately confiscated, but the point was made.

"They will split the Orange movement, Gowan," Sir Harcourt Lees complained to his young *protégé*. It was early evening in August. Ogle was in a new, smaller office in Leeson Street, but already it was messy and the baronet had to move a pile of old newpapers before taking a chair.

Ogle agreed, but was more direct in describing the consequences than was Sir Harcourt. "And if they do, the old guard will take over once again and there will be damn-all room for you and me."

Sir Harcourt did not like this directness in young Gowan. Ever since that disgraceful pamphlet had been published by the printer Bull, Ogle had become less delicate and less refined in his manner of speaking. Sir Harcourt took out a large handkerchief and proceeded to polish a reading lens that he had begun to affect lately. "What they are now doing, young Gowan, is forming so-called Brunswick Clubs — a good name for a bad cause in my view — and they have the Earl of Enniskillen, more fool he, as patron. The Brunswick Society is to be modelled on the Liberal Clubs in England. No oaths, signs, or passwords, and . . . . "

"And — no us.?"

"Correct. They are having a great banquet on the fourteenth of this month, and they plan to collect a 'Protestant Rent,' just as that daemon O'Connell collects his 'Catholic Rent.' "

Ogle was unimpressed. Lately he had come to believe that Sir Harcourt rarely got things right. "With respect, I do not agree." Increasingly, Ogle was taking pleasure in using the demotic. "That bunch won't survive any longer that a maidenhead in a brothel." Sir Harcourt made a face as if he smelled something disagreeable, "The real danger," Ogle continued, "is that the government will let the Unlawful Societies Act lapse, and then the old Orange Order will be revived. That's the group we should be worried about."

Tiring of such a crudely direct conversation, Sir Harcourt took his leave. He and young Gowan, he reflected, were approaching a parting of the ways. The young man's base-born nature was daily becoming more apparent. Reflecting on this fact, the baronet took out his handkerchief and put a scented corner to his nose.

"The old fop is becoming addled," Ogle said to himself after Sir Harcourt left, and he took out an unfinished letter which he had hurriedly thrust beneath a pile of papers when Sir Harcourt had arrived: Ogle was writing to Eustace Chetwood, grand secretary of the English Order. He was on good terms with Chetwood and, in an ingratiating letter, Ogle now suggested that in all probability the government would let the Unlawful Societies Act lapse — "Not, mind you, esteemed Sir, because of any conciliatory sense towards the true Protestants of this country, but in the hope of palliating the ravages of the ignoble O'Connell." Gowan suggested to

Chetwood that the esteemed English grand secretary should revive the Irish order and, in such an event, pledged his support in any way the esteemed secretary should find valuable.

Gowan knew that his unctuous letter was not suggesting anything that scores of old-line Orangemen had not already mooted, but Ogle knew that if the old Order was revived, the Benevolent and Religious Orange Institution would fade into obscurity. Like a circus acrobat, Ogle was trying to jump from one moving horse to another.

He nearly succeeded.

When, on October 15, 1828, the Unlawful Societies Act lapsed, Ogle abandoned Sir Harcourt and the Benevolent Orange Order without a second thought. Four days later, the Irish Grand Lodge, just re-chartered by Eustace Chetwood, met in the courthouse at Monaghan town, and Ogle was there, bustling about, sitting near the meeting's chairman, taking minutes, and handing out drafts of rules and regulations. The Monaghan courthouse, four square and undeniably elegant, resembled that of Wexford town. Ogle did not let that bother him: some days in courthouses are better than others. Upon concluding its business, the now-revived Irish Orange Order, had its new rules and regulations printed. Prominently displayed on these rules was this notice: "All communications upon the business of the Orange Institution are to be addressed to the Assistant Grand Secretary, Ogle R. Gowan, Esq., 2 Leeson St., Stephen's Green, Dublin."

He was on the back of the new and faster horse, but then Ogle had the misfortune to run up against George Nicoll, an Honest Orangeman. Nicoll was a respectable Dublin tailor. A small excitable man, he had a childlike idealism, the sort of innocent honesty that is so terrifying to the crafty. When he talked of something important, such as Orange business, his hands flapped, and one noticed that they were lined with scores of cuts and punctures, the by-product of his tailoring work. Nicoll had held several posts in local Orange lodges, but no national offices. He believed in Orangeism in the same way that he believed in doing an honest day's work for an honest day's pay, and he was horrified to learn of Gowan's becoming assistant grand secretary of the revived Order. Nicoll believed passionately in the revived Order and, if it were to survive, it must be led by men whose character was above reproach. Having learned of the trial to determine the validity of the deed to Ashwood, Nicoll knew beyond a doubt that young Gowan was bad spawn, a bastard child, a forger, the husband of his own half-niece, and a conspirator to defraud. Such a man was not right for a noble movement.

Thus, in a cause that was chivalric, a mission to protect honour, Nicoll went respectfully to residences of the several grand lodge members who resided in Dublin. He accepted the rebuffs of servants who, at their master's instructions, tried to put off seeing him: he waited patiently until he was granted an interview, and then with quiet intensity he went through the trial transcript printed by Perkins Bull. Invariably, the grand lodge leaders promised to give the matter their attention. This could mean anything or nothing, Nicoll knew, but he gratefully thanked his betters for that consideration.

And he succeeded, although not for the reasons that he believed: the grand officers were not upset about the immoral nature of the skeletons in Gowan closet, but rather by Ogle's having become a public embarrassment. Thus, he was removed as assistant grand secretary and two unexceptionable young gentlemen, Messrs. Horan and Kiernan, were put in his place.

And the word about Gowan went out: he was too gamey for the Irish Order to tolerate. This opinion of the Irish lodge stuck: when, in 1835, the United Kingdom Parliament investigated the Orange Order, three seperate items came before the royal commission, indicating the Irish grand lodge's belief that Ogle Gowan was a man of unredeemably bad character.

That was the end: Ogle had to clear out. He had no other alternative. Night after long night he spent talking, planning, worrying with Frances. Finally he decided that they and the family would emigrate. She cried a lot, but Ogle promised her that she would live like a lady in the New World: place your trust in me. She agreed, and Ogle began to believe his own words. Yes, there would be a bright future beyond the horizon.

BOOK II

MINING A NEW LAND

CHAPTER 7

A Very Fast Start 1829-1830

HATH THIS child been already baptized or no?

It is the thirteenth of December 1829, Montreal, Lower Canada. Ogle Robert Gowan, his wife with a baby in her arms, his mother-in-law, one male and one female servant, and four children under ten years of age are standing before the baptismal font of Christ Church, Montreal. This is the family group that Ogle has brought with him to start life in the New World. Even in the Christian sanctuary there is something truculent about Gowan. Moments ago, he entered the church in a strut, not a mere walk, and seemed to be daring anyone to step into his way. Gowan is about five feet nine inches in height, solidly built, with long side-whiskers that carry more than a hint of ginger sheen. His nose is broad and slightly bent to one side, as if it has been broken at some time. While herding his small flock into the church, he several times flaps — opening and closing — the double breasted great-coat that he wears, making himself appear like a large greyling gander, bristling about the barnyard. Under his great coat he bears colourful plummage: a paisley-fronted waistcoat and harmonizing cravat. The modish morning coat that he also wears has padded shoulders. Undeniably, he looks a gentleman.

Dost thou renounce the devil and all his work, the vain pomps and glory of the world, with all covetous desires of the same and the sinful desires of the flesh?

Unlike many Irish migrants (and, especially unlike those

who came during the Great Famine of the 1840s), the Gowan family had crossed the Atlantic in comfort. The family shared two staterooms on board and the party had access to a large dining room for cabin passengers and, weather permitting, the run of the ship. Each stateroom contained a drop-leaf desk, and Ogle had a crew member move the desk from the childrens' room into his own cabin. The two desks, placed side by side, made a large enough area for him to write on and he soon had the space covered with books, bundles of foolscap, and various documents engraved with Orange seals. The Order, he realized, held his future as well as his past.

Dost thou believe all the Articles of the Christian Faith, as contained in the Apostle's Creed?

The baptismal service is being read by the rector of Christ Church, Montreal. Three sponsors are present. The child, a son, born November 24, 1829, is wonderfully quiet, so there is little noise in the church. This is a private baptism, held in the afternoon. Ogle stands close to his wife who holds the baby. The godparents, who reply on behalf of the child, are William Burton, his wife Elizabeth, and John Bacon a young nephew of Ogle's who shipped to Canada on the same vessel. William Burton is from Shinrone, King's County, Ireland. Christenings, Gowan long has realized, are good times to seal alliances.

Burton is potentially useful, for he is well known in the English-speaking community in Montreal, and he and his wife's relative, Arthur Hopper, are co-founders of the civilian Orange Lodges in Montreal. (There are also military lodges, and an acrimonious dispute is in train with the regimental lodges about jurisdiction in that city.) Burton is impressed both with the credentials Ogle shows him from the English lodges, and also with the young man's vigour. He is convinced that the scattered lodges in British North America need a single central organization and, increasingly, believes that Gowan is the man to create such a body.

Name this child.

"Henry Samuel Eldon," replies Ogle. The first two names were chosen by Frances as being among her favourites, but the third, Eldon has great significance for Ogle: the Earl of Eldon, arch-Tory, and former Lord Chancellor of England, had fought steadfastly against any concessions to the Catholics. In Gowan's widely-noised view, Eldon was the most heroic of the opponents to the

Catholic Emancipation Act of 1829. Lord Eldon is a hero of Gowan's for another reason, although he never says so publicly: Eldon had made himself highly respectable, despite a low start in life. As the son of a coal factor, he had little chance of rising above the middle class. Yet, through ability, the possession of a fierce ambition, and by his having the foresight to elope with the daughter of a rich banker, he engaged in a notable legal career.

Ogle wishes to perform the same feat of levitation himself. In the six weeks prior to the present baptism he has been in Brockville, Upper Canada, and has returned the owner of a 400-acre farm. The Brockville area is a natural for him, because the town and surrounding farm countryside is sprinkled with Protestant migrants from county Wexford, people that not only share Gowan's religious and political principles, but know his family, and were willing to help Ogle find a cheap piece of land. Ogle returns to Montreal, nearly broke, but the land, he feels, warrants that he is a gentleman. The property will be named "Escott Park" because it is in Escott township and, "park," of course, connotes a respectable estate. Never mind that it is mostly bush.

We receive this Child into the congregation of Christ's flock and do sign him with the sign of the Cross . . .

Ogle flinches as the rector crosses the baby. This is the one part of the Anglican liturgy he does not like: too Popish.

. . . in token that hereafter he shall not be ashamed to confess the faith of Christ crucified.

I baptize thee in the Name of the Father, and of the Son, and of the Holy Ghost. Amen.

The service is over. Gowan discreetly slips a white envelope with a guinea in it into the hand of the rector, and the baptismal party walks out into a cold and clear December afternoon. Well, Ogle reflects wryly, at least there now is one Canadian in the family.

Given his unfortunate experiences in courthouses, Ogle Gowan might have been expected to avoid them for the rest of his life — but at six in the evening of New Year's Day, 1830, he was descending the steps of the courthouse in Brockville, Upper Canada, a triumphant smile on his face. He wore a new-style overcoat with a velvet collar, and as he talked to a handful of companions he looked very successful indeed. The men who surrounded him were a step above the backwoods rustics that bespeckled the Canadian bush, but they had the tartan complexion of men who had spent some of their years in rougher circumstances than had the young gentleman in their midst. The local courthouse, severe and unimaginative architecturally, constructed of raw, red brick, fitted them perfectly,

Ogle's triumph this day was to have created the Grand Orange Lodge of British North America, and to have placed himself effectively in control of it. Gowan rented the Brockville courthouse and then announced a GRAND OPEN MEETING of all Orangemen. The morning that he brought these men together was clear, with no hint of a storm in the air. In twos and threes, the delegates came up from their hotels and lodging houses on King Street, walked up Court House Avenue, crossed the cobbled square and entered the courthouse. Ogle stood just inside the door, greeting each one by name. He had a facility for remembering names, and had garnered scraps of information on each person attending, so that he was able to call by name and say something appropriate even those whom he had not met previously. In the main courtroom Gowan had arranged for tea or chocolate to be served. The delegates could only conclude that this was a thoughtful and refined gentleman.

Then he called the meeting to order and with compelling directness went immediately to a theme that he knew would appeal to the colonials: he proposed to them a form of Orange association for British North America that was unimpeachably respectable, manifestly gentlemanly, and, in its trans-Atlantic connections, undeniably aristocratic. "Gentleman, I am proud to inform you that the Right Worshipful, his Royal Highness, Prince Ernest Augustus, Duke of Cumberland, Knight of the Garter, fifth son of His Majesty, King George III, has agreed to become the Grand Master of the Grand Orange Lodge of British North America — provided that you gentlemen in your wisdom concur in founding such a noble, loyal, and constitutional association!"

The room errupted with approval.

"By God, that's a fine stroke, Gowan!"

"Agree! Of course we agree, and he a Royal Duke and all!"

"Hurrah for his Highness, the Duke of Cumberland, We couldn't have a finer Grand Master than that!"

Now, in actual fact, the Duke of Cumberland had made no such promise. Admittedly, the Royal Duke was the grand Master of the Irish Orange Order, but this had no direct bearing on the new Canadian institution. Fortunately for Gowan's plans, no one asked him to show the authority for his promise of the Royal Duke's patronage.

To confirm the high respectability of his proposed BNA Orange Order, Ogle next held up a list of names of men whom he proposed to appoint as honorary members of the Grand Lodge. That is, he once again modestly noted, if these names met the approval of his assembled Orange brothers. The names he put forward were men of impeccable credibility in Orange circles in the British Isles — men such as the Duke of Gordon, the Honourable Earl O'Neill, the Earl of Enniskillen, General Archdale MP, and so on, thirty names in all (including Gowan's old friends Sir Harcourt Lees and Chetwood Eustace). Ogle strongly implied that all these men supported his proposed Canadian association, when, in fact, none of them, save Chetwood, directly endorsed it. Also, several of the men on the list had been part of the Irish Orange group that had decreed Gowan was too lax a character for their movement.

Ogle's scheme worked pefectly.

Having established the high respectability of his proposals, he next described an organizational tree on which were hung baubles for everyone. This was important, particularly with the civilian lodges in Montreal: they had valid warrants from overseas, and unless they voluntarily submitted themselves to his new system, they would be beyond the new Canadian discipline. Gowan had already taken an important step in sweetening William Burton, when he had asked him to stand godfather for his newest-born son, Henry. Now he proposed that Burton be made Deputy Grand Treasurer and that a leading Montreal clergyman, the Reverend Fuller Atkinson be appointed Deputy Grand Chaplain. This brought Montreal into the new association.

That flank secure, Gowan took care of local matters. These were important, because the Brockville-Kingston area was a strong natural basin for Orangeism and there already were lodges there. Ogle paid obeisance to local sensibilities by nominating Brockville's leading medical doctor, Robert Edmondson, as Grand Treasurer, and a leading merchant/architect, and land speculator, Arthur McClean, as Deputy Grand Secretary. Both of these men had been pioneer Orangemen, and both were influential in civic matters. The Grand Chaplaincy was reserved for Reverend Rossington Elms, an Irish immigrant who, in the 1820s and 30s, was the Anglican missionary in Leeds county. Like many Irishmen, Gowan knew the value of having a tame priest on his side. And, finally, so as to satisty the dead-keen Orangemen of the Perth area, the Grand Secretary was named: Alexander Matheson, a man of such strong anti-Catholic principles that his home address was "Protestant-Hill, Perth."

In outlining the structure of national offices and in suggesting — always with suitable modesty — the names of men whom he thought should fill the various offices, Ogle left a lacuna so large that even the densest backwoodsman could not fail to notice it. "With no discourtesy, Mr.Gowan, I reckon we are forgetting some things," was how one rough lad from the Perth settlement brought up the matter. "But, you see, I figure we need someone to hold office under our Grand Master, the Duke of Cumberland — a Deputy Grand Master, sort of. A person that could take day-to-day charge of our affairs, because, God himself knows, the Royal Duke has a lot else to do."

Ogle nodded gravely and appeared to ponder this for a long time, as if it were an idea of such novelty to him that he needed to examine it deliberately, like an astronomer observing a new comet.

Dr. Edmondson rose to his feet. "An excellent suggestion." He had been primed by Ogle for this moment. "And would it not be suitable, worshipful brothers, if Ogle Robert Gowan, Esquire, were to hold the post of Deputy Grand Master? Granted, Mr. Gowan is new amongst us, but his experience in organizing Orangemen in Ireland, his high reputation in British circles, and his Loyal and Constitutional devotion make him out ideal man."

"Hear, hear!"

Quickly, Arthur McClean rose and seconded the nomination. He too had been well-rehearsed. "In seconding this nomination, I must add to Mr. Gowan's qualifications that he is a determined Protestant and thus a true friend of both Liberty and the Constitution!"

Soon thereafter, Ogle had the pleasure of announcing from the chair his own election as Deputy Grand Master, by acclamation.

When Ogle and his associates left the Brockville courthouse early in the evening of January 1, 1830. he was justifiably triumphant. Always a man of high energy, he wanted to jump or to sing, but that hardly would have fitted with the thoughtful image he had so carefully projected all day.

Gowan's party ambled slowly towards a hotel where they planned to have a slap-up dinner. On their way, they attracted the notice of an overweight, bewhiskered man, who was working at his desk in the *Brockville Recorder* office. This was William Buell, the MP for Leeds County and the paper's editor. He was, paradoxically, a scion of an old and distinguished United Empire Loyalist family, and a political Reformer. Buell watched Gowan's group with interest, for the presence of the Orangemen in Brockville had been well advertised, but the press had been excluded from their deliberations. In his paper, Buell had pointedly ignored the whole business, but his curiosity was piqued. He waited about forty-five minutes — might as well let the Orangemen take a few hot whiskies, he thought — and then he followed them to the hotel. Buell took a table in the corner of the inn, close enough to hear the discussion they were having. Now well into the hot punch, and exhilarated by their day's work, they paid him no mind. As the restraints of the day's formalities loosened, the Orangemen began to trade stories about past battles with Papists, comments on the near-treasonous stupidity of governmental officials, and tales of superstitious practices among the Catholics. Save for variations in local details, these were the same stories that Ogle had heard as a young Orangeman in his home lodge in Ireland. William Buell, who prided himself on being a liberal Protestant, heard these tales with increasing disgust, but like an unwilling spectator at a *danse macabre*, he could not tear himself away. At last, their meal over, the Orangemen decided to walk up King Street and see if they could find some of their brethren for a real night of revelry.

Buell followed. The whiskey had dissolved the Orangemen's restraint. They linked arms and walked down the middle of the street, six abreast. They began to sing "The Protestant Boys," a tune that in various versions was popular among Orangemen in Ireland, Britain, and the New World. They needed two or three tries before they all agreed on which set of words they would sing, but eventually they formed a stout choir:

By the deeds of their fathers to glory inspired,
Our Protestant heroes shall combat the foe;
Hearts with true honour and loyalty fired,
Intrepid, undaunted, to conquest will go.
In orange and blue,
The soul-stirring music of glory they'll sing;
The shade of the Boyne,
In the chorus will join,
And the welkin re-echo with "God save the King."

This was sung to a tune that had a clear, mesmerizing military beat. Having heard the song through three times, William Buell turned from following the Orangemen and walked hurriedly back to his office. He was a shrewd enough newspaperman to realize that what he had just witnessed was not a news story, but nonetheless was more important than most of the news that he printed: a new force was abroad in Upper Canada.

On the 13th of August, the *Brockville Gazette* had its entire front page draped in black: King George IV had died two weeks earlier and the news had just reached Upper Canada. William Buell was a solemn man, who took reverence for the monarchy seriously. Ogle Gowan also read of the monarch's death with some interest, for it meant, that, under a constitutional custom then universally accepted in the British empire, a general election would be called. And rumour had it that the second MP for Leeds, one James Kilbourn, would be standing down. Hence Ogle, scarcely a year off the boat from Ireland, decided to run for office in Upper Canada.

This, the first of Gowan's many election campaigns, was crucial in determining his political direction for the rest of his life. He assessed the political game as follows: that on a province-wide level there were no real political parties, just special interest groups and broad collections of people with similar attitudes towards government who, therefore, usually voted together. So, politics was chiefly a local matter. Around Brockville, the largest group was the "Reformers," headed by the Buell family. They wanted better and more representative government, but were unclear on details. It would be advantageous to strike a deal with them, and, failing that, at least to attract some of their natural followers; the next largest group was the Sherwood family and retainers, a group of "high-" or compact-Tories" who, in this case were joined by the old loyalist descendants of Ephraim Jones; there was also an important swing-group, the backwoods Irish, who, if they could be mobilized, would support a man from their own background.

William Buell would have nothing to do with Gowan, whom he regarded as a direct menace to social amity, because of his Orangeism. Had it been otherwise, Gowan will might have become a lifelong Reformer, for he had a radical strain in his outlook. Instead of working with Gowan, the Buells decided to run a candidate of their own, alongside William Buell (who was virtually a certain winner), one Matthew Howard. Hence, Gowan's goal became to put together enough Irishmen, disaffected Tories, and breakaway Reformers, to permit his running second behind William Buell. The great thing that Gowan had going for him was the perception among many of the immigrants and backwoods Canadian-born famers that the "Family Compact," was a real and exclusive oligarchy that protected its own interests at the expense of the less fortunate. Never mind whether or not provincial goverment actually was controlled by such a group: it was the perception that mattered. Thus, against this Compact, Gowan came forward as a populist, a leader of the aspiring against the established. As a populist, he had two alternatives: either be a radical ("left-wing," if one prefers) or a reactionary ("right-wing"). The radical postion associated with Republicanism, already was being staked out by William Lyon Mackenzie, so, tactically, Gowan was pushed to the other extreme. That was where his heart lay anyway. He was instinctively patriotic, anti-American, anti-republican, and pro-Empire, and, as his great power over crowds indicated, so, too, were many of the new immigrants to Upper Canada.

Since this was in the days before effective political parties had developed, there were a dozen or more "nomination meetings" in Leeds county. These were assemblies where inhabitants of a town or township, usually men of a single political persuasion, met and solemnly endorsed one or two of the candidates for the two county seats. As soon as the election was announced, Ogle was off to the hinterland like a greyhound after a rabbit, and he had an easy time organizing the Irish. They passed resolutions that declared, for example, that "one third of the inhabitants of Leeds county are of European birth," and "mostly Irish," so that they were entitled to a fair share of the local representation — meaning one of the three local seats (two for Leeds county and one for Brockville). The trouble was, the Irish constituted much less than one-third of the electorate, because many of them had not yet performed the "settlement duties" that were prerequisites for obtaining clear title to their land and, thus, the franchise.

To win, Gowan had to displace Matthew Howard, and here he was characteristically assertive. The confrontation between the two men came on September 18 in a bare, two-storey clapboard-faced hostelry, the Derbyshire Inn, in the township of Yonge. That day, the main room of the inn was packed with upwards of 120 men, most of them clothed in rough woollens, a few in deerskins, all looking for a little excitement. Another two-score rustic political enthusiasts were assembled outside, trying to hear the proceedings through the open door and windows. Gowan had at least forty-five Orangemen present, scattered throughout the crowd. This gathering, chaired by a local farmer, was run with excessive formality. It moved along smoothly, if slowly, towards the point where candidates would be endorsed.

Before that, however, Matthew Howard made a premature move. A devout Methodist lay leader, he had the air of someone about to break into extempore prayer. "Mr.Chairman, I move that the names which I have on this piece of paper be constituted a nominating committee for this meeting and that the meeting resolve to vote for the candidates whom this committee endorses." Howard put forward three pages of foolscap that contained no fewer than seventy names.

Instantly Gowan was on his feet. "Objection! Mr. Chairman! His voice was strong and he could be easily heard by all those outside the inn. "Mr. Chairman, I am sure that each of the men on Mr. Howard's list is a fine gentleman and a wise elector. The point, though, is that this meeting. and the honourable electors who constitute it, should have a chance to vote on *each* of Mr. Howard's proposed committee members. After all, some of them may not be quite as acceptable to the meeting as would others."

"Point for you, Gowan!"

"That's the lad!"

Ogle, sensing general support, quickly moved an amendment that the committee members' names should be put forward separately. This was passed by a voice vote, a victory that Gowan's more aggressive supporters celebrated with reverberating Celtic yells.

So Howard now was forced to move each of his proposed names one by one, and here he made a crucial error. The first name put forward by Howard was that of a preacher, the Reverend William Hallock. Gowan pounced. He quickly objected, pointing out that the cleric should be excluded, because Imperial precedent precluded such political involvement. This was stretching a point, but it hit a raw local nerve: Howard was from a strong Methodist family, and it was claimed by some locals that he therefore favoured political radicalism and social levelling. A voice vote was taken on the question of the clergyman, each side roaring in its turn, like bulls bellowing. In the view of the chairman of the meeting, Gowan's side won. Howard and William Buell contested this and started to abuse the chairman and the secretary of the meeting. These two then decided that they were not willing to take any more railing, and stomped out. Thereupon Daniel Jones, a long-time Compact-Tory and arch-enemy of the Reformers, was moved to the chair. Howard and Buell angrily left the meeting, Howard said something about sin as he left, and Buell, beet-red beneath his heavy whiskers, said something about the power of the press. Thus functioned representative government in Leeds county.

Despite his rivalry with Matthew Howard, Ogle did not wish too clear a line to be drawn between himself and the Reformers. The last thing he wanted was to be labelled anti-Reformer. This was because William Buell, at the top of the Reform ticket, was too strong to topple. Gowan therefore wanted to give the impression that he also was a man of independent mind, and that he was running not against the Reformers generally, but only against Matthew Howard.

As far as the Compact-Tories were concerned, he tried to have it both ways. He accepted a joint endorsement of himself and Henry Sherwood by the electors of Burgess and Elmsley townships, but also accepted a directive of the electors of Lansdowne, who specifically rejected the idea of voting both for Gowan and, as second choice, Henry Sherwood.

Ogle was acting as if he were the Colossus of Rhodes. He thought that by keeping one foot in both the Reform and the

Compact-Tory camps he could hold sway over the electoral situation. He felt sure that his loyal Irish would permit him to control the middle region between those two opposing grounds.

On October 12, Ogle Gowan arrived at the polls, set in the backwoods, about fourteen miles north of Brockville, confident of victory. He appeared at the head of sixty mounted supporters, mostly Irish immigrants. One of the group walked ahead, playing Orange tunes on a flute, and a drummer boy marched alongside. The impression was distinctly and intentionally military, although Gowan's men did not bear arms. They settled in for a long stay, for the poll lasted a week. In such electoral contests, all the votes were cast publicly, and a great deal of gamesmanship was involved. Usually, it was good strategy to sit back and wait for one's opponents to make the opening moves, and then counter-attack. Shrewd electoral tacticians always kept a small regiment of voters back, ready to send forward at a psychologically devastating moment. Since each elector had two votes (two MPs were being elected), the permutations of tactics were complex. Gowan, though, like an inexperienced boxer, came out of his corner too fast, swinging wildly and wasting his resources.

Before the polling began there were formal nomination speeches and sometimes a strong orator could bend undecided voters to his way of thinking."My fellow citizens" Gowan told the electors, "I come before you not as a stranger, but as a citizen of the British Empire, to which we all belong. And I come as an adherent of our excellent Constitution, to which we are all loyal." His voice was strong and as he stood on the hustings Ogle felt confident of victory. The substance of the speech he was about to give he had given a hundred times before in Ireland, and he had only to deliver it with one signal alteration: instread of denouncing the Catholics of Ireland, he attacked the "Americans" — by whom he meant Matthew Howard and his followers. "The great danger to our beloved Constitution comes, not from foreign infidels, but from those within our society who sap our moral strength. Indeed, one of the candidates for election — I shall not deign to mention his name — is so enamoured of the Yankee Despotism, the mob rule, that he preaches its tenets! To you, revered electors, he suggests that he is preaching something called 'Canadian Reform.' No! It is the radicalism and mobocracy of the Republic and he is counseling nothing less than Upper Canadian subordination to that foreign principality to the south!"

"Shame!"

"True, Gowan! More!"

"Lies . . . blackguarding!" Howard's supporters responded.

Ogle continued. "Of course, I believe that one can be a gentleman, however misled, and believe in certain so-called Reform principles. I grant that Mr. William Buell is such a man . . . but . . . but . . . Mr. Howard (there, I've said the name!) is no such gentleman. The Methodistical church, whose levelling beliefs Mr. Howard and his family so proudly promulgate, is not a church of the Empire; it is the American Methodistical society and is given to republicanism in belief and to the foreign control of the Canadian Methodists by their American masters! Could anyone vote for such a man?!"

Ogle was the last of the candidates to speak, and in the voting that followed he had a large squadron of his voters go forward and declare themselves. Thus, at the end of the first day's voting, he had ninety-two votes to William Buell's eighty-six, Matthew Howard's seventy-seven, and Henry Sherwood's fifty. Gowan was exhilarated and cocky. "Victory is ours, lads," he told a group of followers, who joined him drinking hot whiskeys at a local inn.

The second day's results, though, were dismaying. At the end of the day the poll read: Buell 222, Gowan 193, Howard 175, and Sherwood 147. Buell's strength had been expected, but what obviously was happening was that Howard was being pulled along on Buell's coattails. Since Gowan had directed many of his electors to vote early, the outcome now was in doubt. He had hoped that quite a few Reform-minded electors would split their ticket, voting for Buell and for himself. Instead, they were sticking to the Buell-Howard slate.

Ogle now recognized what he should have understood weeks earlier: that Reform voters, almost entirely native-born Canadians of a "liberal" stripe, were not going to vote in significant numbers for a recent arrival with hyper-constitutional convictions. As a correspondent to the *Brockville Gazette* said: "I cannot but deplore that a stranger of Mr. Gowan's description should be able to muster even one vote." Actually, the only possible bargain that Gowan ever could have struck was with the old Family Compact-Tories.

They detested him as an upstart, but liked his reactionary outlook.

So at this late hour, Ogle made a deal with them. He directed his remaining Irish voters to cast each of their two votes for himself and for Henry Sherwood and, in turn, the Compact-Tory candidate had his supporters vote a Sherwood-Gowan combination. The tactic might well have worked if it had been set in train earlier. But now, late in the voting, there simply were not enough Irish and Compact-Tory electors left. So, day by day, as the election continued, Ogle watched his position erode. The final result, gall and wormwood to Gowan, was: Buell, 613, Howard, 567 (these two declared elected), Gowan, 543, and Sherwood, 506.

After the sheriff formally annunced the results, each candidate rose to thank his electors. The two winners were gracious and the losers were expected to be equally so. Ogle, however, let loose a tirade: he had been the victim of slander by his opponents; the object of a conspiracy; the sufferer of deceit on the part of officials. "In robbing me of my justful position as a member for Leeds county of the legislative assembly, these conspirators, deceivers, slanderers, and traducers have robbed the loyal British-born citizens of this county of their rightful parliamentary representation. IT SHALL NOT HAPPEN AGAIN!!" As he said this, his followers, who were surrounding the hustings in a menacing fashion, broke into loud cheers and surged forward. They hoisted Ogle and carried him on their shoulders around the hustings several times, re-enacting in their strange way, the march of the Chosen People around the walls of Jericho.

No, they would not lose again.

Ogle learned several important lessons from his quick start, and early defeat, in Upper Canadian politics. First, he would never again embrace the vice of moderation. In the future, he must stake out a clear, strong, and extreme position. Second, given the character of local politics, particularly the strength of the Buells' Reform-machine, he would never again let the tactical complexities of the hustings unman him: if he could not win playing by the existing rules, he would simply change the rules of the game. And, finally, whenever the next parliamentary election took place, he would be ready, with his gloves off. If local politics was to be a dirty game, that suited him.

Ogle's rocket-like emergence into Upper Canadian life threatened to turn into an equally meteoric crash. He had come so very close to being an MP which, to an Anglo-Irishman of his background, meant being publicly recognized as a gentleman. Though gravely disappointed, Olge kept up a brave face, but daily this became harder and harder to do. His land, which he had so grandly titled "Escott Park," had been bought from one, John Shuter. It consisted of lot fifteen in the first concession of Escott township and lot fifteen in the second, and was already patented, so there were no settlement duties, but the property was mostly bush. Located roughly twelve miles from Brockville and a little farther than that from Gananoque, the two lots had development potential since the main east-west road ran along side them: in fact, it took a jog up one side of the lots, so that Gowan had a great deal of road frontage.

But for the moment, all he really had was a highly mortgaged piece of land: Shuter had sold him the property for £400, and taken back a mortgage of £350. As late as October 1833, Ogle wrote to a cousin that "We have not yet got anything more that the walls of the house up, but I hope they will begin at the roof next week. It is a much more troublesome and expensive thing to get a house up here than you can imagine. Our money is more than run out." As one might have expected, the revenues from Hunter Gowan's estate were not sufficient to bear the charges assigned under Hunter's will. So Ogle and Francis received almost nothing.

What Ogle possessed, then, was high ambitions, an imaginary estate, and an expensive *ménage*. He had to rent accommodations in Brockville for his family and servants that ran him £15 a year. His retinue consisted of a wife, his mother-in-law (Mrs. Colclough), five children, and his servants (Mr. and Mrs. Graham). Then, as happened to so many older immigrants to Upper Canada, Mr. Graham, took a chill, contracted pneumonia, and died. This left Mrs. Graham, ostensibly a servant, but now, equally, a complete and permanent dependent on Gowan. She was a vigorous, trustworthy, and often amusing older lady, but a dependent nonetheless.

Ogle and Frances, still a young couple, modelled themselves on the households of the Anglo-Irish gentry that each had observed while growing up. Frances's life had been more genteel than Ogle's, but he always had been observant when visiting his betters. As in the gentry households, there really were two family circles. Frances spent most of her day in the company of the children and the other womenfolk, while Ogle went about his business. The Gowans made a ritual of having a fairly formal dinner each night and if the pretension often was thicker than the soup, at least they kept their heads high. Ogle sat at the head of the table and, though still in his twenties, was treated like a patriarch. After dinner he played with the children. The two oldest boys, Nassau and Harcourt, were his particular favourites.

Just as the winter set in, the new infant, Henry Gowan, took the croup and died. The brought the ever-mercurial Ogle back to reflecting on his problems: he was going broke, going nowhere, especially politically, and he had a family to protect from fortune's painful arrows.

Where am I to turn? Ogle wondered in moments of despondency.

It was Mrs. Graham who, in her tart manner, suggested an answer. "Ogle Gowan, you should wait on the Word."

"The Bible? I read it on Sundays."

"Not my meaning, foolish man. I mean that, as you did in Ireland, you should enter the business of purveying words. It is the one thing that you do well."

Ogle, though not pleased with Mrs. Graham's near-insolence, realized that she was right, and he knew where an opportunity lay. The *Brockville Gazette* had been founded in 1828 as an ultra-Tory sheet, and as a direct opponent to the Buell family's *Brockville Recorder*. Most of the *Gazette's* money came from its dominant silent partner, Jonas Jones, lynchpin of the local Compact, although there were public partners as well. Because Gowan, in the last stages of the Leeds county election of 1830, had made an alliance with the Tories, it was natural that he work out an arrangement with the shadow-forces behind the *Gazette*. Hence, in the middle of November he became the editor. The paper announced that "We merely mean to tell the public that our paper has got a new editor, but has got no new principles." Perhaps not, but seemingly, Gowan had. In editorial columns he now defended the Family Compact. "Our quarrel," he said, "is with those who maintain that the higher orders are merciless, the magistracy tainted, and the judges corrupt." When taxed by one of his Irish followers with having given up his principles, Ogle replied that defending the rich sometimes was a good way to serve the poor.

CHAPTER 8

Becoming An Immigrant Leader 1831-1833

"DO YOU know what this country is all about my dear?" Ogle asked Frances in one of the post-prandial interludes where he played paterfamilias and sage.

Frances had opinions of her own — they were about mud, drunken louts, insufferable United Empire loyalist ladies who were never home when one called, ponderous brick and stone public buildings, log huts, long-unpainted frame shacks, a cultural wilderness — but she was too shrewd ever to upstage her husband. "What country my dear? All of North America? All of this continent? British North America? Upper Canada?"

Ogle, ever sensitive to the music of domestic irony answered bluffly, "Upper Canada, of course, Frances. Do you know what it is all about?"

"Do tell me, dear husband." She put down the needlepoint that she employed to fill the less demanding moments of her day. She was working on a scene of her own design, a stylized vignette of one of the more unpleasant scenes from the '98 Rising in Wexford.

"It is about Creation?"

"Ex-nihilo?" Frances was not without education.

"No. But here, in what not long ago was emptiness, Creation has happened once again. I mean that here the actions of everyone taken together show in the clearest way, in Creation, what counts in western civilization." Frances nodded. That was all Ogle required. "So first the settlers here secured land and the instruments of making a living. Then they made certain that the state protected property rights. And now, groups are being formed to protect individuals against other individuals — and against the state if it becomes unjust. And of course there is danger . . . "

"Oh?"

" . . . danger that our Irish people will be seduced by false prophets and that the Constitution will be upset or overthrown."

Frances had been through scores of Ogle's discussions of the Constitution. "Yes, you are right my dear. There might be something in it."

By silent agreement they dropped the subject, for Frances had put stress on the word "something." She was referring to the something that they both worried about much of the time: money. Money was one of the Gowan's great problems, for he was much better at spending than making it and especially during his first years in Canada, he spent much more than he earned. While editing the *Brockville Gazette*, he tried to establish an occasional miscellany called *The Sentinel*. This was supposed to appear in the fall of 1830. But in late December Ogle was apologizing for its having been delayed "by want of hands." He promised that it would appear in the new year, and eventually the periodical did see the light of day, but in so few copies and for so short a time that no copies survive.

Things went little better with the *Gazette*. In late January 1831 the paper's shadowy Family Compact owners suspended its publication and Ogle was out of a job. The *Gazette* did reappear in June 1831, but under a new editor, Gowan's friend and Orange ally, Arthur McClean. The paper was decidedly friendly to Gowan, but it no longer was a source of income.

In the fall of 1831, William Lyon Mackenzie was in eastern Ontario, holding public meetings and collecting petitions to take to England against the policies of Sir John Colborne, the Lieutenant Governor, and against the Tory-dominated assembly. Mackenzie held half a dozen meetings in the townships around Brockville in the week of October 13-22, and he was supported by the Buells and by Matthew Howard. Mackenzie's program was radical within the context of its time, but actually was neither republican nor truly democratic. He stood for: fair equal parliamentary representation; parliamentary control of all governmental monies; the abolition of Crown and Clergy Reserves of land; statutory limitations on land giveaways; abolition of all preference for any religious denomination; cheaper and prompter justice, and so on.

Naturally, people of privilege and anyone afraid of swift social change were frightened by his march through the townships, and they did what they could to keep Mackenzie from having a hearing. The sheriff of Leeds county, Adiel Sherwood, turned down an application from either Buell or Howard, the county's two members of the Legislative Assembly, for the use of the district court house for a Mackenzie meeting. (This was the same building wherein Ogle Gowan had inaugurated the Canadian Orange Order.) Thus it was in the Church of the Episcopal Methodists — the denomination that Gowan constantly referred to as "Yankees" — that Mackenzie held his Brockville gathering.

There was no established local orator to defend the views of the local Compact-Tories. The Joneses and the Sherwoods, therefore, encouraged Gowan to be their champion and this they ultimately regretted: this was the first step in Gowan's setting himself up as the leading local opponent of the Reformers and thus, eventually, to displacing the Compact-Tories with his new brand of Toryism based on immigrants from the Old Country.

Mackenzie's Brockville meeting began at eleven and lasted all day. The frame church was packed by ten. The aisles soon filled with youths sitting cross-legged, after having been forced to give up their seats to their elders. Two local men of Reform sympathies, Messrs. Butler and Pennock, respectively, chaired the meeting and served as secretary. To begin, Pennock read a long report of the proceedings of meetings in other districts that had been convened by Mr. Mackenzie. A petition to be considered by this assembly (modelled on that drawn up by Mackenzie's York constituency) was read out. Then came the main attraction: William Lyon Mackenzie rose and spoke for nearly two hours.

Mackenzie's speech jumped from one well-worn groove to another — from the iniquities of the bent justice system, to the Clergy Reserves, to the lack of true representative government — and contained no surprises. But people were not there to be surprised, but to be saved. Mackenzie had the tone of spiritual revivalists, a staccato delivery that sawed away at the listener, a great ability to draw picaresque analogies, and a tangential mode of arguing that allowed him to slip from one subject to another without logical connection, using puns, word-associations, and broad jokes.

Mackenzie was not a handsome man, but he was striking. Short in stature, he had grown massive sidelocks — seemingly in compensation — and his rasping burr of a voice seemed to emanate from this hirsute bush, like the voice Jahweh speaking to his Chosen People. When he became really excited, small drops of saliva splattered forth, and some settled upon his sidelocks, catching the light. Mackenzie did not so much attempt to convince his audience as to wrap it up in a cocoon of rhetoric. With Mackenzie in the pulpit, the congregation in the Brockville Methodist Church, secular though the assembly was, felt that tongues were being called down upon them.

To follow Mackenzie as a speaker would have been hard at the best of times, but was especially hard now because the majority of listeners were strong Reform sympathizers. After Mackenzie concluded his speech, the secretary of the meeting, Mr. Pennock, moved the adoption of the York resolutions. Gowan had little going for him, except that, having been sitting still for nearly three hours, a fair proportion of the audience had to heed the call of nature, and then did not bother to come back into the church. Late-arriving Orangemen filtered in and found seats. Still, it took considerable courage for Ogle to play Daniel in the den of this particular lion.

"Mr. Chairman and Gentlemen of the District of Johnstown." Ogle, unlike Mackenzie did not speak from the pulpit, but stood foresquare in front of his audience. Utterly confident, he had no notes. "At your request and in obedience to call still more imperative upon me — the call of DUTY — I rise to address this numerous, respectable, and intelligent assembly, and in doing so, I call for all that indulgence necessary to be extended to a public speaker, placed in a similar situation with myself. Gentlemen, I have not as yet even read the Address to the King, the Petition to the Imperial Parliament, nor even the Requisition by which this meeting is convened. The document was put into my hand coming to this meeting, by Mr. Buell, one of our county members. And, therefore, I say, of a truth, that I am unprepared . . . to address you upon the subject-matter contained in those documents which I now hold in my hand."

Ogle stopped briefly and looked at William Buell who stared stonily at the floor. Buell had to admit to himself that Gowan was starting out cannily, painting himself as the underdog in this debate.

". . . Mr. Mackenzie has all the advantage of having spoken upon the various subjects now submitted to our consideration for many years. He is quite familiar with them, having delivered the same speech probably twenty times with the last month."

"Eighteen, actually, "Mackenzie interrupted, to the audience's amusement.

Gowan laughed too, good-naturedly.

> Gentlemen, as Mr. Mackenzie has brought forth his Budget of Grievances, containing many burdens under which he and his friends labour, I hope I will not deem it instrusive or presumptuous in serving him up with one of ours, merely by way of ballast; lest the keel of his understanding should overturn. Gentlemen, our first and greatest grievance is that we should be taken by surprise in this district, by the great majority of its inhabitants having never heard of this meeting as yet, and even those who have heard of it, have scarcely had a few hours' notice. That the loyal inhabitants of this district should be *non plussed* . . . is certainly the greatest possible grievance under which we do at present, or could possible labour hereafter.

Mackenzie looked up and smiled broadly in admiration of Gowan's ploy. As one of the greatest natural demogogues in North America, he knew full well what Gowan was doing: redefining the Reform vs. anti-Reform controversy into one of outsiders vs. locals.

Then Ogle, who knew well how to use the Rules of Order to his own advantage, quickly moved an amendment to the original resolutions and these changed the grounds of debate, for now the meeting would first have to deal with Gowan's amendment before getting to Mackenzie's grievances. Ogle resolved,

> that the inhabitants of Johnstown District, ever distinguished for their loyalty to the British Crown, are happy to embrace the present occasion of expressing their devoted attachment to the Imperial Government and their fullest confidence in His Majesty's Repre-

> sentative in this colony and upon whose benevolence and sagacity, united with the cordiality now happily existing between his Excellency and representatives of the people in Parliament, we fully and confidently rely to redress any real grievance . . . .

"Hurrah for Sir John Colborne!" someone yelled while Gowan was completing his motion, and Ogle had to repeat the last part. The point was simple enough: that Mackenzie's various petitions were unnecessary.

Now that he had the floor, Ogle had no intention of relinquishing it. He settled into an hour-and-a-half ramble that, while heavy with sarcasm, simultaneously showed some reasonableness. He made a show of accepting the validity of some of Mackenzie's grievances — he agreed that all public monies should be under the direct control of elected representatives in the London Parliament — but all of these things, he argued, could be sought effectively without the present petitioning mania.

"Besides," suggested Gowan, returning to the anti-outsider line that worked so well with eastern Upper Canadians, "what does it matter if 5,000 Dutchmen from Markham, Whitby, and Vaughan, with 500 Yankees from York, have sanctioned the petitioning?"

"So what, Gowan! You tell them!"

" . . . What does their authority weigh when placed in the balance of common sense?"

An obviously drunk bush savage stood up. "Not much! goddamn them Yankees!" and was pulled back to his seat by his sober cronies.

Gowan paused to let the disturbance pass.

"If 5,000 Dutchmen in the Home District have sanctioned this petition, how many thousand Patriots, Martyrs, Orators, Philosophers, and Statesmen have given their attestation to the excellence of the Constitution, which this petition prays to subject? And how many thousand Patriots have sealed their attestation with their blood, and spent their dearest treasures in its defence, both in Europe and America!!"

This line of argument manifestly made William Buell unhappy, for he turned and glowered at Gowan. Ogle knew that he was hitting a nerve and annunciated a theme that soon was to become a central part of his definition of post-Compact Toryism; that the new immigrants to Upper Canada, particularly the Irish Protestants, were more loyal to the Constitution than were many of the native Canadians and, hence, they deserved to inherit the mantle of true loyalism. "Gentlemen, I am looking over the list of persons who have signed this Requisition. I find that there is but one solitary Irishman."

"Name him!"

"Who is the traitor, Gowan?"

Ogle refused to name him, and instead suggested that they consult the list of petitioners themselves. It was not for him to name individuals, he said. "But suffice it to say that he is not only a countryman, but, nay more, a townsman of my own. Oh! how the heart sickens and the blood recoils at the idea that even one Irishman could be found who, false to his Country, his Religion, and his God, has veered about and united with the Yankee junto of hypocrites, traitors, and knaves who hold their seditious meetings at York . . ."

"Shame!"

"Name him and we will visit the blackguard!"

" . . . However, why need I be surprised at finding the name of one Irishman attached to the pernicious document, when I find the names of so many Canadians, who, false to their country and betrayers of the land of their nativity, have now turned tail and joined with the enemies of the Province in bringing about the ruin and destruction of their own children! OH! YE, HOWARDS AND BUELLS . . . you, whose fathers suffered so much in the defense of those principles which you, their children now seek to destroy, how will you answer for your present conduct . . . ?"

Here, Gowan began raising his boot and bringing it down in cadence at two-second intervals as he talked, like a slow handclap at a cricket match, and soon his supporters picked it up.

"Ye Howards! Will ye thus trample on the principles of your sires?"

The stamping was becoming louder.

"Will ye ignominiously stamp on their graves?"

Louder.

". . . And scoff at the principles for which they were hung on gibbets?"

LOUDER.

". . . And cast their ashes to the winds of heaven?"

LOUDER STILL.

"No! No! No!" he thundered, and with each "no!" his heavy cavalry boot hit the pine floor in unison with those of more than a hundred of his followers. For a full thirty seconds he stopped speaking, while he and his adherents kicked the hard leather of their heels into the pine. A hundred drummers, a hundred soldiers ready to march.

The Reformers recognized that things were almost out of hand. Although there still was a Reform majority in the church, it was possible that Gowan's truculent supporters might tear up the meeting rather than lose a vote. Hence, when Gowan offered them a bargain — that he would withdraw his amendment if Mackenzie's resolution were also withdrawn — Buell, Howard, and Mackenzie huddled with the chairman and secretary of the meeting. They decided, however, to risk confrontation. The chairman ruled that Ogle's amendment would not be voted on at all. Instead a series of local worthies were allowed to make a string of meandering speeches until well after sundown. Gowan's men were content to bide their time, waiting for the original resolution to be voted on.

At last this was done by voice vote. Each side roared, swore, stomped, and whistled when asked to indicate their opinion. Quickly, the chairman declared that the Mackenzie motion had passed — an avid Reformer, he would scarcely have done otherwise — and this so enraged Gowan and his men that they threatenen to do serious damage to the chapel.

Amidst the din, William Lyon Mackenzie went over to the chairman and suggested that they restage the vote, doing so in such a way as to induce Gowan and his followers to leave the church.

"Gentlemen, gentlemen," the chairman called, while pounding a walking stick on the floor as a makeshift gavel. "I propose that we divide again. On the Court House square. And that those who favour the resolutions congregate on the northeast corner, those who oppose on the southwest. Tellers will pass amongst you and tally the division."

A rasher idea can scarcely have been conceived. The tellers could no more obtain an orderly count of the milling men than one could train an eel to stand on its tail. The chairman declared that, once again, the Reformers had prevailed.

But that now was beside the point; by forming the two groups of agitated opponents into groups on courthouse square, the chairman had guaranteed at minimum a gang fight and, at worst, a major riot. Who won the fight depends on who tells the story, as does whether it should be classed as a full-scale riot. The result, in any case, was that William Lyon Mackenzie had come to Brockville expecting a walkover and had been fought to a tumultuous draw by a group of backwoods Irishmen led by Ogle R. Gowan.

In July, 1832, Ogle Gowan, lying pale and trembling in his rented house in Brockville, was told that a file of mourners was on their way to his funeral. He smiled and managed a small laugh. "That is the best news I have had in weeks," he whispered to his physician, Dr. Edmondson.

Ogle had been in bed five weeks, suffering from the "emigrant disease," cholera. In the third week in July word circulated through the back concessions of Leeds county that he had died. Mourners, mostly immigrants, formed a party and walked towards Brockville to honour their dead leader. At Conner's Tavern just outside of town, they learned their mistake, and instead of holding a wake, rejoiced, drank some raw whiskey, and returned home. Gowan recovered remarkably quickly and by early August was once again his robust self.

In a sense, Ogle's catching the dread emigrant disease was the seal on his identification with the migrants from the British Isles. The progress of the disease across Europe had been reported in Upper Canadian papers for over a year and in January 1832 the *Brockville Recorder* had predicted that it would hit Canada when the annual summer flow of migrants from the British Isles arrived. It is commonly accepted that cholera was introduced by persons on the vessel *Carrick*, from Dublin, that landed at Grosse Isle on June 3, 1832, and Ogle was one of the first residents of Upper Canada to suffer. This is not surprising, given that he was a lodestone for migrants from the old Country, particularly Protestants from the south of Ireland.

Equally, Gowan's illness and pain were part of a larger identity: for a full year following the fall of 1831, new arrivals and recent settlers went through hell. The weather was brutal — it was known in local lore as "the iron winter," and the snow accumulation was prodigious. The spring came on cold and backward, and as late as May 4 and 5 heavy snow fell. Then came a burning hot summer, with no rain for weeks. Besides cholera, the fever and ague ran through the countryside. In late summer of 1832, Ogle and Frances Gowan lost another infant child, Charles Ogle Gowan, and thus they shared in the pervasive pain that was wracking their society, especially the foreign-born, the poor, and the vulnerable.

Understandably, the horrors of the cholera epidemic yielded a superstitious and magical response. Curious cures abounded. The *Brockville Recorder* printed the following alchemical remedy for cholera:

> 2 tablespoons of charcoal
> 2 tablespoons of hog's lard
> 2 tablespoons of maple sugar
> Mix and give two spoons full every fifteen minutes . . . when the limbs are cramped, bathe him in warm lye.

This was the cognate of a magical recipe that was circulating in the south of Ireland, where it was widely accepted that the Virgin Mary had appeared at a chapel altar and had left there certain ashes — or "blessed turf" — that was the only effective protection against cholera.

Many native Upper Canadians blamed the new immigrants for the disease. As much as possible, during the height of the epidemic, the local residents stayed away from the towns of Brockville and Kingston, and tried not to associate with newcomers. The Irish, of course, received most of the blame, as they comprised the majority of the immigrants. The more sanctimonious of the townsfolk blamed the disease on the moral character of those who caught it. One remarkable story in the *Brockville Recorder* reported that "one case occurred on Friday last in the person of the wife of Smith . . . which terminated in death in about seven hours. The habits of this woman were such as to render her a fit subject of the disease."

If immigrants had their enemies, they needed their defenders, and that was Gowan's *métier*. Even before the cholera arrived, Ogle was involved in a curious province-wide network known as "emigrant societies." (Note, that, confusingly, in nineteenth-century usage, the word "emigrant" was used not only for out-migrants, but for what today would be called "immigrants" or in-migrants.) Early in the year, Sir John Colborne, Lieutenant Governor of Upper

Canada, had called for the creation of societies to assist immigrants in finding work and places to settle. But like almost every social organization in Upper Canada, these emigrant societies were twisted sharply by local pressures into quite different shapes than originally intended. In Lennox and Addington counties, for instance, political Reformers grabbed control of the meetings, and used them to denounce the government's allowing pauper migrants into Canada. They declared that able-bodied immigrants could well take care of themselves; so no migrant-aid society was necessary! In Kingston, the Conservatives took charge, and used the society as a forum to mount a diatribe against Catholic workers on the Rideau canal.

Earlier in the year, Gowan and some of the Brockville Compact-Tories had presciently recognized this as a chance to strike out at the Reformers and, at the same time, to gain favour with the government. They scheduled a meeting for St Patrick's Day, 1832. Gowan widely distributed portions of a letter by his now-bitter enemy, Matthew Howard, that stated, "the practice, therefore, of removing parish paupers to this country is cruel to the unhappy persons thus removed, and unjust to the inhabitants of the colony." Howard was quoted unfairly and out of context, but Gowan achieved his purpose: on St. Patrick's Day the Brockville courthouse was packed, and, unlike the earlier visit of Mackenzie, most of those present were anti-Reform. The Emigration Society for the Johnstown District was formally established, with the Hon. Charles Jones, the richest and least pleasant of the old United Empire Loyalist representatives, being chosen president. Among the vice presidents were Jonas Jones and Ogle R.Gowan. The secretary was Captain James Gray, soon to become a business partner of Gowan's.

Before long the meeting was a shambles. Andrew Norton Buell tried to articulate the position that the Reformers were not anti-immigrant, merely against too many paupers. Henry Sherwood, Charles Jones, and others, argued the opposite, and soon there was more shouting than debating. A.N. Buell, in an exasperated tribute, said of Ogle: "Mr. Gowan can speak with so much eloquence that he could turn this assembly to be either Government men or rebels." Ogle spoke twice. The first time he talked directly about immigrants and during the second he indicted the Reformers and William Lyon Mackenzie. Eventually claiming that the meeting was stacked against the Reformers, A.N. Buell led a walk-out. Buell and his followers trooped out of the courthouse and towards the Methodist Episcopal Church. As they went, Gowan railed, "Let traitors hold meetings in holes and caves if they wish, but they shall never again hold one in this county. Follow me and we will drive them out!" He led a rush towards the Methodist church but those men whom he bitterly denounced as "Yankees" already had decamped, and thus the public peace was preserved.

This mixture of vituperative rhetoric and threatened or actual violence became a constant in Gowan's move towards power. It is seen a year later at Farmersville (now called Athens) about fifteen miles northwest of Brockville, where he fomented a full-scale riot.

The occasion was an announcement by Gowan's opponents in the 1830 election, Matthew Howard and William Buell, that they would hold a public meeting on March 9, 1833, to discuss the reserves of church land. They proposed selling the Clergy Reserves and using the revenue for some general secular purpose. One would think that this idea would appeal to recent immigrants, for, in theory, it would make more land available for new settlers. In reality, however, in the Leeds county area, the Clergy Reserves gave immigrants a place to rent land cheaply, and thus to get into farming without making large outlays of capital. Besides, most of the local immigrants were Irish Anglicans and they supported this vestigial form of church endowment. Gowan was well aware of the reasons the immigrants favoured Clergy Reserves and had no trouble raising a hyper-Tory force to attack the Reformers. Declaring himself to be a supporter of the "Constitution as in Church and State Established," Ogle printed a handbill:

> If you are desirous that this fine county should again be placed at the feet of Buell and Howard, do not attend this meeting. Let no man be absent who wishes to assert his rights.

Other handbills — of which Gowan later pretended disapproval — called for a paramilitary assemblage. "Britons" (the code-phrase used for British Isles-born immigrants) were to meet a mile from Farmersville where a "GRAND PROCESSION will be formed and the friends of the Constitution will march to Farmersville with *Music* and good *Shilleleaghs*. Up with the Constitution and no quarter to traitors!"

From the very start of this outdoor meeting, Ogle raised hell. Andrew Norton Buell, as convener, opened the proceeding by proposing that David Fairburn, a Scots immigrant and Brockville merchant, be accepted as chairman. Immediately Gowan stood up and objected. Instead he proposed Col. R.D. Fraser, a Tory of United Empire Loyalist background, from Grenville county (who earlier, had tried to convince Ogle to run for Parliament from that county). The convener took Fraser's nominations and ordered that those who favoured Fairburn move to one side of the platform, and those who favoured Fraser to the other, so that each group could be counted. Gowan knew that he and his men were in a minority, so he ordered them to stay in the middle ground where they brandished their sticks and shilleleaghs and hollered that they had a majority.

> "FRASER! Fraser to the chair!"
> "God, King and Country!"
> "Patriots up, traitors down!!"
> "Loyalty forever. To hell with Mackenzie and Howard!"

Several times, A.N. Buell tried to have a vote taken, and each time Gowan's supporters prevented him. Finally, the Reformers gave up and decided to have their own assembly. They moved to a makeshift plaform about fifty yards away and set up an orderly assembly with a chairman and a secretary. Samuel Pennock, veteran of many Reform gatherings, was just reading out the petition concerning the Clergy Reserves when a group of Gowan's supporters, some flailing clubs, rushed the group and mounted the platform.

"Grab that bastard traitor Fairburn!" one of them cried and another knocked him off the platform. Several Gowanites beat Fairburn on the head with shilleleaghs, and one put a heavy farmer's boot into his groin. The Reformers rallied to protect him and, outnumbered, Gowan's men ran off. They augmented their forces, regrouped, and attacked again. Once more they mounted the Reformers' platform and got hold of poor Fairburn. A major riot followed and, undeniably, Ogle's forces won, in the sense that further consideration of ending the Clergy Reserves was rendered impossible.

In fracases like this, Ogle was bonding the Irish immigrants to himself. As an anonymous observer in his opponents' paper, the *Brockville Recorder* shrewdly noted, "It would seem to be his principal interest to enrage the Irish population against any other class of men; and to convince them that they are hated by every other class." Ogle used a vocabulary — Loyalty, the King, and Constitution, versus Treason — straight out of Irish, ultra-Protestant politics. The backwoodsmen of Leeds county had been programmed to respond to these words long before they came to Canada. And his physical postures also were directly imported from the Old Country; his people formed up in procession, they marched with martial music in their van, and they brought and used weapons.

"Family," once wrote an old friend in Ireland, "is like the Constitution. It encompasses everything. My true family is my emigrant [sic] friends, my Orange order, and need I say? my own relations." This clan-like sense of kin explains how Ogle could think of himself as a devoted husband and father and yet invest relatively little of his emotional energy in his immediate family circle. This was something that Frances understood, but did not like. She began to resent the fact that the demands of Ogle's "clan" took precedence over his home life; she was further incensed when, like a feudal magnate, he expected his entire household to give allegiance to his other circles of retainers.

Early in 1832, Frances had greeted Ogle's homecoming one evening with the excited announcement, "Uncle Henry is coming to Upper Canada!" She was dancing and waving a letter as she told him the news. "They say they will leave New Ross in the spring and be here in mid-summer." This was at a time when many Protestant farmers in Ireland were making the same decision. The countryside was agitated once again, and the Catholics in the south of Ireland had started a "tithe war," that is, a guerilla action against payment of tithes to the established (Anglican) church. While this did not immediately affect men like Henry Hatton Gowan, it boded ill. Over fifty when he emigrated, a veteran of the '98 Rising, and of Hunter Gowan's Wingfield Yeomanry, Henry Gowan was no coward. He was an older, hardened version of the man who had captured the legendary Whiteboy leader, "Captain Grant." He was not a man to run away; he was simply making a careful calculation of where the best future lay and acting accordingly.

"Is he bringing the entire family? What about cousin James? I thought he was studying medicine." Ogle held out his hand for the letter and Frances immediately passed it over. She kept talking as Ogle read it.

"Oh yes, cousin James is coming too, and that's wonderful! He was such a shy boy and I was the only one who could make him talk. I wonder if he was changed greatly in the last three years?"

Ogle nodded absently, only half-listening as he read the letter. "Perhaps. Probably, actually. Studying medicine makes a boy into a man very fast." He looked up, walked over to the sideboard and put the letter down and began rubbing his hands together, as he frequently did when planning. "Well, we must make them at home here. They will want a place to stay while looking for a farm to settle. We must look after our own, my dear." He quite enjoyed casting himself as the patriarch of an enlarged clan.

"Of course, Ogle." Frances was briefly silent. "But . . . but, well, can we afford to have them stay for long?"

"Certainly we can. Even if we have to sell the furniture. Mind you, they may wish to settle up by York. If that is the case, then I shall use my influence to find them a suitable situation while they look for an estate."

The influence Ogle was referring to stemmed from his larger "family," the circle of Irish immigrants, Orangemen, and carefully-cultivated provincial civil servants who, though not Orangemen, were well-disposed to the Order's principles. One of the greatest troubles that backwoods immigrants had in Upper Canada was in getting good title to their lands. Once their settlement duties were completed (they had to clear a certain amount of land and pay their taxes), they faced a bureaucratic maze. They needed a big brother and for Leeds county immigrants, Ogle was he. From 1830 onwards, Gowan, on Orange business, journeyed frequently to York (which in 1834 became Toronto, a name that we will now adopt), and he made friends with people in the offices of the surveyor general, the attorney general, and other departments. He set up a regular channel for obtaining the title deeds quickly and smoothly for Leeds county immigrants. The new land owners, who had heard horrendous tales of families who had worked for years to clear their land, only to lose title on some legal technicality, were immensely grateful to Gowan and usually became fervid supporters of his political efforts. Because ownership of land was a prerequisite for exercising the franchise, Ogle was not merely making loyal friends, but literally creating votes. Gowan did not take money for his services. As he once explained, "I do not meddle for money, but merely for the cause."

Ogle used his Toronto connections to find suitable accommodations for his uncle Henry's family and, since they had decided not to settle in the eastern part of the province, to obtain accurate information on land available west of the city. As it turned out, Uncle Henry and family needed all the help they could get, for they had undergone a frightful voyage and had arrived in autumn, late in the immigration year. Although they had engaged a private cabin and had brought with them a domestic servant, their voyage was far from pleasant. They were on a small vessel, only 800 tons, and about a thousand miles out to sea the ship had been dismasted and they had to jury-rig a mast and turn back to Waterford. There the vessel was refitted and they tried again. Eventually, four months after they first had set sail, they arrived in Quebec City. They proceeded directly upstream and, after a family reunion in Brockville, went on to Toronto, impatient to get on with the business of finding land. For a year, Henry Hatton Gowan, accompanied by his angular, seventeen-year-old son James, looked for farms. Finally, with the help of one of Ogle's associates, they found two very nice farms in the township of Albion, about twenty-five miles from Toronto and there they were settled. During this period, Ogle and Frances wrote frequently and with notable tenderness to their relatives, and Ogle helped his cousin Anne find a post as a governess.

Young cousin James was a weedy adolescent and not much good on a Canadian farm. As his mother confided, "He is not at all calculated for the business of this country; he labours too hard for his strength and is in danger of injuring his health." His medical studies in Ireland had been done with an uncle on his mother's side and James had no real affinity for medical practice; it had merely been a way of filling time. So, in Toronto, he was articled to a solicitor, James Edward Small. That was in 1833 and only two years thence, 1835, cousin James Gowan, still a law clerk, became useful to Ogle. James now was able to thread his way through the corridors of the provincial administration and therefore was deputized by Ogle to do "the land business which might otherwise require my presence in Toronto, and thus save me some expense and trouble necessarily attached on such a journey." He explained to James: "There are many good, loyal Old Country people in this part who would support me if they had their deeds."

James, of course, agreed: he understood how family worked. So did Frances, but she did not fully approve of Ogle's pirating cousin James for his own purposes.

" . . . Be it said, however," continued Ogle in his missive ruminating about family, "that betimes the several circles of family lose their proper sense of order, and thus must be restored, sometimes by most vigorous means, to their proper place. Just as the solar system must have its orbits focused about a sun, so the circles of family must fix themselves about their rightful centre."

The circle that was the Orange Order was to Ogle both a joy and a great worry. Undeniably, his movement was a success. Upper Canada — modern-day Ontario — was the centre. In 1833 Gowan reported that there were 11,243 members in Upper and Lower Canada. The figure for 1834 was 12,853. This represented 144 individual lodges, the overwhelming majority being in Upper Canada. The population of males in Upper Canada over sixteen years of age in 1834 was 88,017, so the Order's success is obvious: one out of every seven or eight adult males belonged to an Orange lodge, a much higher proportion than belonged to any other non-religious organization. At first, the appeal of the Order was chiefly to Protestant Irish immigrants, but it quickly attracted Scots and English newcomers, and this crystallized Gowan's status as an immigrant leader. And, as the decades wore on, native-Canadian Protestants joined the Order in large numbers, so that, by mid-century, the lodges in each community were a representative cross-section of the Protestant male population. For the moment, though, Ogle was happy to be able to attract a broad band of immigrants and, since in the 1830s the Irish comprised roughly two-out-of-three immigrants into Upper Canada, most of his Orange followers were his fellow Irish-born migrants.

For Ogle, this success brought difficulties. His past kept

dogging him. In 1830 George Perkins Bull crossed the ocean and continued his war against Gowan. He had set up as a printer in Montreal and immediately began undercutting Gowan in Orange circles. Bull communicated with Upper Canadian Orangemen and they took some notice for, in September 1830, the Orangemen of the Brockville region had convened a kangaroo court to investigate Bull's charges against Gowan. The meeting was chaired by Dr. Edmondson of Brockville, a close friend of Ogle's and Gowan was unreservedly exonerated — but now, two years later, Bull was at it again. His pamphlet, the *Interesting Trial of Hopkins vs. Gowan,* was passed from hand to hand and the Montreal membership, like the Irish Grand Lodge before them, decided that Ogle Gowan was not a fit candidate for high office. They voted, therfore, to repudiate his leadership.

This could not have happened at a worse time for Gowan, for he was having trouble maintaining his legitimacy with the English Grand Lodge (that he avoided communication with the Irish Grand Lodge, with whom he was *persona non grata,* goes without saying). Ogle had applied to the English Grand Lodge to confirm him as deputy grand master of British North America, and this jarred loose a lot of plaster.

April 19, 1832, the Grand Lodge of England assembled at Humber 9, Portman Square in London. His Highness, the Duke of Cumberland, "Grandmaster of the Empire," presided, and on the dais were Lord Kenyon, deputy grand master for England and Wales and the Duke of Gordon, deputy grand master of Scotland. The Grand Lodge examined a mass of documentation and various testimonials that Gowan had submitted concerning his Canadian work, and decided formally to confirm him as deputy grand master "of all the Lodges in British North America, with the dependences, colonies, and settlements belonging, appertaining, or adjacent thereto." The English Grand Lodge also noted in their resolution that Gowan was "certified to be not only a sound Protestant, and most zealous Orangeman, but worthy in every way of filling the exalted and responsible situation to which he aspires and with no less honour to himself than satisfaction to the Brothers, has provisionally exercised." There were further endorsements in this high rhetorical vein, exactly what Ogle wanted.

But trouble began when the authorities of the Irish Grand Lodge got wind of this appointment by the English. Naturally, they disapproved. So strong was their objection that, in June 1832, they sent a special delegate to London to protest: in part, they objected to the English lodge's having appointed a deputy grand master for British North America, but, mainly, they were enraged that Gowan should have been that appointee. He was, the delegate averred, a disreputable character. As evidence of this point, the Irish sent a copy of the report of the committee of the Irish Grand Lodge that had resulted in Gowan's expulsion. Upon receiving this evidence, and after hearing the Irish delegate's testimony, the English Grand Lodge temporarily rescinded their appointment of Gowan. But things had gone too far, they soon realized, for them to back away publicly from their new colonial venture so, with severe second thoughts, they let their resolutions concerning Ogle and the Canadian Order stand.

This particular train of incidents reveals the mind-set of Orangemen and, more important, the kind of institutional thinking that they eventually insinuated into the ideology of English-Canadian Toryism. The Orange Order, and the forms of demotic Toryism associated with it, had their contumacious moments. But equally, they insisted on legitimacy and on a rigid constitutionalism in all institutional arrangements. Just as the immigrant-Tories insisted that the parchment that the Constitution was written on had to be of royal vellum, so the Orangemen demanded that their grand lodge be of direct and documented descent from Old World authorities. As a keen Orange historian of the present century noted regarding the Portman Square resolutions: "The Canadian copy, now on file at Grand lodge headquarters [in Toronto], is the authority under which the Grand lodge of British North America operates and has operated for over a century." No authority, then no Orange Order.

If the English Grand Lodge could not back away from the Gowan appointment it could hereafter remain aloof. As Lord Kenyon later admitted, concerning the appointment of Ogle Gowan, "there has been great misunderstanding about that, and great dissatisfaction felt, not only by the English Orange Institution, but the Irish also . . . ." And because of this great dissatisfaction His Highness, the Duke of Cumberland, was strongly advised not to accept the title of Grand Master of the Orange Order in Canada. The reason, as later explained in bald terms to a parliamentary investigation was that "the deputy grand master was a man of bad character." Thus, unlike the Orange lodges in the British Isles, the Canadian lodge had no royal patron- and, indeed, for an embarrassing period, no grand master at all.

So Ogle was in trouble. The Orange association in Canada was growing and promised to continue expanding, but perhaps without him. The major Grand Lodge meeting for the year 1832 was planned for September at Port Hope, Upper Canada, and there was a strong Montreal-based movement to dump Gowan. Ogle spent the summer rallying his own supporters, and trying to counter the stories being circulated about his actions in the Old Country. On August 20, 1832, he wrote to a brother Orangeman, one Charles Aimes, a gunner in the royal artillery, stationed at Woolwich, England. Gowan had never met Aimes, yet, desperately, he poured out his troubles:

> As regards the equivocal conduct of the Grand Lodge of Ireland towards myself, it is partly attributable to the misrepresentations of a few transient individuals, who comprise a Lodge at Montreal, in the lower Province, and partly to their [the Irish Grand Lodge's] desire, as being the Parent Lodge, to bring us under their subjection, give them a veto in our appointments, transmit them a guinea a warrant, five shillings for a renewal, and one shilling annually from each member — a measure they knew I was hostile to, and in consequence, I have been treated neither very graciously or justly, but no matter if I have suffered, I am consoled when I reflect that it is in a good cause . . . .

Why would Ogle write this way to a stranger? His postscript holds the answer:

> After you read this letter, I will feel obligated by your transmitting it to Colonel Fairman, as I do not know his address and feel happy to communicate with that Gentleman direct.

Fairman had only that spring become deputy grand secretary of the English Grand Lodge, and Gowan was looking for a friend, any friend, in English grand lodge circles.

The Port Hope meeting turned out to be every bit as nasty as Ogle had feared. Several weeks before the meeting, George Perkins Bull had announced his support for a rival candidate for the post of "Grand Master of British North America," one William Green. But Bull's real damage came through his amazingly malicious tongue. In addition to circulating the now-infamous *Interesting Trial*, he told and retold scandalous stories from the Old Country, of the Gowan family's dissolute sexual behaviour, and of its near-fratricidal rivalries. In one incredible flight of fantasy, Bull suggested that after Hunter Gowan had died, Ogle and one of his brothers had exhumed the body, put a live fly in the mouth of the corpse, placed a pen into the dead man's hands, and then signed their father's name to a bogus will. They were then to go into court, and in good conscience swear that this was Hunter Gowan's last will and that it had been signed when there was still life in him!

In fighting this slur-campaign, Ogle took the high road. He played the statesman and cast George Perkins Bull in the role of mud-slinging trouble-maker. More with apparent hurt than with anger, he quietly denied all charges and defended himself as a longtime servant of the cause. And, very cannily, he tied his own defence to improvements in the Orange movement. He noted, for instance, that in January 1831 a bill had been introduced into the Legislative Assembly to ban Orange processions, and, although it had not been proceeded with, legislation against the Order was a distinct future possibility. "Therefore, brothers," Gowan suggested, "we must proceed with dignity and be certain that our governors understand that we are not a danger to the public order. We must affirm publicly our support for our Lieutenant Governor, Sir John Colborne, and we must indicate that we respect the rights of the Roman Catholics — to political freedom — though we necessarily abhor their religious opinions."

Coming from Ogle Gowan, this suggestion that Orangemen endorse the political rights of the Catholics must have struck his listeners like Mary Antoinette advocating democracy, but Ogle knew what he was doing. Grown crafty in the ways of Canadian politics, he had two goals in mind. Ultimately, he hoped to become the spokesman for the entire immigrant population, including the Catholics and, more immediately, he needed the support of the York Orangemen. Many of them were keen on William Lyon Mackenzie and at this time Mackenzie (in his own bid to become the universal immigrant spokesman), was tailoring his program to attract Irish Catholics.

Gowan made his statesmanesque suggestions from the chair of the Port Hope meeting, a position that gave him a considerable tactical advantage over his enemies. He sensed that things were going well and that his presentation of himself as a man above mere petty scandal was being accepted, so he took a big gamble. He tendered his resignation as deputy grand master.

"No! no!"

"Gowan must serve!"

A ground swell rose from the ordinary delegates and Ogle, who had theatrically marched off the podium and taken a seat in the front row of the audience, allowed himself to be brought back to the platform by his supporters. He refused, however, to take his seat as presiding officer. One of his supporters moved a voice vote, that Gowan be asked to remain as deputy grand master and it passed easily. Ogle refused to accept it. Another vote and another refusal followed. Finally, after a third vote, he agreed to accept the chairmanship of the meeting, but not the title of deputy grand master.

Then, under his tutelage, the Grand Lodge passed the most extraordinary set of resolutions in Orange history, in Canada, or anywhere else. These endorsed the suggestions of Sir John Colborne, recommending "a civil reconciliation between this institution and our Roman Catholic fellow-subjects, "asserted" that we have upon all occasions held open our hand to our Roman Catholic fellows . . . and that we never meant or intended that our society should give them the smallest uneasiness, much less wound their feelings, religious or political"; and stated that "it is with feelings of delight" that we "received the manifestation of loyalty and patriotism of our Roman Catholic fellow-subjects and their venerable Bishop." (The bishop, of course, was Alexander Macdonell, who had been with the government troops in the crushing of the 1798 Rising in county Wexford).

Out of this amazing and seemingly bizarre performance, Ogle Gowan won a many-faceted victory. George Perkins Bull and the Montreal dissidents were repudiated, and Ogle was reaffirmed as Canada's Orange leader. More than that, after his repeated refusal to resume the post of deputy grand master, the delegates moved that he accept the title of Grand Master of the Grand Orange Lodge of British North America, and this he accepted. Thus he became the only person in the British Empire, not of royal blood, to hold the title of grand master of a grand Orange lodge. This was a brilliant turn-around: His Highness, the Duke of Cumberland had refused to accept the title of Grand Master of the Canadian Grand Lodge because Ogle Gowan was known to be of disreputable character — and now Gowan himself garnered the title that earlier had been offered to the royal duke!

CHAPTER 9

A REAL WINNER 1833-1835

"THEN YOU won't be coming with us, Mr. Gowan?" The questioner was old Mrs. Graham, the Gowan family's domestic servant. She was wearing her heaviest cloak, as protection against the January cold.

Frances Gowan answered for her husband. "No, Mrs. Graham. He won't. You know that he does not believe in fortune-tellers." Both women smiled slyly, for each knew full well that in his younger days, Ogle had several times visited Irish spae-wives and even now had some faith in them, which he tried to hide.

This was a ritual the Gowans went through every three or four months. Frances and Mrs. Graham journeyed north to Plum Hollow in Bastard township where a famous clairvoyant lived. This was Jane Elizabeth Barnes, an Ulster-born woman of about thirty years of age. She had emigrated to New York when she was in her late teens, married there, and subsequently learned the fortune-telling trade. Eventually, she and her young family moved to upper Canada and through some remarkable feats of prophecy became not merely well known, but famous. Clients came from as far away as Philadelphia to get her advice and, at times in the summer, two or three fine carriages could be seen, their horses tethered to the snake rail fence that skirted the road adjacent to her small log cabin, near Lake Eloida.

Frances Gowan always went to see this white witch armed with a long skein of questions. Mrs. Graham, who always accompanied Frances, permitted herself only one or two queries, and she would brood for days in advance about what these should be.

The witch of Plum Hollow invariably charged twenty-five cents in United States coinage, a fact that Frances kept from Ogle: she reported the equivalent amount in Halifax currency. Each visit, Frances asked at least one question about Ogle's future, and reported the response faithfully to him. He would pretend to scoff, but if some item Frances described was unclear, he would ask her to repeat it.

This time, she return from the trip to Plum Hollow with a message for Ogle that he did not at all like. "Mrs. Barnes says, dear husband, that 'Gray may be a colour for which there is no antidote. You should instead seek governmental allies.' "

"Rubbish" was his only reply. But he thought about it.

The Gray in question was not the colour, but Captain James Gray, with whom Ogle in November 1832 had entered a partnership. If Ogle Gowan can be accurately described as being at times a firebrand, Captain Gray was a true wild man. A sporadically successful Brockville merchant, he held extreme and inconsistent political opinions, was given to violence, and, in latter days, terrorism and arson.

In the fall of 1832, however, he had seemed a plausible business partner and Ogle, as usual, was desparately in need of a friend with capital. The business Gowan planned once again to enter was publishing, and the paper he proposed to establish was to be called the *Antidote and Canadian Sentinel*. The lineage of this periodical goes back of course to *The Antidote* that Ogle had published in Ireland and, beyond that, to *The Antidote,* the famous anti-Catholic pamphlet published by Sir Harcourt Lees in 1819.

Gowan's pitch to Gray was simple. "You see, Captain, we cannot only make a profit from a newspaper, but we can promote our future as representatives of the people." He added quickly, "And, of course, promote sound Constitutional principles as well."

Captain Gray, a half-pay officer and already the owner of a fierce handle-bar moustache, fancied himself as the proprietor of a paper. "Quite right, Gowan. We need an alternative to that Yankee-Reformer paper, the *Recorder.* And the *Statesman* is too milk-and-water Tory." In his bluff way, Gray recognized an important political fact: that in addition to the traditional political interest in Upper Canada — Reform and Compact-Tory — there now was a third force, the immigrant-Tories, and they wanted a clear, indeed extreme, voice. "You're on then, my man!" he said and he and

Ogle sealed their partnership by becoming staggeringly stocious that night: Ogle would be the front man and, officially, the editor and proprietor. Gray would buy the needed printing equipment and contribute £5 a week towards expenses. He would, as well, write the occasional article when he felt like it.

Thus, in early October 1832, Captain Gray and Ogle Gowan had watched with some satisfaction as Gray's merchant stock — hardware, crockery, flannel, dry goods, and guns — was sold at a very successful public auction. Gray publicly announced that in the future he would "confine his business to Importation and Commissions," which, when combined with his silent partnership in the publishing enterprise, constituted a very gentlemanly mode of obtaining a livelihood. Because their own printing equipment had yet to be delivered, the two partners made an arrangement with the Brockville *Statesman* to do their printing, an agreement easily completed as that paper's editor was an Orangeman.

Gowan's new paper had a motto that no Irishman would feel was ambiguous:

COURAGE, FIDELITY, UNANIMITY AND NO SURRENDER

and these he expanded in a statement that read:

> the principles of which it is hoped will give unmixed satisfaction to all those who wish to maintain the Crown, the Law, and the Constitution in all their integrity; and to preserve a close and lasting connexion between the Mother Country and this extensive and important appendage of Empire.

The paper was to be a weekly, published each Thursday. Gowan claimed nearly 500 advance subscribers and promised that he would start publishing on November 5, but the paper did not appear until November 29. It can scarcely have had anything near 500 paid subscribers, and it sputtered along month after month on the verge of collapse.

To Gowan the paper was valuable, even if it barely broke even, for it gave him a platform. To Captain Gray, however, the *Antidote's* editorial policy was a matter of constant perplexity. Weekly, he and Ogle would meet in a tavern and go over the articles and plans for the next week's edition. "By God, these are good hits," he would say in reference to especially cutting remarks about their common local enemies, the Reformers and, particularly snobbish members of the local Compact. These cutting articles went well past what today would be libelous, and Captain Gray loved every word. Inspired by Gowan's vituperation, he wrote several articles himself in the shrill style.

"But Gowan, why is it that you keep inserting this high-flown stuff? This one reads like a petition to the Queen," he would remark, pointing to a notably elevating item. This was the other half of the *Antidote's* editorial policy, and Captain Gray failed to understand that in several columns Gowan wrote over the head of his local readers, specifically to call himself to the attention of the Toronto administration. This was Ogle's statesmanlike posture.

For example, an early issue of the *Antidote* called for "a union of all good loyal subjects, to associate in clubs or societies, particularly the Protestants and Roman Catholics of Ireland." This was a continuation of the concepts put forth in the remarkable Port Hope Manifesto in September 1832, and he followed it with a series of articles praising Bishop Macdonnell and making further suggestions for political alliances between Irish Catholics and Protestants. These ideas made sense, because the wider his base of support the more apt was Gowan to become the outstanding immigrant leader.

But confusing it certainly was, for at virtually the same time that he was ennunciating his ideas for a political alliance with Irish Catholics in Canada, he was writing a private letter to an acquaintance overseas, complaining that he left Ireland because he was driven out by Catholic Emancipation — that is, by Catholics being given the right to sit in Parliament!

For some time, the leading Compact Tory in Brockville, the Hon. Charles Jones, had been thinking of breaking off the tacit alliance he and his old-family Tories had with the immigrants. Charles, the son of the legendary "Commissary Jones" was a portly man with a reputation both as a *gourmand* and a remorseless self-aggrandiser.

It was well remembered locally that, during the war of 1812, he had raised a company of dragoons and then had hied away to Halifax, far from combat and, once the war was over, had returned by way of the United States. Col. Joel Stone, even though a staunch defender of the Compact in the district, nevertheless had noted (in 1816) that Charles Jones, for many years past, had notoriously oppressed the poor: taking away their lands, making himself opulent on their ruin. A typical Charles Jones bit of business was to seize, and order sold for debt, the livestock of a widow lady, then rig the auction so that he was himself the only bidder. Jones, a powerful man indeed, would make either a nasty enemy or an unreliable friend.

On April 1 and 2, 1833, he crossed the Rubicon as far as Gowan and the Irish immigrants were concerned. Those two days were the dates of the election for the Brockville Police Board and Gowan was backing the candidacy of his Orange colleague, Dr Edmonston, against two weak Tory candidates, and two very strong Reformers. When it became clear that the Compact-Tories could not win, Jones had a hard choice: lead the old-family voters towards the Gowan camp, or towards that of the long-hated Reformers. Jones and his voters, to the surprise of the Irish, chose the Reformers. That was as close as the old Compact gentry would ever come to saying directly that they would prefer the devil himself to Gowan and the Irish. Thus. the Orange candidate lost and the election concluded with a serious riot.

On April 4, only two days after the Brockville electoral riot, the *Recorder* reported that the Joneses had arranged for the first Canadian printing of the *Interesting Trial of Hopkins vs. Gowan.* George Perkins Bull, fuelled by his unflagging hatred of Gowan, had written to the Joneses, offering to let them reprint his 1827 Dublin pamphlet. They immediately saw this project as a very good investment in political engineering. So, before the month of April, 1833 was out, Kingston printer, Hugh C. Thomson, had this notable trans-Atlantic artifact made available for public delectation.

Ogle raged: could he not escape that bloodsucking madman Bull? Must he go through life having that accursed pamphlet forever thrust at him? Kingston was an Orange stronghold, and he soon found out who paid for the publication. Understandably, the immediate focus of Gowan's anger was the Hon. Charles Jones. A letter Ogle published in the *Antidote* on April 13 showed what a painful gash had been opened by this re-publication. It had none of the Ciceronian balance that had been so painstakingly inculcated by Ogle's tutors; it was the howl of a wounded and, therefore, aggressive creature:

> Had the individual to whom we allude [Charles Jones] made any subsequent atonement for the DESERTION and HYPOCRISY, with which he stood (and still stands) charged; nay, had he even been content, not to give further offence, we should have allowed his *rashness* and *temerity* to correct themselves . . . . But deeply do we regret to say, that so far from this being the case, the *wretchedly* MALIGNANT and INTEMPERATE man (no doubt writhing under the pangs of his folly), has greatly aggravated his former conduct by a succession of deliberate acts, which any man of reflection and common prudence might well be ashamed to patronize.

And how did the Hon. Charles Jones compare with Ogle Gowan?

> THE BASE AND COWARDLY STATE whose folly now has become sport of every little boy in the county, has dared by his *assassin-like innuendos,* to impugn the character of those who have forgotten more since they entered Canada, than ever he knew in his life, and who have cheerfully sacrificed their time, their comforts, and their property, to maintain their principles, and vindicate the majesty of that constitution, the benefit of which the stupid man is unable to appreciate.

Gowan's howl was too anguished, too bitter, to be a matter of calculation on his part. It also makes evident that Ogle translated injury to himself into injury to the Constitution: if the Hon. Charles Jones was an enemy to Ogle Gowan, he necessarily became a traitor to the polity. Also, when wounded, Ogle instinctively slashed out, his howl of pain quickly transmuting itself into the roar of attack.

The next act in this drama did not occur until Saturday evening, October 20, 1833 and, like so much in Gowan's life, it was farcical in its initiation and near-fatal in its consequences.

"You, sir, are a liar and a coward!"

"And you are sentenced to twenty-four hours in goal, beginning in five minutes!"

The first voice was the hoarse bellow of Captain James Gray. He was on his feet, purple with rage. The second voice was that of Jonas Jones, president of the Brockville Police Board. The scene was the Brockville courthouse. Ogle Gowan, standing beside his friend Gray, tried to say something to him, but Gray was too enraged to hear.

The immediate occasion of this contretemps was risible: an item on the agenda of the Police Board involved an immigrant, William Free, being interrogated about the disputed ownership of a cow. He had a witness, a woman who would testify to his being the rightful owner, and was about to call her, when Captain Gray, who, with Ogle, had been watching the proceedings as protectors of immigrants' interests, stood up, walked over to him, and said something.

"We have not called on you," barked Jonas Jones and banged his gavel. "When we want your information, we will call for it."

Captain Gray, pleased to see Jones irritated, replied cheekily, "I merely wished to advise my friend that the lady witness is out of town and that, therefore, he should ask for a postponement of the case."

"If you want to give advice, you should give it privately. Or in another room. Not in this court." Jones's tone was patronizing.

Captain Gray bristled, but decided to return to his seat quietly. He was just back at his bench when Jones added, "This is not a barroom, or a shebeen, or the *Antidote* office; proper decorum and decency rule here."

Gray wheeled and shouted. "My friends at the *Antidote* at least have served their country! Your whole family is a set of cowards. Did not your brother run away during the late war?"

"ORDER!!"

Insults were rapidly exchanged. Gray stuck home with a piece of gossip long whispered in Brockville. "And did not your brother-in-law seduce his niece?!"

Jones began to pound his gavel wildly, trying to prevent further revelations.

"Americans! Traitors! Yankees!" In pronouncing these epithets, Gray now was joined by Ogle Gowan: in the New World, "American" and "Yankee" had replaced "Papist" and "Croppie" as the vilest words he knew.

"Sergeant at arms! Arrest Captain Gray and, if he interferes, Mr. Gowan as well."

Ogle did not interfere, but Gray spent the next twenty-four hours in the lock-up. Overnight, while Gray was in gaol, Ogle had a handbill printed and distributed, justifying Gray's behaviour and attacking the Compact autocracy.

This indecorus affray set off a most improbable series of events.

Captain Gray owed £9,000, a large sum for the times, to creditors in England, chiefly to the firm of Forster and Smith of London, for which he acted as Brockville agent. To collect this debt, the English firm appointed the appropriately toponymous Mr. Ireland to journey to Brockville. He arrived late in November, bearing two letters, one giving him power of attorney to collect the money, and the other revoking the agency held by Captain Gray. The debt collector and Captain Gray met several times over the course of a week and failed to come to any agreement about terms of payment. Brockville, like most towns its size, was one large gossip matrix. Soon everyone knew of the situation, including Jonas Jones. Cannily, Jones made himself known to Mr. Ireland and — surprise! — was awarded the agency for the London firm that previously had been held by Captain Gray!

Simultaneously, Mr. Ireland, with Jonas Jones's help, set in train legal proceedings to collect the debt and to punish Gray for his defalcation.

Gray fled Brockville and hid in the backwoods of Leeds county. There he brooded about events: his enemy, Jonas Jones, had taken from him his prized London importing agency, and now had forced him to live in a miserable shanty in the back of beyond.

These reflections were inflammatory. Literally. About nine on the evening of Thursday, January 4, 1834, smoke began to rise from several spots in the barn of Jonas Jones, located about a mile east of Brockville. This was a crop-barn, filled with hay, wheat, and other grains, and it had extensive drive sheds attached. The flames moved quickly, much faster than if they had emanated from a single point, and the buildings were consumed before anything could be saved. In an era when insurance was not available for farm buildings, this was a major loss, amounting to at least £1,000.

Sheriff Adiel Sherwood, who happened to be in the area, arrived on the scene quickly. He came upon Francis Gray, the captain's son, bearing pistols, a dirk, and a very guilty air. Immediately, he was arrested. Jonas Jones, who was visiting friends when he heard of the fire, returned home to find the barn burning and Sherwood holding Francis Gray. "Damn the young scoundrel. Put him in gaol and then arrest the *father!* You know as well as I do that he is behind this!" Sherwood swore out a warrant and sent deputies to ferret out Captain Gray.

Meanwhile, Captain Gray, feeling alternatively triumphant and fearful, was in a backwoods tavern in Yonge township, run by a Welshman by the name of Osborne. It was a filthy place, and the smell of the evening meal of rye bread, rancid butter, and glutinous mutton chops hung heavy in the air. Soon the hour was past midnight and, save for his avariciousness, the tavern keeper would have stopped serving the raw whiskey punch that was his specialty and gone to bed. Just as he was deciding to close up, a local farmer named Berry came in with his wife. They noisily brushed snow from their clothes. The tavern keeper was about to tell them to go on their way, that he was not staying open any longer, when Mrs. Berry said, "Ah, there he is!" and pointed to Captain Gray. "We are only just on our road back from Brockville; it's good night for sleighing; and we met three of the sheriff's deputies. They have arrested your son and have a warrant out for you and for some friend of yours."

"Damn the odds!" Gray declared, with a theatrical sweep of his hand and added, grandly, "Osborne! here, another hot whiskey for me and the same for my friend Mr. Berry." He drank this punch and made fun of the whole business: the Joneses, Sherwoods and their lot were fools, parasites, and fornicators with their own families. Gray emptied one jug of punch, ordered another, and worked his way through it, traducing his enemies with increasingly slurred speech. Finally he passed out, his head resting on one of the tavern's long tables, and there the sheriff's men found him next morning. He joined his son in gaol, along with their friend, Niblock, a recent Ulster immigrant. Arson in those days was a hanging charge, and the Brockville authorities had the gaol strengthened in order to prevent the men being freed by sympathizers, particularly fellow Orangemen.

Either by good planning or by good fortune, Ogle Gowan was in Toronto when the arson took place. He returned to discover not only that his business partner was in gaol, but that a member of his own extended family also had been arrested. This was a nephew, one John Bacon, who with Ogle's help had found a job in a retail shop in Brockville. The young lad, upon hearing that there was a warrant out for the arrest of his uncle's business partner, had hired a sleigh and had driven out in the country to warn him. Sheriff's deputies had intercepted him and locked him up. Now, to Ogle's distress, the lad was being held with drunks in the common holding cell in the Brockville gaol. Eventually, he was released, after Gowan appealed to Sir John Colborne.

For the moment, Ogle stayed loyal to Captain Gray. They shared the same enemies, and had similar problems: Ogle, like Captain Gray was in danger of losing a major legal tussle with Jonas Jones.

After the arson, Jones decided to move against Gowan, as well as against Gray, and thus rid the local Compact of its twin tormentors. He purchased a bill-of-hand (that is, a type of IOU) signed by Gray, and then, because Gray was unable to cover the bill, he had Sheriff Sherwood seize the *Antidote's* printing press on the grounds that this was Gray's only property of any value. One of the sheriff's deputies, a hulk of a man named Musson, took the type, gave it to the sheriff for safekeeping, and then, single-handedly, moved the press to the back of a general store owned by a man named Dunbar. This put the *Antidote* out of business. Ogle sued Sheriff Sherwood on the grounds that the type and press belonged to him, not to Captain Gray. The case was put off until the summer term. Gowan was very pessimistic about the outcome. He petitioned Sir John Colborne for a change of venue. He wanted a trial before an "impartial jury," possibly, he suggested, in the Bathurst District "where American predilections are not so prevalent."

The tensions of the Gray affray took their toll on Ogle. He was increasingly snappish around home, and Frances, Mrs. Colclough, and Mrs. Graham stayed out of his way as much as possible. Whenever he came into the house they would make themselves as busy as possible with domestic matters. Gowan found some pleasure in talking or playing with young Nassau and Harcourt, but he could not stay amiable very long, even with them. Rather than remain about the house during the day, Ogle spent more and more time in taverns. He was not a great drinker, but went there for the company and, especially, because he needed an audience. His favourite establishment was a small inn in Brockville's west ward, a district where many Irish protestants were settled. There the diminutive seventeen-year-old barmaid, one Jane Marie, was half-smitten with him: Ogle had a certain physical attractiveness, an energetic magnetism about him, and he treated her with exaggerated courtesy. Once, when the inn-keeper was away for a time, she let him make love to her on a big pile of burlap bags in the store room.

Ogle confided to Jane Marie that he was in big trouble with

some evil men and especially with Jonas Jones. She knew the name but that was all; she did not question Mr. Gowan's judgement. And, so, would she help him against this man? Dimly, Jane Marie agreed to a proposal that Gowan made: she would be well rewarded it she swore out an affidavit that Jonas Jones had attempted to rape her.

Jonas Jones counter-attacked with surprising speed. He and Sheriff Sherwood descended upon the girl, her employer, and her family and threatened, grilled, and cajoled until the truth came out. Then Jones went to the grand jury and had an indictment brought against Gowan. This was for conspiracy to injure one's character. Ogle was arrested and was let out only on £400 bond, a large sum for the times.

Cringingly, Gowan petitioned Sir John Colborne for relief, on the grounds (not entirely fanciful) that the magistrates who would control his trial were highly excited against him: he had been publicly barracking the J.P.s for some time and demanding their "purification." Ogle also argued (quite correctly) that Jonas Jones, by virtue of his being a magistrate, would act both as his accuser and his judge.

The trial was set for mid-February, but was put off and, subsequently cancelled — but only at great cost to Gowan. Jones's friends convinced him to abandon the case, because it would injure him politically, by permanently alienating the immigrant community. He agreed to do so, but only after Ogle signed a written statement admitting himself guilty. This was read in open court.

Now, with no newspaper, his partner in gaol on a hanging charge, a publicly confessed suborner, Ogle Gowan looked to be a real loser.

Amazingly, it was at this point that, instead, he began to be a winner.

He found a *deus ex machine* that disrupted all local equations. Ogle, although willing to fight in the gutter in his home region, consistently had presented himself to governmental authorities as conciliatory towards Catholics, and as an immigrant spokesman of high responsibility. Now, in the spring of 1834, those prudential efforts paid off.

Robert Sympson Jameson was Gowan's saviour. He had arrived from England the previous June, as London-appointed Attorney General of Upper Canada. Prior to that, he had spent four years in the West Indies, trying to reform their judicial system and being frustrated by local slave owners. He was a very compe- competent lawyer, but by tradition, he was also expected to seek and win a seat in the House of Assembly. A general election was expected before the year 1834 was out, and the question became: where would he find a seat?

If — and it was a very big "if" — Ogle Gowan could convince Jameson to run with him in Leeds county, the results would be compelling. The local Compact-Tories, out of deference to the government would not run a candidate against an office holder such as the Attorney General; and, on the other hand, Jameson's reforming activities in the West Indies made him attractive to electors of moderate Reform views. As a bonus, Jameson was in good stead with the Roman Catholic immigrants, because he had gotten himself into hot water with some strict Anglicans, by attending a St. Patrick's day dinner in the company of John Elmsley, the notorious "apostate" to Catholicism.

Convincing Jameson to join him as running mate was one of the most important political tasks Gowan ever assayed. Jameson had the misfortune to be married, quite unhappily, to one of the most engagingly literate women ever to flit across the Canadian stage: Anna Brownell Jameson, author of *Winter Studies and Summer Rambles in Canada*, and correspondent with several European literary lions. She left to the world a picture of a cold, drunken, neglectful husband, and perhaps he was. Unlike her, he had the good grace not to complain publicly about their loveless union. Actually, Jameson's friends found him warm, loyal, and erudite. In addition to being learned in law, he was a competent poet, a friend of Samuel Taylor Coleridge's son, and he had worked on a re-edition of Samuel Johnson's famous *Dictionary*. He craved good talk and good company, the more so because his wife at first refused to join him in Canada.

When Ogle spoke with Jameson — and these conversations took place over several days — he completely abandoned his own posture as immigrant leader. Instead, he acted the part of an Anglo-Irish gentleman. He depicted his political activity in Leeds county as something like fox-hunting: good rough sport that any man of the right sort would enjoy.

Ogle's knowledge of literary Dublin of the 1820s also came in useful. He told stories of men of letters whom he had never met, but in a manner strongly implying that he had known them intimately. In return, Jameson recounted tales of the Romantic poets and the gossip of the London literary world of the 1820s, before he had gone off to be a judicial officer in the West Indies. As they came gradually to know each other, Jameson told Gowan stories of the maladministration of the government of the West Indies, and Ogle talked of Irish governmental fopperies.

By the close of their third meeting, Jameson had quite come to like and trust Gowan: sound man, he thought, fine sense of words, certainly not the wild firebrand some people said he was. And, finally, Jameson agreed to stand for parliament alongside Gowan in Leeds county, subject to only two conditions: that he could stand as a public servant, thus above party, and that he would not have to campaign actively, but only appear on the hustings at election time.

When the news of Jameson's decision hit Leeds county in early May 1834, the local politicos were dumbfounded. Gowan had gone overnight from the excluded middle (that is from being crushed between the Reformers and the old Compact-Tories) to being the possessor of a middle ground that was so broad that potentially it excluded the other two political wings.

"Potentially" — for Ogle still had to clean a lot of dirt from his face, and that was not easy. In fact, for a brief time, things got messier, if that is possible. Whenever he could, Gowan had made a big show of attacking William Lyon Mackenzie, since this helped him present himself to governmental officials as an alternate source of leadership for the immigrant community. The message he transmitted to the government was: trust me, support me, or the alternative is Mackenzie and the radicals. Embarrassingly for Gowan, Mackenzie serialized in his *Colonial Advocate* in June and July 1834, that time-worn document, the *Interesting Trial, Hopkins vs. Gowan.* Granted, in a sense this was the *imprimatur* on Ogle's importance as an immigrant leader (Mackenzie manifestly saw him as a threat that needed to be destroyed), but it hardly raised Gowan's prestige amongst the *haut bourgeousie* of Toronto.

Gowan won a small vindication of himself in a lawsuit against Adiel Sherwood, for seizing the *Antidote's* presses. The case came up in late August 1834, and hinged on whether the press and type, which had been purchased from MacClean of the Brockville

Statesman, actually belonged to Captain Gray (for whose debts they were seized) or to Ogle Gowan. The jury accepted Ogle's claim that the items belonged to him, even though the payment to MacClean had been made by Gray. Hence, the sheriff had wrongly seized the press and type and he had to pay Gowan £7 10s in damages.

Ogle took another step towards respectability by gradually abandoning his friend and ally Captain Gray. Gray came up for trial at the same Johnstown assizes that gave Gowan his verdict against Sheriff Sherwood, and there Gowan, ambitious for his political future, double-crossed Gray. Called to the stand as a defence witness, the character of his testimony was equivocal.

QUESTION: Do you think Captain Gray set the fire in question?

ANSWER: I did not suspect Gray of burning the barn till after my return from Toronto, where I was at the time the barn burned.

QUESTION: Had you any reason to suspect that it was done by his procurement?

ANSWER: I thought that perhaps he might have had some hand in it.

Some defence witness! Some friend!

Despite testimony that left few of Brockville's citizens with any doubts about Captain Gray's guilt, he was judged not guilty. The chief justice, who had conducted this trial himself, gave a three-hour summing up that came down heavily on the side of acquittal. This was because there was only one direct witness (the man Niblock, an Irishman from Islandmagee, County Antrim, one of the conspirators) who turned State's witness and directly linked Gray to the fire: since arson was a capital offense, the chief justice did not want to convict on the evidence of a single witness.

Immediately after being acquitted, Captain Gray, recognizing that Gowan had ratted on him in order to further his own political ambitions, fired off a letter to the Brockville *Recorder* denouncing his "avowed enemy and false friend, GOWAN" who had been engaged in an "attempt to take my life." Gray tried to strike back by offering himself (unsuccessfully) as a candidate in the election that was announced on September 4, only a few days after the conclusion of his trial.

Ogle Gowan's handling of the Leeds county election of 1834 was one of the most tactically brilliant, amoral, and ruthless campaigns in Canadian electoral history. By inveigling Attorney General Jameson to run in Leeds, Gowan had effectively reduced the electoral race from a two-seat contest to a one-seat race (the attorney general was virtually a shoe-in). Ogle's next step, one that proved critical, was to use his increasing influence with the central government to have the hustings moved from Farmersville, where the Reformers were strong, to Beverly (now called "Delta") in the back of Bastard township, about twenty miles northwest of Brockville. This was in the heart of an Irish immigrant area and the Orangemen were very strong there. Each elector had to vote publicly, so voting the wrong way in front of a hostile hometown crowd required some courage. Moreover, Beverly was the bailliwick of an especially effective ally of Gowan's, J.K. Hartwell, Orangeman, Justice of the Peace, Lt. Col. in the militia, and owner of an emporium that was an inn, a grocery store, and a repository of "all kinds of liquors," as he proudly advertised.

Hartwell was the Upper Canadian equivalent of a figure well known to all Irishmen: the gombeen man. He bought and sold anything that had a high mark-up, acted as an auctioneer and broker, and loaned money to locals at exorbitant interest rates. As farmers failed, or drank their farms away, he frequently acquired their lands, and these he later resold to new settlers. A tall, broad-shouldered man, with a horribly pocked face, he was an imposing, slightly frightening figure; not a man to push around. Hartwell recognized that if the Orange Grand Master were elected to parliament, there would be fine pickings for him.

In the late spring, soon after Attorney General Jameson had agreed to join the Gowan ticket, Ogle held a clandestine meeting with J.K. Hartwell. Ogle was fairly confident of what William Buell and Matthew Howard, the Reform candidates, would do, but needed some intelligence on the Compact-Tories and someone to help him outwit them. Hartwell was perfect, for he had several years' acquaintance with the Joneses, especially Charles Jones. Hartwell agreed to become Gowan's cats paw. So, Hartwell wrote to Charles Jones in 1834, "If you ever had any confidence in me, rest assured that *all* things will *end* well, whatever appearance they may seem to have." In the succeeding weeks he transmitted several silly electoral ideas to Jones, allegedly to help defeat Gowan, and several bits of political intelligence concerning Gowan that were intentionally misleading.

In May, Hartwell slipped to the Hon. Charles Jones a plan that purported to provide for Gowan's defeat — but which greatly helped Ogle's cause. (Cannily, Hartwell presented this plan — which was a handwriting immediately recognizable as his own — to Jones unsigned, as if through modesty in the face of its brilliance.)

The idea presented to Jones was this: given that there were 1,500 electors in Leeds county, then there were 3,000 votes. The trick was to break the natural inclination, of those who voted for the attorney general to vote for his running mate Gowan, as well. Hartwell's suggestion was that, since the polling would take five days:

> Let all the Magistrates and other Loyal Canadian Population [that is, the supporters of the Compact-Tories] remain quiet until the *last* day of the Election and till after Gowan's force is done. Then go forward and plump [that is, each cast only a single vote] for the Attorney General.

That would have the effect of electing the attorney general and one of the two Reform candidates, William Buell or Matthew Howard, either of whom the Charles Jones clan preferred to Gowan. Hartwell's note included a denunciation of Gowan:

> The writer detests Gowan as much as you possibly can, and has already made a sacrifice of his feeling for the *sole purpose* of ridding the District of a man whose character is *so infamous* and who caused so much disturbance among his countrymen that were peaceable until he came among them.

The note concluded earnestly:

> Commit this communication to the flames the moment you have read it for fear it may be seen by someone.

The plan matured in the minds of the Compact leaders and they agreed to hold back their voters until the last minute. This must have made Ogle very happy indeed, for he had drafted the note that Hartwell had sent to Charles Jones!

The Leeds election opened on Monday, October 6, a clear,

crisp day with cirrus clouds moving slowly overhead, locks of wool against a blue background. The hustings at Beverly consisted of a rough piece of platform about twenty by thirty-two feet, resting on unpeeled cedar uprights. A set of steps was situated at either end and on the platform were chairs and desks. These were covered by a makeshift canvas roof, where the poll book of eligible electors was kept, and facilities for recording each vote as it was cast. Before the voting began, the hustings made a fine playground for the barefoot children of the village and the odd hen laid an egg under its protective cover. Like most things in Leeds, it was a peaceful, harmless item, as long as the local citizens were nowhere near it.

Robert Sympson Jameson arrived at Brockville a week before the election, his first visit to the area. He came on the steam boat *Great Britain*, and was met at the quay by Ogle Gowan and several well-dressed supporters. After a short speech of welcome, the attorney general was brought to Brockville's best inn. On Tuesday, escorted by Ogle Gowan and J.K. Hartwell, he was taken into the back country, to Beverly, where he spent the next few days holding court. He stayed at Hartwell's inn and each day individuals and small groups of voters, mostly backwoods Irishmen, came to meet him, to converse awkwardly with him and with Ogle, and to go home assured that this Englishman was the sort who could be trusted.

On Monday, October 6, the polls were formally opened by Sheriff Adiel Sherwood. He used semi-archaic language, which fit well with his crusty personality. "Know ye all here assembled that an election for Leeds county is now called. Ye shall elect two members of the House of Assembly." He paused, pleased with the fustian sonorities. "And know ye therefore that nominations now are open."

The returning officer now came to the fore and conducted a venerable formality, one that harkened to the parliaments of late mediaeval England: he asked for nominations and although everyone in the county knew who was running, the candidates were nominated as if their candidacy was being put forward spontaneously. Each man was nominated in a fulsome speech by his chief advocate, and the nomination was seconded by other supporters. There were no surprises. Each candidate made a speech accepting the nomination. Attorney General Jameson claimed to be sympathetic with the Reformers; Ogle Gowan, resplendent in a bottle-green frock coat and a Paisley waistcoat, and wearing thick-heeled boots to make himself appear taller, preached to the "Europeans," and told them to protect the Constitution and Empire against the "Yankees"; Buell and Howard each made pro-Reform statements, but attempted to dissociate themselves from the more extreme views of William Lyon Mackenzie; and Captain Gray spent half-an-hour discussing the iniquities of Ogle Gowan, amidst cries and threats from Ogle's supporters.

Then the real battle began. Gowan and several dozen of his followers, many armed with clubs and some with knives, crowded the hustings. Followers of Buell and Howard had to elbow their way through these men and every time someone tried to cast a vote for the Reformers, Ogle went up to the returning officer and, in a loud voice, challenged that person's electoral qualifications. This meant that the potential voter's land title and tax records had to be checked. By day's end, only twenty-six persons had managed to vote. They cast a total of fifty-one votes, distributed as follows:

Buell 17
Howard 15
Jameson 9
Gowan 8
Gray 2

That night, the candidates and six of the magistrates of the Johnstown district met in a nearby public house, run by a Mr. Lewis, and tried to agree what to do. Buell and Howard pleaded with the magistrates to read the Riot Act and to arrest anyone who interferred with the voting. William Buell, always an abstract thinker, preached to the J.P.s about justice and the rights of electors under the common law, a theme that met with no response whatsoever from the J.P.s. Matthew Howard screeched that, "We are, by God, going to be cheated out of this election, unless something is done — and someone will be hurt, no matter what!" That at least had the ring of concrete reality. Ogle Gowan, when asked for his views, ridiculed the Reformers' fears. "It's only strong country men expressing their opinion and making noise; and that is a citizen's right under our Constitution." The returning officer, a small, worried man, did not wish to be caught in the middle of a riot, and, even less, did he wish to be held responsible for any trouble. He argued, "Gentlemen, my powers extend only as far as the hustings themselves. Whatever happens outside of those four corners is not my responsibility." He turned to Jameson for confirmation. "Is that not correct, Mr. Attorney General?" and Jameson, instantly transformed from an interested party into a supposedly-impartial governmental official ruled, "Yes, indeed my good man. In point of law, any powers you might claim over behaviour outside those precincts would be *ultra vires.*"

"Then *you* must do something," Buell beseeched the magistrates. No hope. These men had been assembled by J.K. Hartwell who, as the local J.P., was directly responsible for maintaining order, and he had asked to be present only men who were known to be strongly opposed to the election of Buell and Howard. This does not mean that they were pro-Gowan, but they were quite willing to let the Gowanites bash the Reformers: it would serve the righteous old whiners right, was the general view.

So the second day of the election was nastier than the first. Ogle's forces developed a very effective technique: this was to crowd the hustings and when a known supporter of the Reformers came to vote, they would let the person part way through and then close in around him, so that he was alone, cut off from his friends. Then they would punch him in the body: not in the face where it left evidence, just fists in the ribs, elbows in the kidneys, nothing so hard as to drop the man, but painful, frightening blows. Often, one of the Gowanites who had a knife would grab the Reformer's coattails in one hand and slash them with the knife held in the other. One massive Gowan supporter (a man so large that the Irishmen in town called him "Hempenstall," in reference to the Walking Gallows of '98), had a trick of grabbing the potential voter by the back of the trousers and lifting him clear off the ground: it was not a comfortable experience to be hoisted by the crotch with rough homespun material. Some few of the Gowan team had taken knitting needles and hat pins from their wives' sewing baskets, and they poked these into the unfortunate Reform electors.

The returning officer looked the other way when these things happened; the magistrates watched, but did nothing; Attorney General Jameson observed without comment; only Adiel Sherwood, as sheriff, showed any concern, and he was shrewd enough to recognize that he could do nothing by himself.

When voters for Gowan and Jameson came forward, they were cheered, and after they cast their votes, often were carried on shoulders around the hustings.

Gowan was very pleased. Not only were the Reformers taking a pummeling, but the Compact-Tories, following the plan sold to them by J.K. Hartwell, were holding back from voting.

The third day, things came to a head. Levi Soper, a major in the Leeds county militia, and an indominitable old curmudgeon, tried to organize a counter-force. Tough, and something of a local legend for his touchiness, he had some chance of success. He called out, "All friends of Buell and Howard, follow me to Mr. Lewis's Inn!" He marched away from the hustings with a number of Reform supporters behind him.

At once Gowan saw the danger. The Reformers were attempting to organize themselves into a gang like his own. "Major Soper plans to attack the hustings, lads!" he hollered. The attorney general took up the cry and quickly, like well-trained storm-troopers, Ogle's men rushed from the hustings and fell on the departing Reformers, beating them bloodily. Levi Soper took special abuse and was severely wounded on the head and face.

The sole response of the authorities was for the returning officer to close the poll for one hour, and then the voting began again. The tally at the end of the third day showed that a total of only 293, of a potential 1,500 electors had cast ballots.

That evening, Buell and Howard wrote a formal request to the magistrates for special constables to keep order. It was ignored.

On the morning of the fourth day the two men wrote a protest (chiefly as the basis for a future appeal that the election be voided), and retired from the contest. At that point only 445 persons had cast a total of 889 votes:

Gowan 311
Jameson 311
Buell 108
Howard 107
Gray 62

The Reformers were out of the race, and now it was too late for the Compact-Tories to do anything. "Plumping" for Jameson would work as a tactic only if there were a second-place candidate who could beat Gowan, and with Buell and Howard out, there was no one.

Gowan had won. There was no sense in keeping the polls open any longer and the returning officer announced in his reedy voice, "I declare that the duly elected Members of Parliament, to hold seats in the lower House of Assembly, for the county of Leeds, are Robert Sympson Jameson and Ogle Robert Gowan." With manifest relief, he added, "I now pronounce the polls closed." After these words, he collected the poll book and scuttled for his carriage with the staccato speed of a sand flea caught on an open beach.

Ogle and the attorney general stood drinks for their supporters in Mr. Lewis's inn and spirit-grocery, and promised them a big dinner, perhaps an ox roast, in the future.

Ogle immediately began signing his business correspondence "Ogle R. Gowan, Esq., MP" and such was the Upper Canadian deference to political institutions that even William Buell's newspaper, while abominating Gowan's behaviour in graphic detail, dignified him with the title of esquire and member of parliament.

Ogle, undeniably, was a winner.

On February 14, 1835, a select committee of the Upper Canadian House of Assembly brought in its report, instigated by Buell and Howard, on the contested Leeds county election. Upwards of eighty witnesses from the county had been called, and the report was almost like a rural Social Register. Anybody who was anybody was listed amongst the witnesses. The report declared that "insult, interference, riot, force, and violence were used to such a great extent as to interfere with and prevent the freedom of election," and that the supporters of Buell and Howard were "deterred and prevented from exercising the Elective Franchise in peace and safety . . . . Neither the magistrates nor the returning officer had done their jobs; the view that the returning officer had no jurisdiction beyond the limits of the hustings was wrong. For all these reasons the election of Gowan and Jameson was voided and, because their defence was judged to be "frivolous and vexatious," they had to pay the costs.

New elections for the Leeds seats were set for early March,

1835, and Gowan, having worked out a technique for winning, intended to keep to the path of success. Gowan and Jameson still had purchase with the central government and they convinced Sir John Colborne once again to make Beverly the site of the polling. Thus, the new election would again take place in a backwoods stronghold of Irish Protestant immigrants.

As the election approached, the attorney general began to get cold feet. In an address to the Leeds electors, he politely requested that "in order *not* to run the risk of being dragged . . . . into an affray that they either stay away from the hustings or foreswear violence."

When Ogle read these words, he laughed.

The only person in authority who acted practically in the face of the impending election was Sheriff Adiel Sherwood. He designed a special set of hustings, unique in Upper Canada: they were intended to be riot-proof. These hustings sat in the middle of the road that ran through the centre of Beverly and looked like a large shanty, put together by a madman. The basic structure was a raised platform, square, twenty-five feet per side. Each side had a seven-foot wall around it, with a window cut into the wall and a set of steps leading up to that window. The whole business was covered with canvas. The idea was that the supporters of the four candidates — Gowan, Jameson, Buell, and Howard (Captain Gray had dropped out of electoral politics) — would be kept apart. Each voter would make his choice known only at the window designated for his candidate. Since the electors had two votes, they would vote at two windows. The theory was that this would keep the factions apart and the election orderly.

A fine theory, but on Monday, March 2, 1835, reality intruded.

The four candidates, as usual, were nominated and addressed the throng before the polls were officially opened. Jameson and Gowan complained of unfair treatment and injustice to them in the House of Assembly, and when Buell and Howard tried to speak, the Gowan-Jameson supporters set up a chant that prevented their being heard. The returning officer recognized this chant for what it was, the death-knell for any chances of an orderly election, and went inside his little fortress, the hustings, and took a long drink from a jug of whiskey.

Buell and Howard gave up trying to speak. So, fortified by another secret splash from the whiskey jug, the returning officer went out and explained to the electors how the poll would be conducted. He began, "To ensure fairness gentlemen . . . "

"We'll make it bloody fair!" a Gowan supporter interupted,

" . . . to make it fair gentlemen, we will take votes for each candidate in rotation. We will do so in the following order: Jameson, Buell, Howard, and Gowan."

The idea was to keep the parties separate by forcing them to concentrate on the mechanics of organizing their own voters, so that an elector would be ready to appear at the proper point in the sequence. This worked for one round:

"Jameson."

"Buell."

"Howard."

"Gowan."

But then a line of Gowan and Jameson supporters began to edge in on the electors assembled at the Howard window. They pushed forward in a row, like the Hoplite phalanx of ancient Greece, each man protecting the flank of the other, and each doing something nasty to the Reform supporters: a punch, a kick, a poke with a knitting needle, a knife brandished, a cosh brought down on the exposed forearm or unprotected shoulder. The returning officer, now relying openly on the whiskey jug for courage, several times came out amongst the electors and each time the Gowanites backed off. But the moment he went back inside the hustings, they again pushed forward. Jonas Jones, trying to protect public order, acted nearly heroically. Twice he jumped out of the Howard window smack into the middle of the Gowan-Jameson forces, and his presence momentarily quelled the attacks. But only momentarily. Finally, Jones demanded of the returning officer that the polling be adjourned for an hour, and this he happily did. "Jesus, what a day!" the poor official reflected. "and it not yet noon!"

By the time the hour's truce was up, the returning officer was thoroughly doited, for he had spent the time industriously drinking. He announced a new procedure. "Gentlemen, we'll continue to proceed in rogation. I mean in rotation. I shall take five votes for each candidate." Only a desperate and drunken man could have conceived of this idea as being eirenic. "The first window to receive votes will be that of Mr. Buell. Then Mr. Howard. And so on."

Buell's first five votes indeed were cast, but immediately the trouble at Howard's window began again and this time it developed into a general gang fight. Jonas Jones once again leaped out of Howard's window into the scrum, but this time his presence did no good. In fact, now the Gowan-Jameson supporters turned on him. "Get the old bastard out of here!" one man yelled and nearly broke Jones's shin with a hard kick with a hobnailed boot. "The old ho'er is a goddman Yankee, any road!" another hollered and smacked Jones so hard on the ear with his open palm that it nearly burst an eardrum. Other Gowanites slashed at his clothes with their knives. They were practised with these instruments and shredded his clothing without drawing blood. At last, his head ringing, his clothes badly torn, Jonas Jones scrambled back up on to the hustings, safe from the immigrant-Tories of Leeds county.

"The poll is adjourned until tomorrow morning!" screeched the returning officer, who had been yelling so much that he was beginning to lose his voice. "No more votes!" he piped. "Closed! Done! Adjourned!" He grabbed the poll book and, observing that nobody was near Gowan's side of the husting, since the Gowanites all were rioting elsewhere, scuttled off towards Mr. Lewis's tavern. He threaded his way the 300 yards up the road, terrified, unsteady, in search of shelter. In Lewis's he ordered more whiskey, drank nearly a half-pint in a gulp, and went upstairs to collapse on a lumpy tick bed.

The candidates who, as well as the returning officer, had all been allocated rooms at Lewis's inn, arrived soon after the little official, followed by a few Reform supporters who were seeking asylum. A crowd of Gowanites marched towards the inn and the innkeeper quickly barred the door. For a time Gowan's men satisfied themselves with clubbing and beating the few Reform supporters they could catch, but then, with the hope of laying their hands on Buell and Howard, they broke the tavern windows. When Mr. Lewis went out to plead with them to stop, they clubbed him senseless. They then broke down the door and rushing inside, grabbed any supporters of Buell and Howard they could find. "Let's burn out the Yankee hoor's-melts" one animated Gowanite cried and, taking a burning brand from the stove, he started to charge upstairs where Buell and Howard had sought refuge. He was stopped by Mr. Lewis who had recovered consciousness and now blocked the stairway. Lewis pleaded with the Gowanites not to destroy his means of livelihood, and not to burn a building that housed innocent women and children. This latter note struck a chivalric chord in the Gowanites and the pyrophile was told by his fellows to put the firebrand back in the stove.

At last Jameson and Gowan came down from upstairs. Standing on the first step, Jameson told the men that they must desist. He talked of Order, Honour, and of not giving the Reformers a chance to steal this election by lodging protests. Then Ogle came down and gave much the same speech. It was a very near thing, but the rioters calmed down. They went away, uttering threats against Buell and Howard.

In fact, Buell and Howard were ahead at the end of this first day of polling (Buell 62, Howard 60, Gowan 52, Jameson 50), and they were not beyond a bit of sharp practice of their own. They demanded of the returning officer that the election be stopped because of the violence, and that they be declared the winners.

The returning officer reflected on this demand just long enough to let him imagine what the Gowan-Jameson forces would do to him if he announced such a decision, and replied, "You must be mad."

So, Buell and Howard announced their retirement from the contest.

And the returning officer opened the polls the next morning knowing full well that his job was to effect a Gowan-Jameson majority as soon as possible and then to get home to safety and never again be involved in a Leeds county election. He let the polling continue until the immigrant-Tories were well ahead of the Reformers (Gowan 115, Jameson 109, Buell 69, Howard 65). and then he closed the polls and wrote the names of the winners on the official returns.

Another victory for Ogle.

It had two immediate local effects, one comic, the other tragic.

The first occurred in Lewis's tavern. Several of the Reform supporters went there after the hustings were shut, to drink heavily and swear revenge. A band of Gowanites shortly entered and soon a full-scale brawl was in progress that threatened to wreck the place. No magistrates were present and all the candidates had already had left for Brockville. Mr. Lewis showed the ready wit that ever is the tavern-keeper's best friend. He yelled

"Fire!" and when the combatants tumbled outside, he barred the doors.

Another group of Buell supporters, having been beaten at the polls (in several senses), found their way to the tavern of James Philips about three miles north of Beverly, at a site now called "Philipsville." James Philips was a prosperous and respected member of his community, and something of a local legend. He was as keen a Reformer as Gowan was an anti-Reformer, and William Lyon Mackenzie was his hero, although he thought Mac a bit soft on some issues.

The beaten Reformers drank whiskey punch for a while, and Philips commiserated with them. With each jar of drink they became angrier at what had been done to them. Just as they were leaving Philip's tavern, these Reformers spotted two Gowan supporters, easily recognizable by the white ribbons they wore. "We'll take those ribbons and pin then on Ogle's arse!" one of the Reformers suggested and, waylaying the Gowan men, after a brief tussle, stripped them of the insignia.

There the matter should have ended, for what are mere campaign ribbons anyway? Answer: everything. Just like a flag to a batallion, these ribbons were of importance, particularly to men raised in the Irish tradition of party flags and faction colours. In a sense, the Gowan supporters had been unmanned, and they had to recover their honour. So they went for help and returned with ten sleigh loads of supporters, mostly non-voters from Lanark county, who were in the area more for the fights than the politics. The Reformers, seeing that they were outmatched, hid in a gulley behind the tavern, and for a time they and James Philips listened as the Lanark men vandalized the tavern.

At last Philips could stand it no longer and he went berserk. Wielding a wooden claymore, he charged out of the gulley and singlehandedly cleared the tavern, a roaring dervish who could be stopped by nothing short of a musket ball in the brain. The Lanark men fled.

In the debris lay one Edward Cusak, a Gowan supporter whom the Gowanites claimed, Philips had clubbed to death.

Winning, of course, always has a price.

CHAPTER 10

Local Hero, 1835-1836

TO SEE Ogle Gowan on the streets of Toronto, one would have thought that he had just been knighted. He had a new suit of clothes made, one with a double-breasted waistcoat. He had gained weight during the political campaign and in his new suit he really looked a banty rooster. He loved being in Parliament. Seeing the words "Esquire," and "MP" after his name gave him sheer pleasure. And there were practical benefits. He could frank his letters and, more important, government functionaries had to take him seriously. His fellow Orangemen were gratified by his eminence and this strengthened his hand as Grand Master.

Ogle, still cramped for funds, stayed in the Black Horse Tavern on the west side of Church Street, a full mile from the parliament buildings. The owner, a Mr. Brown, was an Orangeman and friend of Gowan's and charged him half-rate for the room. Brown also was a trusted intermediary — in the past he had held valuable land documents for Gowan — and now ran a letter-drop for him. When, because of pressing business, Ogle could not meet with his cousin James, who was doing a lot of land work for Leeds county immigrants, Brown took care of passing on instructions. Also Brown, like most innkeepers, had seen a lot of the sins of the world and had learned the value of discreetly tolerating mankind's venalities. When, once or twice a week, Ogle brought some young girl to his room, Brown said nothing. The girls were very young, though, Brown noticed. On occasion, the inn-keeper would catch

Ogle's eye and the two men would nod to each other, brothers in an unspoken conspiracy.

As a new boy in the Legislative Assembly, Gowan realized that he was expected to be quiet and he was, though, in fact, his long experience in various Orange matters had given him more experience with formal meetings than was possessed by most members of the house.

He did well to keep his head down, because he was the centre of unfortunate attention in any case. On March 9, in a characteristic bit of grabbiness, he put in for a supply of official stationery. The clerk responsible for it refused to give him any until it was certain that Ogle would be permitted to take his seat.

The farcical incident led into another one, when it was found that Sheriff Adiel Sherwood, who had to certify the election returns for Leeds county, had made a cock-up of the election results. He had sent in a writ of election without signing the actual election returns. Whether he did this on purpose or not is unclear. The Lieutenant Governor wrote to Sherwood telling him to come to Toronto immediately, to sign the writ. This executive action, in turn, offended the sensibilities of some of the members of the House of Assembly, who considered Sir John Colborne's actions in this instance to be an interference with the privileges of the assembly! Hence, the assembly appointed a committee of five members to look into the matter and, finally, on March 21, 1835, Gowan and Jameson were allowed to take their seats.

That kind of attention Ogle definitely did not need.

Nor did he need the worry of an investigation that was taking place in the spring of 1835 into the hotly contested Brockville parliamentary election of the previous year. This should not have involved Gowan, but it did. In late March 1835, it became public knowledge that Ogle had taken a bribe the previous year of £60 to vote for Henry Sherwood. This rippled through the provincial papers, and eventually a parliamentary committee confirmed that he had indeed taken the bribe and, therefore, his name was struck off the Brockville voting list.

What next? Ogle wondered — and must have known. On April 11, a parliamentary report on the election of Gowan and Jameson concluded that they had used extreme force, and that their elections should be voided. Three days later, this was done.

Thus far, Ogle had won two parliamentary elections and had managed to remain an MP for a total of less than two months.

Once things start to roll downhill, they pick up momentum. That's what Ogle thought, and no matter how hard he tried to change things, his luck would not improve.

At home in Brockville, Ogle found his name, and that of his political party, constantly being besmirched in various legal tangles. For example, in late August, 1835, James Philips, tavernkeeper and destroyer of Gowanites, was brought up for murder. Attorney General Jameson himself prosecuted the case (so much for the myth of juridical impartiality), and Ogle sat next to him at counsel's table and frequently advised him on points of testimony to pursue. The trial was long and bitter, and accusations against Gowan and his followers were thrown about like Jovian thunderbolts. Once the evidence was heard, however, the jury took only five minutes to reach a verdict: not guilty. While the verdict cleared Philips, it implicitly loaded the blame for the Philipsville riot and the accompanying manslaughter onto the shoulders of the Gowanites, who had begun the disorders at the hustings.

This implicit judgement was confirmed explicitly in a separate civil action, wherein Philips was awarded £50 in damages and costs against the Gowanite outriders from Lanark county who had broken up his tavern. "I will send half this amount to William Lyon Mckenzie," Philips announced, loud enough for Gowan and Jameson to hear.

Messier, and highly embarrassing to Ogle's claim to be a gentleman, was a matter raised at the same September assize by Gowan's old partner and present enemy, Captain James Gray. In an earlier court case, a witness, Arthur McLean, had sworn that the printing press — the one seized by Sherwood — had belonged, not to Gray who at the time was in prison, but to Gowan. On the basis of that testimony, Ogle had won a judgement against the sheriff. Now, Gray went before a grand jury and swore: (1) that he had at one time given Gowan a letter of power of attorney; (2) that McLean, editor of the ill-fated Brockville *Statesman*, had sold the printing presses not to Gowan, but to Gray; (3) that McLean owed Gray £400; and (4) that Gowan had improperly used his power of attorney to give McLean a discharge from all the debts that he owed Gray. This was (5) in return for McLean's perjured testimony that the presses had been sold to Gowan, not to Gray.

The alleged behaviour was tawdry, ungentlemanly, and worse, potentially felonous. Gray pressed the grand jury to indict McLean for perjury. He was shrewd enough not to ask for an indictment against Gowan at this point, but rather against the more vulnerable McLean. Since McLean was a ranking Orangeman, anything that besmirched him would hurt Gowan too. And if the perjury were clearly proved, then perhaps Gowan himself could be prosecuted next.

But here, for once, the system protected Gowan. The usual practice was for a provincially appointed official to look at the grand jury recommendations, and decide if a prosecution should occur — and that person was Attorney General Jameson, who had a personal interest in seeing that his political partner, Ogle Gowan, was not damaged. So the attorney general refused to attend the grand jury sittings while this matter was at hand. On the last day of the assize, the grand jury decided to draw up a bill of indictment on its own, without the attorney general's approval. By then, however, McLean had left town and the matter died. That was a big break for Gowan (and to a lesser degree for Jameson), for the Gray family had compelling documentary evidence of Gowan's complicity in committing perjury.

William Lyon Mackenzie was never charitable to Gowan, but sometimes he was accurate. In October 1835, his Toronto newspaper observed that the "poor creature Ogle R. Gowan is like 'a hair on griddle.' "

Ogle had one further problem that he did not know about. Frances, his wife, was having an affair with his young cousin, James Gowan.

James was now well settled in as a law student in the office of Mr. Small in Toronto, and was in an attractive transitional state from weedy youth to the forbiddingly pompous judge he later became. In these years as a law student he became, briefly, a warm and attractive personality, and a dapper, worldly young man. He dressed well, learned how to drink without making a fool of himself, and chased women.

Both he and his sister Anne were up and down between Toronto and Brockville fairly frequently, and they stayed with their cousins, Ogle and Frances. Ogle had a great deal of trust in young James, who looked after sundry legal matters for him without charge. In turn, Ogle used his influence to find governess posts for young Anne, who was lazy and not willing to work unless pushed.

During one of James's visits in 1835, Ogle was in Toronto, and Frances and James stayed up late in the evening, talking about family matters. She began teasing him about the girls in his life, and, did he know what to do with them? One thing led to another, and they spent the night making love.

That should not surprise anyone. Frances — James used the old family nickname "Fanny" when he was in bed with her — was still only just thirty, and combined an endearing and surprising coltishness with breasts that belonged on a much larger woman. Frances was very sexually responsive, but Ogle, as he became more and more involved in the depressing wrangles of political life, paid her less attention. He was also spending increasing amounts of time with girls of tender years and minimal virtue.

And, considering the family's background, one should not be surprised that they were keeping sexual relations within the clan. The Anglo-Irish, being very thin on the ground in many parts of the Old Country, respected the Restricted Degrees of family interbreeding more in theory than in practice. Cousins, and even half-brothers and sisters frequently engaged in beneath-stairs dalliance. In the particular case of the Gowans, the family was sexually remarkably close: after all, Frances's mother was Ogle's half-sister.

This little tryst between Ogle's wife and their mutual cousin was repeated at least twice in 1835. Because they had the sense not to knock the plaster from the wall in their dalliance, the other adult inmates of the house (Frances's mother and old Mrs. Graham, the longtime family servant) tactfully ignored the proceedings.

At first it was James who was smitten with his cousin, and she played the coquette. They wrote to one another, and in James's letters one gains a feeling both for the nature of his young ardour and for the ribald character of their conversations. In a letter to her written in May 1836, he said:

> I really believe that it is only those who know the difficulty of finding real friends of the opposite sex, beyond the pale of their im-

> mediate family, the delight experienced from even an epistolatory communication and exchange of thought with them, and the feeling of full confidence which a mutual connection of the sort which naturally engenders between the persons who stand in such relations toward each other . . . .

That is not a great opening, but he was a student of the law, a discipline frequently deadly to the spirit. He continued:

> I assure you I feel much gratified by your letter . . . and I will for this once forgive you for praising me so much.

Frances had asked James in a previous letter if most women felt ennervated after making love:

> You ask me, do not all wives act "heavy" after a *battle*. It is certainly often the case at least with those "who love their Lords."

And, as Frances had mentioned the possibility of his coming to live in Brockville, James replied:

> As you remark, there might be a good offer for me at Brockville and I would be happy to be surrounded by friends.

And then he referred to an inquiry Frances had made of him concerning a recent wedding party:

> The circumstances you mention I am not in possession of. I think they must have transpired in the Bridal Chambers, but one very funny thing occurred which is so funny that I must mention it. After my mother and sisters Anne and Susan had come down from laying the Bride out and had gone to their own rooms, the Bridegroom by his brothers' order was proceeding with great deliberation to undress in the drawing room and performed the operation with such celerity that he was almost in a state of nudity before my father could stop him. With much exertion, however, we got his brothers to compromise with him for giving a *ball* when he went home instead of dancing the gallop in his pelt four times up and down the room.

This affair between Frances and James was good fun for both of them, but nothing more. It gradually cooled and they kept writing each other. But from late 1837 onwards, the correspondence was friendly, not sexually provocative.

On February 10, 1836, Frances gave birth to Frances Jane Gowan, and on November 13, the next year, to John Hunter Gowan, who died young.

Without a doubt, the father of both of these children was a Gowan.

Attorney General Jameson, though he still felt a personal loyalty to Ogle Gowan, had had enough of the rough policies of Leeds county, and decided not to run in the special election that was called to fill the Leeds seats.

Ogle, in contrast, still lusted for battle. "We will defeat them — that Yankee party! — again and again. Sooner or later, Buell, Howard, and those Mackenzie-lickers will retire back to their republican caves." He made this statement at the opening of a meeting of the British Constitutional Society for the County of Leeds, held in mid-January 1836. This formerly moribund society had been revived by Gowan, specifically for his own personal benefit. He had founded it in 1831-1832, but in those days it had largely been a paper organization. Now, near noon on Saturday, January 23, nearly 300 electors crowded into the ballroom of Mair's Stone Building, Church Street, Brockville.

Mid-winter was the easiest time of year for back-country people to travel, because the lakes and swamps were frozen over and they could sleigh easily, and two-thirds of those present were from the back concessions. The travellers from the backwoods were good-natured and animated, like children at a carnival. The clothing of those present varied immensely, as did the membership of the political coalition that Ogle was trying to cobble together. The backwoodsmen who had been in Canada for some time wore garments mostly of homespun cloth; brown and grey were the dominant colours. More recent immigrants wore the black outer coats that they had brought with them across the sea. Men aspiring to be gentry wore frock coats on the British pattern. The best-dressed people in the room were those who were standing for nominations: Ogle Gowan (who as organizer of the event was a shoe-in), Col. Richard Duncan Fraser, Jonas Jones, and one, John Gardiner.

Promptly at two in the afternoon, Col. Fraser took the chair. This was the closest thing to a Tory political convention that had yet taken place in the county. There were two delegates from each concession of the county, as well as delegates at large. "You, the loyal and true electors of Leeds county, may be considered as fully, faithfully, and impartially representing the political opinions and principles of the British population of the country," Fraser declared. "It is your task, then, to nominate, support, and elect for this constituency, two candidates for parliament."

"And, by God, we will, Colonel!"

Four candidates were quickly nominated and, Fraser being one of them, he vacated the chair. It was then filled by the veteran political manipulator, Col. J.K. Hartwell. There was no doubt that Ogle would be nominated, or that he would control the choice of his running mate, but, cannily, he kept the issue open until the last moment, when he indicated that his choice was Col. Fraser. The convention overwhelmingly ratified this choice, and a significant one it was, since it indicated the future direction of Tory politics in the region: Fraser had been one of the first of the old Loyalist figures to see that the future lay with Gowan and the immigrants; that Jonas Jones, representing the Compact-Tories had been willing to run in the second spot on the Gowan ticket was revealing; that he was rejected, even more so.

Of course, the one thing that Gowan had to fear was a fair election. William Buell and Matthew Howard were again chosen to carry the colour of the Reformers and this time they were formidable. Electoral arrangements favoured them. During February 1836 a special Leeds Election Bill passed through the legislature, and received royal assent on March 7. Instead of a single hustings, to which access could easily be limited by a band of thugs, there would be four voting stations; and each would have a deputy returning officer in charge. Frances Gowan declared, doubtlessly reflecting her husband's view, that these arrangements were to "please the Yankoos," her word for Upper Canadian Reformers. Despite these arrangements, Ogle was confident that he would win easily.

He could not have been more wrong. In a large turnout (2,451 votes were cast), the results were:

Buell 700	Gowan 547
Howard 691	Fraser 513

Victorious at last, the Reformers put on a big celebration, aimed as much at emphasizing Gowan's humiliation as rewarding their own followers. An entire ox was roasted at Busher's Hotel, Brockville. This was an Old Country custom, but novel in this part of Upper Canada, and it attracted attention from people who simply stood and watched the great beast rotate on the spit. One of the Reform electors christened the beast "Ogle" and someone put up a crude hand-lettered sign over the hearth saying:

OGLE: ROASTED TWICE.
REFORMERS, HURRAH!

About five-thirty in the afternoon, the carcass was cut up and put on tin plates that were set in front of guests. Speeches, toasts, and more toasts followed well into the evening.

Ogle Gowan, the collar of his coat turned up, walked past Busher's Hotel several times that evening, being careful to avoid recognition.

He was not quite at his wit's end. He still believed that he was only one trick, one ingenuous idea, away from being an MP.

Like his great nemesis, Daniel O'Connell, Ogle Gowan had a genius for finding a gimmick. Now, in mid-1836, with a bit of wit and an equal amount of luck, he turned himself from a local-joke back into local-hero.

Sir John Colborne, having alienated virtually every faction in Upper Canada, left, unlamented, for Lower Canada and on January 15, 1836, Sir Francis Bond Head took office as Lieutenant Governor of Upper Canada. Head was the British Empire's equivalent of the Holy Fool. Bond Head's accomplishments admittedly were painted from a large palette: he was one of Upper Canada's best horsemen (he had twice ridden across South America, from Buenos Aires to the Andes); was the province's most able exponent of the lasso (for the demonstration of which, it is said, William IV knighted him); and, in mid-1836, was Canada's most astute election strategist.

This latter propensity coincided with Ogle Gowan's self-interest. To telescope sharply Sir Francis's actions: after a brief political honeymoon, in which he convinced important Reformers to join the executive council, he fell out with the Reformers and they resigned, followed soon thereafter by the Tory councillors. This had a contagious effect on the House of Assembly and soon Bond Head was at war with a legislative body he considered to be Reform-dominated and, perforce, honeycombed with crypto-republicans. He decided to consult the people directly, through a general election.

An election fought against the republican menace, to repel American influence, to promote patriotism, Constitution, and Empire, would have been well-tailored for Gowan at any time, but at this moment it was perfect. Ogle guessed (correctly as it turned out), that "a great reaction in the public mind is now taking place in this part of the country" and he began readying himself for yet another election. In mid-April, Bond Head prorogued the legislature, and everyone knew that a general election soon would be called.

Now Ogle made a series of moves, so smooth, so quick, that he seemed a magician. The first of these was the forming of an alliance with one of the hated Joneses — Jonas. A deal was struck for merging the Compact- and the immigrant-Tories into a single conservative ticket. Ogle would run with Jonas Jones. This was high realism on the part of both factions. The old Compact-Tories recognized that they were losing influence and that a coalition was necessary if they were not to be displaced. In turn, Gowan realized that unless the entire Conservative bloc could be mobilized, it would be impossible to beat the Reformers. So, Jonas Jones momentarily forced himself to forget that Gowan had written dozens of merciless attacks upon his character, and had once been an ally of the arsonist Gray; and Ogle forced to the back of his mind the fact that the Joneses had financed the reprinting of that hated pamphlet, the *Interesting Trial*.

Then, on May 24, Ogle orchestrated one of the most unctuous scenes in Upper Canadian politics. In Toronto, he and fifteen other worthies, associated with eastern Upper Canada, assembled at one in the afternoon at the New British Coffee House. There the owner set up tots of his best liquor, a French brandy that he had not yet watered. A pot-boy cleaned the glaur off of their boots and trousers: it had rained in the morning and the streets were muddy. Ogle convened a brief discussion of the tactics and they marched off, sixteen worthies, for an audience with Sir Francis Bond Head.

As they approached Government House, they formed themselves into a pre-arranged pattern. They entered in pairs and, as in ecclesiastical procession, the persons of the highest rank came last. Col. Fraser and J.K. Hartwell were the first, then six sets of local notables (including Jonas Jones, George Sherwood, and Henry Sherwood) and, finally, like a bishop and his coadjutor, Attorney General Jameson and Ogle Gowan.

Sir Francis received them in the large, elegant library. Out of habit, he was standing with his back to the fireplace, even though no fire was lit at this time of year. Like most proconsuls of the British Empire, he instinctively took the favoured spot in any room he entered, and he assumed that the locals would appreciate that this was part of the natural order.

The attorney general stepped forward and, acting as *chef de mission*, introduced the mysterious men from the east. As each name was mentioned, Bond Head bowed slightly at the waist and said something pleasant: having decided to throw himself on the will of the people, he was trying hard to win as many friends as possible. Ogle was introduced last and, as previously arranged in the New British Coffee House, he took over speaking for the group. For over twenty minutes, Ogle laid on the flattery with a trowel: Sir Francis's sagacity as a governor was applauded; his anti-republican stance was praised; the "pain and indignation" felt by all loyal persons when they heard Bond Head being vilified by those of "American" persuasions was voiced; the "happy connexion existing between us and the Mother Country," was vaunted.

Sir Francis, well trained in the military virtues, remained almost perfectly still, giving his undivided attention to Ogle. Occasionally, he nodded in recognition of a particularly telling encomium. The eastern worthies, not professionally versed in the need for immobility, shuffled their feet. Col. Fraser stroked his moustache. Jonas Jones checked surreptitiously in his pocket for his coins, and J.K. Hartwell tried to scratch himself without being detected.

When Gowan was done, Bond Head said, "Thank you gentlemen. You opinions are most illuminating and I assure you that they will have their effect." He bowed deeply, and the delegation left the library in the same order that they had entered, Ogle and Jameson last. Just as Jameson was going through the door, Sir Francis called to him. "Stay behind, if you would, Mr. Attorney General, as I have a matter to discuss with you."

This was exactly what Gowan and his associates had hoped would happen. Behind closed doors, the lieutenant governor asked the attorney general exactly what it was that the men wanted? and Jameson told him.

And Sir Francis granted it.

Namely: when Bond Head appointed a returning officer for the Leeds county election scheduled for June 1836, the man was Col. Joseph K. Hartwell, Orangeman and henchman of Ogle Gowan. And the poll was not to be held at four sites, but at Beverly, the home of Col. Hartwell, the place where Gowan and his forces had banged heads so successfully in earlier contexts.

The visit to Bond Head had taken place on May 24, and one might think that Gowan had done enough to assure his electoral victory. But having been over-confident in the previous polling, he was not going to fall into that error again. The next day, Ogle presided as grand master over a meeting of the Grand Lodge of British North America (most of whose representatives were from Upper Canada). There he explained to his fellow Orangemen that, for once, they should take a lead from a Roman Catholic, specifically, from Bishop Macdonnell, who had sent to Bond Head a letter assuring him of the support of the Catholics of Upper Canada in his fight against republicanism. Gowan drafted a long manifesto that proposed Macdonnell. "Such conduct," it declared, "merits our cordial approbation and thanks," and went on to state that the Orange Society never had intended to give the least offence to Catholics, much less to wound their feelings. The loyalty of the Catholics to the Empire and Constitution was recognized.

Ogle here was setting up what rightly has been called the goddamndest alliance in Canadian history. The Irish Protestants and Irish Catholics would temporarily set aside their mutual distaste and fight together against evil: radicalism, Reformers, and republicanism. Ogle Gowan was antithetical to everything that smacked of American republicanism and Bishop Macdonell, ever since his days helping to suppress the '98 Rising in Ireland, had abhorred anything too French, too democratic, or atheistic.

"It is with no small gratification that I here acknowledge having received from Orangemen unequivocal and substantial proof of disinterested friendship and generosity of heart," Bishop

Macdonnell stated in an address he issued to the freeholders of Stormont and Glengarry. In quick response, the Orangemen of Toronto sent him an address on their own behalf, praising his personal qualities and hoping that in the approaching test "for the maintenance of the British Constitution," Roman Catholics and Orangemen would march side-by-side.

Given that the '98 Rising in Ireland still was a living memory among the Irish in Canada, both Protestant and Catholic, the Bishop's response was nothing short of amazing:

> When I tell you that I passed four years in the most disturbed parts of Ireland from 1798 to 1802, you will not be surprised that the flattering address of the Orangemen and the expressions of their kind wishes to me in my labours to promote the interest of the Roman Catholic Church in Upper Canada, should fill my heart with a joy and gratification beyond the power of language to express and almost too big for my heart to contain. Irishmen in Canada see the necessity of putting shoulder to shoulder and standing forward in defence of the British Constitution and British liberty against a host of crafty and designing enemies.

In a final response and tribute to the Catholic bishop, the Grand Orange Lodge of British North America offered up the ultimate Orange sacrifice: they cancelled the July Twelfth parades for that year.

Considered province-wide, the Orange and Green alliances probably moved six to nine seats in the sixty-odd-member House of Assembly from the Reform column to the government side.

In Leeds county, however, there were relatively few Catholics and even with both the Macdonnell and the Jones alliances, Gowan probably was not in a majority. As the election of the spring of 1836 had shown, most of the electors still were Reformers.

The solution was simple enough: do not let them vote.

The election began at Beverly on Monday June 27 and closed on Wednesday, when Buell and Howard retired in protest. To again recite the pattern of intimidation, head-banging, clothes-slashing, vituperation, and vilification inflicted on the Reformers by the new Tory alliance would be tiresome: we have seen it often before. The clearest indication of the extent of the local intimidation is that, whereas in the spring election, 2,451 votes were cast, now only 1,048 were. (The results: Jonas Jones 362, Gowan 349, Buell 169, Howard 168.)

The Reformers now were both beaten and bowed. Buell and Howard knew that the newly-elected assembly was Tory-dominated, and would not pay much heed to their protests. They let the matter drop and dropped out of politics themselves.

CHAPTER 11

Loyalism Incarnate, 1836-1838

THE THIRTEENTH, and last, Parliament of Upper Canada was convened on November 8, 1836. (It ran through five sessions, finally being permanently dissolved on February 10, 1840.) Ogle was there at Parliament's opening, and took in everything with great avidity. From the very first, he was active. He was always on his best behaviour and at times was almost courtly in demeanor. Each day that the assembly was in session he walked from his lodging almost a mile along Front Street, tipping his hat with grave courtesy to all ladies whom he met, including those who passed by in carriages. The parliament buildings sat on a square at Front and Simcoe, and when Gowan reached them he invariably stopped and raised his hat before passing the flag that flew on a pole near the central entrance. One of Toronto's long-time residents observed him doing this and suggested that, in his act of devotion, he resembled John Strachan's brief nod to the altar as he passed from Gospel side to credence table.

The 1836 election that finally put Ogle Gowan into Parliament, cost William Lyon Mackenzie his seat. Mackenzie could scarcely comprehend losing an electoral contest to Conservatives, and he began a series of erratic distracted agitations which, in their myriad intersecting orbits, resembled not so much the activities of one man, but the swarming of a nest of vexed bees. He founded a new paper, the *Constitution* and, after several false starts, began organizing political action groups whose purposes, though never clearly stated, at minimum involved the replacement of Bond Head and of the Conservative House of Assembly, and, at the other extreme, the possibility of the introduction of an entirely new form of government in Upper Canada. No one, least of all Mackenzie, knew for sure what was in train. For Ogle Gown, Mackenzie was a worrisome phenomenon to be watched closely. Ogle not only read Mackenzie's newspaper carefully, he also received regularly pieces of intelligence from inn-keepers, barmen, and hansom-cab owners, who often, in the course of their activities, dealt with Mackenzie and his followers.

Ogle understood full well that the motives of Mackenzie's followers were close to those of his own supporters. They were sick to death of the various *élites* whom they believed held them down. Therefore, Mackenzie's near-republican radicalism was a potent rival, among the alienated, to Gowan's hyper-loyalism.

All the while Ogle was keeping an eye on Mackenzie, he was also serving as a good member of Parliament — good, in the sense that he took care of his Leeds county constituents, and also did a fine job of burnishing his own political image. Parliament had been in session only one full day, when he gave notice of a bill to connect the village of Beverly to the Rideau system, and later a £6,000 grant to a local group, called the Wiltsie Navigation Company. Much of his work was tinted with overt loyalism. For example, in late November he introduced a bill to give free land to members of the British army and navy, if they moved to Upper Canada. This failed, but it publicized his loyalist interest.

His real *coup de théâtre* along this line was his bringing in a bill, slightly later in the same session, that would have required the enrolment of all men sixteen to sixty capable of bearing arms, presumably to meet the threat of international republicanism, and of an American invasion. In time of war, these men were liable for six months of active duty anywhere in the province. The fine for not doing one's duty, Ogle Gowan suggested, should be £20, or six to twelve months in gaol. Militia men should be put to death for desertion. (This, considering that one-quarter to one-third of the militiamen in Gowan's own constituency had deserted during the war of 1812, would have drastically reduced the population.) And, if any militiaman spoke disrespectfully of the Royal Family, he was to be court-martialed. Such a bill had no hope of passing through the House, but it dramatically called to the attention of the highest governmental officials that Ogle Gowan was undeniably loyal.

How did Ogle appear to his contemporaries? Walter Cavendish Croften, a civil servant and a close observer of the members of the House of Assembly, at the time described him this way:

> This gentleman has for eight or nine years occupied a prominent position in the politics of the country, not only as the head of a powerful body, but in consequence of talent he possesses of engaging the minds of popular Assemblies, and leading them with him. He is very ambitious.
>
> As a speaker he is fluent and energetic, very powerful in his appeals to feeling, and evidently he speaks for the audience more than the House. His sarcasm is bitter, and possessing great evenness of temper, you seldom see him ruffled at any remarks which may be made.
>
> He is an active, well-made man, rather low, with a prepossessing face and easy insinuating manners, very mild in his address, and with talent which, if rightly applied would soon raise him to an eminent situation.

As had happened before, when Ogle was in the public eye, an enemy published once again the fateful *Interesting Trial*. This third full edition was printed in the spring of 1837, by William Lyon Mackenzie who, in 1834, had run a serial version of it. The re-publishing struck Gowan at one of his most vulnerable points. He tried to refute the pamphlet's charges, but he could list only a dozen or so errors in it, and none of these central. In response to these minor points, Mackenzie published a certified statement, made under oath by George Perkins Bull, averring that the originally-published version of the matter was a direct copy of the original transcript, as set down by a commissioner appointed by the Lord Chancellor of Ireland. The Brockville *Recorder*, still owned and published by the Buell family, rubbed salt into Gowan's wounds: why, the paper asked, if the pamphlet is untrue, did Gowan not prosecute the Honourable Charles Jones and his brother Jonas, who had financed the second full edition years earlier? Indeed, why did he not now prosecute Mackenzie or George Perkins Bull? The answer, of course, is that the transcript of the trial was substantially correct.

Significantly, although the pamphlet once again made Ogle a laughing-stock, it did not undercut his position with the government. This was because, in singling out Gowan for attack, Mackenzie confirmed to Bond Head that Ogle was, therefore, a man of some importance in keeping eastern Upper Canada Loyal.

During the summer of 1837, disaffected "Patriot" groups in Lower Canada drilled their volunteers openly, and although it is problematical how much direct influence this had in encouraging rebellion in Upper Canada, it certainly encouraged counter-insurgency. Loyalists of all stripes — from descendants of U.E. Loyalists, to recent immigrants from Ireland and England — began planning counter-measures. Mackenzie now talked openly of armed rebellion and, if the little man was characteristically unclear about what he had in mind, many of his followers were not. Using the Orange Order as an intelligence network, Ogle Gowan heard of all these plans and more: Irish Protestants, living in New York State, sent him information on American groups that were planning to invade Canada. Ogle knew that he had to act.

"Men! You are loyal and brave soldiers; you will serve your Lady Sovereign well!!" Gowan, mounted on a large white gelding, was addressing the Brockville Invincibles, a volunteer company that was completely independent of the local militia. Gowan formed the corps in the late fall of 1837. When addressing them, he consciously imitated the Duke of Wellington, no mean task for a journalist of medium height, ginger-black hair, and softening features. Most of his men were immigrants. "You men know full well the danger that stalks this portion of our British Empire. Many of you have seen, or your fathers told you of seeing, the rapine, pillage, and unhappiness that follow from permitting disloyal and treasonable persons — such as Wolfe Tone, such as William Lyon Mackenzie — to go about the land preaching sedition!" The reference to the '98 Rising was not a rhetorical allusion. Ogle believed that the '98 was about to be repeated in Canada.

At this moment in his life, Ogle's personal advantage, his highest principles, and his fantasy life all perfectly coincided. In Brockville in 1837 he founded a newspaper that became the most successful journalistic effort of his life: it ran until 1851. The paper's title, *The Statesman*, is as direct an insight into his fantasy life as one can get. Directly under the head: *The Statesman* ran in large type, BY OGLE GOWAN. The paper's motto was taken from Lord Bolingbroke and was as ultra-loyalist as possible could be:

> Those who are preparing to build up a Government should recollect that the Kingly power ought to form the basis and the popular, the superstructure: for if you place a Republic as the basis, and afterwards building a Monarchy upon it, your building will fall into ruins on the slightest shock.

That may not be a very catchy slogan, but it tells one unmistakeably where the paper's editor stands.

In founding the Brockville Invincibles, Ogle felt the hand of Hunter Gowan on his shoulder, for he was doing in 1837 what his father had done in '98: organize a paramilitary force, to preserve the Constitution against republicanism. He told his men, "You will receive no pay, and you will perform guard duty at important points on cold nights and in pelting rain. Hardship will be your constant accompaniment. You will, brave men, have the satisfaction of serving in a volunteer company, the first in the province and we will set an example for the rest of the Britons of our land. GOD SAVE THE QUEEN!"

"God save the Queen!" Lt. Col. Grant took over at this point and started to drill the enthusiastic volunteers.

Ogle returned to his newspaper office and began composing a long letter to Sir Francis Bond Head. Gowan had good intelligence sources and had been closely analyzing Mackenzie's actions: he knew a rebellion was at hand. Head, however, was being insanely perverse: by the time Gowan's letter was in Toronto, the lieutenant governor already had sent the Province's last two companies of Red Coats to Lower Canada, to deal with the "Patriot" problem there. Sir Francis read Gowan's long and impassioned plea for readiness and did nothing, except to have his aide arrange to have Ogle appointed a captain in the second regiment of the Leeds militia. Ogle loved having the rank, but he knew it was intended to keep him quiet rather than an indication that his warnings were heeded.

On Tuesday night, December 4, 1837, Mackenzie was gathering his men outside the city of Toronto, preparatory to attacking the city. That same night, Gowan's Brockville Invincibles, under the command of Lt. Col. Grant, marched from Brockville to Kingston to protect a steamer bearing 800 small-arms and ammunition.

When he heard of Mackenzie's rebellion, Ogle became possessed of preternatural energy. He issued an address to his fellow Irishmen and not only published it, but went about Leeds county, reading it to any body of men that he could assemble:

TO THE LOYAL IRISH OF THE COUNTY OF LEEDS

By the Blood of your Fathers, the Heroes of old;
By the Honour and Courage, that never were sold;
By the Laws you respect, and the Crown you revere,
UP *Irishmen,* UP, *and in phalanx appear!!*

That dramatic start was followed by a moment of silence. Gowan bowed his head, as if in prayer, then slowly looked up until his gaze was fixed over the heads of whatever audience he was addressing, like a prophet annunciating a vision:

COUNTRYMEN AND BROTHERS

The hour, the important hour, has at length arrived, when every Briton's cry should be "to your tents O! Israel."

Martial Law has been proclaimed in Lower Canada . . . .

The Rebels of the Province are in arms. The have shed innocent blood; stopped the Mails, burned Houses; and already the scourge of Insurrection is to the suburbs of the City of Toronto.

There is no longer room or time to 'halt between two opinions,' — we must now act, either as Britons, or as Rebels.

With adjustments for items of local geography, Hunter Gowan could have made these same remarks in Gorey, Co. Wexford, in 1798. Under pressure, Ogle, like his father, also thought in extremes. One was either a friend or an enemy. Choose!

In the present emergency, give me leave to offer you the following suggestions.

> Let there be a volunteer company formed in each Regiment. BEFORE VOLUNTEERING KNOW THE NAMES OF THE OFFICERS UNDER WHOM YOU ARE TO SERVE . . . and let no man, friend or foe, wheedle you out of it.

"Too right, Gowan! We won't serve under those Yankoo colonials. If we march, we march with our own!" Ogle understood his audience perfectly. They, like him, distrusted most of the militia officers, who were of United Empire Loyalist extraction.

> Having organized your Companies in the several Regiments of the County, your next duty will be to get formed into a BATTALION OR ROYAL IRISH BRIGADE . . . .

This was a radical suggestion, for Gowan was mooting the creation of an *élite* unit within the militia, one that would not be responsible to the regular militia officers. Therefore, he played down its innovative character:

> The plan I have suggested is not new. In the army we have our English, Irish, and Scotch Regiments; and our German Legion. The same course is now being pursued in Lower Canada . . . and the city of Montreal has its First or Royal Irish; its Royal British Company and its Fourth Company of Royal Scots.

Then his plan having been put forward, Ogle would end his recruiting talk with blood and thunder:

> Fellow Countrymen, remember that it is better to fight the enemy at the commencement, and at a distance; than do so by our own door. . . . In the one case we should have to contend against our foes while they are yet weak and inexperienced. In the other, not only would our lives by exposed to peril, but the demon of war would be brought to our own doors — our wives and families — our homes and properties — all would be exposed to the horror of bloody insurrection.

"Not here Gowan!"
"Let the rebel bastards try!"

> Our bereaved families, our smoking dwellings, our slaughtered cattle, our fields of blood would all upbraid us that we had not kept the

> war away — that we did not attack the enemy at once, and on his grounds, instead of waiting for him to attack us, upon ours! "HURRAH! And three cheers for the Queen!"

The meeting would be over, and Ogle would press on to the next tavern or inn where he could muster a crowd.

From this fevered recruiting in December-January 1837-1838 emerged a regiment called the "Queen's Own Rifles." This body was sanctioned by Sir John Colborne, who was commanding the loyalist forces from his base in Lower Canada. Gowan did the recruiting, and Sir John placed a recently-retired, regular army officer, Lieut. Col. Macmillan in charge. R.D. Fraser and J.K. Hartwell, longtime outriders of Gowan's, were appointed majors. Nine companies were formed, and Ogle was himself made captain of one of these. He had sixty-eight men directly under his command.

Mackenzie's Toronto rising of early December 1837 failed miserably. His followers were poorly armed, badly led, and less than heroic. Mackenzie and his fellow leaders easily escaped, however, for many of the locals were sympathetic to radical politics, if not to actual rebellion. With their escape, the focus of trouble shifted from domestic to foreign soil. Mackenzie proclaimed a provisional government for Upper Canada with himself as "Chairman, *pro tem.*" Necessarily, this became a government-in-exile, and at first its seat was Navy Island in the Niagara River and later, various addresses, mostly in New York State.

These external locales fit perfectly with the mindset of Ogle Gowan and his immigrant-loyalists, for it merged into a single evil the phenomena of domestic rebellion and American republicanism. The U.S. authorities, Gowan argued, were covertly supporting Mackenzie. Thus, one could perceive eastern Upper Canada, not as a quiet frontier, but as a battle-front in the American sector.

Embarassingly, there were more potential heroes in Leeds county than there were battles to ennoble them. Chances for action improved, however, when on February 12, a nearly breathless Elizabeth Barnett burst into the Gananoque premises of the MacDonald mercantile firm, and began blurting out a warning of an American attack. She had been in Clayton, New York, and there had heard talk of a force that would be mustering secretly on an island in the St. Lawrence. She had quickly put on warm clothes and driven a sleigh across the ice to Gananoque, to spread the word. Her alarm at first was treated skeptically, because she was an American, and had lived in Leeds county only since 1836. Her words held conviction, however, and soon despatches were being hurried to all available units between Brockville and Kingston.

Hickory Island, the centre-point of this episode, lies less than three miles below Gananoque and is about equidistant from the American and the Canadian shores of the St. Lawrence. It had no military significance in itself, but had been secretly taken by troops loyal to Mackenzie's republic. What they had in mind is unclear. Either they were intent on pillaging Gananoque, which had virtually no defences save an old blockhouse, or planned to feint towards Gananoque, and then descend on Kingston. Whichever it was, Gowan and his men at least were to have a chance of glory.

"It's that deformed Dutchman, Van Rennsselaer and Pirate Johnston. Pass it on." That was the word that went from one member of Gowan's company of the Queen's Own Rifles to the next. Van Rennsselaer, created a general by William Lyon Mackenzie, was of no consequence in the view of the Leeds men, but William Johnston demanded some respect. He was a legend on both sides of the St. Lawrence, and now, in his late sixties, was hard and gnarled as a bough of hillside ironwood. Johnston had served on both sides of the war of 1812, though preferring the American, and after the war had become a notoriously successful smuggler. In that trade he was unstoppable, and finally, authorities on both sides of the border decided it was safer to look the other way than try to apprehend him. Now Pirate Johnston was engaged in the romantic task of "freeing Canada."

Not until February 22 were the Canadian forces ready to strike. Seven miscellaneous companies, including a party of Mohawk Indians, were assembled at Gananoque. Joseph K. Hartwell was the senior officer present, and was thus in charge, at least until that afternoon when a Major Fitzgerald arrived from Kingston, with orders from the military authorities to take over. Hartwell was livid. "I shall not yield! My men are ready. I have arranged for an immediate attack and heaven and hell themselves won't remove my hand from my sword!" He went on for quite a time. Major Fitzgerald, a regular army officer, was by turns contemptuous ("Do you expect, my man, to lead a regiment, you of no military experience?") and tactful ("I should of course call upon you for advice, were you to withdraw in my favour.") Eventually Hartwell gave in. The regular army officer had all the cards. Hartwell retired to an inn and spent the Battle of Hickory Island sulking.

Actually, the Canadian forces probably would have done better with Hartwell in charge. Major Fitzgerald was determined to do everything by the book: this included parading the troops, and thereby putting off the attack for a day. The various militia officers, men of substance in their own communities, who were accustomed to being heard, pressed him for an immediate attack. Finally, he compromised. He sent out a reconnoitering party that evening and agreed that after it returned, a surprise attack on the Americans would be planned and executed.

While all of this arguing was going on, several more units straggled in, including the company of the Queen's Own Rifles under Ogle Gowan, and a militia unit under the Hon. John Elmsley, Catholic convert and *colporteur*. Ogle greeted him warmly, for Elmsley, like Bishop Macdonnell, was a trustworthy loyalist.

That night, it was all the officers could do to keep the men in the ranks from mounting an attack on their own. "The whores will be gone if we sit here on our ass," was the general — and, indeed, correct — view. The men had to be satisfied with the knowledge that the Hon. John Elmsley and fourteen of his men were reconnoitering, as was a party from Kingston. "Might as well send them a calling card, as let those dandies from Kingston try to sneak near," remarked Gowan to one of the Mohawk Indians, who was spending the evening in complete silence, perhaps envisioning the battle to come. Everyone in the rank and file stayed awake through the night, and in early morning there came word from the advance party: "The enemy are retreating. Hurry or they will be gone!" Only then did Major Fitzgerald order an attack, and when the decamping Americans became aware of the vastly superior Canadian forces, they scattered in all directions. The victors captured pikes, muskets and ammunition and took five prisoners. A man who was instantly recognized by Gowan and several of his Leeds countymen, but was not among the captured, was James Philips, former tavern keeper and Reform lodestone from the county.

Five prisoners. A lilliputian result, about as consequential as a music-hall melodrama. And, indeed, for a time after the Hickory Island fracas, it seemed as if everyone involved was a character in some broad *grand guignol.*

The central authorities made as much propaganda as they could out of the victory and formally commended all of the units in the Hickory Island affray. Then, on April 19, they disbanded the Queen's Own Rifles, on the grounds that their services were not needed. The men were told to return to their own militia units. Clearly, the government recognized the danger of keeping an *élite* unit, composed almost solely of Irish immigrants under arms. The Irishmen responded by trashing and rioting in Brockville.

Sir Francis Bond Head, replaced by Sir George Arthur as lieutenant governor of Upper Canada, kept up the mad galloping that was his trademark. He decided to return to England by way of the United States and, in late March 1838, he galloped through hostile territory. He started out in New York State, at first accompanied by Jonas Jones. He tried to pass incognito, but in Watertown, New York, he was rumbled: at the moment he was recognized, he was trying to disguise himself by sitting on a wheelbarrow in the street, like a costermonger. Once sighted, he got back into the saddle quickly and galloped off.

On the night of May 29, William Johnston, pirate and American patriot, burned a new steamboat, built at Brockville, the *Sir Robert Peel*.

Meanwhile, James Philips, that bitter and disillusioned rebel, invaded Canada briefly on July 4. He crossed the river east of Gananoque and, with a small group of men, intended wrecking part of the Rideau Canal. He was detected and scurried back across the St. Lawrence.

During the summer and early fall of 1838 the government worked hard at convincing itself that all danger of rebellion was past. Sir George Arthur made a show of pardoning scores of former rebels. Many of them then hied off to the United States, where they worked on plans to invade Upper and Lower Canada. One of the points of concentration of potential invaders was directly across the river from Brockville, and people in Leeds county had good intelligence on what was taking place. Ogle was particularly upset by the growing concentration of enemies, and in the *Statesman* was nearly hysterical in his trumpeted warnings.

He was very apprehensive about the Hunters Lodges (named, some say, after an admired republican, Dr. James Hunter of Whitby). These were dedicated to breaking Canada away from the

British Empire. Ogle believed that there were 217 such lodges in Lower and Upper Canada in the fall of 1838 (a quite preposterous number, for the total number of Orange lodges in Upper Canada was only 245). In fact, Gowan was convinced that the entire countryside was honeycombed with treasonous enemies, clandestinely organized, set in lodges that had a hierarchy of degrees and a panoply of secrets, not unlike the Freemasons or, actually, the Orange Order. In reality, there were very few Hunters Lodges in Gowan's vicinity. One of these few was in Kemptville, and it was wiped out by an informer.

But Gowan now was living in a world where the backwoods, he construed, were filled with secret republicans. He had spent his whole adult life organizing religio-political bodies that were semi-secret, and he was convinced of their effectiveness. Because he believed, not only in the realities of Orangeism, but in its shadows and vapours, he was also predisposed to imagine endless conspiracies and secret societies among his enemies. His agitated state was heightened, when he found that the *Freeman's Advocate*, a republican paper, published in Lockport, New York, had included in an editorial of October 9 a screed that Ogle took to be a threat of assassination. The paper mentioned Orangeism and Gowan by name and declared:

> We bid them beware! The arm of the Patriot is not yet withered, nor his energies palsied. Beware! Let all the slaves beware; but especially we say, let the haughty leader who chains his thousands to the chariot wheels of tyrannical Britainia, beware!

About this time, William Lyon Mackenzie made a long-shot gamble, one that was ultimately unsuccessful, but wonderfully imaginative: he wrote secretly to Gowan. Mackenzie had been reading Gowan's *Statesman*, and knew that the Orange master was convinced that the government was paying scant heed to his warnings. Thus, he suggested that Ogle ally himself with the Hunters Lodges, as a first step towards providing a government for Upper Canada that would yield just recognition to men of ability. Quite properly, Ogle passed the letter on to Sir George Arthur, but it did make him reflect — reflect that perhaps his enemy, Mackenzie, understood him better and recognized his talents more clearly than did the Imperial governors.

Ogle was convinced (rightly, it turned out) that the next republican invasion of Canada would occur in his own district, and that either Prescott or Brockville would be the point of attack, and he kept saying so in the *Statesman*. Finally, Sir George Arthur responded to Gowan's editorials, and allowed the formation of two companies of *élite* volunteers from the Johnstown district in mid-October, to aid the local militia. Even so, Sir George did not believe that there was a serious threat of invasion; he just wanted to keep the locals happy. In his view, the republicans were making a lot of noise and were deliberately starting rumours; they had, he believed, no intention of invading.

These opinions filtered back to Gowan and he nearly went berserk. Did not that priggish idiot understand anything?! Was the British Empire to begin to break up because of a snuff-inhaling, brandy-drinking, powder-haired catamite such as Sir George?! Ogle, named to command one of the companies of volunteers, began organizing it with manic energy. His unit, not surprisingly, was entirely composed of Orangemen.

In the latter part of October and in early November 1838, Ogle was whipsawed by two opposing forces, and these left him unable to sleep, except for brief naps in a chair. One of these forces was the continual arrival of intelligence from across the St. Lawrence, news that men were drilling openly and preparing for invasion. Reports came independently from many spots, Cape Vincent, Alexandria Bay, Sacketts Harbour, and a dozen other places, right across from Brockville. This information made Gowan recruit volunteers and drill them more animatedly than ever.

And second, Sir George Arthur and the Earl of Durham continued to make the defence of Upper Canada maddeningly difficult. Durham was a special case, a man who made every Orangeman boiling mad. He was on his whirlwind tour of the Canadas as governor and investigatory commissioner. This lasted from late May to November 1, 1838. Durham had the precise mixture of liberal beliefs and patronizing snobbery that would most offend the Orangemen. The following incident was passed on to Ogle by James Gowan in July 1838:

> You have heard before now of the reception L'd Durham met with in Toronto, but his short stay here gave very general dissatisfaction . . . .
>
> Some of the country Orange Lodges came in procession to

> Town with their usual insignia. This, I have been informed, was mentioned to L'd Durham in the presence of Sir G. Arthur of whom he enquired, "if he had been aware of it."
>
> Sir G. declared his ignorance.
>
> L'd Durham then s'd, 'Such things — in the 19th Century — it ought not to be — it must not be.'

Now, late in October, Durham, this same liberal ponce, this tool of the enemies of the Empire, issued a general amnesty in Lower Canada! And, following His Lordship's example, Sir George Arthur on October 25 did the same thing in Upper Canada! My God, man, the countryside is infested with vermin and those imbeciles open the sewers! Where will it end?! Ogle in his worst nightmares, now saw the burning of Mount Nebo being re-enacted up and down the St. Lawrence frontier.

Then, abruptly, the official posture changed. Sir John Colborne, commander in chief of the military forces in the Canadas, stopped accepting the politicians' vapouring and November 1, sent an order to the commander at Cornwall, stating that Canada was "threatened with an attack from the American frontier by a horde of rapacious brigands." He therefore called on everyone who could bear arms to "repell the wicked and unprovoked invasion."

Immediately arrangements were made to form an *élite* corps within the Leeds militia (in addition to the two volunteer units already formed). This group, known as the Ninth Provisional Batallion, was to be on full pay. It was commanded by Ogle Gowan who, simultaneously was promoted to the militia rank of lieutenant colonel, a distinction that he prized.

On the evening of November 11, Ogle was sitting alone in the drawing room of the house he rented in Brockville. In self-conscious preparation for the battle that he knew would soon come, he was reading one of the classic battle scenes set down by Herodotus. A loud banging started at the front door and Gowan was pleased, for surely it meant important news. The hammering was by no less a person than Adiel Sherwood, longtime sheriff of the Johnstown district. As Gowan opened the door, Sherwood fairly burst in. "The Patriots are massing at Crooked Creek! About a hundred of them. Led by Pirate Johnston and General Von Schoultz. Good leader that one. Only thirteen miles away, Gowan. Better do something quickly!"

Not bothering to put on a coat, even though it was a miserably dark and cold night with low scudding clouds obscuring the stars, Ogle hurried down the street to where his sergeant major lodged. The man quickly put into operation standing orders for summoning the men. He roused four line-sergeants, and they in turn wakened half a dozen corporals who collected the private soldiers. Within half an hour, the men, with their arms and ammunition, were gathered in front of the Brockville courthouse, awaiting orders. They were a hard lot, not pretty to look at, but keen. They were not in uniform; each wore his own bush clothes, but they each had been issued with a heavy leather belt that criss crossed the chest and with a government musket and ammunition pouch. The battalion resembled the units that were mustered on the American frontier to fight Indian wars.

For once in his life, Gowan eschewed bombast. "You will defend Brockville tonight against invasion by a force superior to you in numbers. Your sergeants have been told where to position each of you along the waterfront. Go quickly now lads, and God be with you!" Ogle's men disappeared at once. They spent the night and early morning in an unnatural silence, for ice-fog crept in after midnight and muffled everything. Gowan went from post to post, saying a word to one man, giving another a pat on the back, and so on.

In fact, it was not Brockville that needed defending, but Prescott, a dozen miles downriver, where the republicans had already arrived. (They, incidentally, called themselves "Patriots"; Gowan called them "rebels." To avoid confusion, we will continue to use "republican.")

Their original plan had been to have a steamship pull two schooners, filled with men, artillery, and ammunition, across the St. Lawrence River, and to cut them loose near the shore, so that they could silently slide up to the wharf at Prescott. There they would unload men and stores, and move as quickly as possible to nearby Fort Wellington, a military target worth taking. The plan was sound — lashed together, the two schooners came within shouting distance of the wharf before they were detected. A small band of militia officers was on the wharf and they called out "Who goes there?" "The *Charlotte* of Toronto" was the reply and the crew of one of the schooners threw a rope over one of the wharf's bollards. It slipped off. The seamen tried again and again, but the rope, being stiff with ice, slipped off. Finally, the schooner moved off. So dark was the night, and so well hidden below the decks were the republican soldiers, that no one on the wharf guessed that this was the invasion force they all feared.

The two schooners glided silently out of Prescott harbour. They separated, and one of them, captained by Pirate William Johnston, ran aground in the darkness. Men and military gear had to be taken off it by scow. Johnston never reached Canadian soil. He had himself taken back to Ogdensburg, where he blustered about for a time, and then surrendered to American authorities.

Coupled with this farce was genuine danger and, eventually, a loss of life. The republicans decided to attack a secondary target, a large stone windmill. The regular army authorities transmitted the alarm to militia units as far north as the Ottawa River, and told Gowan to prepare his men to attack. Ogle's troops were cold and hungry and had been on their feet for an entire night. "I'll not mistreat my men," he told the regular army colonel who commanded Brockville. "They're not beasts of burden, you know." Gowan made certain his men were fed and given extra rations before marching towards Prescott. He left Brockville at about one in the afternoon. The small army consisted of Lt. Col. Gowan in the lead, his Ninth Provisional Battalion, followed by the Brockville Independent Company and some "gentlemen volunteers," whom he was temporarily commanding.

The fall had been a wet one and the roads were in terrible shape. Wagons had churned deep ruts in even the most solid sections, and any small declivity was a mudhole. Gowan was on horseback, but his men slogged away on foot, alternately sloshing through mud and then, in the hard, rutted sections, twisting their ankles on the treacherous track. Since there was no means of knowing where the enemy actually was, Gowan had to proceed slowly, watching out for ambushes. Advance scouts moved ahead of the main body of troops, and only when they were certain the path was safe, did the men move forward. Just outside of Prescott they found that the invaders had broken down the bridges, so they had to build a makeshift structure. They arrived in Prescott just before dark, and the inhabitants treated them like liberators.

Prescott, like Brockville, was under the command of a regular army officer. Morale of Gowan's men dropped precipitously when he ordered the Ninth Provisional Battalion to do picket duty.

Gowan protested, "My men have been on their feet for nearly twenty-four hours; they need rest." It availed not. That night it rained hard, the sort of black, penetrating rain that comes in November, just before the onslaught of winter. Ogle joined the men on picket duty and intentionally grumbled aloud about this goddamned weather and those ramroad-arsed regular army officers. The men appreciated this: their colonel was a decent skin, not a martinet.

During the night, other loyal units arrived at Prescott, and the colonel in command ordered an attack on the enemy at the windmill for the next day.

Tuesday, November 13, was miraculously clear. The storm had blown itself out and the St. Lawrence was mirror-smooth. Against that glassy backdrop, the wind-powered mill stood out like a fortress. "Dear God, it looks like something the Moors put up," said Walter Ebbs who acted as aide-de-camp to Gowan. The windmill was built of heavy field-stone and resembled a Celtic round-tower. It was 100 feet in circumference and 80 feet high. With walls three to three-and-a-quarter feet thick, it was not going to be taken easily. Various stone buildings were contiguous to the mill, and the whole thing was surrounded by a stone wall. A more desirable defensive position is hard to imagine. "Perhaps we ought to say a prayer, Colonel," the aide-de-camp suggested to Gowan. In civilian life, Mr. Ebbs was sexton of the Anglican church that Gowan attended. Gowan ignored the sexton.

For the attack, the tactics of the Upper Canadian troops was simple. The available regular army troops were put in the centre of the battle order, the left wing was taken by militia, mostly from Grenville county under Col. Fraser, and the right wing by militia from Leeds County under Gowan. The 170-200 republicans in the windmill were outnumbered by seven or eight to one, but had the advantage of a superb tactical position and the knowledge that they were fighting for their lives.

About noon, the Canadians commenced firing. Seemingly, the most impressive fire came from heavy guns mounted on steamboats that had been brought down river and anchored close to the mill. The barrage continued for two hours, but long before it was concluded it was clear that the guns were not heavy enough: in fact, the balls just drove the wedge-shaped stones of which the mill was constructed closer together! During this bombardment the whole Canadian line moved forward, Gowan and his men moving up the beach. "Remember the Boyne!" one of them yelled. "No surrender!" "God save the Queen!"

Many of the republicans hunkered behind a stone wall and their small-arms fire took a nasty toll. Ogle and his men soon adopted the tactic of throwing themselves flat on the ground, firing, then slithering forward a few more yards, trying to hide in any hollow or behind any big piece of driftwood or stone outcrop they could find.

Then, when they were within twenty-five yards of the wall, Ogle stood up, called "Follow me lads; for God and Queen!" and his men roared forward. They carried the wall and were about to charge one of the stone out-buildings when a small body of republicans, held in reserve for such an emergency, opened fire on them with great effect. The republicans then charged with fixed bayonets. Ogle turned to flee, but not before he had recognized that the man commanding this small party was James Philips. One of Phillip's men fixed on Ogle as a prime target and went for him, bayonet ready. Ogle turned, and tried to throw himself back over the recently-won stone fence. His coat caught. He was, he believed, a dead man. "Dear God, help me!" he screamed, and screamed louder when the enemy drove his bayonet into Gowan's lower buttocks. He was preparing to finish him, when Mr. Walter Ebbs came running and bayoneted the republican in the back.

"You see, Colonel, prayer works," Mr. Ebbs noted laconically.

Gowan and his men retreated. The attack in the other sectors had been equally unsuccessful, and the Canadian officers fell to planning what they should do next. Gowan also spent some time reflecting on how he would explain a bayonet wound in the arse.

Wednesday, November 14, there was no fighting. An hour's truce was arranged so that each side could bury its dead. Ogle had cat-gut sutures put in his buttocks, and spent the day standing up.

Little happened on Thursday, but reinforcements for the Upper Canadians poured in, including four regular army companies and two eighteen-pound field-pieces. Still the Canadians waited.

Finally, at three-thirty on Friday afternoon, the heavy guns opened fire. Even the heaviest had little effect on the windmill itself, but soon some of the outbuildings started to crumble. The regular army, with the militia on its flanks, advanced. On Gowan's wing, the stone wall was taken easily enough, but then the attackers were stopped. The republicans held out stubbornly in their small buildings. Only when the artillery barrage set the roof of one of the buildings on fire, did they break. As the fire spread from house to house, the invaders were forced outside and there they were easy targets.

"Up boys! Now is the time — remember your Country!" Gowan led his men toward one of the stone houses that was not yet on fire. Because of his previous wound, he moved slowly, ramrod straight and was a tempting target. As he and a handful of men prepared to bash in the door of the building, Ogle caught a musket ball on the side of his knee. The wound was superficial, but the large ball, fired at close range, hit him with terrific force. He went rolling backwards as if poleaxed. Again, it was Walter Ebbs who looked after him, pulling him behind a sheltering wall and tearing a strip from his own shirt to bind the wound. "Christ's foreskin," Gowan remarked to Mr. Ebbs as he recovered himself, "this fighting wars certainly takes the stuffings out of a man."

Ebbs agreed.

The republicans finally put out a white flag. They marched out to lay down their arms to a background of fires crackling through the outbuildings, with the huge mill standing behind them, grey and adamantine against a darkening sky.

Gowan and several other officers went into the mill to see what had been left behind. There were 10,000 rounds of ammunition, 200 reserve guns, three cannons, and a hand-made silk flag, bearing an eagle surmounted by a star. It bore the optimistic legend, "Onadaga Hunters — Canada Liberated."

In one corner they found James Philips, recently a brigadier-general in the republican army. Dead.

Glory and vengeance are the two by-products of battles and the Windmill was no exception. Ogle was mentioned in despatches and his regiment, the Ninth Provisional Battallion, became the "Queen's Own Royal Borderers." Two of Ogle's men composed "Colonel Gowan's March:"

> *Ho! men awake, the call it has gone forth;*
> *And echoes loud along the woods of north.*
> *Awake free Sons of the wide forest land,*
> *Awake in your might, the struggle's at hand.*

Come forth Caledonia, Sons of the Gael,
Come Lads of the Shamrock, Erin's green vale.
On men of the rose, be true to your fame,
Britons! let God and the Right, *be your aim!*

One hundred and sixty-seven ambulatory republican prisoners were taken. They were tied to a rope, single file, and paraded before the townspeople of Prescott, who threw things at them and used words rarely uttered outside of shebeens and cow byres. One of the republicans was found to be carrying a list of prominent Prescott citizens who were to be hanged when these representatives of American democracy took the town.

Onward to glory, for now is the hour,
Onward each phalanx, in strength and power.
"United we stand, divided we fall,"
Be this the watchword, the password of all.
Push forward as Brothers, leagued in one cause,
For Queen, *for* Country, Religion *and* Laws.
Up, up for the Truth, *whatever betide,*
O' think of the Wife, you once made a Bride.

The prisoners were loaded onto a boat at Prescott and taken to Kingston where they again were paraded before a jeering populace. A band, with hilarious intent, played "Yankee Doodle." The republican leaders were tried, the star case being that of Nils Szoltevky von Schoultz, the thirty-one-year-old Pole who had led the force. Tall, dignified, understandably morose, he tried to plead guilty, even though he knew that meant hanging. The court martial refused to accept the guilty plea and instead heard evidence against him and then, after pronouncing him guilty, sentenced him to be hanged. Von Schoultz was represented at this proceedings by a twenty-three-year-old Kingston Lawyer, John A. Macdonald. the only substantial concession Macdonald gained for his client was to have a special gallows erected for him at Fort Henry. Nevertheless, Von Schoultz was so grateful for Macdonald's help that he tried to leave him 100 United States dollars in his will. Young Macdonald, who already had visions of a political career, shrewdly turned it down.

Rebels have 'dream'd,' and in phrensy they spoke,
That Loyalty now, must bend to their yoke!

> *The taunts of their chiefs fling back to the air,*
> *Unfurl the flag,* "Let them come if they dare!"
> *Come forth, come ye fast, rise in your might,*
> Pro Aris et focis, *honor and right.*
> *By sons yet unborn, by sires in their graves,*
> *Up brother Britons! be Freemen, not Slaves!*

And, in mid-December, Lt. Col. Gowan, surveying his past two months' activities, wrote to his cousin James;

> "I have lately received a very kind letter from His Excellency, Sir George Arthur, from which I infer that I stand pretty well in that quarter."

That, of course, is what it was all about.

BOOK III

JUST REWARDS

CHAPTER 12

The Brass Ring, 1838-1841

"FANNY, I do believe, I am a success at last!" Ogle stood in the drawing room of their rented house in Brockville, while Frances made chalk-marks on the side and front of his waistcoat. Ever since the Battle of the Windmill, he had become very conscious of his appearance and Frances was engaged in converting the garment from the double-breasted style to the new single-breasted fashion.

"Yumsdarrh."

"What was that?"

Frances took the tailoring pins from her mouth. "I said, 'yes dear.' And it's only time too. I was worried that you never would be treated fairly in this bush-Eden!" She had grown ironic, even sarcastic, about Upper Canada, referring to it as Paradise, Eden or, sometimes, Blissful Heaven. Often she wondered why they had left Ireland, but of course she knew.

These months, the last ones of 1838 and the first few of 1839, were the second-happiest in Ogle's life. They rivalled those first months of 1824 when all Dublin, all the world, seemed to be at his feet. But with one difference: now, unlike those earlier years, he knew how quickly failure could follow success, how deep despondency could be in the wake of euphoria. Always now there was a tiny, private hesitancy in the back of Ogle and Frances's minds about accepting his apparent triumphs.

Publicly, Ogle and his family were expansive, and why not? He was a member of parliament, was head of the largest non-religious association in British North America, and his newspaper, the *Statesman*, was doing well. Over the editorial columns still was printed, "All kinds of country produce received in payment for the Statesman at this office," but that was a reminder of harder times. Now the Gowan's older children, Nassau, Harcourt, Frederick William, and Elizabeth Jane, were useful around the paper, the older ones writing minor items, and setting type, the younger running errands. Frederick showed particular aptitude for typesetting and, in fact, eventually became a professional printer. If Ogle hollered at the children like a colonel giving orders to a regiment, well, that was the way a patriarchy worked. Gowan realized that the older sons, Nassau and Harcourt, promising lads, could not stay around Brockville forever. Eventually they would have to be trained for some genteel profession in Kingston or Toronto.

Frances was once again pregnant. Two years later, the Gowan's tenth and last child, Emily Jemima was born. Of all the children born to Frances and Ogle, seven survived through infanthood. That was not a bad rate for the era, and Ogle and Frances did not grieve too long for the lost ones, but were pleased that the survivors were quick and healthy. Historically, it is difficult to ascertain what children were alive during any given period, because on census and other records Ogle had the habit of misrepresenting their birthdates, as well as those of himself and his wife.

The only really irreplacable loss was that of their faithful domestic servant, Mrs. Graham. The harsh winter of 1839 proved too much for her failing health, and she died after a prolonged illness.

Ogle now was self-consciously patrician. On his rides into the countryside, he particularly liked to stop at a tiny Irish-Protestant settlement, Charleston Lake, in Escott township, for there he was treated with as much fawning as if he were an Irish landlord in deepest Connaught. Several of the locals actually called him "Your Honour," and took off their hats upon seeing him. He held court in the NO SURRENDER INN, an establishment owned by David Hamilton, an Orangeman from Ulster, who was a regular advertiser in the *Statesman*:

NO SURRENDER INN

> The undersigned avails himself of this opportunity to inform his friends and the public generally that he still continues to keep constantly on hand at his old stand at Charleston, a large supply of the following liquors . . . .

> Common Whiskey, Morton's Proof Whiskey, Scotch Whiskey, Brandy, Gin, Rum, High Wines; Temperance drinks; Greighoon's Premium beers; Wines, Peppermint. *No liquors sold on the Sabbath.*

Gowan liked to take a seat by the large stove and accept a glass of brandy. Slowly the locals would filter in and would ask for a boon, just as they would have done from a landlord in the Old Country: could Mr. Gowan help them obtain clear title to their land? Did His Honour know someone in Toronto who would help their son find a job? Could he recommend a physician in Brockville who would take payment in kind rather than cash? Ogle listened gravely and dispensed advice and aid and, sometimes, spiritual counsel. As he sat in the NO SURRENDER INN, he frequently re-read the owner's printed notice hanging on the pine-plank wall:

> We keep on hand Dr. Booth's Celebrated Thomsonian Medicine, which Mr. Hamilton will dispose of at manufacturers price, and *better than that,* he keeps a large and general supply of Bible and Testaments from 6d to 2s for Testaments, and £1 to £1/9d for Bibles.

Ogle often recommended to his petitioners that they purchase one of Mr. Hamilton's Bibles.

He found that the best part of being a success was that it allowed him to be a patriarch where it really mattered, within his own family. Ogle was delighted to dispense jobs to his relatives. His greatest coup was to be able to be magnanimous to Mary Hopkins — his half-sister. She was now the widow of the man who had instigated the lawsuit concerning Hunter Gowan's will, which, in turn, had led to the Wexford assizes, to the *Interesting Trial,* and, actually, to all of Ogle's troubles. In the spring of 1838 Mrs. Hopkins, her five children and the wife of her eldest son, arrived in Brockville and threw themselves on Ogle and Frances's charity. Ogle thus could savour the pleasure of giving aid to his former enemy. Besides sheltering the family, Ogle found Mary's oldest son, Nicolas, a job: Ogle, as an MP, had sponsored an act to begin the macadamizing of the road out of Brockville and, naturally, obtained a seat on the board of directors. Now, in December 1838, he had his nephew appointed toll collector. Gowan realized that the Apostle Paul was right — the sweetest revenge is to pour hot coals on the head of one's enemy by being forgiving.

Ogle was becoming the head of quite a little clan. His younger, illegitimate sister, Margaret, in late 1837 married a Dr. Buchanan and, a year later, they arrived in Brockville. Ogle used his political connections to have Buchanan's medical licence transferred to Upper Canada.

Gowan still was supporting his mother-in-law, Mrs. Colclough, who lived *en famille*. Moreover, Ogle's elder, illegitimate brother, William, had also come to the New World, and in 1837 had begun shopkeeping in what Frances called "a very remote part of the country." He kept a wide range of goods, did reasonably well, and married a girl from Lansdowne, not five miles west of Ogle's land. Here, Ogle had finally completed his house (in 1835), although he seldom lived in it. William had three children. Ogle was able to throw some trade in the way of his brother.

To a man like Gowan, who carried the weight of illegitimacy with him from the Old World, the freedom to become a patriarch in the New World was the equivalent of emancipation. He saw himself transformed from a bastard cub into, as he wrote in his own genealogy, "the more prominent head of the family in America." That was real success.

Nevertheless, when, in December 1838, Ogle had written to his cousin, reporting that he stood well with Sir George Arthur, he was setting himself up for an embittering disappointment. Sir George had no intention of doing anything for Gowan. Arthur was one of the fussiest men to pass through the halls of Upper Canadian government. He had served as an officer in the Argyll Highlanders during the Napoleonic Wars and had been lieutenant governor, first of British Honduras, and then, of Van Dieman's Land. Sir George came to Toronto with a mind-set determined by years of fighting Frenchmen, of disciplining slaves and slave owners, and keeping felons at forced labour. He was not the sort of man to take any sauce from the colonials.

Soon, to Ogle, he became "Goddamn Sir George." That was because he refused to give Gowan a farthing of patronage, much less the major posts he desired. "He does not recognize that we are God's own people," Ogle explained to Frances at the family table one evening. "We save the country, defend the Constitution, we preserve Law, and what does goddamn Sir George do? Ignore us!"

Sir George's reason for doing nothing for Ogle was that he was attached to the Orange Order, for which the lieutenant governor had a strong dislike. It was a cause of disorder, a disturber of the neatness that he demanded in all things, from the Government House gardens to social intercourse. Although the Order was legal in British North America, it again had been made illegal in the United Kingdom, so anyone associated with the Order was, in Sir George's mind, doubly besmirched. No, he would not promote Gowan.

Mrs. Colclough, Ogle's mother-in-law usually sat quietly during family dinners, but here she interrupted. "Yes, Ogle, of course he ignores you." Everyone paid attention, for, not only did Mrs. Colclough rarely speak on these occasions, but when she did she employed a *Grande Dame* manner, left over from the great houses of the eighteenth century. "He is a remarkably silly man, but one I have seen many times. They are all the same." She raised a very old and tarnished lorgnette to her eyes.

"And?"

"And the man is a military man and a centurian, the sort that the Romans sent out to small colonial outposts. He is quite incapable of understanding the matter of Loyalty and how the battles of 1837 and 1838 changed things." Here the old lady was immensely shrewd. Sir George indeed was incapable of understanding what every alert politician in Upper Canada had recognized at once: that by being hyper-loyal during rebellion times, the Orangemen (who may have constituted as much as one-half of all men in active militia units), had been naturalized and their organization legitimized. Whatever the Order's status in the home countries, in Upper Canada the Orangemen were major defenders of the established order. And now, like the Loyalists in the war of 1812, they had a patriotic myth that justified, by virtue of the sacrifices they had made, their obtaining a fair share of the province's baubles.

Gowan sat silently. The dowager continued. "And also, Ogle, you know that your silly Sir George is a blockhead — because he cannot count."

"Oh?"

"If he could count he would see that one out of every five adult men in the province belongs to your society. And that now the members are not solely good Protestants from Ireland, but English and Scots, and men born in Canada. Locking out the Orangemen is just as foolish as trying to dam the St. Lawrence with a dyke of reeds."

Ogle addressed his mother-in-law as if she were an oracle. "Then how should I deal with this blockhead?"

Mrs. Colclough, recognizing the role she was being asked to play, pushed back her chair and walked slowly to the dining-room door. There, like an actress giving her last lines just before an exit, she said, "Wait, Ogle. Do nothing. That man will be gone soon and your time will come. You will still be in Parliament and he will be, God knows, in the South Seas." She swept out.

This was some of the best advice that Ogle ever received, and he ignored it. Instead of sitting still and letting events work naturally for him, Ogle enmeshed himself in two of the most disruptive issues to surface in Upper Canada in the late 1830s and early '40s: the Clergy Reserve question and the issue of Responsible Government.

"The Clergy Reserves question is the most tiresome one in public life," a prematurely jaded John A. Macdonald told Ogle Gowan during a chance encounter outside Macdonald's law office in Kingston.

Gowan and Macdonald had first met in Kingston at a session of the Celtic Society, a largely, but not exclusively, Scottish group, to which Gowan had been invited by a a merchant friend, an emigrant from Ayrshire. Macdonald, twenty-one years old at the time, was an apprentice lawyer and secretary of the Society.

Macdonald was a reedy figure, given to bobbing about and obsequiously asking the opinions of anyone whose favour he wished to curry. He had unusually long arms and none of his coats fitted him properly. A long expanse of white arm stretched out from his cuffs, leading to a set of hands whose fingers never were still, drumming, twiddling, twisting constantly.

An ambitious young man, Macdonald used the Celtic Society as a means of meeting men of influence — Bishop Macdonnell, for instance, was a member — and the energetic Gowan obviously was a man with a future: an MP at age thirty-three, and the head of a large, province-wide association. So, following the dinner, Macdonald had made a point of singling out Gowan and inviting him to the Grimason for a jug of punch to finish off the evening.

There Ogle waxed expansive on the Constitutional cause and young Macdonald nodded gravely and drank more than was customary for a man of his age. Macdonald tried to look senatorial, but this was undercut by his unfortunate habit of wiping his nose with his fingertips. Would he wish an introduction to one of the Kingston lodges of the Orange Order? Gowan asked. Macdonald considered it and said, no, not now, as he was just settling into Kingston society after having been away for quite a time, and, yes, perhaps he would join someday. "You will, my good man, you will," Ogle stated with certainty.

"The man who puts the Clergy Reserves from public view will be a public benefactor," Macdonald continued. "But like the giver of most benisons he will be forgotten by those who should thank him and will be remembered only by the few whom he shall offend."

Instead of recalling the opinion of the young sage, Gowan charged into the Clergy Reserves question. He was named head of a Legislative Committee on the Clergy Reserves and, on April 8, 1839, he presented a recommendation that the Reserves be divided equally among all legally recognized Christian denominations. This idea suited the Roman Catholic bishop, Alexander Macdonnell nicely, but it was a sharp switch for Gowan, who always had been a stout Church of England man. The idea had merits, granted, but it shook many of Gowan's Orange supporters, for here was the Grand Master pushing an idea that was vaguely associated with the radicalism of William Lyon Mackienzie and, more directly, with the demands of the Romanists.

About a month later (in a decision unconnected with Gowan's stance on the reserves issue), Sir John Colborne, still Governor of the Canadas, ordered Ogle's regiment disbanded. This was sensible, as there was no longer any military need for the unit, but it was an extreme blow to Gowan's pride. The Queen's Royal Borderers was not merely a military unit to him, but one of the pieces of parchment on which his social legitimacy was engrossed. It hurt Gowan grievously to be reduced from being a lieutenant colonel, in command of his own regiment to captain, second-incharge of the second Leeds militia.

Ogle interpreted his downgrading as a snub, engineered by Sir George Arthur. He believed that Sir John Colborne — "that gallant old veteran" — was merely an innocent catspaw for Sir George.

Consequently, he set out to hurt Arthur any way he could. Earlier, Ogle had been flirting with the idea of Responsible Government and now, as a means of attacking Sir George, he came out full-fledged for it.

"Responsibility" was a live issue at this time because the Durham Report had just appeared. This followed upon the indecently rapid visit to Canada of John George Lambton, First Earl of Durham, and son-in-law of Earl Gray of First Reform Bill fame. Durham had arrived in Quebec City May 27, 1838, had completed his survey of Canadian governments, and was back on board ship for England by November 1 of the same year. A select committee of the Upper Canadian Assembly waspishly (and incorrectly) noted that "His Lordship's personal observation was confined to his passing up the St. Lawrence River and crossing Lake Ontario in a steamboat occupied exclusively by his family and suite, a four-day's sojourn at the Falls of Niagara, and a twenty-four hours' visit to the Lieutenant Governor at Toronto." Durham's final report was completed on January 31, 1839. It was then printed, released to the United Kingdom parliament and, eventually, became known in Upper Canada. The text was that rarity amongst government publications — it was a highly documented and a fascinating amalgam of apercus and silly bits of hearsay. The document's actual recommendations were considerably less interesting than the text. At heart, Responsible Government meant that the Executive Council (the forerunner of the Cabinet) was to be selected from the party which secured a majority in the assembly, rather than being appointed from among the provincial *élite* as hitherto, and therefore would be quite independent of the electoral process. Now the Council was to be responsible to the people, through having been elected, and therefore having the confidence of the House. In general usage (if not in strict logic) Responsible Government was associated with the uniting of the parliaments of Upper and Lower Canada.

Inevitably, responsibility would result in the effective demotion of the lieutenant governorship, and acceptance of the idea of Responsible Government would be a tacit judgement that the existing office holders somehow had failed. Thus, Gowan saw Responsibility as a means of going for Goddam Sir George's throat. This was not lost on contemporary observers. A printed set of thumb-nail sketches of upper Canadian Legislators noted concerning Gowan:

> He is very ambitious and had a most favourable opportunity at one time of forwarding his views, for no man was more highly esteemed among the Conservatives; but in an unfortunate moment for himself, he took offence at some private wrong, supposed to have been inflicted on him by Sir George Arthur, and fell from defending the government, and warmly espoused the cause of "Responsibility."

Ogle's quick change on Responsibility, like his rapid shift on the Clergy Reserves, shook his Orange followers. Instinctively conservative, they were predisposed to be suspicious of any constitutional change, especially if it reduced the colony's ties with the Mother Country. They were particularly unlikely to listen to any idea coming from the Earl of Durham, for he had gone out of his way to insult them in his report. In Orange lodges, in country taverns, around stoves in backwoods spirit groceries, Orangemen were enraged to read the following:

> The Irish Catholics complain very loudly and justly of the existence of Orangeism in this Colony.

"And well they might, for aren't we the first defenders of Law and Constitution?"

> They are justly indignant that, in a Province which their loyalty and bravery have materially contributed to save . . .

"True enough there: they were loyal in '37 and '38."

> . . . their feelings are outraged by the symbols and processions of this association.

"Yes, we just have a parade once a year; and they come out to watch it as much as anyone else"

> It is somewhat difficult to understand the nature and objects of the rather anomalous Orangeism of Upper Canada. Its members

> profess to desire to uphold the Protestant religion, but to be free from those intolerant feelings toward their Catholic countrymen which are the distinctive marks of Irish Orangemen. They assert, that their main object, to which the support of the English Church is subsidiary, is to maintain the connexion with Great Britain.

"It is, by God! For Crown and Country and No Surrender!"

> . . . And at their public dinners, after drinking the 'pious, glorious and immortal memory,' with all the usual formality of abuse of the Catholics, they toast the health of the Catholic Bishop, Macdonnell . . . .

"Whyever not? Bishop Macdonnell, Romanist or not, is one of the loyalist men ever to live in Upper Canada!"

> It would seem that their great purpose has been to introduce the machinery, rather than the tenets of Orangeism; and the leaders probably hope to make use of this kind of permanent conspiracy and illegal organisation . . .

"It's not illegal in Canada! Even an ignorant earl should know that!!"

> . . . to gain political power for themselves. It is an Irish Tory institution, having not so much a religious as a political bearing.

"Of course we are Tories, for who could trust the Reformers? But not just Irish — look at all the English and Scots and born-here Canadians that have joined!"

For Gowan, the timing was unfortunate. A truncated version of the Durham Report was published in Egerton Ryerson's *Christian Guardian* on April 6, 1839, and, within a month, the full version had percolated through the countryside. This was just at the time when Gowan's plan for the Clergy Reserves was in the air, so when he began making affirmative comments about Responsible Government, Gowan's Orange followers were doubly upset. The Grand Master seemed to be becoming unsound on two matters that related to the Constitution.

For another reason this was a bad moment to shake the faith of his Orange constituency — the seat of the Grand Lodge was in the process of being moved from Brockville to Toronto. This move made sense for practical reasons — membership in Toronto was booming, but it meant that Ogle's day-to-day control over Orange business was reduced. Now a group of Toronto Orangemen, led by Alderman Armstrong and George Duggan, began to question Ogle's leadership. They were aided, from Hamilton, by George Perkins Bull and by that quiet watchdog, George Nicoll, "Is Gowan really *sound*?" they asked.

Ogle responded to this challenge with a power-move. Just before the Grand Lodge held its annual meeting in mid-June to elect officers for the next year, he told his brethren that he intended to resign as grand master. Actually, he had no such intention, but this was the only way he could get the Grand Lodge to endorse his views on Responsible Government. So great was his prestige, that rather than lose Gowan as grand master, the Orangemen endorsed a resolution that most of them did not believe in:

> Resolved: That the errors into which the Right Hon. the Earl of Durham has fallen . . . so far as they relate to the numbers of the Roman Catholic population of Upper Canada, and to the alleged hostility of Orangemen, while they are subjects of regret to the Grand Lodge: yet they cannot at the same time prevent the Members of this Institution from expressing their assent to the general accuracy of His Lordship's statement, and their desire to see many of his suggestions carried into practical effect, *particularly, a thorough local responsibility upon all matters of domestic government.*

This came from men who had, as recently as six months earlier, labelled Reformers who promoted the same views as treasonous. So great — for the moment — was Gowan's prestige.

"Ogle, dear, is there not a chance that you are going ahead too fast for your brethren?" Frances asked soon after this victory.

"I have never been a man of half measures, and I know what is right for my Orangemen." He was very full of himself, confident to the point of arrogance: he seemed to think of himself as a royal duke amongst commoners. "I shall lead them to much bigger rewards under Responsible Government than we will ever receive from the likes of Goddam Sir George Arthur."

Disgruntlement in the ranks, however, was hard to stifle. A Leeds county follower wrote: "Our slogan or war cry that used to excite such deeds of daring at Beverly and Farmersville has been long abandoned. 'Loyalty, church and state, the sceptre and the throne, British supremacy, No Surrender — have given place to 'Equal division of the Clergy Reserves, Family Compact, and Responsible Government.' "

Nevertheless, Ogle went ahead writing a set of "Letters" advocating Responsible Government. These appeared in his *Statesman* in late August 1839 and were re-drafted into a pamphlet. It was a long time, more than ten years, since Ogle had written a pamphlet, and when he started he was afraid that he might have lost his touch. He need not have worried: His *Letters on Responsible Government* is unusual in Canadian political writing of the period in that it is literature. The first part is measured exposition of the argument that Responsible Government was simply the British Cabinet system moved abroad, and the second part is a set of replies to various objections to Responsibility. The second half had an intentional *ad hoc* character, but the first is truly distinguished expository writing. It was written in the contemporary British pamphlet tradition, not the Canadian or American: it is allusive, subtly structured, and is immediately recognizable as having been composed by someone who has had a sound classical education. For once in his Canadian career, Ogle took the high road.

Late in 1839, that unusual Irishman, the Toronto reforming journalist Francis Hincks, put out the *Letters* in pamphlet form, and in that form they caught the fussy eye of Sir George Arthur. He thereupon had Ogle removed from his post as Crown lands agent for the Johnstown district.

In 1841, central Canada received the form, if not the full substance of Responsible Government. The new Governor-General, Charles Poulett Thomson (Baron Sydenham, 1840), saw to that. So was not Ogle Gowan on the side of the victors and thus, once again, a winner?

No. And only partly because his nemesis, Sir George Arthur, stayed on under Sydenham as Lieutenant-Governor of Upper Canada.

The real problem was that Ogle, like a juvenile card player, did not realize that high-ranking cards usually are not much good unless they are in the right suit. For instance, his pamphlet was a fine card, a queen or a king, in the Responsibilty line; but since Gowan had spent most of the last decade developing the hyper-loyal Tory suit, the pamphlet could do no more than take an isolated trick. So, like a player who leads away from his strong suit, playing the Responsibility card cost him heavily in the long run.

In December 1839, the House of Assembly reconvened and the Speech from the Throne was delivered by the speaker on behalf of the new governor of Canada. It was a big moment, the first full session of parliament after the Durham Report's appearance. Gracelessly, the speaker noted that he had "procured a copy" of the speech, "to prevent mistakes." The speech was notable chiefly for its omissions: union of Upper and Lower Canada was discussed, but no mention was made of Responsible Government or anything that even smacked of it.

Ogle listened with the restless energy of a schoolboy who has been kept inside too long. He fidgeted, crossed and uncrossed his legs, turned sideways in his seat and exhaled noisily at parts he did not like. When the members of the House of Assembly left the Legislative Council chamber at the end of the speech, he moved agitatedly from member to member, looking for allies who would join him in opposition. Most members rejected him and he resembled a large bee in a field of flowers, moving from plant to plant with little satisfaction. He found a few allies at last, but had he found none, it would not have mattered, for now he had a chance for getting back at Sir George Arthur. "A little salt in Goddam Sir George's wounds is what is required."

Next day, the Assembly passed, without division, fourteen uncontentious resolutions, approving the Governor of Canada's intentions, as expressed in the Speech from the Throne. An amendment to the fifteenth resolution, however, went for the throat, and though it was not moved by Gowan, it bears the unmistakeable stamp of his authorship. This amendment affirmed the loyalty of the Crown's subjects, and agreed that no rebellion was presently at hand, and then veered brutally towards Sir George, by adding that the "*adoption of more prompt measures by Her Majesty's Ministers at the very outset of these aggressions* would have effectively prevented their renewal and that to their *ill-timed forebearance* are chiefly attributable the subsequent violations of Her Majesty's territory, the murder of her loyal subjects, and the destruction of their property . . . . "

This was as close as it was possible to come to a vote of no-confidence regarding the way that Sir George had handled events after he took over from Bond Head. It was also tantamount to blaming him for having let the republican invasion of 1838 take place. When on the division, Ogle cast his vote, his face was beet-red with excitement. Lord, what joy! Never mind that the amendment was overwhelmingly defeated, thirty-eight to seven; never mind that he now was openly at war with the lieutenant governor of Upper Canada; the moment was one of pure pleasure and to be relished.

But this condition of euphoria was not of long duration. Ogle's confidence, so overweening at times, now began to ring increasingly hollow. One civil servant wrote: "He [Gowan] is losing ground among many of his best friends, and unless he retraces his steps, and that quickly, he will sink in public estimation. Even now, he is not regarded with much confidence by either party."

Ogle was assailed by slight doubts about his position and tried, with terrible awkwardness, to retrace some of his steps. For instance, he permitted several friends of his in the legislature, headed by Colonel John Prince, to petition Sir George Arthur on his behalf.

> The Undersigned Representatives of the People respectively beg leave to bring under your Excellency's notice the gallant conduct of Lieutenant Colonel Gowan, in defense of this Province; and they beg to express to your Excellency their conviction that, should your Excellency confer on Colonel Gowan, some mark of your Excellency's favour, it would not only be an act of justice to that Officer, but to be gratefully received by the Country he so gallantly defended.

This petition was presented January 25, 1840.

Colonel Prince was, as James Gowan noted, "a colleague and fellow-helper of Mr. Gowan," but he was also a well-known maniac with duelling pistols. He had blazed twice in the four months that followed the Battle of the Windmill, and in the second of those affairs of honour, had neatly blown away his opponent's head.

Ogle started to run scared. He found that he had underestimated the defections from his leadership among the Orangemen and now it was all that he could do to keep them from dumping him. Little things started to get out of hand. For instance, some of his enemies in the Order started a rumour that he was making a considerable profit printing up Orange resolutions, notices, and warrants. Doubtless this was true and all the more damaging for being so. Grand Lodge minutes were printed in batches of 500, and the rules and regulations of the Order in runs of 1,000 in those days.

This was big business for a Canadian printer, and Gowan, like most newspaper publishers of his day, made as much money from job-printing as from journalism. Typically, when he heard the rumour, Gowan replied with self-righteous outrage: he did not wish to profit from his high office and therefore in future would refuse to print any Orange material! Of course he was not serious and, in the end, an agreement was struck whereby half the Orange business in future would be printed in Toronto, the other half in Brockville.

At the Grand Lodge meeting of 1840, a resolution "regretting the principles advocated by the Grand Master on the subject of Responsible Government" had to be beaten back.

For the moment, his hold on the reins was tight enough to keep him in uneasy charge. What bothered him most was the appearance as an overt enemy of that silent watchdog of Orange morality, George Nicoll, the little tailor from Dublin. Nicoll now informed the members of the Grand Lodge that he had documentary evidence of Gowan's having been expelled from the Irish Order, and these charges were repeated in a letter in the public press (*Patriot* 11, February 1840). The devastating suggestion was made that not only had Ogle been expelled in Ireland, but that the documents he had produced for earlier inquiries made in Upper Canada were the products of his own press. The only thing that kept Ogle from being discredited among the brethren was that Nicoll refused to recognize the authority of the Order in British North America (for it stemmed from an illegitimate Gowanite, line, he believed) and therefore would not testify directly, but instead referred the Canadian Orangemen to the Irish authorities for documentation. That little terrier, Nicoll, could be kept at a distance for a time, Ogle knew, but he feared that sooner or later the wee beast would really get his teeth in.

Things were slipping fast locally as well. In November 1840 Col. R.D. Fraser, one of Ogle's longtime allies, walked into the *Statesman* office and in front of one of Gowan's sons upbraided Ogle for lacking spine and for failing to keep to the principles of true loyalism. A fool: that's what Ogle was for talking Responsible Government, and a worm for wishing to lick the boots of Sir George Arthur. Ogle responded histrionically, by challenging his old friend to meet him with pistols at twenty paces. As befitted old friends, each man was as afraid of winning the duel as of losing. After face-saving intervention and negotiation by the two men's seconds, the matter was compromised.

Increasingly, Ogle lost his taste for Brockville. He took to spending as much time as he could in Kingston, forty miles away. This city was on the rise and next to Toronto, it was the nexus of political and governmental intelligence. Gowan established a regular round of calls on lawyers, municipal officials and, especially, medical doctors: he had learned earlier in his career that physicians are an excellent source of gossip, provided one permits them to pretend to preserve their ethics by using indirect references rather than personal names.

Ogle set up what was effectively a second office for his *Statesman* on a large pine table in the Grimason House on Store Street. There he frequently wrote the editorials for his paper and checked proofs. The narrow, brick-faced house had little to recommend it outwardly, but inside was always a warm fire, a full-proof whiskey punch, and a lubricious barmaid. It was the favourite tavern of the lawyer, John A. Macdonald, and Ogle and he frequently met. There was a certain social distance between them, but each man recognized the other as someone who might someday be useful. Several times, Gowan reminded Macdonald that he would be welcome in the Orange Order. Mostly, they talked about politics and they agreed that the new capital of the United Canadas probably would be Toronto, and, also, that despite the difficulties he faced, Ogle would win re-election.

Frequently, both watched with appreciation a buxom girl who made a salacious performance out of everything she did. Macdonald, now in his mid-twenties, threw off a few off-colour jokes to show Ogle that he was knowledgable about such things. The girl, no more than fourteen or fifteen, was no innocent. She put on a particularly coquettish performance each time she brought a fresh glass of punch to Mr. Gowan, the MP and his friend, the lawyer.

Early in February 1841 the long-awaited official announcement of the new capital of the United Canadas came: it would be Kingston. John A. Macdonald and Ogle Gowan both were surprised, although quite pleased. Each said that, of course, he had been certain all along that it would be Kingston.

The union of the Canadas was to take place on February 10, 1841, and a general election was to follow in about six weeks. "Should an election take place," Ogle had told his cousin James in June 1839, "I believe my return *without opposition* is certain." Things now, however, were different; for the election was held under new rules, the most important of which was that Leeds county became a single-seat constituency. James Morris, the junior Member for Leeds county, ran against Gowan for that seat. He was an undramatic man, who had stayed at home, done his constituency work thoroughly, and had built up a loyal following. To the government, Morris was infinitely preferable to Gowan as an MP. This was very important now, for in this election, Lord Sydenham electioneered as heavily as any governor in Canadian history ever has done.

The Leeds county electorate considered Morris's solid constituency work, noted the government's disdain for Gowan, and recalled the way Ogle had strayed from the path of true Toryism, by favouring Responsibility over Imperialism, democracy over deference, and the electorate responded: Ogle lost his seat.

CHAPTER 13

A Certain Bluff Humanity, 1841-1844

"THIS IS not a social call, Doctor." Ogle was sitting in the Brockville consulting room of his brother-in-law, Dr. Charles W. Buchanan. "It is a medical matter. It must be kept in confidence."

"Certainly. I never discuss my patients' medical problems with anyone." Buchanan, an Irishman from Omagh, County Tyrone, was tall and slightly greying. He was every inch the medical professional, the sort of man who was driving the old leech-and-quacks from the healing profession. On the wall behind him were rarities for Canadian medical men of his era — diplomas — one for passing the examinations of the Royal College of Surgeons of England, the other, an M.A. degree from Glasgow.

"I mean, it must not be discussed with my sister Margaret."

"So, Ogle, it is a very personal problem?"

"Yes, and well, damn it, it's hard to talk of." Gowan actually blushed.

Dr. Buchanan waited for him to continue.

"Well, goddamn it, doctor — it *stings*."

Buchanan immediately had a fair idea of what Ogle's problem was, but he still waited, his countenance grave.

" . . . I mean . . . it's my man-peg. It stings half the time and every now and then it drips. Strange stuff. It's horrible!" Ogle blurted this out quickly, and, having done so, he visibly relaxed. His colour returned to normal and his confidence also began to return. He did not hesitate when Dr. Buchanan suggested that the offending appendage be examined. In fact, once Gowan had dropped his trousers to the floor he had one of those emotional *volte faces* that characterized his entire life: he now began talking as a man-of-the-world about his sexual experiences. "Yes, as you can see, I am being punished for having achieved an intrigue with one of the opposite sex. She was, alas, not a virgin. Young, fresh, glorious . . . but not virginal."

"Or hygienic," added Buchanan.

"Decidedly not."

"Have you been treating this yourself?" Buchanan asked severely. Even in those days of early medical professionalism, it was well recognized that the greatest danger to the profession was the patient who cured himself.

"In fact, Charles, yes I have." Ogle was now so fully recovered in his self-esteem as to use Christian names. "But to no avail, I'm afraid. By chance, I mentioned the problem to a friend of mine, a young attorney in Kingston, and he procured for me an injection of white vitriol and water. This, and violent exercise, he had been told, would cure the problem."

"But it did not?"

"No. In fact, the white vitriol felt . . . " Ogle searched for a word. " . . . it felt *keen*."

"Might as well apply a mustard poultice and a branding iron," Buchanan commented.

"So, Charles, if you could prescribe a course of treatment rather more effective and considerably less painful, I should be in your debt forever. Perhaps something of a cooling mixture."

Buchanan was about to reply atrabiliously that he was not a wayside pox-doctor for every rake who passed along the King's Highway, but, remembering that in part he owed the establishment of his practice in Brockville to Gowan, he held his tongue. "Certainly, my friend, certainly. I know just the unguent for you and shall compound it at once. Healing, cooling and effective. Use the salve daily."

He turned away to search among his reference books for the precise formula, saying over his shoulder, "Yes, use it daily. Now pull your trousers up." As an afterthought, he added, "And try to keep them up."

Infelicitous as it may be from a purely literary standpoint, Gowan's mild case of the pox turns out to be a suitable metaphor for the problems that plagued his career in the 1840s. Ogle would often seem to be on the road to real and permanent success, when a relapse into bad judgement and self-destructive behaviour would bring him low.

As his popularity had waned during the years 1840 and 1841, the circulation of the *Statesman* had dropped, and Gowan's first task now that he no longer was a member of parliament was to put his personal finances in order. In the spring of 1842 he sold his putative "estate," Escott Park. Considering that, as previously mentioned, he had had a house built and a good deal of the land cleared, he actually lost money on the ownership of this property. But at least the sale gave him some cash-in-hand, and freed him from having to maintain a farm that cost more than it produced. Ogle paid some of his debts, but as usual cash burned a hole in his pocket and he bought more parcels of third-rate land. For the moment he was all right financially, but he had nothing set aside for an emergency — and his life was one long emergency.

Gowan decided to re-build his reputation within his old parliamentary constituency, so that he could run successfully in the next general election. As part of this plan, he took up local small-time politics in a big-time way. Here he was lucky, for on January 1, 1842, nothing short of a revolution in local government occurred. Before then, local civic affairs were run by central-government appointed justices of the peace in an arrangement closely based on English mediaeval precedents. Now, suddenly, civic affairs were put into the hands of locally elected councils. In Gowan's case, the relevant council was that for the Johnstown District, which consisted of Leeds and Grenville counties and a few sparsely populated northern townships. He represented Elizabethtown township.

With his parliamentary experience, Ogle stood out. William Morris, the brother of James Morris, MP for Leeds, was the warden: the first wardenship was appointed by the central government, rather than elected. When Morris could not attend, Gowan usually was elected temporary chairman. Although in experience and oratorical ability, Gowan stood head and shoulders above the other local councillors, this was a mixed blessing, for it made him an easy target and there were a lot of people who enjoyed shying rocks at him. When the wardenship of the district became elective, Gowan campaigned hard for it. He did not win the post until 1847, however, and that is a good indication of the local resistance to him.

The other territory that Gowan now worked assiduously was Kingston. Even though he no longer had a parliamentary seat, he needed to keep on top of governmental gossip and to maintain his contacts with officials, particularly the middle level of civil servants who were frequently Orangemen, and thus good sources of information. Now that the capital had moved from Toronto to Kingston, things were much more convenient for him. Ogle was much more at ease in Kingston than he was in Toronto. Unlike most outsiders who come to that cold and grey place, he actually liked Kingston. Perhaps Robert Baldwin was right when, in 1843, he described Kingston as an "Orange hole," but that suited Ogle perfectly.

Kingston was in the midst of a building boom — there was activity everywhere and money to be made. Over 400 buildings, some of them very substantial, were built in the years 1841-1844. Gowan was tempted to move his newspaper from Brockville to Kingston, for not only was there plenty of room for an Orange-tinted sheet, but there was lots of money to be made from governmental printing contracts. In the end, Ogle decided that to move both his family and his business from Brockville would be too difficult. Still, he loved the city. In particular, he like to take long walks from the Kingston harbour, all the way out to Portsmouth, inspecting the construction sites along the way.

At the start of one of these rambles, he encountered an Englishman, a quiet man of middle height, who had a notebook protruding from the breast pocket of his topcoat. From the existence of this journal, Ogle surmised that the fellow was either a land speculator or a fellow-journalist, and from the velvet collar on the top coat and the unwrinkled tailoring of the garment, that this was a man of substance, and therefore worth knowing. As with most middle-class Englishmen abroad, the stranger did not give his name or occupation, but was quite willing to listen to Gowan's chitchat, becoming an unwitting consociate on Ogle's guided tour of Kingston.

The town had undergone a severe fire recently, so that it looked half-burned; and, with there being so much construction, the rest of the place seemed half-built. This the visitor took in without comment. Gowan showed him "Summerhill," a massive house built by the Archdeacon of Kingston: the "Archdeacon's Palace" Ogle wryly noted. Now it was being cut up into apartments, to house government officials. After that, the two men walked through a bit of open countryside before coming to Alwington House, which Lord Sydenham, the Governor General had taken over as his official residence. Its size and character impressed the English visitor. He took out his notebook and wrote something in a squiggling hand that Ogle took to be shorthand. Presumably the Englishman had heard of Sydenham's Olympian philanderings, for he said dryly, "The villa seems eminently suited for irregular congress." That lapidary phrase told Gowan that his companion was a writer.

The Englishman was more impressed with the gaol at Portsmouth than with anything else that he saw. He proposed to gain admittance, speak to the chief keeper, and interview some of the prisoners. Ogle declined to join him, so with courteous small bows, the two men parted, neither having learned the other's name. That is a pity, for being mentioned in Charles Dickens's *American Notes* would have guaranteed Ogle Gowan an immortality that he struggled unsuccessfully his entire life to achieve.

In Kingston's early days as the seat of government, Gowan spent a great deal of time in the company of John A. Macdonald, who, as a young bachelor, had plenty of free time and a wide range of friends. Most important, Macdonald had that elusive quality: he was "good company." The two men had a pilgrimage that they sometimes took of a late afternoon, a route named by Ogle as "the Rogation of Barriefield." This consisted of a slow walk from Macdonald's law office to the "Penny Bridge" that led to a path to Barriefield village which, in the early 1840s, comprised eighty-four families and nine public houses. There they had a jar in each tavern and then dandered unevenly back to Kingston for a meal. Young Macdonald was in the habit of standing in the middle of the Penny Bridge and singing some lines of Thomas Moore's about the "meeting of the waters," while he urinated. Ogle always laughed at this and said that's about all he thought the poetry of Ireland's national bard was worth.

A sign of Gowan's influence on Macdonald was the young

lawyers's finally joining the Orange Order in 1841. (Curiously, this is ignored in the standard biography of the future prime minister.) This important decision had been announced jocularily. "Well, Gowan, I've decided that it is safer to embrace your principles than your mistress!"

The friendship between the two men was close during 1841. That was the year of great public ceremony in Kingston and the city abounded with public spectacle, exactly the sort of event that politically-interested people like Macdonald and Gowan liked to attend and, equally, to ridicule. They particularly enjoyed the ceremonies held on June 15, when the first Parliament of the United Canadas met in a converted section of the Kingston General Hospital. It was a day for high pomp and low puns.

The Gowan-Macdonald friendship was truncated, however, by Macdonald's taking ill in the fall of 1841. He decided to go to Great Britain to recuperate and he was gone for the first half of 1842. When Macdonald returned, they spent nights drinking at the Grimason House and, sometimes took turns going upstairs to enjoy the services of a new and uncontagious barmaid. Then, in the spring of 1843, Macdonald fell in love with his cousin. He was married on September 1, 1843 and for a time did not circulate in the company of dissolute males.

The time that Ogle spent in Kingston in these years was not entirely wasted. He wrote a good deal of newspaper copy on parliamentary matters and also was engaged in the serious task of lobbying for the Orange Order. Despite its great and growing popularity among central Canada's Protestant men, the Order was an embarrassment to colonial administrators and a thorn in the flesh of reforming politicians. In particular, the Reformers, Louis LaFontaine and Robert Baldwin, who became executive councillors and *de facto* joint prime ministers in the autumn of 1842, were committed to the suppression of the Order. They had two measures in mind, one, a Processions Act that would prevent the Orangemen from parading, and the other, a Secret Societies Act, that would force the dissolution of the Order. Gowan fought these two measures vigorously and the knowledge that the Order was in danger temporarily stifled assaults on his leadership within the association.

Now that Macdonald was married, he and Ogle Gowan were

not to see much of each other socially, but events of the summer and fall of 1843 threw them into a close alliance, and, through some complex political physics each of them became an ally, if an uneasy one, of the Governor General. This occurred because a new governor general, Sir Charles Metcalfe, arrived late in March 1843. Kingston had been hard on the country's chief administrators. Lord Sydenham had died in the fall of 1841, after being thrown from a horse, and his successor, Sir Charles Bagot, had suffered a debilitating illness and, having requested recall to England, died soon after getting there. Metcalfe arrived in Kingston to find that the coalition of Baldwin and LaFontaine had gone much further in the direction of Responsible Government than the Imperial authorities had contemplated. He tried to apply the brakes to what he thought was a wildly careening carriage.

Thus, early in July, Ogle Gowan was invited to a private dinner at Government House, as Alwington House was now called. It was the kind of evening for which Ogle had been preparing when, as a boy, he sat in a corner of Mount Nebo and absorbed the conversation of his father and Sir George Ogle. His apparently genteel behaviour and his telling of amusing (if, by now antique) stories, assured Sir Charles that, however Gowan might act when surrounded by Canadian backwoodsmen, he was, at heart, a gentleman. After dinner the two men adjourned to the library and had a long talk about politics. The Governor General wanted advice on how to rearrange the ministry so that the Reformers would be displaced, and he wanted the Orangemen to keep quiet and, in particular, not to parade on the approaching Twelfth. Ogle agreed to quash the Kingston parade and he provided Sir Charles with a plan for re-organizing the ministry. Both men thought the meeting a great success. Sir Charles wrote to Lord Stanley, the colonial secretary, that the local Orange problem was diminishing; and Gowan wrote a confidential memo to his business partner saying that "I have no doubt *my plan* has been approved, and that Baldwin, and the Reformers are on the way out."

Both men were wrong. Although there was no Orange parade in Kingston that year, an attack on the Orange Hall caused a riot, with loss of life. Then, to make matters worse, Gowan had a falling-out with his business partner and the letter he had written describing his secret conversations with the Governor General was leaked to the press. This made it nearly impossible for Sir Charles to move against the Reform ministry.

As if Sir Charles did not have enough of a problem in his attempt to tame the Reformers, he had another one: where should the seat of government be? Kingstonians apart, no one was very happy with the location of the capital, and Sir Charles himself had no liking for the place. Throughout the summer and early fall, rumours spread that the executive council had decided to move the seat of government to Montreal, subject to parliamentary approval. Kingstonians of all political persuasions fought the move, but the most vocal group was a band of young Conservatives, and one of the most prominent of these was John A. Macdonald. Ogle Gowan, sensitive to the fact that any move to Montreal would be a loss for the entire eastern half of the province, joined the opposition. It was all to no avail. After a vituperous debate, the House of Assembly voted on December 3, by a majority of fifty-one to twenty-seven to abandon Kingston.

As Macdonald told Gowan during a chance meeting at their mutually favourite tavern on Princess Street (Store Street had just been renamed for the Princess Royal), the only good thing was that Samuel Harrison, the MP for Kingston, had resigned his seat in protest against moving the capital. "That leaves a seat for a good man," Ogle said portentously. "And, it's best that it should be a trustworthy young man with the right principles." Macdonald permitted himself a slow, wide, smile. Gowan raised a glass. "To the right young man."

Meantime, like a foaming team of horses pulling a brakeless sleigh, the Baldwin-Fontaine ministry still was pulling Sir Charles's government in a direction he did not want it to go. On October 9, the ministry introduced two measures of consequence, one to ban Party processions, the other to outlaw all secret associations, save the Free Masons. Members of secret societies (meaning, chiefly, the Orange Order), were to be made legally incapable of holding any elective office or to serve on juries; inn-keepers were to lose their licences if they permitted their premises to be used for the meetings of such societies. The Reform majority in the assembly was massive, so that the Secret Societies Bill passed the third reading overwhelmingly: fifty-five to thirteen. This was on November 5. Throughout the province, Orangemen boiled in anger. In Toronto, effigies of Baldwin and Hincks were placed on a gibbet, hanged, and burned. In Kingston, Gowan directed a lobbying crusade, with the goal of convincing the Governor General to reserve the legislation, rather than permit it to receive the royal assent. John A. Macdonald, now an Orangeman himself, helped. In the end, Sir Charles Metcalfe temporized: he permitted the Party Procession Bill to become law (it stayed on the books for eight years, then was repealed), but he reserved the Secret Societies measure, and it never became law.

Although Gowan and Macdonald had worked together on the issues of location of the capital, and on the protection of Orange rights, these essentially were matters of sectoral interest. What each man sought was an issue of high principle, one that would resonate through the wider community. The Baldwin-LaFontaine administration gave it to them; the Reformers got into a wrangle with the Governor General about patronage appointments. The Reformers declared that, in accordance with the principles of Responsible Government, patronage appointments should be made in agreement with the wishes of the elected representatives, not according to executive preference. Soon nine of the ten members of the executive council resigned, in a power play that was nothing less than an attempt to bring the imperially-appointed governor general under domestic suzerainity.

John A. Macdonald immediately began a Kingston campaign devoted to the principle of protecting the Royal Prerogative in general, and Sir Charles's position, in particular. Gowan began a similar effort among his Orange associates and most particularly in his former parliamentary constituency of Leeds county. Together, Macdonald and Gowan were forming a strong conservative network in eastern Canada West. Both now identified with the plangent and high principles of the protection of the Canadian Government against the patronage-scavenging of the Reformers.

Sir Charles Metcalfe prorogued Parliament and governed without it throughout most of 1844. A general election had to come sometime. In March of 1844, the Kingston Conservatives decided to ready themselves and to select a candidate. John A. Macdonald ran against Samuel Harrison, and garnered the nomination. Because Kingston was solidly conservative, unless shamelessly gerrymandered (as Lord Sydenham had done in 1841 to elect the Judas-goat Anthony Manahan), Macdonald had good odds for winning the seat.

Gowan's preparations were less smooth. But, then, nothing in his life ever was glassy. In March, while John A. Macdonald was lining up votes for his own nomination, Ogle was working at getting a pistol shot at the Reformer, MP, and journalist, Francis Hincks, who had recently begun a paper, the Montreal *Pilot*. On March 8, an anonymous correspondent to Hincks's paper wrote about Queen Victoria's famous refusal to accede to Sir Robert Peel's demands to replace her Whig ladies-in-wating with Tory ladies. The *Pilot's* report was that eventually Peel's "demand was complied with, though Col. Gowan falsely asserted the contrary at Kingston." This was not a major insult by contemporary standards, but it stimulated an archaic Anglo-Irish response in Gowan. In his youth, the Irish gentry "blazed." That is, fought duels, and the best occasion for blazing was when one's honour had been impugned. And, in this case, Ogle's honour was in some vague way tied up with that of her Britannic Majesty. So, like Don Quixote preparing to mount up for a glorious tilt, he wrote to Hincks, quoting the offending phrase and stating that;

> As it is impossible that I can suffer the application of such terms to me, when published in a paper under such sanction as yours, I have to request that you will give me the name and address of the author.

Ogle wished to challenge the correspondent to a duel, but if Hincks refused to name him, he threatened:

> Should you, however, decline to accede to my demand, I beg to inform you that I will hold you personally responsible for the publication in question, and in such an event, I beg you will refer me to a friend on your behalf, to meet Captain Weatherly of this city (Kingston) who will arrange a meeting between us.

The two men's seconds met and compromised matters.

That problem behind him, Gowan turned to curry-combing his Leeds County constituency. An election was called for October and inevitably it would be a difficult one for Gowan, the moreso because under the new general election law, the poll was not to be held at a single site, or even at four sites, as in some previous elections. Instead, there would be a separate polling place in each township. Ogle triply hated this law: first, because it meant that he could not use his Orangemen to rig the voting as he had done in the past; second, because the measure had been framed by the hated Robert Baldwin; and, third, because the model that Baldwin used was the special Leeds Election Act of 1836. This had been drafted by none other than Andrew Norton Buell, a man whom Gowan believed had been a traitor during the rebellion and invasion years of 1837-1838. Gowan, thus, went into the election fighting mad.

The one thing in his favour was that the sitting member, James Morris, took himself out of the contest. This occurred because Sir Charles Metcalfe, wishing to leave an electoral path open for Gowan, let Morris understand that if he withdrew from the race for the lower house, he would be appointed to the Legislative Council after the election. (Metcalfe indeed made the appointment in November 1844.)

Four candidates ran in Leeds: two Reformers, William Buell and his nephew William Buell Richards, and two Conservatives, Ormond Jones and Ogle Gowan. This pattern is bizarre, considering that Leeds now was a single-seat constituency. The two Reformers split the Reform vote and the two Conservatives, the Tory, Ormond Jones claimed that Ogle had pledged him his support and only later joined the contest. Whatever the truth of that assertion, Gowan, running on a platform that blandly avowed his being "in favour of the views of the Governor General on Responsible Government," won. It probably was the first time that he won an election by fair means.

Of course the Buells protested, but this was a reflex action — they protested every time they lost. In December, an investigation by parliamentary committee confirmed Gowan's victory.

In Kingston, John A. Macdonald swept the hustings, receiving seven votes for every one that his Reforming opponent garnered. Gowan and Macdonald were part of a Conservative sweep in Canada West. In Canada East, LaFontaine's Reformist party had triumphed. Some explosive parliamentary debates seemed certain.

Gowan and Macdonald went down to Montreal together to attend the opening of Parliament in late November. Ogle, now aged forty-one, was a bit jowly, but he still looked to be a man one would not want to fight. Macdonald, aged twenty-nine, was tall and slender. Despite their disparate appearances, they were a well-matched team. Each was entering the Parliament of the United Canadas for the first time; each represented a Conservative constituency in Canada West; and each man had vices which, if he were unlucky, would keep him from realizing his potential.

CHAPTER 14

A Fine Chance, 1844-1848

"THIS PLACE looks like a fishmarket," John A. Macdonald remarked to Ogle Gowan as they approached for the first time the legislative building in Montreal. It was located just off McGill Street in Place Youville. Ogle now was beginning to grey, and strands of silver twined in his beard. Macdonald, though still thin of figure, was filling out and at last he was a mature adult, rather than a spindly youth.

"Too bloody right, my friend," Ogle replied, and he was not joking. The structure, a long and narrow limestone edifice once had been a market-building and all sorts of fishmongers, butchers, and green-grocers had been evicted so that it could be refurbished. "One surveys this place," Ogle added archly, "and one queries why our colleagues were so dissatisfied with the Kingston General Hospital as a meeting place." The new parliament building had a pillared portico at each end, but no one would have thought it classical. The ground floor was given over to offices for the civil servants, and resembled a rabbit warren. On the next floor were debating chambers for the Legislative Council and for the Assembly. There were robing rooms, a bar, and a library. The theme running through the *décor* was vulgarity.

"Can you imagine their having spent £600 for a mace?" Macdonald asked, sounding very Scottish indeed. He was referring to the eight-foot-long, parliamentary mace that was used for ceremonial occasions and which required the strength of caber-thrower to manage. Macdonald looked forward to the inevitable day when the mace tumbled out of control.

"Still, I wish we had been here for Metcalfe's entrance on St. Jean-Baptiste day. They say that the man actually had palms strewn in his path." That was not quite the truth. On June 24, Sir Charles Metcalfe had arrived in Montreal and had been greeted by flag — bearers and marchers from every organization in town. He took this as homage to his rank, although it also was a traditional celebration day. Flowers indeed were thrown in his path as he progressed in state to his official residence.

However derisory the attention Gowan and Macdonald paid to matters of style, it counted. In public debates, Ogle was largely engaged in a series of dramatic presentations, a set of tableaux that was intended to leave his parliamentary colleagues, the governmental authorities, and those who read his speeches in the papers, with a clear impression of himself: most important, although Ogle supported the government, he always strove to present the image of a man of independent and courageous mind. This he did through a variety of means, but most effectively by becoming a stalwart defender of the integrity of Parliament. He pushed for procedural reforms. He was a member of the Standing Committee on Printing and Binding. And when he learned that bills were sometimes introduced into the house with large parts missing — in some cases totally blank save for the title — he pushed for their being given a first reading only when they were printed in full. In February of 1845, Gowan went so far as to introduce a bill to secure the "independence of Parliament." As it turned out, this was chiefly an excuse for Ogle to give a three-hour speech, in which he argued in defense of the holders of twenty-six various offices (mostly "placemen" in the eighteenth-century sense, sundry clerks, and law officers). By recent legislation they had lost their right to sit in Parliament, and Ogle insisted they be allowed to do so, if elected by a constituency. To ban them, he declared, was to fly in the face of the electors' rights, and upon those rights hinged the integrity of Parliament. Having had his time at centre-stage, he then withdrew the bill.

Second, whenever in doubt on an abstract issue, Ogle put himself forward as a person of unimpeachably British outlook. Although the Parliament might be forced to sit in a godawful French and Papist city, Gowan could at least fight to maintain Imperial standards of conduct. He became particularly insistent on procedural and constitutional matters, where he argued, if at all possible, that things should be done as "in the Kingdom of Great Britain and Ireland." And, even when moving an amendment to the Speech from the Throne, that might have embarrassed the government by being excessively enthusiastic about Responsible Government, he played the True Briton: "And this House now hopes to see the Provincial Administration speedily completed on the true principles of the British Constitution."

Ogle was a strong speaker, not an eloquent one. On occasion, provincial papers noted that he had given the best speech of all the legislators on some specific issue. He could be cruelly sarcastic, not truly witty, but amongst the political journeymen of the United Canadas, this counted as wit. In late February 1845, William Henry Draper, member for the town of London, was about to take his seat in the Assembly for the first time. Before Draper entered, Ogle was speaking and was referring to a comment by a Quebec member:

"Sir, the Honourable Gentleman reminds me of a fable that I read when a boy, of a lion and a tomtit."

Just then Draper entered and the member for Quebec City said derisively, "Here comes the tomtit!"

Gowan's caustic reply was: "The Honourable Member for Quebec remarks that the tomtit has just entered the House, but, Sir, I tell that Honourable Gentleman that the tomtit was in the House before the Member for London entered."

Heavy sarcasm indeed. So too was a typical sally that followed a few minutes later.

Ogle again is speaking: "The Honourable Member for Quebec has told them that when His Excellency came to the Province, the Members on this side of the House looked upon those of the late administration, if not as gods, yet as demi-gods."

Interruption: "Tomicods."

Ogle: "An Honourable friend has helped me to understand the mistake under which the Honourable Member for Quebec has laboured — yes, that must be the case — they were not considered as Demigods, but as Tommy Cods — their error was easily made. (Loud laughter from the members.) " 'Tomicods' . . . is a more appropriate expression and quite in keeping, for we say, 'Oh, ye gods and little fishes.'"

That was not a bad spur-of-the-moment pun, but it was about

as subtle as Ogle ever became. When newspaper reports of his abusive jokes were read aloud in a Toronto tavern or in a backwoods inn, they always exacted a guffaw from the hard men present. That Gowan, they would say, he sure can flail the back off those Frenchies.

In his parliamentary performances, Ogle looked strong, independent, and well able to take care of himself.

There was, however, a private counterpoint. Often he sat alone in his boarding-house room in Montreal, either unable to sleep or incapable of rising to full consciousness. He frequently experienced a sense of depression, one that settled around him as the daylight failed each day. Ogle learned to hate the approach of nightfall, for the gloaming often brought a feeling that his spirit had been riven.

Ogle had real problems. Being alone in a strange city for long periods of time is disorienting to anyone; and middle-aged men are easy prey to psychic anomie. Also, the stresses of managing a newspaper by long-distance mail, and the financial pressures and family obligations that every day pressed in on him all affected his outlook. Yet, these things explain only part of the problem.

Ogle's social disease affected him both physically and emotionally. The complaint did not respond well to treatment, and he was constantly after his brother-in-law, Dr. Charles Buchanan, to come up with something better. Buchanan had moved to Toronto in July 1842, and Gowan found an excuse to visit him three or four times a year, and when he could not get to Toronto, he pestered the physician by mail.

Since the original salve no longer worked, Buchanan's most effective remedy now was an oral compound that included morphine, and this did nothing to make Ogle mentally energetic. But even without the opiate, Ogle would have had his black moments — syphilis itself exacted a neurological toll.

From the mid-1840s onward, Gowan became an unpredictable mixture of energy and purposiveness, and of a strange ineluctable lassitude. To an external observer, he resembled a machine, one of those behemoths of which nineteenth-century industrialists were so proud, one that badly needed mending. It was as if a massive engine had half of the teeth of its gear broken, so that one moment it moved forward surely and powerfully, only to stop in place the next instant, before once again shuddering forward.

When he was in gear, Gowan conducted private political negotiations in a style as purposive and goal-directed as were his public speeches. For example, there were those dealings he conducted with the Honourable William Morris, registrar general, and, for 1846-1848, president of the upper house. Morris was a wealthy Perth merchant, and, by virtue of his position, operated as something of a co-premier. He had both patronage and power at his disposal. Nearly a score of letters survive from these years, and they show Gowan at his most direct. Ogle mixed discussion of party politics, public policy, and patronage (both for himself and for others), in a hard-edged, graceless style. Gone, now, is the smooth, classically-derived tone that characterized Ogle's letter writing in the 1820s and early 1830s. Now his transitions are rough and his phrasing frequently awkward. He still has a standard of literacy above most of his colleagues, but there is no doubt that he has regressed.

His first letter to Morris in May 1845, begins abruptly: "Mr. Joseph is named as the new Registrar for the County of Hastings. I think this appointment would be highly improper and against the true principles of Responsible or Representative Government . . . I am clearly of the opinion (and I told Mr. Draper so) that Mr. Benjamin (a leading Orangeman and later-to-be rival of Gowan's), should have this appointment." He jumps to querying why the appointment of an inspector general has so long been delayed, and then to the idea of abolishing the office of solicitor general for Lower Canada. In some sense, these all were patronage matters and thus belonged together, but then, out of nowhere, Gowan asks, "Why are not the clergy reserves in all the districts put up for sale as originally designed?" Again, without transition, he goes on to talk about frauds committed against the revenue department. Even granting that Gowan knew Morris quite well and that great literary polish was not demanded, this is a strange, strobic communication.

Ogle follows this in late July with a gnomic missive that can only have left Morris puzzled. Only a paragraph long, the note warns Morris of " 'signs of the times' — a storm is in the political atmosphere here, you cannot but see its approach . . . . Respect for Lord Metcalfe stifles opposition at present, but the time will come, unless speedily averted, when even that barrier will burst." William Morris, replies in quizzical, but diplomatic form:

> I have heard the sound of the blast you speak of, for some time, and I anxiously await the receipt of your fuller explanation. In the meantime, I shall cherish the hope that, if the present Government is laid prostrate before the coming storm, it will be succeeded by men who have ever stood by the Red and the Blue.

This gives Ogle a chance to up the ante. He long had been a supporter of the government, but has little to show for it. So, in a long letter of August 2, 1845, he suggests that unless things change, he will be forced by his conscience "either to resign my seat, or to go to Parliament and oppose the Government." He then puts forward four foolscap pages of complaints about it, ranging from its management of the Crown Lands Department (a pet subject of his, and one connected to his desire for an appointment in that department) to the need for the Montreal authorities to make local appointments only with the approval of the local MP. In the midst of this attenuated shopping list, Ogle makes a comment that can only be construed as suggesting that he would himself be an appropriate choice for a Cabinet post. He tells William Morris that, "you must certainly know that, without meaning to derogate one iota, from either yourself or Mr. Draper, Upper Canada will not be satisfied with only two Representatives in the Cabinet."

Morris does not even deign to indicate that he has seen the bait. His reply to Gowan is very formal, but to a political colleague, John Bland of Brockville, he writes: "I shall deeply regret if under any circumstances Mr. Gowan shall feel it necessary to resign his seat. He has been a powerful supporter of Lord Metcalf's Government, and I know that his services are duly appreciated and will, I doubt not, be rewarded."

How rewarded? If a Cabinet seat is too much for Ogle to expect realistically, then at least something could be found for his sons: their welfare and future prospects are a constant worry to him. Thus, in mid-October, William Morris tells Gowan that "I have long been anxious to do something for your son and I think I now see my way clear for doing so . . . . " He offers to give Ogle's eldest son, Nassau, an appointment in the customs at Kingston at an annual salary of £150.

Ogle replies, yes, he would like the post for his son, and then, in his now-abrupt style, lunges into a discussion of the need to change the township laws; to the necessity of firing two ranking public servants, one of whose "incompetency is notorious"; and again jumps to the problem of the Crown lands agency. "This *abominable department*," Ogle says, "tends to no earthly good except indeed *the lining of the pockets* of Land Agents, *expense and procrastination* to the Parties, and fomenting *great and general dissatisfaction* throughout the country." Gowan concludes by once more implying that he can be had, for a price:

> As regards myself, or rather the wish you have expressed for my continuation in the House, I can only say that I have no feelings of hostility, but every desire to assist the Government of Lord Metcalfe, and if I be assured that the necessary Reforms I have from time to time presumed to suggest, would be carried out . . . I would even yet yield my own inclinations, and sacrifice my own private interest to give to it whatever little support it might be in my power to afford.

Morris responds by finding a government job for Gowan's second son, Harcourt Potter Gowan, and early in January 1846, writes to Ogle suggesting a post — "an indoor situation" — in the Customs in Toronto. So, Ogle stays in the House of Assembly, and another son enters gainful government employment.

The correspondence continues, always with Ogle dealing with political issues — Repeal of the Corn Laws, the representation of the colonies in the Westminster Parliament — and always in the background is the unspoken question: what is Ogle seeking for himself? Posts for his sons are useful, yes, but they are mere appetizers. Would Gowan settle for a Cabinet seat and nothing less? for the headship of a civil service department? or less?

He is fussy. In the middle of June 1846, Gowan visited Toronto on private business and he travelled there in the company of William Cayley, an on-the-make Tory, soon to become inspector general. Cayley mentioned that Draper had spoken about offering Gowan the post of an arbitrator under the Board of Works. Doubtless this was a try-on: Draper did not wish to offer something unless he were sure that he would accept. The triviality of the post mentioned offended Gowan's sense of dignity. "I cannot express to you," he tells William Morris, "the supreme contempt I felt at such an offer, and though a poor man, and with a large family, I trust I am not so poor in spirit as to receive such a sop . . . . " Morris on behalf of the Government, quickly backpeddled. Cayley had been out of line in mentioning the post; it was solely Cayley's own idea, and, no, Mr. Draper never had entertained such an insulting suggestion.

The year 1846 ends with Gowan in Parliament, still supporting the Government, and still owed something for that support.

The pushing, cajoling, threatening of Morris, the continual assertion of his right to attention, and ultimately to reward, were characteristic of the old Ogle Gowan, the ruthless breaker of heads in backwoods elections. But now, simultaneously, there was a noticeable absence of spirit. This was not merely a matter of age. Notoriously, the search for power and patronage energizes politicians until a very late age. For a politician, Ogle still was young. His episodes of lassitude of the will were sporadic and showed themselves only on certain matters, but two of these are very surprising: relations with his long-trusted cousin James, and Ogle's own position in the Orange Order.

Cousin James always had been a useful agent for Ogle, but there was more to their relationship than that. As James grew older, Ogle increasingly treated him as a potential *protégé* and, alternatively, as a junior partner. After the invasion of 1838, James moved away from rigid Toryism towards an advocacy of Responsible Government and finally became what was known as a Baldwin Reformer. This did not alienate him from Ogle, who himself favoured Responsible Government, and Ogle continued to entrust James with major pieces of Orange business and he found James a seat on the council of the Grand Lodge of British North America.

But, gradually, James shoved Ogle to the edge of his life, and, finally, all the way out. In August, 1839, James passed his final bar examinations and, at that point, took over almost all of the work of his law partnership. His senior partner, the Honourable James Small, was counsel for the University of King's College and for the solicitor general. His legal duties brought James into frequent contact with the Honourable Robert Baldwin and, in December 1842, Baldwin, then Premier of Canada, offered James the judgeship of a new judicial district being formed in the Simcoe region. James accepted and began his duties in January 1843. He was only twenty-eight years old, and of barely three-and-a-half year's standing at the Bar. It is said that at the time of his appointment, he was the youngest man ever entrusted with a Royal Commission as a judge, either in the United Kingdom or in the colonies.

As James became more and more successful, association with Ogle — his rough edges, his illegitimacy, his frequent and embarrassing litigation, and, ultimately, his gamey sex life — became undesirable. James Gowan, like so many of the Canadian *bourgeoisie*, was becoming "Victorian" in the sense of valuing public decorum and of avoiding the organic, the disruptive, and the undisciplined. So, with his increasing success, James put more and more distance between himself and Ogle.

Ogle understood what was happening and yet he could do nothing at all to keep the ever-fewer threads that tied him to his cousin from fraying and snapping, one by one, until there were none left. In the worst of his depressions, in those twilight hours spent staring out the window of his boarding house, surveying the darkening city, Ogle agreed with James: he was not, indeed, quite respectable.

Ogle's withdrawal from leadership of the Orange Order was even more surprising, for the Order was one of the points of leverage on which he had based his entire career. Granted, at one time, his association with the Order had been a block to promotion, but as the Order's membership ceased to consist chiefly of immigrants and, instead, came to be a representative cross-section of the entire Protestant male population, it no longer was politically harmful to be one of its leaders. Now, influential men, businessmen, politicians, bankers, and lawyers, joined as a way of establishing their *bona fides* as good Protestants. Paradoxically, then, it was just at the moment that his leadership of the Order ceased to harm him politically, that Gowan decided to let his hands slip from the Orange reins.

In an action that smacks of nothing so much as symbolic

suicide, Ogle proposed at the 1844 Grand Lodge meeting, held in Hamilton, that the Order be dissolved, and he tendered his own resignation. This was not a power-play, but a tortured attempt to abnegate his own main achievement in life. The Grand Lodge, by a standing vote, rejected both ideas and reluctantly he continued as Grand Master.

During the next year, Ogle let Orange business slide. He rarely attended Grand Lodge meetings and few new warrants to establish new Lodges were issued. Observers said that he appeared discouraged and anxious to give up office. When the annual Grand Lodge convocation took place that year, he tried again to resign. While the election of a grand master was being carried out, he left the hall and wandered off aimlessly, head down, not knowing where he was going or, it seemed, where he had been. The election and its associated debate took two hours and finally a deputation was sent to ask him to continue in office. The deputation had trouble finding him, and when they did, he seemed dazed and unresponsive. With a shrug and a vacant stare he agreed to take office again. This tortured interview took so long that all the other Grand Lodge officers had been elected by the time he dragged himself back into the hall.

Both Nassau and Harcourt Gowan now were junior Orangemen and quite devoted to the grand old cause, and Ogle's admirers asked them to intervene with their father. When he was at home in Brockville they would try to get him to pay more attention to Orange business. For a time he would heed their pleas and work energetically, but then he would withdraw again. Frances Gowan did what she always had done when faced with a weakness, failing, or vice, on her husband's part — she ignored it. She put a good face on things and managed the household as usual, but she worried a lot. Her mother had died within the past year, and Frances missed her.

In 1846, Ogle resigned as Grand Master and made it stick. He was replaced by George Benjamin of Belleville, a great bear of a man, tall, corpulent, of Loyalist family. Gowan did not approve of his successor, but, after some brief sputterings, withdrew into gloomy silence. He attended only one Grand Lodge meeting (that of 1849) between his resignation and the year 1852. Considering that Orangeism had for so long been a vivifying force in his life,

Ogle's actions can only be taken as a desperate rejection of much that was himself.

While Gowan was undergoing these personal crises, his friend from Kingston, John A. Macdonald, was experiencing personal pain of his own. He too hated the city of Montreal, the people with their unfathomable language and the long hours in lonely lodgings. Macdonald's however, was greatly increased by domestic anxiety. Isabella, his wife, became mysteriously ill in July 1845, and had to be taken to Savannah, Georgia, for a cure. There she stayed for many months. Later, when back home, Isabella continued to have a disconcerting array of symptoms that kept her bedridden most of the rest of her married life. She died, eventually, in 1857. Her symptoms included the signs of tuberculosis, violent headaches, extreme fatigue, numbness in one or more limbs, uterine complaints, and mental confusion.

Macdonald's chief biographer has shrewdly noted that the twelve years of his marriage twisted Macdonald's whole life. "He had become a family man whose home was a hotel or a lodging-house; a bachelor husband who had to go for companionship to bars and lounges and smoking-rooms; a frustrated host who drank too much on occasion, partly because it was the only way he could entertain, and partly because it passed the empty time, and because it was an easy way to forget."

There was more to it than that, even. John A. Macdonald's marriage put him on an emotional roller-coaster that would have upset anyone. When he met her, Isabella was living in an isolated farm house, three miles outside of Douglas on the Isle of Man, with a widowed elder sister and an unmarried younger one. She was thirty-four at the time she married her cousin, John, and he twenty-eight. She was a spinster, called upon to leave her native isolation and to settle in a strange new land, and there to perform what was euphemistically known as her wifely duties.

Isabella had two pregnancies and was normally fertile. Whatever their aetiology, her mysterious diseases allowed her to limit John's access to her body. The dramatically wasting character of some of her symptoms provided her with a great measure of emotional influence over her husband, and the episodic nature of the attacks precluded his ever taking her health or their domestic situation for granted. An hysterical personality, combined with dependence on opiates left her with a perpetually saintly smile on her face. Her seemingly supererogatory optimism and enduring patience were a marvel to her husband, and she wore those characteristics as a veneer, even as her body atrophied from her self-imposed exile in bed or a divan.

In order to be successful in Canadian political life in the Victorian era, one's vices had to be manly. Macdonald responded to his loneliness, sexual frustration, and emotional vulnerability by taking up "manly" sins. He drank a lot. He occasionally visited whores. And in the 1850s he kept a mistress at the Grimason House in Kingston, the same tavern where he and Ogle had caroused in earlier days. None of these were considered admirable actions, but among men-of-the-world they were understood and winked at. Macdonald's heavy drinking was widely known, but his sexual life was carried out discreetly, and the few who knew of it accepted that he still was a young man and needed outlets for his frustrated energies.

In contrast, as they developed in the 1840s and were embroidered in the next decade, Ogle's vices — that is, his ways of dealing with his fears and dolorous experiences — were not manly, as understood by his contemporaries. His increasing withdrawal (whether from the Orange leadership, or into the brooding silence of a darkening room) was not the sort of proud, head-up masculinity that his contemporaries expected. And there was always the ticking time-bomb: Ogle's habit of relieving boredom and sexual tension by seeking surcease in the bodies of ever-younger girls. From the mid-1840s onwards, fourteen-year-olds were his common sexual fare, and he was vulnerable both to arrest and blackmail.

So, if one considers a public man's immoralities to be one of the limiting constraints on his career, John A. Macdonald's vices were much less apt to ruin his future than were Ogle Gowan's.

The careers of Macdonald and Gowan intertwined in the '40s and then they diverged permanently. Implicitly, the two men were working together to form a fresher, broader Tory party, one unlimited by the shackles of the old Compact-Toryism. On some matters, such as those directly affecting the Kingston and Brockville regions, they worked well in concert.

There was, however, a basic difference in their styles. Gowan usually bargained as an Independent, that is, from a position of potential opposition to the Government (as he had done in his dealings with William Morris). Macdonald, on the other hand, furthered his own career by becoming subserviently loyal to the Government. He made himself an acolyte of William Henry Draper and it worked, for in 1846, Draper decided to appoint Macdonald to the commissionership of Crown Lands. Macdonald refused, because he needed to return to Kingston and earn money at his legal practice, but another plum in the future now was inevitable.

Gowan meanwhile kept pressing from his semi-independent position for a lucrative governmental post and in March 1847, was verbally offered the post of assistant commissioner of Crown Lands. Before this appointment could be made, however, the increasingly shaky character of the Ministry gave Ogle a shot at a bigger prize — membership in the Cabinet, which would follow upon Draper's trying to broaden his political base. In this situation, John A. Macdonald worked hard at getting his friend, Gowan, a ministerial post.

Macdonald, who had been visiting important local personages at Gananoque, Leeds County, wrote a private letter to Gowan on March 22, 1847, suggesting that he start an active canvas in Leeds county, "as if for the general election." The "as if" was because, in reality, Gowan would have to seek re-election upon taking a Cabinet post. "But," advised John A., "tell only your confidential friends of your taking office *just now*. Get *your own* returning officer, a *true man* selected, and *all your deputies*." Macdonald added, "I am ready to do whatever you want me to do in *any way*. Command me and I will do your bidding."

John A. Macdonald was sincere in pushing Ogle for a Cabinet seat, but he was outgunned by the Compact Tories, especially by the Speaker, Sir Allan MacNab. William Morris, though not hostile to Gowan, did not support the idea of a ministerial post for him. Ogle did not help his own case by his bad taste in publishing in his *Statesman* in early April that he had turned down an official office (the assistant commissionership of Crown lands), worth £500, and with it the promise of an easy retirement into private life. More harmful was the recirculation by his Compact opponents of material from the *Interesting Trial*. John A. Macdonald told Ogle that "the trumping up of this old story against you, which has been raked from among the dust and ashes of by-gone times by the Family Compact is merely an excuse to put you off." But, in fact, the material from the pamphlet went to the heart of the charges against Gowan: HE WAS NOT RESPECTABLE. The old Irish scandals were circulated not as definitive proof, but merely as illustrative of that fact.

When he realized that his friend had been both shabbily treated and his appointment blocked, Macdonald was outraged. he wrote to Ogle from Kingston that,

> . . . situated as I am on account of Mrs. Macdonald's health, I had almost made up my mind not to go down [to Montreal] during the beginning of the session, but under the circumstances, I shall certainly do so and as perhaps the last act of my short political career, protest against the Family Compact party who with little ability — no political principle, and no strength from numbers, contrive by their union and active bigotry to override the conservatives and to make us, and our whole party stink in the nostrils of all liberal-minded people.

The last act of my short political career. Certainly, defending Gowan was not that for young John A. Macdonald. In fact, he quickly overcame his repugnance for working with the Compact Tories when offered the receiver-generalship early in May. This offer came because the Ministry's chances of survival depended upon bringing in a representative of the popular Toryism of Canada West, and if Gowan was unacceptable to the Compact-Tories, then Macdonald was the only major alternative. To his credit, Macdonald laid down as one of his conditions of accepting office, that some political reward be found for Ogle Gowan. He was worried about losing Ogle's friendship, and very soon after joining the ministry, he wrote to him explaining why he had accepted the offer. More important, he copied out the text of a letter that he had written to William Morris, championing Ogle's interests. Macdonald told Morris: "Gowan thinks himself aggrieved, and I think with justice . . . . Whatever his enemies may say against him, he has long been gladly received and welcomed by all sections of our party as an Ally, and during the present parliament been courted by every ministerialist. We cannot expect to obtain his services and refuse the reward and, highly as I appreciate his powers of benefitting us, I confess I fear his opposition more."

Morris replied. "*We* will take care of *Gowan*."

In effect, Macdonald was asking Ogle to forgive him for accepting office. "Thus, you see, my dear Gowan, I am fairly in the scrape and have entered into a mess of troubles in which I fear the selfishness of the Family Compact more than the opposition of Baldwin or the French. But I thought that if I did not come forward, the Family would force themselves into power and Morris out of the council and thus ruin the party."

That was the turning point of both of their lives. Macdonald assumed a Cabinet position and moved through a series of ministries in a governmental career that was monumentally successful. Ogle Gowan never again came as close to a seat in the Cabinet as he had in the spring of 1847.

Gowan still had to be paid for his services, however, and as a downpayment, his bastard brother William was given a job in the customs in early November 1847. At the same time, John A. Macdonald told Ogle that "I have just drafted a letter to be sent you by the assistant secretary offering you the Superintendency of the St. Lawrence Canals and Navigation. You will observe the office is offered, '*when created*.' These words have been put in to prevent your letter of acceptance being operative in any way . . . as you would vacate your seat prematurely. Your appointment is at your own disposal."

It was a good post, worth £500 a year, but whether Ogle actually intended to take it and to slide quietly into private life is unclear. In any event, he decided to run for office in the general election that took place in late December and early January, and he lost to the Reformer, William Buell Richards, a nephew of his old enemy, William Buell. Then he accepted the canal appointment.

In Kingston, in contrast, John A. Macdonald won handsomely. Thus, the two men who had travelled down to Montreal for the parliamentary session as a well-matched team, left it very differently.

CHAPTER 15

The Black Flag, 1848-1852

IN AN age that was ever-mindful of geneaology and of family ties, Ogle Gowan's own sensitivity to such matters remained as extreme as ever. When James Bruce, eighth earl of Elgin and twelfth earl of Kincardine, arrived in Montreal in 1847, the first thing that Ogle commented on was that Elgin had married the daughter of Lord Durham, whose insults to the Orange Order were still widely remembered. Never mind that Elgin was a man of considerable personal charm, nor that as a colonial administrator he had wide experience and a reputation for being able to make decisions: he had been a forceful governor of Jamaica. (And, in later life, as envoy extraordinary to China, ordered the burning of the Emperor's summer palace at Peking, a barbaric, but not ineffectual form of diplomacy.)

Elgin came to Canada pledged to carry out the policy of the Colonial Secretary, Lord Grey (who, not so incidentally, was the uncle of Elgin's wife), and this meant completing the establishment of Responsible Government. In practical terms, Elgin was committed to staying out of purely domestic matters which, under the Responsibility doctrine, were held to be under Canadian parliamentary control. Thus, when, in early 1848, the Reform party won a decisive victory at the polls, he at once accepted the parliamentary mandate and invited La Fontaine to form a ministry.

This election, which took place in the winter, December-January, 1847-1848, doubly hurt Ogle Gowan. Not only did he lose his seat for Leeds county, but in the new government were several of his longtime Reform enemies, notably Robert Baldwin and

Francis Hincks. Given his principle of not meddling in local affairs, Lord Elgin let matters of domestic patronage fall entirely to the government of the day. Gowan, as superintendent of tolls on the St. Lawrence River was vulnerable, for, unlike Lord Metcalfe, Elgin would not protect patronage bargains made by previous governments. It was only a matter of time, therefore, before Ogle's Reforming enemies settled into office and got around to having him discharged.

The axe fell in mid-June 1848. Instead of dismissing him from his post, the Government took the easier road of simply abolishing the position altogether. Upon receiving this news, Ogle tried to lure the government's confidential secretary into an indescretion. He asked for an explanation of why this decision had been made. Of course Ogle knew why, and this was merely an attempt to get a governmental representative to say something against him that might be actionable. Shrewdly, the civil servant replied that there had been no complaint from any quarter relating to Gowan's character, conduct, or discharge of office. The change was being made for reasons of efficiency and to save the public purse.

In a sense, sacking Gowan was breaking the rules, for the practice that had governed eighteenth-century English politics had been generally (if not universally) accepted in Canadian political life until that time. Patronage plums, given by one administration, were not retrieved by the next, and the Governor General in Canada (like the monarch in eighteenth-century England) was responsible for seeing that these rules were maintained. Twelve years later, in 1860, John A. Macdonald still waxed indignant when he reflected on this matter. "Gowan and I served in Parliament, elected in 1844, together, and acted cordially together. He was appointed to office by the Government of which I was a member and if I remember rightly I drew the minutes of Council myself on which he was appointed. He was most improperly dismissed by Hincks and was so dismissed on account of his Conservative Principles." About a month later, Macdonald told another correspondent that "Gowan . . . was most unjustly and oppressively deprived of his Canal superintendency."

Ogle himself felt enormously aggrieved, believing that Lord Elgin, acting as viceroy, should have protected the integrity of governmental appointments. Elgin became a name Ogle could not say without seething.

In the later years of the decade, Ogle continued to experience periodically the blackness and depression that had affected him so heavily in the mid-1840s, but now something more was added. He became increasingly bitter. Always a man to nurse a grievance, in the past he usually had been able to turn his anger into purposive (if, often, crude) action. Now, a free-floating, imputrescible bitterness afflicted him, a sense that his universe was controlled by the Elgins and the Reformers of this world which, to him, meant by cowards and by traitors. As in the mid-1840s, Ogle still was able at times to escape dramatically from his depression and to act with purpose, but now many of his active moments were tinctured with the peach-pit bitterness that also filled those long darkling hours when he brooded.

Losing the canal superintendancy hurt Gowan financially, for the £500 a year was enough to keep him ahead of his many creditors. On the basis of the expected income, he had run up bills both for his family and for his newspaper. In 1849, Ogle was unable to find either the financial backing or the personal energy to keep the *Statesman* running, so he temporarily discontinued it.

Bad times for Ogle, certainly, but also bad times for the country. The nation was in a severe commercial depression, and, at the same time, Canada West had to assimilate a large body of Irish immigrants who had fled the Great Famine. Gowan's *Statesman*, like most papers in Canada West, traced the course of the Irish tragedy, from reports of the crop failure first published in October 1846, to horrific accounts of the universal blight of 1847 and accompanying epidemics. Then, finally, came reports of the arrival of masses of Irish immigrants in Canada in 1847, '48, and '49, and of the diseases that the newcomers brought with them to the New World. During those years, over 150,000 emigrants from Ireland arrived in British North America (and approximately three times that number shipped directly to U.S. ports). Most of them were physically drained and financially impoverished. Although inwardly the immigrants were frequently individuals of great personal courage and considerable economic acumen, their outward appearance was of shoddy clothing and vacant-eyed ill-health. They elicited both pity and disgust.

Ogle printed the news concerning these people responsibly, but he stayed cool about it personally. Almost all of his Famine material was borrowed (as was the common journalistic practice of the day) from other newspapers. His main individual involvement with the story was the printing of cheap ballad sheets that took advantage of the immigrant market.

How could Gowan stay so cool? In part, because the mixture of depression and bitterness that enveloped him periodically also numbed him emotionally. But there was more to his coolness than that. He recognized that there was a backlash against the Irish immigrants and he did not want to be associated too closely with them. He and his Irish followers came from an earlier wave of migration, one whose members had now worked themselves into the middle levels of society. In part, the general reaction against the Irish took the form of avoiding them, because they were a health hazard. In the fall of 1847, Brockville and Kingston were emptied of people who were frightened of typhus, and those town residents who could do so sent their families to the countryside. Rumours circulated, some of them manifestly absurd, such as the canard that many of the immigrants came to Canada with considerable sums of money concealed on their persons, and that they only pretended poverty, so as to be shipped onwards from Montreal at governmental expense. Such a rumour, of course, would provide justification for mingy behaviour on the part of someone who was not inclined to be charitable to the incoming poor.

There was a certain shrewdness behind Gowan's coolness, for Ogle believed that most of the Irish who arrived in Quebec City or Montreal eventually would settle, not in Canada, but in the hated Republic to the south. As long-term patterns of settlement became clear, he was proved to be right. Most, but far from all, Famine emigrants from Ireland to Canada drifted through Canada on their way to the United States. That most of this pass-through population consisted of Roman Catholics did nothing to recommend the migrants to Ogle's charity. Still, there were many Irish Protestants amongst the Famine migrants who settled in Canada West, and to the extent that they commanded Ogle's attention, he referred them to a local lodge of the Orange Order.

A series of national political events snapped Gowan out of his lethargy in the winter and spring of 1849, and for weeks at a time he operated vigorously before falling into despondency. It long had been held desirable to compensate people who had suffered in the rebellions and invasions of 1837-1838: that principle was one with which Ogle agreed. The problem was that no one could suggest to everyone's satisfaction who was eligible for compensation. A commission had been set up in 1845 to decide the matter, but nothing came of it. Essentially, there were three categories of persons to be dealt with: those who had loyally supported the Crown by serving in the militia or in a paramilitary force; those who had taken up arms against the government; and those who had been effectively neutral. The first group obviously would be compensated, the second not. But what about the third? In a bill heatedly debated in the Canadian parliament in February 1849, the Baldwin-La Fontaine ministry proposed that these neutrals should be compensated for damages to their property, caused either by rebels or by government troops.

"Blackguards!" roared Ogle upon hearing this, using the archaic vocabulary he sometimes employed when affronted on political matters. "This means that anyone who wasn't actually convicted of rebellion can claim government money! La Fontaine is a scoundrel! He would pay money to rascals like that quack Dr. Nelson!" Ogle was referring to one Dr. Wolfred Nelson, member of the Legislative Assembly for Richelieu. He had tried to lead a group of Rebels in 1837, but had not actually been convicted of an act of rebellion and, in 1845, put forward a claim for £12,000 damages against the government.

The Rebellion Losses Bill hit Ogle and men of his background at one of their most sensitive points. Their actions (and, in many cases, their heroism), in 1837 and 1838 were what had made them fully naturalized as Canadians — their extreme loyalty to the British Crown had fused at that moment with their allegiance to their new homeland. Anything that derogated their actions in 1837-1838 struck at the lynchpin of their loyalty to the Canadian constitution. "Scum! the whole lot, Baldwin, Frenchie Fontaine, traitors to the Crown and to the memory of our loyal dead!"

Gowan's enraged cries were echoed throughout English Canada. The Rebellion Losses Bill passed both Houses of Parliament after a particularly nasty debate — in the lower house, Sir Allan MacNab and Edward Blake had tried to punch each other out in the centre of the chamber. Two questions arose immediately after the bill's passage: would Lord Elgin sign it and if he did sign it, what would the enraged loyalists do?

For Frances Gowan, the month of March 1849 began with one of the strangest experiences of her life: on horseback, she led a procession. She did so in a costume that would have looked smart even upon the wife of the Governor General: a striking female riding habit, with a very long-trained skirt, trousers just showing beneath, and military-style braiding on her bodice. Of course she rode side-saddle and she wore a top hat and veil.

Attending her on foot, a militia sergeant bore a home-made flag, and did so with the same seriousness and dignity that he would have used if he had been carrying the royal standard before the Governor General. This flag was black and it had been woven by Mrs. Gowan (and, therefore, somewhat infelicitously, it passed into folklore as "Mrs. Gowan's Petticoat"). The black flag bore the inscription, "Down with Elgin and his Rebel-Paying Ministry."

Immediately behind Frances, like the Prince Consort behind Victoria, rode Ogle Gowan. He did not look as preposessing as his wife. He slouched in the saddle on a big strawberry roan. His hair needed trimming and the pinched waist of a military-style frock-coat that had fitted him years ago, now bunched uncomfortably. He waved to spectators and most of them waved back. Many, though, avoided looking him in the eye.

A makeshift flute and drum band marched along behind, playing a mixture of patriotic airs and Orange tunes. Next came a group of militiamen, in mufti, but marching in reasonably close drill. After that, anyone who wished to do so was free to join the procession, and by the time the train had woven its way twice around the central streets of Brockville, nearly 300 persons were in the parade and several hundred more were on the streets, watching. Finally, the flag-bearer turned the procession towards Brockville harbour, where a large crowd was assembled. They were waiting for the arrival of James Bruce, eighth earl of Elgin and twelfth of Kincardine.

It was one-thirty in the afternoon, and Elgin's ship, a shallow-draught steam vessel, already was in view. As it approached the wharf there was a dissonant mixture of cries:

"Hurrah for his Lordship!"
"Traitors go away!"
"God bless the Governor General!"
"Paymaster of Rebels!"

The split was chiefly on Party lines, local Reformers being keen on the Governor-General's presence, and Conservatives opposed. Local officials, led by the Honourable James Morris, were anxious to minimize embarrassment, so a carriage was brought right up to the gangway and his lordship was taken away quickly to Brockville courthouse where he held a *levée*. Gowan had a petition to present to Lord Elgin, but he waited until four-thirty in the afternoon to do so, just moments before Elgin was scheduled to return to the harbour and depart. He intended to embarrass the Governor General, but Elgin wrote a reply as his carriage jolted down to the harbour, thus avoiding any hint of offense.

As Elgin's vessel left the harbour, the same mixture of cries of approval and of denouncement that had greeted him, echoed across the water. He had stopped momentarily at the top of the gangplank, bowed slightly to the civic officials who stood below, beside the official carriage, and then was gone quickly to his cabin.

As soon as the vessel was out of sight, Ogle re-formed the procession and they once again did a circuit of Brockville before stopping at courthouse square for a series of short speeches, the showpiece of which, of course, was Gowan's. "We presume that it will be freely conceded by all men," he began, "that the removal of LORD ELGIN is an *indispensable preliminary* to the return of tranquility to this nation."

"Amen, Ogle!"

"Without peace there can be no prosperity and that peace cannot be procured so long as the HATED FOOT . . . "

"You mean the traitor Elgin!"

" . . . HATED FOOT presses the free soil, or his LYING LUNGS . . . "

"Damn the rebel-loving bastard!"

" . . . LYING LUNGS breath the pure air of Canada!!" Ogle continued along these lines for fifteen minutes and then concluded. "We demand JUSTICE for our loyal citizens. And JUSTICE will only come when the TRAITOROUS NECK is stretched and the INFAMOUS ENTITY forever consumed, as by fire."

This was the signal for the militia sergeant who earlier had served as flag-bearer, to bring forward an effigy of the Governor General — a dummy made from a man's suit, stuffed with straw, with a burlap head attached, so that the figure resembled a large rag-doll. A rope was tied around "Lord Elgin's" neck in a hangman's knot.

The crowd cheered.

Another militiaman had gone to a nearby inn and taken some cooking coals from the hearth. He placed one at the bottom of each leg of the figure and soon it was ablaze.

The crowd cheered louder and Ogle broke into a laugh that might have been considered maniacal. After the fire died down, the crowd dispersed, except for some children who joined hands and danced around the flickering ashes, as if it were a Guy Fawkes bonfire.

Soon thereafter, like an unexpected meteor shower on a summer's evening, a strange, predictive event occurred — a large part of central Toronto burned. About one-thirty, on the morning of Saturday, April 7, a fire started near what is now Jarvis and Duke streets. It began in some frame outbuildings attached to a tavern and spread rapidly, consuming an entire city block and jumping across streets until, finally, a dozen to fifteen acres in the heart of the main business district were in ruins. The city market was destroyed, as was St. James's cathedral. Fortunately, only one life was lost, that of Richard Watson, former publisher of the *Upper Canada Gazette*. He perished while helping some printers remove materials from the office of the *Patriot* — a newspaper which, in 1852, Ogle Gowan purchased.

That transaction was in the future, but much more imminent was another conflagration, one that probably never would have taken place, had not the great Toronto fire fixed in the mind of English-speaking Canadians the avenging and purifying power of uncontrolled flames. On April 25, Lord Elgin, acting in fealty to his principle of allowing Canadians to exercise Responsible Government in domestic matters, gave the Royal Assent to the Rebellion Losses Bill. Even before Elgin could leave the parliament building in Montreal, a small crowd had assembled and he was hooted as he left. His carriage was pelted by stones and garbage as he drew away. Elgin noticed that the crowd, despite its unruly behaviour, seemed to be drawn from persons of the "respectable class." That should have scared him, for it meant that he was not dealing with recreational violence of the sort practised by hooligans, but with the concentrated outrage of most of the English-speaking community in Montreal. The crowd in front of the parliament building grew, and incited by several angry speeches, broke into the building, where members still were sitting. Windows were shattered, tables and chairs smashed, and the gas pipes that provided for light were gashed open. Thus, when a fire was started, it roared through Parliament as if a bomb had been set. Soon nothing was left of the remodelled Montreal markets, save a shell that, despite all the cosmetic efforts of the architects, still looked more mercantile than Ionic. Only a portrait of Queen Victoria was saved. Several days of rioting followed the fire. The mob is usually described as being Orange and Tory, but in its abhorrence of the administration and of Elgin's pusillanimity, it reflected the beliefs of most English-speaking conservatives of all sorts.

When he read of the Montreal fire and of the indignities to Lord Elgin, Gowan laughed for the first time in months, a reedy, staccato bray that had its origin in his spleen.

Vicariously cathartic as it was to many conservatives to read of the humiliation of Lord Elgin, the entire skein of events was very unsettling. Many conservatives, among them John A. Macdonald and Ogle Gowan, began to worry about the viability of the Canadian constitution. As Gowan expressed it: "Ever since 1846, when Free Trade replaced the old system, the Mother Country has done us no good in trade or in a mercantile way. And, now under the Elginite policy of not interfering with the Reformers and radicals, the Home government does Canada no good in our public affairs. We are loyal — but to what end? Something *must* change."

But what? Soon after the notorious Black Flag march Ogle began a more traditional, but, ultimately, no more controlled, mode of political self-expression: he formed yet another local society. "The Anglo-Saxons of this community must unite to prevent ourselves being governed by Frenchmen — and by their allies, the traitorous Reformers and the cowardly Elgin." Thus, the first branch of what became known as the British American League was formed in Brockville. Although virulently anti-French in its origins, the association adopted a respectable veneer in that it focused on constitutional issues — always an acceptable matter of political debate in Canada — and especially on ways of legally protecting English-Canadian interests. In Brockville, this society attracted a broad range of conservative support, from old Compact die-hards to prospersous new Conservatives, such as George Crawford, and William Stone Macdonald of Gananoque. Like a grass fire, a league of similar societies spread across Canada West. Gowan did spend a fair amount of time going from town to town in missionary work, but he was preaching to the already-converted. The British American League spoke to the anxieties of a significant section of the population, and its growth was virtually spontaneous.

Although most of the League's members were in Canada West, the most energetic branch was in Montreal. This is not surprising, given the level of anger against recent constitutional practices, as shown in the Montreal riots. There, an influential and moderate Conservative, the Honourable George Moffatt, took charge and under his leadership a national convention of the British American League was called for Kingston in late July. The roughly 150 delegates assembled in the city hall, an embarrassingly grand structure now that the capital was elsewhere. They were as ill-assorted and as mixed in motivation as members of any group could be. Some were there out of hatred for the French; some out of distaste for the Governor General; others came to push for a union of all the Canadian colonies; and still others to push for the annexation of Canada by the United States; some came to press for the promulgation of commercial protection laws and for high tarriffs; others for free trade with the United States. The delegates were men of middle stature in their own communities, successful businessmen, large farmers, lawyers, frequently active Tories, the sort of persons who were looked upon as substantial citizens, but not as great community leaders. John A. Macdonald was the only person attending who had cabinet experience.

"There are only two ways of proceeding," Gowan told a meeting of the league's branch for Elizabethtown township (Brockville) that selected him as their delegate. "Either we press hard for a true improvement of the constitutional situation — by protective tariffs and a reform of the legislature — or we must face the danger of

Annexation." Ogle was referring to the opinion of some leaguers, especially those from Montreal, that annexation by the United States was the only real solution to the present constitutional crisis. "I say, however, that no power will ever be so abused, to the extent of provoking reflective men to contemplate an alliance with a foreign power." Ogle was animated. "I predict that the time will never come when no British hands remain to hoist the flag of England on the rock of Quebec, and no British voices survive able to shout, 'God Save the Queen.' "

"Right, Gowan! Take that message to Kingston!"

So, on Thursday, July 26, Ogle and John A. Macdonald walked together to Kingston city hall. Ogle came primed to fight the annexationists, as well as to press for constitutional reforms; Macdonald came without a personal agenda, save the goal of protecting his own brand of moderate conservativism against any *rivanche* by the Compact-Tories. As it turned out, Macdonald was quiet for most of the three-day session, and this was because of political savvy. He recognized at once the disparate backgrounds and motivations of the delegates and he knew that the Honourable George Moffat was inept at running meetings. Macdonald smiled wryly when he saw that it was necessary to post two heavies at the door of the debating chamber in order to exclude the press — this league was in danger of running out of control.

At the very onset, a strange quarrel broke out between the Compact-Tory faction and the moderate conservatives. A resolution was introduced in favour of making the legislative council of the Canadas elective. This appealed strongly to the men from Montreal who, with the Rebellion Losses Act in mind, were keen to remove all undemocratic control over the council. The upper house, they said, should be protected from interference by the ministry and free to act in accord with public opinion. Most of the delegates, however, were swayed by an amendment, written by Ogle, but not moved by him, that plumped for the "true principles of the British Constitution," meaning a rejection of an elected upper house: that, after all, was too much like the Senate of the United States. The debate on this item was long and remarkably ill-tempered.

The second day, Gowan was the star turn. Ogle arrived with a fresh haircut and with his beard neatly trimmed. In his pocket was a set of resolutions on economic matters and these came to have a resonance later in Canadian history. "Resolved. That in the opinion of this convention, all the inhabitants of Canada have an equal right to protection of good government, not merely in the suppression and punishment of crime, but also in the guidance and direction of public affairs . . . and this should conduce to public quiet which is the sure and only foundation on which public prosperity can rest . . . . " That was a rare prescription for the mid-nineteenth century, a call for positive state involvement in economic affairs, in an era when the dominant dogma in the British Empire was becoming that of laissez-faire. Ogle argued that most of Canada's economic woes came from the United Kingdom's having abandoned preferential tariffs for the colonies in 1846, in favour of unfettered free trade. "That dogma, that mistake, introduced by as great a man as Sir Robert Peel. Oh! a mistake, no, not a mistake! A Calamity! A Disaster!!" Several subsequent speakers lustily condemned the British government before Gowan's motion was unanimously passed.

But what was the state to do if it was to act positively, rather than merely be a passive force? Ogle, speaking in a self-consciously homey fashion, explained that the most trustworthy markets for farmers was the farmer's own local town market, and that as long as the farmer was free from unfair overseas competition, then he would fare very well, thank you. And the town markets would be there, if Canada came to do all of her own manufacturing, rather than importing finished products. So Ogle proposed a protective tariff be erected to protect home industries and farm markets. This resolution was adopted with enthusiasm, in part because a gesture of retaliation against the British for having dropped Imperial Preference appealed to the delegates' sense of vengeance. However, some observers have seen in this proposal the kernel of the National Policy later adumbrated by John A. Macdonald.

That was a good morning's work, and if Ogle had sat down at that point, everything would have been fine. But in the afternoon he overreached himself: "Resolved that the present expenditure of the civil government is disproportionate to the resources of the Province and that great economic retrenchment may be safely introduced without impairing the efficiency of the public service." A whisper ran through the audience the moment Ogle read this resolution. Had it been moved by anyone else, it might have been taken at face value, but most delegates knew that Gowan had been only too willing to take half-a-years's salary as superintendent of tolls on the St. Lawrence Canals, and that he would still be accepting the stipend, had he not run afoul of the Baldwin-La Fontaine government.

Some delegates actually laughed, and Gowan, taking them to be partisans of the Compact-Tory faction, turned on them. He remembered only too well his being barred from Cabinet office by MacNab and his high-hatted cronies. "Of course, the honourable delegates may laugh; I could remind them that the Compact jackals, living off the body of the Upper Canadian people, those sluggards, fools, and parasites, put into office by their own incompetence in administration, the present Reformist and radical ministry. Laugh! They should be in sack cloth and abject tears!"

Feet stomped in approval, cries of "Shame! Shame!" arose. Several delegates from the Compact wing of the Tory party immediately were on their feet. It took the Honourable George Moffatt five minutes to sort out the order of speakers and then, one after another, the Compact supporters upbraided Gowan and, implicitly, attacked the new-style moderate conservatives. John A. Macdonald, realizing that this could hurt his own position, intervened and made a conciliatory speech that calmed everyone down. Gowan's resolution then passed.

No one at the convention was a partisan of Lord Elgin, but Ogle let his personal bitterness take him too far when he tried to have the convention call for Elgin's impeachment. Eventually, he accepted a less-abrasive demand for the Governor General's recall. Still, the resolution was something both Elgin and the government of the day remembered and eventually they took their revenge.

On the convention's third day, a major constitutional issue was discussed: the union of the British colonies in North America. This idea was presented by a Toronto delegate as the best alternative not only to French domination, but to annexation. A far-seeing idea, but the Honourable John A. Macdonald, suggested that the scheme was premature and impractical! Ogle Gowan argued that the federal union of the existing provinces actually would aid French domination of the English-speaking people in the province of Quebec. To him, the only useful form of federation would occur if the country were divided into a number of small provinces and these units then merged into a federation. Gowan and Macdonald later changed their minds about Confederation (Gowan within days, Macdonald considerably later), but neither had been intuitively shrewd about it.

Within a year, Gowan's British American League had faded into memory. Most of its members now contributed their political efforts to the Conservative Party. In later life, John A. Macdonald claimed that the principles laid down by the British American League "are the lines on which the Liberal-Conservative Party has moved ever since." From a virtually-spontaneous, short-lived, chaotic, and ill-controlled organization, that was an enduring legacy.

Gowan's immediate inheritance was quite different. In late October 1848, Ogle was dismissed as a justice of the peace and from the militia. He had held the rank of lieutenant colonel and commander of the second regiment of the Leeds militia since November 1846. To someone raised on the Anglo-Irish idea that being a J.P. and an officer (whether in yeomanry, militia, or regular army), was the *sine qua non* for being a gentleman, dismissal was a real and terrible punishment. It heart-sickened Gowan and he did not react to these dismissals with dignity, but carried on virulent correspondence and editorial campaigns concerning them: all to no avail, of course, for his attacks on the Governor General had been too telling, his venom too acid, for him to be ignored.

Frances Gowan, gone gray with middle-age and with the strain of her episodic life with Ogle, now became a reproach to him. Not that she said anything, but rather that she did not. With quiet no bility she took care of the household and gave her attention to the younger children. She did not tax Ogle with his failures, even as he was being stripped of his epaulettes. She was, indeed, a perfect lady, and that for him was the problem. When Ogle was at home in Brockville, the family still had the traditional evening meal together, with Ogle at the head of the table, the family arrayed before him. Now, when the children left the table after dinner, Frances and Ogle sat in silence. Frances occasionally tried to make conversation — of late, she was even more interested in fortune-tellers, and also in unusual diseases and folk-medicines — but her husband said little and when the curtain of silence fell between them he found that he could not look her in the eye.

It was during this period of their domestic life that Ogle became involved with an unusual Toronto girl, Eliza McCormick.

Undeniably, she was different. She was fifteen when he first met her, tall, with very dark hair and aquiline features. She looked older than her age, and had Gowan not been feeling particularly libidinous when he encountered her in a Toronto hotel, he would have passed her by. Something attractively aggressive in her posture attracted his attention, and once he had started a conversation with her, he found her slow way of talking and her low voice arresting. They spent the night in her room and Ogle ended up exhausted, feeling as if he had just spent the night in a footrace with a well-conditioned whippet. Money well spent, he reflected.

The next time Gowan was in Toronto, he looked for Eliza in the hotel that served as her brothel, and when she was not to be seen, he asked the bartender where Miss McCormick might be. "In the corner. She's been sitting there for the last hour." The barman smiled ironically. Eliza indeed was there, but with a short haircut and in a suit of clothes that was so obviously male that Ogle overlooked her. He affected not to be surprised, and for the usual fee, had a pleasant afternoon's exercise. He said nothing about her attire. Just as he was about to leave her room, Eliza asked, "Would you like to see my wardrobe?"

"Your clothes closet?" Ogle was puzzled.

"No, silly man! I mean my clothes. Would you like to see all of my clothes?"

Ogle wasn't sure. "Well, I . . . well, yes, certainly. Are they particularly interesting?"

"You tell me!" She opened the door to her closet and revealed her prized belongings: two dresses and seven suits of men's clothes.

This was the beginning of an unusual friendship, one that made Gowan uneasy, but that he felt driven to continue. As she came to trust Ogle, Eliza would try on her costume for him, usually between bouts of love-making. Sometimes she was a law student, and other time a clerk in a dry goods store, another a medical student, another a messenger boy, or a tailor. The costumes were authentic, the details perfect, and each time she put one on she engaged in a performance, an act of perfect mimicry of how each one of these men would act. Then she would slowly take off the clothes and slide back into bed with Gowan.

One afternoon after he had known Eliza McCormick for about a year, she said, "Ogle Gowan, you are a trustworthy man. And I feel so lonely sometimes. So, I shall trust you with my closest secret."

Ogle sat up. Eliza's mode of address was cloying, but intriguing.

"Do you know why, really, I own all those man-clothes?"

Man-clothes? A strange term. Ogle shook his head: no.

"Because there is one game in the world more enjoyable to me than any other. What do you think it is?"

Ogle was about to guess, but he would not have been even close.

"I love to seduce girls. But only when I am in those clothes."

He was about to say something, but, with unusual coquettishness, Eliza placed a hand across his mouth. "Shh, dear man! I shall tell you what I do." She took her hand away and sat cross-legged on the bed. "Once a month or so, I go to Hamilton, or to Kingston, or to Galt, for three or four days. Then I go to a dress-making establishment, usually, and soon find a little poppet who is willing to walk out with me of an evening. I wear a hat and keep my voice deep, and they think I am a beardless, charming, young man of seventeen or eighteen. Sometimes I have to visit these young darlings over a period of three or four months. Others can be dealt with in a night or two or three. But always they start talking of marriage, or of sharing a house, with flowers by the doorstep and when that talk starts, well then . . . "

She faltered.

" . . . then I know that I can have my way with them."

"Your way?" Ogle was not sure what that was.

"I mean, with my hands of course. They let me play inside their blouses and almost always under their skirts. Some of the darlings go quite crazy, I can tell you?" Ogle was fascinated, but Eliza took his intense stare as a sign of disapproval. "And, I can tell you, believe me, that none of them have been virgins! They're all little trollops, I tell you . . . so, when I just disappear and am not seen again, the little hussies haven't lost anything that they hadn't lost a long time earlier!"

Eliza stopped and looked at Gowan. "You won't inform on me, will you? You're the only person I've ever told of this. Please tell me you won't!" Ogle promised and he kept his word. He continued to visit Eliza as often as he could, even though he knew that in doing so, he was delivering hostages to fortune.

They made a strange couple, client and hooker, confessor and sinner, and they developed a routine to fit their relationship. Ogle would pick Eliza up in the bar of the hotel out of which she worked. Invariably now she wore "man-clothes." They would make love in her room and then she would dress herself in the clothes she had worn while conducting her latest seduction. The gifted Eliza would then put on a drama for Gowan's benefit, playing both herself in male clothes and the wee girl she had seduced. All this was accompanied by graphic descriptions of the victim and of the physical details of the seduction. Then Eliza would quickly undress and Ogle, excited by the pornographic drama, was asked to complete the seduction, doing to Eliza what she had been unable to do to her victim.

This mixture of sex, drama, and fantasy, was addictive to Gowan, though he knew that he was an accomplice to a set of felonious sexual assaults, could not stop himself. He was terrified when he learned in 1852, that Eliza had been apprehended in Hamilton and charged. He worried throughout her trial, but she said nothing about him. In her way, she was true to her man.

In the past, when Ogle Gowan had encountered setbacks to his national political ambitions, he had recouped by concentrating on local politics and using these as a spring-board back to national prominence. This time, however, he could not gain mastery of local affairs.

Undeniably, Ogle revelled in holding incidental local office such as serving as chairman of the grand jury and as chairman of the board of the Victoria Macadamized Road; the latter had great patronage possibilities. Real local power, however, resided in the Johnstown District Council (renamed, in 1850, the Council of the United Counties of Leeds and Grenville). Gowan served as warden of this council from early 1848 until the beginning of January 1851, but his hold was weak and, eventually, he lost it. To illustrate the decline in Gowan's control over local matters, consider his downfall in early 1851.

It takes place in the council chamber, Brockville. Gowan now has served three terms as warden of the council of the United Counties of Leeds and Grenville and wishes to be re-elected. He has not done much tactical planning, however, and his opponents have. The council chamber is full, for the word has spread that something interesting will happen. The day's task is to elect a warden for the year 1851 and Ogle, who was warden in 1850, proceeds to the warden's chair and gavels the meeting to order. Immediately a councellor stands up and asks by what authority Gowan occupies the warden's chair. Ogle tries to brush him off. "I will show that presently." The counsellor will not accept that. He has consulted an attorney and Gowan is acting *ulta vires* if he takes the chair before being elected. One of the Sherwoods, old Family-Compact enemies of Gowan's, rises and says that the county clerk should act as chairman of the meeting until the warden for 1851 actually is elected. Long arguments follow, but in the end, Gowan's bluster is of no use and he has to put the matter to a vote. The council votes fifteen to eight to put the clerk in the chair. Then two men are nominated for warden, Gowan and George Sherwood. The result is fifteen to three for Sherwood, with several abstentions. Gowan is out.

That is loss of control. Gowan's fall from local power is confirmed almost simultaneously by the results of his running for town councillor for the west ward of Brockville. He runs sixth in a six-man poll.

Ogle did not read the signs. By the late summer of 1851 it became clear that there would be a parliamentary election in December, and Ogle hit the campaign trail with more enthusiasm than perspicacity. In mid-August, for instance, he paid a visit to Cole's Ferry, and despite the visit being well advertised, only seven people turned up and two of these were Reformers who were there out of curiosity. Ogle lectured this group for a time and then asked for an endorsement of his candidacy. Four people voted and Ogle was endorsed three to one! That was a sign.

Ogle's opponent was the Reformer and sitting member, William Buell Richards, who was very well organized. As might be expected, the Brockville *Recorder* supported him, but now it did so with unrestrained vigour. William Buell, W.B. Richards' uncle, had sold his interest in the paper in June 1849, and whereas under his editorship the paper always had a tone of gentlemanly reserve, the new owner waded into the fight against Gowan with a claymore:

> Who is Ogle R. Gowan? A man, whose first act, after he set foot on Canadian soil, was to set one class of his countrymen against another. With a soft voice, a ready tongue, a deceitful heart, large ambition and inordinate self-esteem, he has laid siege to religious

> and political feeling to exalt himself; and now bankrupt in political character, and steeped in trickery, he is loudly appealing to men whom he has often duped, to range themselves under him once more, seeking to blind their judgment by new colors hoisted at the masthead of his shattered vessel. But his colors are false. The true flag of the pirate is black, and that flag the Reformers of Leeds are well aware was hoisted at his command, to insult the most enlightened and constitutional Governor-General Canada has yet known. Let the Reformers of Leeds remember Gowan and his black flag when they are asked, "Who are you going to vote for?"

Remember Gowan and his black flag . . . In December 1851, the electors did. He lost to W. Buell Richards, 1,205-1,072. His losing margin was up from sixty votes in the previous election to 133. The trend was obvious: finally, Ogle got the message.

While W.B. Richards and his followers were celebrating the victory with a parade of sleighs through Brockville and a feast at Wilson's Hotel, Ogle was sitting alone and bitter in a darkened bedroom of his Brockville home. Members of his household tiptoed downstairs. They spoke not a word to each other, and even the family dogs were mute. At last Ogle came to a firm decision. He would move his family to Toronto and start over. Thus, early in the new year, 1852, he bought the weekly edition of the Toronto *Patriot*, sold the press and type of his Brockville *Statesman* and became a Toronto journalist and publisher.

CHAPTER 16

Big City, 1852-1856

IN APRIL of 1852, a small, ferret-faced man in a black suit and starched wing-collar moved from shop to shop, hotel to tavern, boarding-house to factory in Brockville, talking unsmilingly to people and then discreetly jotting down what he had learned. This was the man from Dun and Company, an American credit investigation service that did most of the credit-ranking of central Canadian businesses. His task was to pick up gossip, to learn about unpaid accounts and planned investments, to discover who had a drinking problem and who was a shrewd investor, to weigh this information, and, finally, to suggest who was worthy of credit and who was not. His laconic manner, black garb, and omnipresent notebook led local businessmen to call him the Recording Angel and, though his presence made them nervous, they knew that his good opinion often was the difference between being in business and not. When he came to the building where the Brockville *Statesman* had until recently been published, he tried both doors, and, finding them locked, peered through the windows to see if any of the furnishings or the printing presses still were there. They were gone. He then went to several shops on the street and asked questions about Ogle Gowan. His report, succinct in the extreme, was an epitaph to Ogle's more than two decades in eastern Ontario. "O.R. Gowan . . . Gone to Toronto; little or no means."

For a man of Ogle's background, moving to Toronto was a natural and sensible decision. Except for Kingston, Toronto was the most Irish town in what is present-day Ontario. In 1851, just under thirty-seven percent of the city's 30,000 population had been born in Ireland, and when one realized that there were many second-and-third-generation Irish persons in the city, it is clear that people of Irish background comprised the majority of the population. Most persons of Irish ethnicity were Protestants and, among them, Anglicans were the largest group. The United Church of England and Ireland (often misdenominated the "Church of England") bonded together large numbers of Irish Protestants to other Protestants of English extraction: in 1845, 43 percent of Toronto's population subscribed to that denomination, making it the largest Protestant group. After 1847, there was a growing Irish Catholic presence in the city, both in absolute numbers and as a proportion of the total population, but until well into the twentieth century, the Catholic vote in Toronto was submerged in the Protestant tide. The Toronto business community was dominated by men who belonged to the Freemasons or to the Orange Order and whose wives served on the women's guilds of the Anglican, Methodist, and Presbyterian churches.

In a general sense, Protestantism was the great popular cause in Toronto in the 1850s. The same vocabulary that Ogle Gowan had brought with him from Ireland — the touch-words of Liberty, Constitution, and Loyalty, the very watchwords of Irish Protestantism — also dominated Toronto's ideological life. For a newspaperman this was a godsend, for Ogle could write as he talked, quickly, forcefully, mixing sarcasm, irony, and diatribe, with those high-principled Protestant code-words, and he could know that his vocabulary would find an immediate resonance with his audience. Gowan's weekly *Patriot,* once a Compact paper, now became a democratic-conservative sheet, aimed at people with strong Protestant feelings, but avoiding the more extreme Protestant positions (such as the opposition to Catholic separate schools).

Toronto seemingly was ideal for Gowan for another reason: it gave him a chance to rebuild his political base. Local politics in Toronto was a big-time business and he could look forward to being an alderman. And Toronto sent two MPs to the House of Assembly and that too was a prize worth seeking. Toronto's population was extremely loyal in outlook and that also suited Gowan. Anybody with a shrewd eye could not have missed the import, for example, of the Queen's birthday celebration, held on the grounds of Government House in 1854. Fully a quarter of Toronto's population assembled to toast Victoria: middle-class men in top hats, their wives in wide skirts; workers in clean suits and cloth caps, their wives wearing their best shawls, all showing loyalty, respectability, and Protestant good sense.

If one notes that in the 1850s there were fifteen Orange lodges in Toronto and that they enrolled about 1,000 to 1,200 active members — fifteen percent of the adult male Protestants in the city — and that, in addition there were many men who had been Orangemen but now were inactive, then it is clear that Ogle had a potentially strong political base. And the municipal corporation of the city of Toronto was a particularly rich source of patronage. Jobs-for-the-boys were available in large numbers. Equally important, the corporation controlled the licences to enter into the cartage and cab businesses and to run an inn or tavern. Toronto at this time had seventy-eight taverns, which works out to one for every 120 adults. Municipal government, obviously, was a field with a great deal to offer.

Just before the Gowans moved to Toronto, Frances suffered an ulcerated leg. At first it seemed to be a minor affliction, but the ugly circle spread. To Ogle's horror and France's great distress, the leg became gangerous. The course of disease would have been terrible at any time, but Frances, always a believer in fortune-tellers, freets, and nature-cures, had become a devotee of homeopathic medicine. Nothing that Ogle could say would persuade her to see a conventional doctor. Even when Charles Buchanan made a special visit, she would not permit him to prescribe for her. Homeopathy, as practised on Frances, was a treacherous illusion. It operated on a presupposition that was magical: namely the belief that one treated a disease by giving the patient a drug which, if administered to a healthy person, would induce the same symptoms as produced by the disease in question. On occasion this worked, but the success was random. Thus, during her last tortured months, Frances faced acute pain without the aid of palliative drugs. Her leg throbbed and she could not tolerate sitting in a chair or bear being transferred from bed to sofa without emitting wrenching cries of pain. Death, which occurred in the spring of 1852, was no unkind release.

For Ogle, Frances had been the one constant in a life that had begun with the almost-feudal social assumptions of post-'98 County Wexford and had then moved into the age of telegraph, steam, and the confusing social flux of the New World. In mourning her loss, he was mourning as much the passing of his own youth and all its possibilities, as he was grieving for her.

For a time, Ogle decided to be faithful to her memory, but, inexorably, this resolve faded and he became servant again of the old thorn in his flesh. In mid-1853 he took to visiting harlots again. A disorderly boarding-house on King Street that served as a home for actors, whores, circus performers, and black musicians became his favourite haunt. The owner specialized in very young girls and Ogle now pleasured himself with twelve- and thirteen-year-olds. But the memory of his late wife had one lasting effect. Now, when he served the needs of the flesh, he somehow felt that he was being unfaithful to her; he carried with him a sense of guilt, something he never had experienced when she was alive.

The King Street brothel had several entrances and the owner was discreet. It was, however, a business of some size, and it required credit, just like any other business. It was a particularly risky sort of business, which explains why the man in the dark suit, the Recording Angel of Dun and Company, made a close study of it and of its customers. One of the items jotted in his notebook concerned the visits of a certain "ORG."

"The great thing about the Toronto corporation," Gowan once remarked, "is that all the rascals can be changed every year." He was referring to a situation that prevailed from the beginning of 1851 onwards: terms of office for aldermen and councillors had been reduced from twenty-four months to twelve. Everyone came up for election every January. This made Toronto city politics very volatile and, for someone like Gowan, it made it much easier to wedge his way into municipal office.

Moreover, to Ogle's advantage, a new ward, St. John's (the seventh created in Toronto), was established and in January 1853, elected its first aldermen and councillors. It was ideal for Gowan, because it held a large number of Irish working-class Protestants. Ogle began preparing for a municipal election as soon as he moved to Toronto. He made it a point to visit all the Protestant businessmen in the area that would form the new ward, and did so once a month. He asked after their families and, if they were Orangemen, he inquired if there were anything he could do for them. He began attending meetings of the Orange Lodges held in his ward, appearing in the role of elder statesman of the Order. Often he would give a brief talk when introduced, one that mentioned, as if in passing, the need for loyalty, true Protestantism, and good citizenship at all levels of government, including the municipal. His campaign worked. In the election held in early January 1853, he ran first (albeit by only five votes), in a four-man poll for alderman of St. John's ward. In his good moments, Ogle told himself that, indeed, he was on his way again.

As an alderman and as a newspaper editor, Gowan simultaneously pursued two special interests (in addition, of course, to the pervasive loyalism, constitutionalism, and Protestantism that was the ground-base of all of his politics): he was mad keen on railroads and he supported his fellow-Irishman, Mayor Bowes, during the scandals that wracked his administration. The first half of the 1850s saw the start of the great railway age in central Canada and by the decade's end, Toronto was tied into the rapidly reticulating North American rail network: "Getting in on the ground floor of railroads will make a man rich — richer than canals, richer than steam ships." He did not himself have any money to invest, but he knew that by creating a bit of trouble for the railway magnates, he stood a good chance of being co-opted, as a means of keeping him quiet. Hence, in the Toronto city council he fought unsuccessfully against the Toronto and Guelph Railway's appointing an agent to sell stock in England: this on the grounds of financial responsibility. More effectively, he appointed himself as the defender of the public demense: he pushed for a general plan to coordinate all railways coming into Toronto, with the special view of preserving the lake frontage of the city. These activities were essentially insurance, in case his political career faltered. At minimum, the railways would give him a job, just to keep his mouth closed.

Equally calculated was his alliance with John George Bowes, who was mayor of Toronto from 1851 until the beginning of 1854. Along with the then-premier Francis Hincks, Bowes was involved in the "Ten Thousand Pounds" scandal: they had used inside knowledge to buy and sell at £10,000 profit, city of Toronto debentures issued for the Northern Railway. From the very beginning, Gowan defended Bowes. In February 1853, for example, he had inserted into the city council minutes a long report that was favourable to Bowes. He supported another councillor's motion that 3,000 copies of this report be printed and distributed (considering that the population of Toronto was 30,000 at the time, this must have meant one copy for every second family!). Later, Gowan used his considerable experience in parliamentary tactics to impede council investigation of the Bowes scandal. Ogle, in his weekly *Patriot*, was the most prominent journalist defending Bowes and Hincks. His paper claimed that the city council proceedings were "a full, complete, and triumphant vindication of RIGHT and TRUTH against the assaults of CALUMNY and FALSEHOOD." One thing was certain — when the scandal died down, both Bowes and Hincks owed something to Gowan.

Ogle's support in this instance for the Reformer Hincks (whom, one recalls, he had once challenged to a duel), moved him away politically from the more extreme sort of demotic conservatism. This seeming political catholicity was an image he had been preparing for himself since the late 1830s, when he had entered the temporary Orange-Green alliance with Bishop Macdonnell. Of course, Ogle still polished his hyper-loyal image whenever possible. For instance, in the city council he secured a committee to stage a celebration of the Queen's birthday. And he still delivered baubles to his Orange friends whenever possible: little things, such as obtaining free of charge the use of the city's premier meeting place, the St. Lawrence Hall, for charitable Orange benefits.

There was now one crucial question in Gowan's political career. Could he gain the same degree of control over the Toronto Orangemen that he had possessed over those of Eastern Ontario, while, at the same time, maintaining his statesmanlike and reasonable posture towards some of the Reformers and some Roman Catholics? In April of 1853, he found out.

One of the two seats in the Legislative Assembly for Toronto came open, because the incumbent had been disqualified. Gowan, keen once again to be a member of Parliament, was the first candidate to throw his hat into the ring. There was some intelligence in this, as the Toronto members were elected in an at-large election for the entire city, and Ogle needed all the time he could get to make himself known outside the boundaries of his own ward. He rented the assembly room in the St. Lawrence Hall and held a meeting to promote his candidacy. This was the perfect venue, for the hall, like the candidate, was *nouveau*. The building was a hulking three-and-a-half-storey structure, standing at King and Jarvis streets and it was the embodiment of Toronto's self-image: sturdy, expensive, and ornamented by respectable and totally inappropriate neo-classicisms, such as a cupola, columns, and carved stonework. Ogle orchestrated the meeting in the St. Lawrence Hall very well. The following week he placed advertisements in several Toronto papers, stating that "It is to me a source of great satisfaction that at one of the most crowded meetings ever held in the great hall of this noble city, a very large majority expressed their confidence in my integrity and of their desire to confide the Representation of their interest in Parliament to my keeping." Yes, he would heed their call to duty and, yes, he was an ardent proponent of "Civil and Religious Liberty," a code phase that meant that, indeed, he was a True Blue Protestant.

The Reformers in Toronto were, at this time, split between supporters of Robert Baldwin and those of Francis Hincks and no candidate could be found who was suitable to both factions and who was willing to stand. So it became a straightforward battle between Conservatives. Henry Sherwood, mayor of Toronto 1842-1844, came forward, a doubly ironic occurrence, because, as Gowan himself noted, as long ago as twenty-three years earlier he and Gowan had stood at the hustings in the Leeds county elections. Moreover, Sherwood now presented himself as a hyper-Protestant and therefore, this scion of the eastern Compact cut into Ogle's traditional constituency of Orangemen and Irish Protestants. The formal nominations took place on April 10 at husting erected in the market square. The old and the new Toronto were nicely tied together at that moment. Sheriff Jarvis controlled the nomination rituals with a virtually mediaeval touch, while the backdrop was the brand-new market building, an Italian Renaissance structure, occupying the square bounded by what today are Jarvis, Front, and Market Streets, a monument to burgeoning mercantile prosperity. The general election was set for the end of April and Ogle, now snapped from his frequent lethargy, ran hard, holding meetings in each ward and spending his days glad-handing voters.

Now, a further irony tinctured the campaign. That old radical,

William Lyon Mackenzie, pardoned by the government, was back in Toronto, editing the *Message* and he endorsed Ogle! "Mr. Gowan," Mackenzie told the Reform electors, "is the more progressive of the Tory candidates." Then, irony-upon-irony, George Brown's *Globe* urged Protestants to vote against Ogle, on the grounds that he was not sufficiently anti-Catholic! "Mr. Gowan has been intriguing to make an alliance with the Roman Catholics to break up the school system," the *Globe* charged. "He, a professing Orangeman, would bow down so low as a hound before his master, in the papal Church. That is why we would have every Liberal vote for Mr. Sherwood."

The allegiances of the Orangemen of Toronto, therefore, were split. George Benjamin, Grand Master of the Order in British North America, let it be known from his home in Belleville that he did not favour Gowan. Ultimately, most Orangemen voted for Sherwood. Ogle lost by a nearly two-to-one margin — 833 to 423.

When the results were declared on Thursday, April 28, Ogle made a characteristically caustic speech of concession. Next time he would not be beaten, he declared. This time he had been beaten by two Popes — the Pope of Rome and the Orange Pope, Mr. Benjamin, the Grand Master.

The one thing that now gave Ogle real pleasure was being an alderman, and he was one of the most regular attenders at city council meetings. Every time he approached the white brick city hall on Front Street, he felt good; he liked to bounce up the spriral staircase to the mayor's offices on the second floor, to strut in and be given a hearty handshake by Mayor Bowes. And in the overly-large council chambers (75 x 100 feet in area), he took great pleasure in taking a seat before the large, arched windows and ostentatiously putting his feet up, like a railway baron.

His journalism gave him little pleasure, but for a time things seemed to go well. In May 1853, he bought the daily edition of the *Patriot*, thus completing his takeover of that publication. This transaction brought around the ferret-faced Recording Angel from Dun and Company, who discovered that Ogle had had to take a silent partner. This man the notorious John G. Bowes, held a "controlling interest" and the Recording Angel concluded that Bowes was the "real proprietor" and Gowan merely the editor and "nominal proprietor."

Despite this private financial backing, Ogle was broke, which led to a great humiliation early in 1854. He did not own his own house, and he, and those of his daughters who still lived at home, often found themselves in places that were just short of being condemned. He was re-elected alderman for St. John's Ward in January 1854, took his seat, and was appointed to three committees he desired to be on. These were applications-for-office, railroads, and walks-and-gardens. His property qualification, however, was questioned. Aldermen had to possess real property in their own name, worth £80 per year or more and, for those who leased, rather than owned property, it had to be of a value of £80 a year, and to have been rented for at least one year. Ogle and his family, it turned out, had lived as tenants in three houses during the course of the previous year, one on Ann Street, leased at £35 per annum, another on Adelaide Street at £45, and a third in King Street at £65. To meet the property qualification, Ogle had claimed tenancy of all three houses, as if he had rented all three for the entire year, even the tenement in Ann Street that had been torn down shortly after he moved out. Furthermore, the King Street premises were not held solely by him, but jointly with Samuel Thompson, a sometime member of the Toronto city council.

The case against Gowan went quickly up to the court of Queen's Bench and Ogle experienced a deep humiliation: it was proven that he could not meet the minimum property qualification for sitting in council, that he had misrepresented his holdings, so he was deprived of his aldermanic seat. That was the end of his career in Toronto municipal politics. He had seen Corporation politics as a means up: it had just brought him lower.

Yet, he kept trying to get back into Parliament. A new parliamentary riding was created for Ontario North in the general election of 1854, and, like a punch-drunk fighter, who thinks that all he needs is one more chance to get back into the bigtime, Ogle entered the race. He took another pounding.

Strapped for money, Ogle spent the fall of 1854 selling his remaining land holdings in Leeds County. These were unimproved or barren lands. He sold most of them in a single transaction for £400, but had to take back a mortgage from the purchaser to cover most of that amount. So he still was short of cash, for the money he received as downpayment went to ward off his creditors. Selling his land was a blow to Ogle. Although most native North Americans would not have been bothered by having to unload a few hundred acres of swamp, rock, and bush, to Ogle, who thought of himself as landed gentry, it hurt.

And still the debts accumulated. He shuffled creditors, put off some of them, wrote bad bills-of-exchange to others, fighting hard to keep ahead of complete insolvency. Of course, the Recording Angel heard about these transactions, and he investigated. His conclusion was flint-eyed: "Don't think him worth the Confidence of any hon. man."

Finally, in early December 1854, Ogle sold his newspaper interests to James Beatty, who merged the *Patriot* with the Toronto *Leader*. And that should have been the end of the matter.

Except that Ogle was arrested and held to bail for an alleged scam connected with his selling of the paper. During the fall of 1854, when he had been trying to sell the *Patriot*, he had talked to certain members of the Conservative Party about their buying it and leaving him in control. The result would be that they would have a Party paper of their own in Toronto. The idea had some merit, but nothing came of it. Nevertheless, Gowan went around stating that £400 was needed to keep the *Patriot* running, and he approached several prominent politicians, including George Wright of Brampton, a former MP for the county of Peel. Wright coughed up either £25 or £100 (accounts vary) to help keep the paper running. Later, when Wright learned that Gowan had pocketed the cash and sold the paper, he was outraged, and had him charged for obtaining money under false pretences. Eventually, in the cause of Tory unity, the charges were withdrawn, but not before many Party followers came to suspect that Wright had not been the only prominent Tory to have been fleeced.

With no political office, no newspaper, and no cash, how did Ogle support himself? His interest in the railways finally paid a small reward: he was made a clerk in the office of the Grand Trunk Railway Company.

Somehow, while his political, financial, and personal problems mounted, he managed to carry on a Holy war within the Orange Order. His jihad possessed a minimum of strategy and a maximum of aggressive tactics. "The Grand Lodge meeting is in Kingston this year," Gowan told Richard Dempsey, a Toronto lawyer and small-time politician, "and I plan to become Grand Master again." Dempsey, who knew Gowan well, was pleased. The Old Master, as he called Gowan, seemed focused and purposeful again; his frequent moroseness might be behind him. Dempsey was optimistic. "I'm not as young as once I was," Ogle told Dempsey, "so I expect you to have some strong lieutenants, men of substance, men who will plan and carry out this purification of the Order." The lawyer nodded agreement.

The war, in large part, was a battle of the bearish Grand Master, George Benjamin, Upper Canadian to the core, against the Irish bulldog, Gowan, but it was more. In part, it became a contest of Toronto, as represented by Gowan, against Belleville and eastern Ontario, as represented by Benjamin. The Benjamin phalanx was more genteel, more white-collar, and more Canadian. Gowan's men were more apt to be working-class and Irish-born. The Benjaminites tended to be Anglican, the Gowanites, broadly representative of the whole Protestant spectrum. Gowan's forces were less concerned than Benjamin's with maintaining Anglican privileges, so were willing to accept some compromise on such things as the Clergy Reserves and the separate schools. In essence, the Gowanites' political philosophy was that of the emerging new conservatism of John A. Macdonald.

Nasty: that described the Grand Lodge meeting held in Kingston in June 1853. Very nasty. Gowan's lieutenants packed the session in order to pledge delegates to their cause. The Benjaminites were well prepared, however. They of course had copies of the famous *Interesting Trial* distributed. They also spread around copies of the evidence from the United Kingdom parliamentary investigations of the 1830s, which dealt with Gowan's having been adjudged a man of disreputable character by the Irish Grand Lodge. In a ploy, notable for its viciousness, they brought George Nicoll to Kingston. Though not in good standing with the Canadian Order, and thus unable to attend any meeting, he was set up in a downtown hotel. Benjamin's men then brought wavering delegates to him and he provided them with further evidence against Gowan.

Kingston was an Orange city, so the Grand Lodge was given the use of the city hall's large council chambers. The first day of the three-day session was filled with routine business inside the hall, and vespine attacks outside. On the second day, it came time to elect the Grand Master for the coming year. As Grand Master for the past year, George Benjamin was in the chair and, foreswearing ritual modesty, he openly solicited re-election. Then, with great symbolic probity he retired from the room, while Angus Bethune, senior deputy grand master, and one of Benjamin's supporters, took the chair. Immediately Benjamin was formally nominated and then, Richard Dempsey, the junior deputy grand master and Gowan's chief lieutenant, put forward Ogle's name. Unlike Benjamin, Gowan stayed in the meeting room, so that he could direct his forces.

"What about proxies?" someone called from the back of the room, and a long debate followed as to whether or not proxies should be allowed. Admittedly, this was a procedural question, but it also was the cock-pit of the battle. The Benjamin people had collected several proxies from lodges in Canada East, and particularly from Montreal (where, since the 1830s the Lodges had been leery of Gowan's leadership). Without these proxies, the Benjaminites knew they would lose; even with them, the vote would be close. The debate was ugly and Bethune, as chairman, lost control of the meeting. Instead of ruling from the chair on the proxy question, he permitted one of Gowan's lieutenants to move that the proxies be not accepted and, when this motion passed, Bethune left the chair. Immediately, Richard Dempsey, as deputy grand secretary, seized the gavel and called for a vote on the question.

Just then, George Benjamin, having been summoned by the distraught Bethune, returned to insist on his right to resume the chairmanship of the meeting, and to decide the procedural point himself. Not so, said Dempsey and the Gowanites. They argued that, technically, during an election there was no grand mastership. Benjamin carried the point, however, and pledged that he would simply make the procedural ruling and would then again retire from the room. Of course, he ruled that the proxy votes were permissible. This led to a lot of yelling, some impressive obscenities, and a fist-fight in the corner.

Benjamin might just have survived as Grand Master had he had, at this point, the presence of mind to prorogue the meeting for an hour or two. Instead, in the hope of quieting things down, he fell into a Gowanite trap: he permitted the moving of a resolution that declared, in effect, one lodge, one vote; in other words, no proxies, despite the earlier ruling. Two hours of the most indecorous debate followed. Rather learned discussions of parliamentary procedure were interspersed with vile harangues, with much stamping and hollering. Both Benjamin and Gowan were vilified. Near the end of the "debate," several of Gowan's supporters began pushing and shoving Benjamin's people, in a mild version of the sort of intimidation that had won Ogle several parliamentary elections in the 1830s. Many of Benjamin's supporters left, either from fear or disgust. Finally, the vote could not be put off any longer and Gowan's forces won handily. Proxies would not count.

Benjamin retired from the chair. This time, it was not for the sake of form, he left with all but three of his followers in tow. Ogle Gowan was quickly elected Grand Master of the Loyal Orange Association of British North America, and Richard Dempsey, tactician and major domo for Ogle Gowan, was rewarded: he became senior deputy grand master.

A victory for Ogle, or just another clutched straw? For months it was not clear. The Benjaminites formed a rival association, claiming to be the true Loyal Orange Association of British North America, and they published some devastating material about Gowan, using the ever-present George Nicoll to further blot his name. They dug up the old question of Nicoll's expulsion from the Gowan-controlled Orange Order in February 1840. Then, his charges about Gowan's being expelled from the Order in Ireland had not been sufficiently substantiated. Now, a "Committee of Correspondence of the Grand Lodge of BNA" reopened the case, and published not only Nicoll's evidence, but many new pieces, proving that Gowan had not been an Orangeman in good standing when he left Ireland in 1829. (These pieces of evidence are accurately presented in the Benjaminite report; they correspond to historical records found in other, independent sources). Most devastating of all, was a letter, not previously printed, sent from the then-deputy grand secretary of the Orange Institution of Ireland to an Orange master in Canada:

> I cannot conclude without cautioning the Brethren against a man named *Ogle R. Gowan* who has recently emigrated to America. He is not a member of the Society and should not be associated with by any Orangemen. I will send some papers about him in a parcel.

The letter was dated 22 December 1829 and was not received in Canada until well after Gowan's formation of the Orange Order in Canada on New Year's day in 1830. Its content was confirmed by a resolution — also printed by the Benjaminites — of the Grand Lodge of Ireland, dated November 17,1830:

> That this Grand Lodge has heard with extreme surprise that a person called Ogle R. Gowan has declared himself to the Orange Lodge of Canada to be one of our secretaries, whereas the said Ogle R. Gowan is not even a member of this Institution. This resolution to be communicated to the Grand Lodge of Canada.

That was going for the jugular. Had the full facts been known in 1840, George Nicoll never would have been expelled from the Order, and Gowan would have been in deep trouble. Had the facts been known in 1830 or 1832 he would not have been head of the Order.

For his part, Gowan went out about the countryside, taking the high road when it suited, the low otherwise. He had a stock sermon entitled, "God's Judgement against Rebels," in which, without once mentioning the name of the Benjaminites, he expatiated, with rich biblical and historical allusions, that "rebellion has introduced disorder and misery into the world and every calamity under which the sons of man stand, may be traced to it, as the undoubted source." That went down well in public gatherings, especially if the press was present. In closed sessions he went, detail-by-detail, through the Benjaminites myriad iniquities. And, wherever he found himself, he tried to encourage the formation of new lodges. His energy, though, came in fits and starts, and he oscillated between melancholia and extreme agitation. At the Grand Lodge meeting of 1855, for example, he sat through a discussion aimed at blackening his enemy, George Nicoll, and became increasingly unable to concentrate. Finally, Ogle had his deputy take the chair and later arranged for the official record to show that he had left the chair because of illness.

In the report of the same Grand Lodge meeting for June 1855, Gowan is found declaring victory: 363 of 513 lodges in Canada West followed him, as did thirty-six of seventy-six lodges in Canada East, and all of those in the Maritimes. But if this was victory, where was the peace that should follow? Ogle wondered.

There was no victory in heading a social sect that had two Popes. Ogle had studied enough of the history of the Catholic Church to know that the Avignon papacy of George Benjamin, weak though it was, discredited the whole movement. Until the Order was re-united, it would be of no use to Ogle in his political career. Thus, in 1855 and early 1856, Ogle encouraged his lieutenants to carry on conversations about re-uniting the Order. The Benjaminites were anxious to come back into the fold, but they were stubborn and fully able to hold out on one point: they would come back only if Ogle Gowan were not Grand Master.

Which is to say the Ogle's dream of again being head of the Orange Order in Canada was impossible to obtain. He brooded about it and finally surrendered. His lieutenants arranged an artful compromise that made him look good: he would be elected Grand Master at a great reunion meeting in June 1856 and then immediately he would resign and be replaced by George Lyttleton Allen, grand secretary, and a man acceptable as leader to the Benjaminites. That is exactly how it was staged. Ogle was rousingly re-elected Grand Master and then, in a gesture that moved many of his followers to tears, renounced, seemingly spontaneously, the mastership, in order not to stand in the way of reunion. To complete the theatrics, Allen was elected Grand Master on the motion of *both* of Ogle's sons, the Reverend Nassau C. and Harcourt Gowan. As a further salve to Ogle's pride, his son Harcourt was elected the new grand secretary and Nassau, deputy grand chaplain.

After his campaign was over, Ogle's position was exactly what it had been before he started. He was past grand master of the Order and nothing more.

CHAPTER 17

RECESSIONAL, 1856-1876

THE MOMENT that Ogle dramatically announced his retirement from the Grand Mastership, a transfiguration occurred: his brethren turned him into an icon. Now that he was removed from real power within the Order, he was treated as an elder statesman, even though he was still in his fifties. He was the Order's Canadian founder, after all, and he could speak well, so now he was displayed, front and centre, at every ceremonial occasion. Thus, on July 12, 1856, shortly after the Orange reunion, he joined the new Grand Master, George Allen, in reviewing the parade in Toronto that was said to be two miles long. About eleven o'clock that morning, the Lodge members, in full regalia, preceded by several bands, colours flying, began marching past their officers. Ogle, in full scarlet robes, ranked just behind the present Grand Master in precedence and he enjoyed himself. The review over, the procession moved to Government House where the Governor General, Sir Edmund Walker Head, accepted a loyal address. That evening, Gowan was the featured speaker at the "Virgin Lodge," a group originally made up solely of bachelors (not, one hastens to add, comprised of devotees of the BVM), and he made a speech apostrophizing the viceroy, Sir Edmund, who in his official capacity had earlier received the Orangemen. This was a far cry from the black days of Arthur and Durham and Elgin.

On his better days, Ogle sometimes thought of himself as the Orange equivalent of the Governor General. He took to referring to his rented house in Toronto as "Nebo Lodge," a reference, of course, to his place of birth in Ireland. He addressed his correspondence as coming from this imaginary palace, just as he had done in the 1830s from his pretended landed estate "Escott Park." His social round actually was quite diverting, and helped to reduce the time he spent dwelling on his troubles. He received frequent invitations from country lodges to their soirées and ceremonies. He especially enjoyed events, like the one held in Barrie on New Year's Eve, 1856, where he could bring his two younger daughters, Frances Jane and Emily Jemima, and make a light speech before a supper and dance. He enjoyed such soirées and, besides, they provided a good opportunity for the girls to meet eligible men. And he revelled in the free steamship trip to Quebec City in June, 1857 for the Order's annual Grand Lodge meeting, which was held in Lower Canada that year. A boat, the *Highlander*, was chartered by the Orangemen and, as the delegates embarked at Toronto, Gowan and Grand Master Allen received their homage like dignitaries in a reception line. A band played and the boat steamed off to cheers and Orange tunes.

As an icon, Gowan was expected to be a repository of Orange folklore and this, too, he enjoyed. He was able to toss off a two-hour talk on a subject such as "Orange Halls" with the same ease as if he had been simply talking at table. On some of his visits to country lodges, Ogle was joined on the dais by one of his sons, Nassau or Harcourt, both now well-known Orangemen in their own right. These occasions were among the proudest in Gowan's later life.

If only . . . if only Ogle had been satisfied to slip into a dignified retirement from public life . . . if only he had been satisfied with being an elder statesman of Orangeism . . . if only he could have lived on his salary as a Grand Trunk clerk . . . if only his free-floating hatreds, his depression, his bent sex drive could have been controlled.

Gowan badly wanted back into Parliament. He recognized that his middle-of-the-road political conservatism left him open to the accusation, from more extreme Protestants, of being soft on the Catholics. Hence, in July 1856, he launched an attack on a long-time *bête noire*, Egerton Ryerson, on a straight pro-Orange, anti-

Catholic issue. The provincial education department, headed by Ryerson, had a rule against employees taking part in public processions. One, William Howe, had been in that year's Twelfth parade in Toronto, and the deputy superintendent had dismissed him from his job. Ryerson, who had the good sense to know that fighting the Orangemen was a losing cause, quickly reversed the dismissal.

At that point, Gowan entered the picture. With his friend and lawyer, Richard Dempsey, he visited Ryerson's office. Ogle literally pounded on Ryerson's desk, and called him a handmaiden of Romanism. Gowan refused to take in Ryerson's explanation of events, deliberately ignoring the fact that the man in question now was back at work. Instead, he and Dempsey staged a protest meeting in the St. Lawrence Hall. They spread the word that not only had an Orangemen been victimized, but that Ryerson allowed Roman Catholics to walk in procession on St. Patrick's Day. That Gowan was on to a good issue is indicated by the fact that Toronto's mayor, John Beverly Robinson Jr., a man of as pure Compact background as one could find, agreed to be the official convener and chairman of the session. Because there had been no real problem to begin with, the whole event was a Punch and Judy show. But it had one direct result — it allowed Ogle to remind the people of Toronto that he long had been a staunch defender of Protestant interests.

In the fall of 1856, Ogle's daughter, Frances Jane, married a prosperous Cookstown merchant, Thomas R. Ferguson, whose family came from County Cavan, Ireland. Ferguson was an enthusiastic Orangeman and held conservative political views of the same stripe as Gowan's. As a municipal councillor, Ferguson was building a strong local base and Ogle calculated (correctly) that his new son-in-law soon would be in the Legislative Assembly.

Gowan used the wedding ceremony as a lever for his own political ambitions. He hired a Spadina Avenue estate and, after the ceremony, was host to what one guest recalled thirty years later as "the first garden party ever given in Canada." Perhaps it was not the first, but it was opulent, and even though he had to pay the caterer in monthly installments for a year thereafter, it was worth it. John A. Macdonald, Attorney General and *de facto* premier, fellow Orangeman, and old friend of Ogle's was the lion of the party. Anybody who was powerful in the conservative party was present. Macdonald arrived early, proposed one of the toasts to the new bride and groom and eventually had to be bodily lifted into a diligence for the trip back to his lodgings.

The temporary respectability among conservative MPs that Ogle won by this social association with John A. Macdonald was reinforced by a legal victory, short-lived though it was, over that now-omnipresent hell-hound, George Nicoll. In response to the implacable Nicoll's continuing to spread information about Ogle's disreputable activities in the Old Country, Gowan had written some things about Nicoll that had led, in turn, to Nicoll's bringing a libel suit in January 1855. Nicoll won the libel judgement in the fall of 1855, but immediately Gowan counter-attacked, by charging Nicoll with perjury. The gravamen of the charge was that Nicoll had lied when he had testified that he had not been up before the Johnstown grand jury on a perjury charge in the mid-1840s. This had been a case tried at the Brockville assize, and Nicoll defended himself by arguing that it was his no-good son who had been up for perjury. Gowan had a very strong witness, one William Tucker, who claimed to have been present on that occasion, ten years earlier, and in the absence of accurate court records (a common failing at the time) his testimony was crucial. The jury believed Tucker and, in the fall of 1855, Nicoll was sentenced to three months' imprisonment. Although this did not clear Ogle of the original libel decision, it effectively discredited Nicoll his perpetual tormentor.

When Nicoll heard the sentence, he cried out, "I would rather go to my grave than to the penitentiary," and he pulled out a pistol that had been hidden in his coat. He was in the act of priming it when the High Constable of the court seized him. So Ogle had the joy of seeing Nicoll led away, screaming, to serve his time.

But George Nicoll resurfaced. Three months in the penitentiary had turned incandescent his wrath against Gowan. He had been wrongly convicted. He vowed he would prove it and would show up Gowan as a blackguard as well. The little tailor set about investigating the witnesses at the trial, particularly William Tucker. He also chased down all the men who had been foremen of the Johnstown grand jury in the 1840s. Fortunately for him, all of them still were alive. By mid-summer, he had put together an airtight case and he had William Tucker charged with perjury. At the August 1857 assize in Brockville, the case went quickly. Gowan's chief witness had been lying, the jury decided, and Gowan's prosecution of Nicoll for perjury had therefore been based on a fabrication. Thus, Ogle was again badly soiled. Moreover, Nicoll swore that he would prosecute all those who had led to his own wrongful conviction. For the moment, he could not prove that Gowan directly had suborned William Tucker, but he would keep trying, and this was something more for Ogle to worry about: can I never shake this mad bulldog?

This extremely bad publicity preceded, by less than three months, yet another attempt by Gowan to win a seat in the Legislative Assembly. He ran again in Ontario North, and there he conducted a most unusual campaign. His chief piece of electoral propaganda was a long political litany, of which the following is a sample:

> To a union of the British American Provinces,
> I say NAY . . . .
> To a repeal of the Legislative Union,
> I say NAY . . . .
> To vote by Ballot,
> I say NAY . . . .
> To the Annexation of the Hudson's Bay Territories,
> I say YEA . . . .
> To the abolition of the property qualification for members of parliament,
> I say YEA . . . .
> To railroads and interior improvements,
> I say YEA . . . .

It was a most eccentric performance. After each of the phrases that included NAY or YEA, he would adduce a reason, but these frequently were bizarre, such as his rationale for opposing the federation of the British North American provinces: "An improvident man might seek to replenish an exhausted exchequer by a union with a rich bride but 'tis certain her dowry would not be increased by the alliance."

Ogle's other new tactic was to seek Irish Catholic votes in the riding by quietly indicating that he approved of separate schools for Catholics. He tried to cover himself with the extreme Protestants by declaring, "To scriptural education, I say YEA," by which he meant only that the Bible should be read in all of the common schools. His tacit support of the separate schools earned him denunciations as a crypto-Papist. In a straight two-man race, he lost to a Reform coalition, (broadly labelled as "anti-ministerialists,"), by 469 votes.

The year 1858 began with a major change for all Canadians. Halifax currency, a sub-species of Imperial currency that employed the traditional pounds, shillings, and pence, was replaced on New Year's day by dollars and cents. Ogle did not see this as a good omen for the year. He complained about abandoning the Empire's system of money. But, in fact, the year was doubly good to him. His son-in-law, Thomas R. Ferguson, won a seat for Simcoe South and, finally, Ogle found another parliamentary seat for himself. Gowan's success came in his old lair, the back concessions of eastern Ontario, specifically, the north riding of Leeds and Grenville counties.

This was a solid Tory seat in a district dominated by people of Irish descent, and it had gone in the January election of 1858 to Dr. Basil R. Church, who died in the spring. At the time that his death occurred, Ogle had recently quit his Grand Trunk clerk's job and was serving as one of the commissioners appointed to investigate charges against the former Crown lands agent for the Huron area. This was a patronage plum from his old friend Macdonald, now, with Étienne Tasché, joint premier of the United Canadas. It was worth ten dollars a day, which Gowan desperately needed.

Nevertheless, he realized that the electoral opportunity was too good to miss, so he dropped the commissionership and spent April and May among the people he knew so well, the hard and hyper-loyal farmers and labourers of the marginal lands of the old Johnstown District. He knew many of them from the old days and other, younger electors, were easy to approach because they had heard of him from their parents. In a straight fight against an old-fashioned Reformer, Ogle knew what to do. He sounded the old tocsin: Loyalty and the Constitution against crypto-Republicanism and the American menace. To this well-worn motif he added a new wrinkle. He took George Brown's famous demand for "Rep. by Pop." and made it "Rep. by Pop. and Territory," a conception that virtually precluded definition. In this election, as in his previous unsuccessful attempts in Ontario North, he somewhat played down his own Protestantism and tried to pick up Catholic votes. This, once again, earned him the denunciation of the *Globe* for being "an uncompromising adherent of the priest party." (Then, as now, being railed against by a Toronto newspaper is the best thing that could happen to a candidate for office in rural Ontario.) In any case, Gowan won handily, by 257 votes in a total poll of 1,701.

Never one to be charitable, George Brown summarized the purported reaction to Ogle's election. "There is very little rejoicing over the result in Ministerial circles. Mr. Gowan is universally detested and Ministers look at his advent in the House with apprehension and dread."

"I've made more maiden speeches than has a thirteen-year-old whore," Ogle told Richard Dempsey on the eve of his first attendance in what was the sixth Parliament of the United Canadas. To be sure, he had an adequate background for making such a comparison.

The Legislative Assembly now was meeting in Toronto, although under the awkward arrangement prevailing at the time, Parliament and administration were scheduled to move back to Quebec City in 1859. The seat of Government then being in Toronto not only was convenient for Gowan, but, because of his popularity with many Toronto people, it gave his parliamentary activities a resonance they never could have had if the capital were in a French-speaking area. Also, there now were several Orangemen in Parliament and the number was growing: two members of the upper house, plus, in the lower house, John A. Macdonald and Sidney Smith, the post-master general, and at least ten other members of the Assembly. That scared a lot of people, including members of the governing Conservative Party.

Their fears that Ogle might not be a responsible addition to Parliament were not allayed by his performance on his first day in the house. He did not merely walk to the parliament building from his home, though that would have been easy enough to do. Instead, he arrived in a carriage, proceeded by a band that played military marches and Orange tunes. Gowan wore a large rosette in his buttonhole in the Tory party colours. Many of his Orange supporters took seats in the gallery, and they too wore party rosettes on their coats. Ogle was not long in his seat before he heard one of the Reformers attacking him for wearing party ribbons. He rose and said that he had not intended to say anything that evening, but he was proud of the rosette. He made a few more remarks and sat down. It was not much of a maiden speech.

Ogle came to feel aggrieved towards his old friend John A. Macdonald, and he acted in a very self-destructive way. Now that he was Premier, Macdonald necessarily had less time for social life, but even so, he did not hold himself aloof from Gowan's social circle: he was pleased to be invited to dinner at Gowan's Toronto lodge; he promised political plums for Ogle's son, Nassau; he dined with Gowan's chief lieutenant, Richard Dempsey, and with Ogle's son-in-law, Thomas Ferguson.

So it was Gowan, not Macdonald, who truncated the friendship. In mid-September 1859, Macdonald invited Ogle to dinner for a post-prandial "quiet talk" about what Gowan wanted, but Ogle declined and went into an unexplained sulk. Macdonald wished to straighten things out, and two months later he wrote to Thomas Ferguson (doubtless he knew that Ferguson would show the letter to his father-in-law)

> I have always been anxious to serve Gowan from old acquaintance sake, and for the service he has done for the party. He has, however, held aloof from me and when I invited a full and unrestrained talk for the purpose of removing any political or personal misunderstanding, if any such existed, he, I may say, declined it. My own idea was that he should serve out the present parliament and that if he desired to retire from political life, he should be provided for in some position worthy of his acceptance.

This was neither ungenerous nor impractical thinking on Macdonald's part.

Yet Ogle continued to sulk. Macdonald asked Ferguson to try to get his father-in-law to meet with him personally for a "straight up and down talk," but Gowan, now in one of his deep depressions, merely wrote to Ferguson in January 1860 with a long litany of grievances that Ferguson then passed on to Macdonald. The Premier was honestly surprised to learn the depth of Gowan's bitterness: Ogle's complaints went all the way back to the mid-forties when he had lost his militia officership, his J.P. status, and his canal job. Macdonald was amazed to hear that anyone could care about such trifles. Ogle charged Macdonald with abandoning him and this hurt Macdonald: "I have always been ready to take care of him if he wanted to retire into private life, and at one time I offered him the registrarship of North Ontario, but he refused it." To George Allan, who as a ranking Orangeman served as an intermediary in dealing with Gowan, Macdonald promised that if Ogle wanted to retire from Parliament, either at the end of the present session or at the end of the life of the present Parliament, he would have a job worth £300 to £400 a year and, of course, he could have his militia rank and his J.P.'s commission back. All he wanted Gowan to do was to meet him in a friendly spirit, and things easily could be resolved.

Ogle, though, was in an emotional death spiral, and comparing his own failure with Macdonald's success only made him feel worse. In 1860, instead of attending the full parliamentary session in Quebec City, he remained much of the year in Toronto, living alone in "Nebo Lodge." When he was not immobilized by depression, he worked on the second and third volumes of his *Orangeism: Its Origin and History* (of which, if they ever were published, no copies are known to survive.) The first volume had appeared in 1859 and had been widely advertised in the Toronto papers. It had made him a few dollars, but, chiefly, it had been a labour of love.

In the late spring, Gowan took to sitting in the mid-day sunshine and this lifted his spirits. He was a sad sight. As a concession to vanity, he had begun to dye his hair an unconvincing black. Incongruously, he wore carpet slippers and padded about with small, hesitant steps. He had a small flower garden, and as spring came, he took some small pleasure in the plantings. Often he would sit for two and three hours at a time. Because his housekeeper and cook worked only part-time, the house was often empty and lonely. He preferred being out in the sunshine to being indoors.

One afternoon, a young girl entered the garden and cheekily

inquired, "Please, sir, may I see the Lodge Goat?" Ogle, who had been drowsing, came awake, slightly befuddled. "Sir, I mean the goat you keep in the case." She was referring to a stuffed animal that had been given to Gowan as a half-joke, half-serious tribute by one of the rural lodges. It was a perfectly stuffed and quite superb buck, with agate eyes, an arrogant four-inch-wide tail, and its private parts preserved. It was mounted in a glass and mahogany case and it suited Gowan's humour — a puckish humour, he liked to say — to have it placed outside on fine days.

"Certainly, my dear. But I did not hear you introduce yourself. And the goat requires that all introductions be made properly." He looked her over. Obviously she was working-class.

"Janet, sir." She wiped her nose with the back of her hand.

"Janet. A nice name. But Janet what?"

"Janet Stock." She tried to make a curtsey, but obviously was unused to such high manners. She wore a simple dress, much like a smock, with several smudge marks.

"Well, come with me." Ogle led her to a corner of the garden where the buck goat reigned. The taxidermist had preserved him with his head held aggressively high, like a bull elk surveying his harem. Ogle took the girl's hand and with mock formality presented her to the goat. "Lodge Goat, I have the honour to introduce to you Mistress Janet Stock." He looked at her fingernails and noted that they were dirty. "And, Mistress Stock I have the pleasure of presenting to you, the Lodge Goat." Ogle bowed.

Janet Stock giggled.

Ogle noticed that her hair was greasy.

"Now, Janet Stock, may I ask if there is anything else I might do for you?"

"Please, sir. A glass of water."

Gowan seemed not to hear her. "How old would you be, young lady?"

"Twelve, sir."

Ogle observed that her figure was just beginning to bloom. The nymphet age, he thought. Despite her being a bit dirty, she would clean up nicely and would be . . . .

"Please, sir. I asked if I could have a drink of water."

Ogle snapped out of his reverie. "But of course, my dear." He took her hand again. "Follow me, please." He led her into the empty house and, keenly aware of her social origins, took her into the scullery, where a kilderkin of drinking water and a ladle were kept for the housekeeper's convenience. "Here, drink from this." When she was done, he suggested, "Why don't you wash your hands and face and I will find you some nice cakes?"

The promise of the sweets made Janet agree to washing; manifestly it was not one of her favourite activities. Ogle took half a dozen small sugar cakes from the biscuit box, arranged them on a plate, and carried them towards the drawing room. "This way please." Janet followed. He placed the plate of cakes in the middle of the divan. She plunked herself down at one end and started greedily working her way through the provender, while Ogle, at the other end of the sofa, watched her. He knew that the next step was inevitable, that he could not stop himself even if he wished to and, God help me, he thought, I don't wish to be stopped.

Quickly and expertly he discovered she was not a virgin. "Well, do I get more cakes?" Janet demanded, as Ogle slowly returned to an awareness of where he was. "Yes, yes of course." He scuttled away, and brought back more cakes which Janet, her dress now pulled down, ate with a certain langorous slowness, as if she knew that for the moment she was mistress of Nebo Lodge. She seemed to enjoy the situation. "Of course I won't tell anyone," she volunteered. Ogle, who had been trying to think of a way to exact just such a promise from her, was immensely relieved.

"I am going to come back some day, for some more cakes," Janet announced, very much in charge.

"Well . . . ."

"And, I am going to bring a friend with me."

Ogle nearly panicked. Her father? Her older brother? A policeman?

"My friend is named Alice, and she likes sweet cakes ever so much."

"I don't think that . . . . "

And sometimes Alice and I play games with each other with our skirts up."

Ogle changed his mind. "Yes, bring her of course. But only if I am alone in the garden with the Lodge Goat."

Janet nodded, understanding fully.

Alice Kenny, aged twelve, lived in a tenement with her mother and her father, a partially disabled military pensioner. He leased the entire house, subletting parts of it to two other families, and two widowed women. These rentals, his pension, and the money he earned fishing on Lake Ontario kept him in drink and the family in food and clothes, but just barely. Alice was much more reserved than was Janet Stock, a passive follower rather than a leader. She had a pale, potential beauty. She might some day be a lovely woman, in the pellucid, tubercular style so beloved by the Victorians.

In early June, Alice came to her mother to tell her that something was wrong and burst into tears. There was a white discharge coming from between her legs.

Mrs. Kenny, a woman nearly broken by years of trying to keep her family decent in a tenement world where filth of all sorts surrounded them, did not know what to do. She told Alice to keep quiet and that she would think of something. Alice, very frightened, took to sitting on the front steps, alternately sobbing and staring silently into space. One of the people who sublet rooms in the tenement was a massive woman, Mrs. Lettitia McCord, a nosy gossip, a bully, but still known locally for her big heart. She saw that something was the matter with Alice and asked her mother what was so wrong. Mrs. Kenny at first tried to say nothing, then to lie, and finally, in tears herself, she told about the vaginal discharge.

Mrs. McCord, a sergeant-major in the regiment of tenement women, immediately gave orders. "Fetch Alice at once. We must discover who gave her such a terrible disease." Mrs. Kenny obeyed, and Alice, sobbing hysterically, was sat down at the kitchen table, the two women facing her, like a police detective and his assistant.

"Now, dear, we must know. Has anyone been touching you?" The interrogator was Mrs. McCord. Mrs. Kenny sat dumbly.

Alice just sobbed.

"Well, has there?"

Alice gulped hard and managed to say "no" between sobs.

Silence held for a full minute and then Mrs. McCord's hand shot out, slapping the girl on the face. Mrs. Kenny did nothing. She could have been made out of wood.

More sobs came from Alice and then she blurted out, "Janet."

"What?"

"Janet Stock. Sometimes when her mother and da' are out at work we go to her place. And . . ."

"Yes. Speak up!"

" . . . and we take turns touching ourselves and then touch each other." Alice started to cry again. "We don't mean any harm, really!"

Mrs. McCord turned to Mrs. Kenny. "So that's where she caught the disease!" She uttered the observation as if she had been pronouncing a judicial decision. And, as if passing sentence, she added, "Well, tomorrow you must take the girl to Dr. Howson for an examination."

The next morning, Thursday, June 21, Mrs. McCord brought Mrs. Kenny and Alice to Dr. Howson. She ushered them in like a goose with goslings, and insisted on being present while Alice was examined. Dr. Howson asked Mrs. Kenny if that were all right, and the mother just nodded.

The physician asked Alice the same questions she had been asked the preceding day and received the same answers: she had acquired the disease from Janet Stock. He was willing to accept that, and was about to tell the girl to put her shift back on, when Mrs. McCord put a question. "Your mother wants to know, Alice, if you ever have been in the company of boys?"

"No, ma'am."

Mrs. McCord continued, putting questions as if from Alice's mother. "She means, girl, have boys ever done anything to you, touching or anything else?"

"No,no ma'am."

"Well, you dirty little girl, I have a suggestion to make." Dr. Howson stood up, as if to stop Mrs. McCord, but she was a Juggernaut. "You have been making free with some man, have you not?"

Alice broke down and, amidst tears, said yes, but that he had only touched her and not put his thing into her, and that he had only done that to Janet, and that he had called them pretty little girls and given them a York shilling. Mrs. McCord sternly asked for the man's name and Alice gave it.

Immediately thereafter, the three females left Dr. Howson and went to the police magistrate to lodge an information against Ogle R. Gowan. The magistrate, George Gurnett, proceeded with great propriety and efficiency. He had the girl examined by a police physician and set two police officers to investigate the case.

The result was that on Thursday, June 28, Ogle Gowan found

himself on trial in the Toronto police court for criminal assault. This was an omnibus charge, used for everything from mugging to assault with intent to commit buggery. In our day, the charge probably would have been either sexual assault or child molestation.

The Toronto police court, of the mid-1800s, was a cross between an eighteenth-century English assize and a bear garden. It was a court of summary jurisdiction, which meant that a single officer of the court, the police magistrate, made all the decisions. In 1851, a full-time stipendiary magistrate had been appointed and he sat in judgement on an amazing range of cases: vagrancy; drunk and disorderly conduct; an endless variety of assault cases; and violations of the city's by-laws and licensing regulations.

The court was conducted with a minimum of formality. Most defendants did not have counsel and when lawyers were present they did not wear wigs or gowns, only ordinary suits. Attorneys, as well as their clients, frequently engaged in slanging matches that would not have been permitted in a higher court. The dock always was full of prostitutes, drunks, and debtors, many of whom appeared at such frequent intervals that they became old acquaintances, almost friends, of the policemen and magistrate who dealt with them. All this made the court one of the best bits of theatre in the city, and the galleries were often packed with spectators who clapped and hooted as if they were in a music hall.

This Hogarthian ambience was reinforced by the physical character of the court. Toronto city council, while happy to have the police court housed in a separate building of its own, was reluctant to spend any money on it or even to keep it clean. As one observer noted, the physical surroundings were better calculated to inspire nausea than awe. The stipendiary magistrate complained that the courtroom usually was chock-full of people in an unclean condition, and that the air was so bad that it was undermining his health.

In a case such as Gowan's, the magistrate had a wide variety of alternatives. He could find the defendant either guilty or not guilty, or he could dodge the issue by bringing in a Scotch-verdict of insufficient evidence, or he could recommend that the case be taken over by a higher and more formal criminal court. Obviously, in a court such as this, everything depended upon who the magistrate was.

In this case, it was George Gurnett, sixty-eight-years old, an

Englishman by birth and a former journalist. Gurnett was a long-time city alderman and had twice been mayor of Toronto, most recently in 1848-1850. (He had lost an earlier mayorality bid, in 1841, when it was discovered he was renting out one of his houses to a brothel-keeper.) Gurnett had been a strong Tory party adherent before being stipendiary magistrate in 1851. During the mid-1830s, he had been an ally of Ogle's, when Gowan was trying to woo the York Orangemen away from their infatuation with William Lyon Mackenzie. In the 1840s, however, Gurnett had quarreled with several leading Orangemen, so what his feelings were towards Gowan is uncertain, as, indeed, is the entire question of whether or not he wanted to do justice in this particular case.

Two people, however, certainly did not wish to see justice done: John A. Macdonald, and, of course, Ogle R. Gowan. Gowan, despite his recent sulks, was still a trustworthy Conservative and an old friend. Most important, his conviction on such a tawdry charge would be a major embarrassment for both the Party in general and for Macdonald in particular. Fortunately for Gowan, Macdonald was serving as attorney general, as well as Premier, and this gave him some direct leverage. As attorney general, he was expected to name a Crown Observer who would report to the higher courts on whether or not a major prosecution should be launched in this case. Macdonald did not demur when it was suggested that Richard Dempsey, a longtime barrister and even-longer-time henchman of Ogle Gowan, be appointed Crown Observer. This virtually guaranteed that, whatever might happen in police court, there would be no further trial. Which is to say that the damage to the Tory party would be limited. In this way, Macdonald virtually cleared his political debts to Ogle.

Despite the rigging of the Crown Observer, Gowan had a serious problem in the lower court — he had two witnesses against him. Thus, he clandestinely hired an Orange lawyer of protean ability, one A.D. McDougall, and gave him simple orders: try to stop both of the girls from testifying, but in any case prevent at least one of them from appearing.

McDougall called first on Mr. and Mrs. Kenny. They would not talk until Mrs. McCord joined them, but then they were easy to deal with. Mr. Kenny was an Irish Protestant and had been in military service. McDougall reminded them of what a fine man Mr. Gowan was, how much he had done for the Protestant cause, and suggested that their daughter was a delicate girl and that the trial might be harmful for her. In fact, wasn't it likely that someone other than Mr. Gowan had molested her? The Kennys, neither one of them of strong character, seemed to agree.

The Stock family was a harder lot. Mrs. Stock believed her own daughter's statements about Gowan and wanted revenge on the "filth" who had seduced her. McDougall then tried another tactic, going back to the Kenny tenement to enlist Mrs. McCord in his cause. For a small fee, she called several times on Mrs. Stock and tried to convince her to take young Janet to the country, along with Alice Kenny, for the duration of the trial. It would be best for your child if all this were not made public, she advised. (Never mind that Mrs. McCord had contributed greatly to the imbroglio by raising Gowan's name in the first place.) Would a little money help? If so, Mrs. McCord would find four or five dollars to pay for the trip.

Mrs. Stock made no promises.

Therefore, the first question to be answered when the police court convened for Ogle's trial on June 28 was whether there would be one, two, or no witnesses against him. The courtroom was packed and, as Magistrate Gurnett feared, smelled like the monkey-cage in a travelling circus. The prosecution was led by a police investigator named McMichael, with support from Sergeant Ferris, a large, laconic man from County Antrim, who had done most of the legwork on the case. Gowan was represented by a lawyer who answered to the apposite name of Boomer. Because of his extensive courtroom experience, Ogle planned to conduct much of his defence himself.

Magistrate Gurnett gavelled the court to order. He knew it was not going to be an easy trial. First he asked if the complainant and witnesses were present? Mr. McMichael answered that Janet Stock and her mother were. There, pointedly, he stopped.

"And is the Kenny girl here?"

"Her mother is."

"And the girl?"

"Not at present, sir."

Applause and hoots of derision came from the gallery at this revelation. Ogle smiled broadly. With only one uncorroborated witness, he had a strong chance of escaping punishment.

"Sergeant Ferris! To the bench, please!" The magistrate was miffed. "Did you not serve the summons on the girl and on her parents?"

Sergeant Ferris, a man of some dignity, would not permit himself to be hectored. With exaggerated slowness, he explained, "I handed the summons to Mrs. Kenny. She wept. She said that she would never be compelled to prosecute Mr. Gowan. She said that she had never made a voluntary statement against Mr. Gowan, and that they had been forced to say it. She averred, sir, that Mr. Gowan was not the right man and that the man who hurt her child has left the city."

"Did she name this man?"

"No, sir."

"That may be and then it may not be. It is for the court to determine guilt. But where is the Kenny child? And where is her father?"

At that point A.D. McDougall arose. "If it please the court, I appear here on behalf of Kenny, whose wife is in the court."

Though this did not satisfy the magistrate, he calculated that he had better get on with the trial before the crowd in the galleries became restive. He gave a nod to Mr. McMichael, who began the prosecution. Instead of calling a witness, he turned on McDougall, attorney for the Kennys. "Mr. Kenny is not here I presume?"

"No, I cannot tell where Mr. Kenny is now. I saw him fishing on one of the wharfs a couple of days ago."

McMichael looked skeptical. "And where, Mr. McDougall, is the child, the girl Kenny?"

"I do not know where she is at present." "Rubbish!" someone called from the gallery. McDougall blushed red and stammered, "I heard she had gone to several places. The last time I saw the child she was playing up at her father's house, but I cannot say anything about why she is not here."

Sergeant Ferris rose and, tiptoeing up to the prosecutor, whispered something to him. McMichael framed his next question on the basis of what the sergeant had told him. "Is it true, Counsellor McDougall, that the girl was brought down to your own house last week?"

The courtroom exploded, for this was tantamount to an accusation that the attorney had suppressed evidence. Magistrate Gurnett called for order and McDougall, careful not to leave himself open to a perjury charge, answered, "I cannot tell whether the mother brought the child down to my house or not. I was not there. But on Sunday I asked the mother where the child was and I have never asked her since."

Seeing where this line of questioning was leading, Counsellor Dempsey, who was supposed to be sitting as a strictly neutral Crown Observer, interfered. Mr. McMichael, he said, was taking up the court's time in asking useless questions. The magistrate disagreed, however, and Counsellor McDougall was forced to stumble along, all the while trying to keep from losing his licence to practice law. "I know nothing about the child and know nothing about her going away from Toronto nor where she went to." He was perspiring now and compulsively brushed back his off-red hair, time and time again. *"I do not want to incriminate myself."* He was nearly screaming. "I had *nothing* to do with the removal of the girl from Toronto. I will not admit that I ever heard any conversation in my presence as to getting the child removed." When McDougall at last was permitted to stand down, he slumped gratefully into a chair and mopped his brow.

Prosecutor McMichael called Mrs. Stock. Instead of going into the question of sexual molestation at this point, he spent his time laying the groundwork for a possible charge of subornation of justice. "Were there proposals made to you to remove your child from Toronto, instead of letting her give evidence?"

"Yessir. I was asked to allow her to go away, along with Alice Kenny. Mrs. McCord, a friend of the Kennys, offered me money to allow her to go. She said she would take the children and pay for everything."

"When did this occur?"

"Last Monday or Tuesday."

"Did you consent to let your child go?"

"I did not."

What indeed had happened to Alice Kenny, the second key witness? A little later in the trial, her mother took the stand. She spoke quietly and was on the verge of tears. Several times, Magistrate Gurnett had to interrupt the questioning to ask her to repeat her answers. "Mrs. Kenny," the prosecutor began, "do you know where your daughter is?"

"Yes, I mean, no. That is, my husband took the child out fishing on Tuesday morning and now it is Thursday, and they have never come back since."

"Do you have any idea why he did that?"

"He said that she was far too young to bring into court. And that she would only get a bad reputation by being seen with that Stock girl, who has a bad character."

"Mrs. Kenny, is there any chance that your husband is not fishing, but that he has taken the girl someplace in the countryside?"

"No. He took no trunks with him. He went fishing, I know."

"Are you not afraid that he and the girl have drowned"

"No. No, he has not. He is in the habit of going away now and then. He often is gone several days when he is at the fishing. He sleeps on the boat if the night is calm, or ties to some pier or dock if it is not."

"Was Mr. McDougall, the attorney, ever at your house about the child?"

"Yes."

"Did he ever offer you money to take the child away?"

"No."

There, for juridical purposes, the trial ended. There was only one direct witness, a twelve-year-old girl whose testimony would be tied in knots by a clever cross-examiner. Even though there was an extremely high probability that the second direct witness had been suborned, there was not enough evidence on this point to charge either McDougall or Gowan.

But the rest of the trial ruined Gowan for life. Even though the evidence subsequently presented by Mrs. Stock, Mrs. Kenny, the voluble Mrs. McCord and by Dr. Howson, all necessarily was indirect and not sufficient for conviction, it permanently besmirched him. The trial proceedings became a circus. The harridan McCord was so vigorously rude in her replies to interrogatories that the magistrate had to warn her that she would be sent to gaol herself, unless she learned to behave. That possibility brought cheers from the galleries. During the remainder of the trial, two interesting developments arose. One was that an alternate suspect was introduced, namely the gardener of Sir Adam Wilson, the Mayor of Toronto! This, like a good joke at a music hall, brought down the house. It was not seriously pursued as a possibility, however. Second, at one point, Gowan took over his own defence and said that the whole matter was a conspiracy against him from beginning to end, and that Sergeant Ferris was at the heart of it. Ferris stood up and asked to be allowed to explain what his investigation actually had shown; that is, he asked to be called as a witness. Immediately, Gowan and his counsel, the resonant Boomer, objected. New witnesses could be introduced at this point only with the acquiescence of the defendant and his counsel. The magistrate agreed with this argument, and thus a major source of evidence was elided.

Ogle himself conducted the cross-examination of twelve-year-old Janet Stock and although she unwaveringly identified him as the man who had molested her, Gowan made a great deal about her having the time of day wrong, and of the "fact" that one could not get in and out of his house without being seen and that his domestics were "never absent." This kind of pettifogging was the sort of thing that would have worked well in, say, a homicide defence, where precise timing and locale are crucial, but in a child molestation case, the central matter is one of identification and on that the girl had no doubts.

As the trial edged towards its conclusion, magistrate Gurnett increasingly wore an expression of extreme distaste, He could stand the physical smell of his courtroom, but the emerging moral stench of this case was abhorrent. Still, he knew that the case against Gowan was unprovable on the basis of the available testimony and he said as much. "No jury will convict Mr. Gowan on the evidence adduced."

Before Gurnett transformed this opinion into an official verdict, he took the extraordinary step of calling a short recess, during which he called Counsellor Dempsey, the Crown Observer, into his chambers. They agreed what the verdict should be. "It has been my duty," Gurnett told the expectant courtroom audience, "to review the evidence before giving a decision. I have discussed this matter with the Crown Observer. It is my opinion, and he concurs in it, that there is nothing left for me to do but dismiss the case. I am obliged to do this because no jury would convict Mr. Gowan on the basis of the available evidence."

This was the most damning acquittal possible. Granted, Ogle got off scot-free, and had the further comfort of Gurnett's having announced, in open court, that the Crown Observer saw no reason to take the matter to a higher criminal court. This was a great relief, certainly, but a long way from a verdict of "not guilty." Whatever his failings as a jurist, Gurnett's judgement actually carried an important sub-text: in effect, that even though there was only one direct witness to the crime, and she a juvenile whose testimony had been attacked hard by legally-sophisticated adults, even so one could not adjudge Ogle Gowan "not guilty." The only judgement that could be made was that there was not enough evidence for a jury to convict him.

Anyone with even average awareness, anyone from John A. Macdonald down to the Orangeman who read the newspapers, understood what the results of the trial meant — the end of Ogle Gowan's public career.

Soon after his trial, Gowan loudly made it known he was a victim of a conspiracy and that the chief conspirator was the demon tailor, George Nicoll. Hence, five days after the trial Nicoll, who was walking through the streets of Toronto, was set upon by a group of Orangemen. They started to rough him up, but a constable appeared and dealt with them.

Ogle sent a long, self-pitying letter, full of legal quibbles to the *Globe*, which did him the disservice of printing the entire document, for the letter raised more questions than it answered.

The most telling summary of the case was found in a letter to the editor, written by George Nicoll. He asked a devastating series of questions:

> — why was the witness, Kenny, who it seems had knowledge of the crime and charges against Gowan allowed to abscond?
> — who furnished the money to pay her expenses?
> — was her evidence in favour of Gowan or against him? If against him, he had an interest in her absence; if for him, why did he not secure her? He has friends enough in the Police that would have prevented her escape by either steamboat, stage or railroad.
> — let Mr. Gowan bring her back. If he is innocent it is a duty he owes himself . . . till he does, he must lie under the censure of having spirited her away to prevent her giving evidence.

And, to this, one must add the editorial query of the *Globe*: why did not Gowan prosecute for perjury the girl, Janet Stock, and her mother, for they had testified against him? Certainly, in the recent past, Ogle had been willing to use perjury charges as an instrument to try to clear his name.

There could be no reply to these queries. Ogle had finally been hung out to dry.

For a time, he put a brave face on things. When, in early September 1860, the Toronto *Freeholder* published a report that he was about to be required to resign his seat as a member of Parliament because of his morals, he quickly had his supporters in Leeds and Grenville North organize counter-measures. The Conservative Party in the township of Elmsley called a meeting to pledge their faith in Gowan: they did not believe a word of the charges put forward "by an abandoned female." They would vote for Gowan at the next election, and they requested his presence at a public banquet. He wrote them from Nebo Lodge, expressing pleasure that they would not accept "the attacks made upon my character by the unfortunate and misguided juvenile . . . . " He would be pleased to attend a banquet some time in the future.

That, though, was whistling in the dark. Ogle knew that he had no chance of winning an election, even in an overwhelmingly Tory area and, in any case, he had long wanted to retire into a safe patronage job. The difficulty now was that John A. Macdonald already had paid most of his debt to Gowan by his benevolent neglect of the sexual assault case. And Macdonald was disgusted by the Gowan story. Ogle would not get much from him.

In February 1861, a rumour spread briefly that Gowan would be made registrar of Grenville county, but no offer was forthcoming and, to save face, Ogle announced publicly that he would not accept the post if it were offered.

An election was probable in the early summer that year and as it approached, Gowan became worried. It would be a waste of time to run again. He needed a job badly. Would John A. Macdonald abandon him completely? No. This was not because Macdonald felt any residual warmth towards his old friend, but because he wished to be absolutely sure that Ogle did *not* run again. To prevent this, he offered Gowan a job as inspector of money orders in the post office. This was a position that Ogle would have loftily refused a year earlier, but now he grabbed it. Even after accepting this post, he tried to get more out of Macdonald, but the great man would have nothing more to do with him. Gowan complained bitterly and wrote a spiteful letter to Macdonald. "This is probably the last letter I shall ever address to you," he scribbled in February 1862, and there the friendship ended.

Ogle did not stay long in the post office, because his Orange allies on the Toronto Corporation, waxing sentimental about the Old Master, found him a local plum: he became inspector of licenses for the City of Toronto at $1,200 a year. This entailed his walking about for two or three hours a day and checking that taverns and spirit groceries were licensed and meeting various bylaws. There were myriad opportunities for making the odd dollar by winking at violations. The job was easy, but even so, in 1867 he hired an assistant at his own expense to do most of the work, just like an indolent clergyman in an eighteenth-century English parish would use his curate as a hireling.

Thus, once he was out of Parliament, Ogle had plenty of time on his hands. On a typical day he would call in at city hall about eleven in the morning and then would walk to Orange headquarters, where he was treated as an esteemed elder statesman. After a lunch at some tavern, which of course was free to the city's inspector of licences, he would amble homewards, where, with nothing else to do, he would listen to the clock tick, watch the day end, and brood. No sex: his disastrous trial for sexual assault had finally broken this thralldom to the flesh.

Only Ogle's sons and his son-in-law Thomas R. Ferguson brought him much pleasure. Nassau was an especial joy, because he had become a virtual missionary for Orangeism and for another Protestant society, the British Order of Good Templars, a temperance group. He lectured all over Ontario on these causes, and founded both Orange Lodges and temperance societies as far east as New Brunswick and Nova Scotia. Nassau spent the late winter of 1865 lecturing in the Maritimes and had only just returned to Ontario when disaster struck. He was travelling on a Grand Trunk Railway train from Sarnia when it left the track and rolled down a forty-five degree embankment. Nassau's spine was broken and, from the third rib downwards, he was paralyzed. A telegram was sent immediately to Ogle who came at once, accompanied by his brother-in-law, Dr. Charles Buchanan, and by Nassau's brother, Harcourt. Although Nassau was conscious and recognized all the relatives, he nevertheless died. The one comfort was that he had not been in pain, for the snapping of his spine had cut off all sensation from his lower body.

As an analgesic for his emotional pain, Ogle re-married, but the new Mrs. Gowan (*née* Alice Hitchcock) was little more than a housekeeper to him. There were times Ogle could not even remember her name. The only person who still could command his undivided attention for any length of time was Thomas Ferguson. With him, Gowan would talk Tory politics and recall old victories and even older grievances.

Unfortunately, whatever slight improvement in his spirits his marriage achieved, it was quite offset in that same year by an event of the first magnitude: the Fenian invasion of Canada. Silly, inept, half-comic as the Fenians were, Ogle saw in them a Sign of the Times, an indication that the anti-Christ and his army of Philistines were preparing to smite the unwary in their beds. Gowan spent more and more time with his Bible now and he concentrated on the Book of Revelation. It fitted the present times he knew.

He tottered into his seventies, a shuffling old man, frequently unshaven and, because his feet pained him, often in those carpet slippers. Early in 1874, his post as tavern inspector was cancelled. He pressed hard for some back salary owed to him, and then was content to withdraw to Nebo Lodge. He knew that the end was coming, and he looked forward to seeing Frances and Nassau again.

A brief spark came to his eye in the fall of 1875, when a group of Catholic "pilgrims" walked in procession through the streets of Toronto, visiting several churches in one day. It was a "Jubilee Year" declared by Pius IX, and believers were promised a special indulgence and escape from all temporal punishments for their sins, if they would make fifteen church visits over a set period of time. The first day of these pilgrimages led to a riot. Gowan, nicely cleaned up by his wife, attended a meeting at the St. Lawrence Hall, presided over by the mayor of Toronto. He spoke, deploring the rioting and, simultaneously, warning the Catholics not to conduct any more pilgrimages or bloodshed might ensue.

Further riots did follow and they reminded Ogle of old times.

On a Sunday morning early in August 1876, Ogle was being taken to St. George's church for morning service when he had a cerebral stroke. He was paralyzed throughout most of his body, but he could speak and, though very tired, was lucid. His family and representatives of the Orange Order gathered at his bedside. His old physician and brother-in-law Charles Buchanan (himself apparently healthy, but actually only two months from his own death), attended him. Ogle died, aged seventy-three, on Monday August 21, 1876, and was buried four days later. His funeral, one paper said, was attended by so many men in strange robes, aprons, sashes, and clanging metals that it would have done honour to the last lay cardinal of the Roman Catholic Church.

EPILOGUE

The Gowan Legacy

OGLE GOWAN'S entire life was a drive for respectability that his actions continually repudiated. Yet, if he did not find respectability in life, he achieved it in death through the successful achievements of his relatives and descendants. His cousin, James Gowan, became nineteenth-century Canada's most respected jurist. At the time of James's appointment to the bench in 1843, he was the youngest judge in the British Empire. He was John A. Macdonald's counselor and draftsman on legal matters and, after Confederation, oversaw the revision of the system of Canadian statute law. If, in later life, James shied away from admitting much knowledge of Ogle Gowan, the family name nevertheless benefitted, particularly because of James's being knighted and being named to the Senate.

Two of Ogle's daughters, Frances and Emily, married into the Ferguson family of Cookstown, Ontario and that family rose to unimpeachable respectability. Thomas Ferguson, husband of Frances Gowan, was an MP, and Tory party stalwart. Emily Gowan married his brother, Isaac, and through their line rose two of the most respectable figures in twentieth-century Ontario. One of these was their son (Ogle's grandson), George Howard Ferguson, political fixer and Tory Premier of Ontario from 1923-1930. His sister, Emily Gowan Ferguson Murphy, wife of an Anglican clergyman, became one of the stars of Canadian women's history. Under the name of "Janey Canuck" she wrote successful travel books and articles. She was an early proponent of suffrage, and in 1916 was appointed police magistrate for Edmonton, the first woman magistrate in the Empire. It was she who brought the famous case to the United Kingdom Privy Council that in 1929 resulted in the ruling that women are persons under the Canadian constitution and thus are eligible for all political offices. It is fascinating to see how in four generations, from Hunter Gowan to Emily Murphy, a bloodline could go from a hellbent bigotry, that everyone would like to forget, to a feminist icon, immortalized on a postage stamp.

Respectable indeed, and as the real Ogle. R. Gowan faded into folk-memory, his life became more and more respectable. A recent memoir of one of his descendants, for example, has accepted with credulity the family tradition that Ogle was a "wealthy politician"; the owner of a country estate of four hundred acres; the "Father of the House of Commons"; and, because of his journalistic career, the "father of the press" in central Canada. Ogle, a man of strong imaginary powers, would have loved this gloss on his life.

In Ireland, within twenty miles or so of the former Gowan estate, Mount Nebo, the family name is remembered still, and there are Gowan collaterals who are well thought of by both Protestants and Catholics. But Hunter Gowan himself remains sufficiently alive in the folk-memory that there are people who will not mention his name with first clearing their throat and spitting.

By an historical irony that Ogle Gowan would have hated, Mount Nebo eventually passed into the hands of the Benedictines who, for a time, ran a fashionable Catholic boarding school there. One of the most famous students of that institution was Sean MacBride, a man who in a protean career managed to be, during the 1930s, Commander-in-Chief of the Irish Republican Army; a virulent anti-Protestant; later, the head of Amnesty International; and, finally, winner of the Lenin Prize and the Nobel Peace Prize. Rechristened Mount St. Benedict, the Gowan estate became a monument to the triumph of Irish catholicism and nationalism over protestantism and loyalism.

In the New World, the Gowan legacy was more enduring, for, in Canada, loyalism and protestantism prevailed. Ogle Gowan was only a highly visible and influential part of a larger phenomenon, and his obsession with Catholics was part of an attitude that pervaded much of Protestant Ontario in the nineteenth century and, in a vestigial form, continues to exist in the twentieth. Most modern historians and social scientists have played down the Protestant-Catholic split, in part because it offends against the academic sense of rationality, and in part because the fissure does not fit easily into present-day analytic and ideological categories. Therefore, the legacies in our own time of this nineteenth-century social division often are missed. Witness, thus, the surprise of a contemporary political scientist who, after spending scores of thousands of dollars in survey research, learned what anyone living in rural Ontario could have told him for the price of a cup of coffee: that Protestants usually vote Tory, Catholics vote Liberal or NDP. The stream of religious division runs quietly and underground. It becomes weaker year by year, but it still is real, and its origin can be traced clearly and unambiguously to the British Isles and, most especially, to Ireland.

Of course, Ireland was not the only fountainhead of religious tension. One can scarcely forget that the French-Canadian presence in the country was also an important stimulus to anti-Catholic agitation. Moreover, Scotland and England hardly had exemplary records of inter-faith amity (at mid-nineteenth-century, the United Kingdom Parliament had responded to the Catholic church's establishment of a diocesan structure in England, with the notorious Ecclesiastical Titles Act). However, one must remember that the chief source of what is misleadingly called the "English-Canadian" population of Ontario was Ireland. Until the 1850s, emigrants from Ireland to British North America exceeded in number the total of emigrants from England and Scotland *combined*. In Ontario, the Irish were the largest ethnic group from the early 1830s to at least the late 1880s. In the enumeration of 1871 (the last census of Ogle Gowan's lifetime) somewhat over one-in-three (34.5 percent) of Ontario's population, listed Irish as their primary ethnic affiliation. Although persons of Irish Catholic and of Irish Protestant backgrounds differed in many ways, they had their origin as components of a single, sectarian system, and it was their relationship that made the Irish, considered as a single ethnic group, so influential in this regard. Ogle Gowan, by introducing the Orange Order, influenced not only Irish Protestants, but also Irish Catholics, for he triggered a well-programmed response on the part of the latter.

In another light, it is possible to view the Irish Protestants and Irish Catholics as two separate ethnic groups. From this viewpoint, the Irish Protestants (who comprised roughly two-thirds of the Irish ethnic cohort), are especially significant. During most of the nineteenth century, persons of Irish Protestant ethnicity in Ontario, equalled or exceeded both the English and the Scots, but their numerical preponderance is not as important as was the character of their cultural baggage. The Irish Protestants were the perfect Upper Canadians, trained by their experience in the Old Country to revere the Crown, and Constitution, to exalt Law over justice, to be anti-republicans and thus Canadian nationalists, all the while invoking the symbols, flags, and ritual of Old Country loyalism.

They were also predisposed to become historically invisible. This stemmed from their dual historical identity: on the one hand, they thought of themselves as being Irish, but, simultaneously, they were British. They willingly lost themselves in the "English-Canadian" identity; they did not mind being called British or English or having their political beliefs presented as being those of the English constitution.

When Ogle Gowan organized his Irish Protestant followers and then bonded them with English and Scots Protestants in the Orange Lodge, he was performing one of the central acts in the creation of the "English-Canadian" identity. As the single largest voluntary society in nineteenth-century Ontario, the Orange Order was influential in purveying the *mélange* of British Colonialism, Protestantism, Loyalism, and Constitutionalism, that was the kernel of the dominant Upper Canadian mind-set. But, simultaneously, what was occuring in hundreds of individual Orange Lodges was only a synecdoche of a process that was taking place in thousands of churches, friendly societies, and civic groups. Canadian historians have done an excellent job of tracing the intricacies of party formation during the nineteenth century, but too often, in concentrating on the veneer of high-level politics, they have overlooked a forgotten fundamental sub-stratum of popular realities. The Order and its fusion on an Irish-Protestant base of an Upper Canadian *mentalité*, was both influential in itself and a metaphor of a larger, more pervasive phenomenon.

Gowan lost control of the Orange Order in the mid-1850s, just when it was coming into full stride as a patronage network. For roughly eight decades — until, approximately the end of World War II — it was hard to get anywhere in Toronto politics or civic life, or obtain even the smallest patronage job in many rural areas, unless one were a member of the Order, or at least well-spoken of by its members. During the 1930s, one could not expect to become even a Toronto corporation binsman without the Sash's imprimatur. Over half of Toronto's mayors through the years have been

Orange, an amazingly high percentage, considering the Order's sharp decline after the Second World War.

In a sense, the Order dwindled because it became redundant. In the 1940s, '50s, and '60s, the Order's principles were better and more directly served by a more efficient machine: the provincial Tory party. What had once been Protestant-Irish and Orange, now was simply part of the general political culture of Ontario.

Sometimes politicans, no less than historians, forget the historical roots of present realities and get into trouble. In 1985, more than four decades of Tory rule in Ontario came to an end because Conservative politicans forgot the limits on their behaviour set by their Orange heritage. To their great surprise, their plan to provide full funding for separate (meaning, effectively, Catholic) schools, resulted in a voters' revolt, led by Protestant religious leaders. The Tories, trying to escape from their Orange legacy, lost heavily. Anyone familiar with the life and times of Ogle R. Gowan could have told them that that would happen.

AFTERWORD: # A NOTE ON SOURCES

THE READER of a fictional biography has the right to ask how much actually happened and how much is made up? The principal characters all existed, looked and acted, pretty much the way that I have depicted them. In the case of minor characters, whose actions are known but whose name is lost from the historical record, I have created an identity: the chief example is the "Recording Angel" of Dun and Company, whose credit reports on Ogle R. Gowan are found in Baker Library at the Harvard School of Business, but whose name is nowhere recorded. The odd minor character, such as Eliza McCormick, is moved a bit in time, but, other than that, also comes from the historical record. The people who count in this book, and particularly Ogle Gowan and his family, are as accurate as I can make them within the limits of the available evidence.

So, actually, the reader here is not dealing with anything daunting. A conventional biography (either a scholarly or a popular one), like a fictional biography, consists of a series of statements about historical personages that have varying levels of probability of being accurate and true. In a scholarly biography, these are clearly labelled with phrases such as "it is highly probable that . . . ," "it is believed that . . . . ," and "one conjectures that . . . . " In popular biographies, these labels often are left out. But in all cases — fictional biography, scholarly biography, and popular biography — one is dealing with a series of informed guesses about how real people acted in the past, nothing more.

If the reader looks up Professor Hereward Senior's article on Ogle Gowan in the *Dictionary of Canadian Biography* he or she will note a number of differences between the story as presented here and that version: such as Gowan's illegitimate birth, his frequent unethical and illegal behaviour, his expulsion from the Orange Order in Ireland, and his political demise after the child molestation case. On all of these matters, the historical evidence is clear. It was only a lapidary tactfulness on Professor Senior's part, not any deficiency in historical craft, that led him to exclude these facts from the DCB. I am, indeed, grateful for the assistance the he so kindly gave me on this project.

Two other general matters: occasionally I have intentionally used anachronisms. These instances are limited, but in the case of the "Anglican church" a term not widely employed in the last century, and of the odd political word — "lobbying" for example — their economy makes them acceptable, for their early nineteenth-century alternatives are cumbersome. As for dialogue, people did *not* speak exactly as I have depicted. Anyone who has read a verbatim transcript of a present-day conversation knows that it reads badly and, despite its literal accuracy, lacks literary authenticity. What someone writing modern fiction or good journalism does, is filter out the accidental and extraneous elements in a conversation, leaving the substance. With historical dialogue one not only does that, but also translates archaisms and idioms into something that, to the modern ear, sounds old, but still intelligible. This is important, because if we were to hear a recording of, for example, Ogle Gowan talking to a backwoods immigrant in the 1830s, we would understand, at most, half of what was being said. A complex technical linguistic literature on this matter exists, but if one wants to gain a feeling for one of the dialects that Gowan had to deal with, see my article, "Listening to Rural Language: Ballycarry, Co. Antrim, 1798-1817" in *Canadian Papers in Rural History* vol. 2 (1980), pp. 155-172.

The major sources of information on Ogle R. Gowan are the Ferguson family papers on the Public Archives of Canada, Ottawa, and the James and Ogle Gowan Papers in the Archives of Ontario, Toronto. Ogle Gowan's own writings are not without value. (The listing of them in Henry J. Morgan's *Bibliotheca Canadensis* [Ottawa: 1867] is wildly inaccurate.) See Ogle R. Gowan, *The Annals and defence of the Loyal Orange Institution of Ireland* (Dublin: 1825); *Orangeism: Its Origin and History* (Toronto: 1859); and his *Letter on Responsible Government* (Toronto: 1839). (The suggestion that this pamphlet actually was written in 1830 is a canard.)

CHAPTERS ONE AND TWO

There is a rich contemporary literature on the 1798 rising, much of it readable, and most of it highly partisan. Before engaging the literature, however, one would do well to consult the 1840 Ordnance Survey map of County Wexford, available in the National Library of Ireland, and the Linen Hall Library, Belfast. At a scale of six inches to the mile, it gives accurate topographical details, and is a necessity for making sense of what happened. As for contemporary accounts, see James Alexander, *Some Account of the First Apparent Symptoms of the Late Rebellion in the County of Kildare and an Adjoining Part of the King's Country . . . with a succinct Narrative of the . . . Rebellion in the County of Wexford* (Dublin: 1800); *Memoirs of Miles Byrne edited by his widow* (published in 1863, second ed. Dublin: 1906); James Gordon, *History of the Rebellion in Ireland in the Year 1798* (London: 1803); Richard Musgrave, *Memoirs of the Different Rebellions in Ireland*, 2 vols. (Dublin: third ed., 1802).

Of particular interest to Canadians is George Taylor's *A History of the Rise, Progress, Cruelties, and Suppression of the Rebellion in the County of Wexford in the Year 1798*. This was an eyewitness account, originally published in Ireland and republished (third edition) in Belleville, Canada West in 1864, by McKenzie Bowell, who eventually became Prime Minister of Canada (1894-1896). The dedication of this Canadian volume was to George Ogle Moore, then MP for the city of Dublin. The first two editions, published in Ireland, had been dedicated to "The Right Hon. George Ogle of imperishable memory."

Ogle Gowan's history of Orangeism includes a good deal of material on 1798 that is not available elsewhere. Like all contemporary evidence, it must be used with caution.

For modern historical works see: H.F.B. Wheeler, *The War in Wexford* (London: 1910); Charles Dixon *The Wexford Rising in 1798: Its Cause and its Course* (Tralee: 1955); Thomas Pakenham, *The Year of Liberty: The Great Irish Rebellion of 1798* (London: 1969). A very incisive article is Thomas Powell's "An economic factor in the Wexford Rebellion of 1798," *Studia Hibernica*, no. 16 (1976), pp. 140-157. There is a good deal of information on Wexford in the late eighteenth century in L.M. Cullen, *The Emergence of Modern Ireland, 1600-1900* (New York: 1981).

CHAPTER THREE

Ogle Gowan's illegitimacy was clearly established in a Chancery suit of the mid-1820s. See documents in the Public Record Office of Ireland, Dublin, M5584. In later years, Ogle claimed that his mother and Hunter Gowan had married, though this was patently false.

There are two versions of the Gowan family lineage drawn up by Ogle. These are found in the Ferguson papers, (PAC).Sir James Gowan had a more accurate version drawn up. See Henry H. Ardagh, *Life of Hon Sir James Robert Gowan, K.C.M.G., LL.D., Senator of Canada* (Toronto: 1911), pp. 275-328. See also, Arthur H. Colquhoun, *The Hon. James R. Gowan . . . A Memoir* (Toronto: 1894), pp. 10-13.

On early Orangeism, the standard work is Hereward Senior, *Orangeism in Ireland and Britain, 1795-1836* (London: 1966). A good deal of Orange material germane to Ogle's life is found in his *Annals and Defence* of 1825. For the structure and ritual of Orangeism, at the time Ogle was initiated, see *The Orange Institution: A slight sketch with an Appendix containing the rules and regulations of the Orange Societies of Great Britain and Ireland* (Dublin: 1813), found in the Henry Collection, the Queen's University of Belfast.

Material on the bandit, Captain Grant, and on Henry Gowan, is found in the family geneaologies mentioned above. For a scholarly reference to Grant, see James S. Donnelly, "Irish Agrarian Rebellion: The Whiteboys of 1769-1776," *Proceedings of the Royal Irish Academy*, ser. c., vol. 83, no. 12.

On early nineteenth-century Catholic sexual mores — which were markedly less strict than were post-famine patterns — see Sean Connolly, *Priests and People in Pre-famine Ireland, 1780-1845* (Dublin: 1982).

As mentioned above, in later life Ogle prepared two separate versions of his own genealogy. In the one he included the date of his marriage, 20 August 1823, but made no mention of children. In the other, the children of his marriage are mentioned (albeit with their birthdates cannily omitted) and the marriage date is specified as "in 1822"), a useful back-dating. In neither of these documents is his blood relationship to his wife clearly noted (see PAC, Ferguson papers).

CHAPTER FOUR

That Hunter Gowan had to get married is shown by comparing the birth date of his eldest child (see PAC, Ferguson papers) with the Dublin Diocesan Marrige License of John Hunter Gowan and Frances Norton, 1771. See *Twenty-Sixth Report of the Deputy Keeper of the Public Records of Ireland*, p. 356, and also Geneological Office, Dublin, MSS. I am grateful to Ms. P. Beryl Phair, Glasnevin, Co. Dublin for these references.

On Frances Gowan's family background, see the family geneological items mentioned above. On the Duffrey, her family's home locale, see Philip Herbert Hore (ed.), *History of the Town and County of Wexford* (London: 1900-1911, esp. vol. 6, p. 341). More evocative material is found in the locally specific work of Patrick Kennedy such as *The Banks of the Boro: A Chronicle of the County of Wexford* (London: 1867); *Legends of Mount Leinster . . . Bantry and Duffrey Traditions* (Dublin: 1855); *Evenings in the Duffrey* (Dublin: 1869). For an evaluation of Kennedy's work as a nineteenth-century folklore collector, see Caoimhin O'Danachair, "The Progress of Irish Ethnology, 1783-1982," *Ulster Folklife* (1983), pp. 5-6.

The prosecution of Ogle for theft of the silver cup is mentioned in the testimony found in *Interesting Trial* (Dublin edition), pp.4-5. See below for the full title of this pamphlet.

Concerning Hunter Gowan's last will and testament, see the documents in the Public Record Office, Dublin, T6293 and T13269. I am grateful to Ms. E. Ellis, Sandyford, Co. Dublin for these references. See also, the documents in the Public Record Office Dublin, M5585, items 1-5.

CHAPTER FIVE

Maurice Craig's *Dublin 1660-1860* (Dublin: 1969), remains the most vivid depiction of the city in which Ogle and Frances Gowan lived.

Sir Harcourt Lees's activities are sprinkled throughout the Dublin newspapers of the era. His variegated pamphlets are found in the Joly Collection of the National Library of Ireland.

An incomplete run of *The Antidote*, 1823-1825 is found in the British Library, Newspaper Division, London. Copies are found in Ireland as well, but I have been asked not to make their location public.

The letter to Lord Wellesley is found in draft form in PAC,

Ferguson papers. Various circumstantial details of Ogle's work with Protestant proseletizing societies are found in the Ferguson papers, PAC. For general background on the societies see Donald H. Akenson, *The Irish Education Experiment.* (London: 1970), pp 80-107.

On the internal politics of the Orange Order during the 1820s there is a good deal of material in Gowan's *Annals and Defence.*

The evidence for the 1826 Chancery case is found in remarkably full detail in "Dominical of Depositions of Witnesses," Public Record Office, Dublin, M5584 (2). Related items are found in M5584 (1), and (3-5). See also, as background, M5545. The depositions provide a good deal of insight into the tensions between the legitimate and illegitimate sections of Hunter Gowan's family.

CHAPTER SIX

The full title of the pamphlet of the 1827 trial is *Interesting Trial, Hopkins v. Gowan, Wexford Spring Assizes, March 14, 15, 1827, before the Hon. Judge Burton, and the following special jury* [twelve jurers are listed as well as counsel for both parties] (Dublin: 1827). It is found in the Joly Collection, National Library of Ireland. Comparison of the original with the versions printed in Upper Canada, show that the texts were the same, although William Lyon Mackenzie's 1837 version was prefaced with new material from the United Kingdom Parliamentary papers on Gowan's being expelled from the Order in Ireland.

Was the *Interesting Trial* accurate? I think yes, within the limits of the time. It was not a direct transcript of the testimony (this was before the era of shorthand writers in county courts), so it consists largely of indirect discourse, as do the reports of parliamentary debates of the era. Documentary evidence in the form of letters is quoted in full. For what it is worth, George Perkins Bull later gave a statement under oath, before justices of the peace, as to the accuracy of the transcription. Bull's record was not spotless (he had spent time in prison for libeling a Catholic priest), but he must have been fairly confident of the accuracy of his transcript, as he risked imprisonment for perjury if he were forsworn.

Given that one is dealing with a reasonably accurate trial transcript, that does not mean all the accusations made against Ogle were true, even though, manifestly, the jury was convinced of the validity of most of them. I have made my own judgements about the accuracy of various charges on the basis of the evidence presented and, especially, the degree to which it corresponds with the best external source of information, the Chancery depositions of 1826. I am grateful to John Blackwell, Kingston, Ontario, for advice in finding the various Upper Canadian versions of *Interesting Trial.*

On Daniel O'Connell, the classic study is Sean O'Faolain's *King of the Beggars* (Dublin: 1938). It is a piece of good history and fine literature.

On the Orange Order in the period, see Senior's study, cited above, and: *Rules and Regulations of the Orange Institution of Ireland adopted by the Grand Lodge at a general meeting held in the courthouse in Monaghan, Wednesday, the 9th of October 1828* (Dublin: 1828); and *Laws and Ordinances of the Orange Institution of Ireland* (Dublin: 1828). Both of these items are found in the archives library, PAC, Ottawa.

CHAPTER SEVEN

The baptism of Henry Samuel Eldon Gowan is recorded in the register of Christ Church, Montreal, held in the *Archives Nationales,* Montreal. I am grateful to Dr. Bruce Elliott for providing me with this reference. The item is accurate, but one should be aware that, because Ogle was an habitual liar, many of the public documents concerning him are not. For example, in the 1851 census he claimed that he was forty-three years of age when he actually was forty-eight, and that his wife Frances was forty, which would have meant that he was fifteen and she twelve years of age when they married ("Census of Brockville, West Ward, 1851," Archives of Ontario).

The outlines of the Orange organization Gowan established are found in *Rules and Regulations of the Orange Institution for British North America adopted by the Grand Lodge at its first meeting held in the Court House, Brockville, Upper Canada* (Brockville: 1830), in the archives library, PAC, Ottawa. There are interesting anecdotes of early Orange history in William Perkins Bull, *From the Boyne to Brampton* (Toronto: 1936) and in Walter McCleary, *One Man's Loyalty* (Toronto: 1953). On Arthur McClean see the article on his life in the *Society for the Study of Architecture in Canada. Selected Papers,* vol. 3 (1978), pp. 24-42. Snippets of Orange historical tradition in the early years are found in *Orangeism in Canada, 1830-1860,* by

Leslie H. Saunders (Toronto: 1973), and in the special edition of *The Sentinel* (the Orange newspaper), of 3 July 1930.

Work of a more scholarly character is found in the several essays of Hereward Senior, including: *Orangeism: The Canadian Phase* (Toronto: 1972); "Ogle Gowan, Orangeism, and the Immigrant Question, 1830-1833," *Ontario History*, vol. 66 (1974), pp. 193-206; "The Genesis of Canadian Orangeism," *Ontario History*, vol. 60 (1968), pp. 13-29; "Orangeism takes root in Canada," *Canadian Geneologist*, vol. 3, no. 1 (1981), pp. 13-22; and "The Character of Canadian Orangeism," in *Thought from the Learned Societies of Canada, 1961* (Toronto: 1961), pp. 177-189.

A series of articles, dealing with early Orangeism by an Orangeman and professional historian, W.B. Kerr, appeared in The *Sentinel*, 19 January 1939, 2 February 1939, 16 February 1939, 2 March 1939, 16 March 1939, 6 April 1939, 20 April 1939, 4 May 1939, and 18 May 1939. I am grateful to the archival authorities of the Grand Lodge of British North America, Toronto, for providing me with copies of these items, which are unavailable elsewhere.

A radically different analysis of the Order is presented by the historical geographers, Cecil J. Houston and William J. Smyth, *The Sash Canada Wore* (Toronto: 1980).

Statements about Gowan's landholding are based on the Leeds and Grenville County land records in the registry office, Brockville.

CHAPTER EIGHT

The political events involving William Lyon Mackenzie and those involving the Buell family of Reformers are found in local newspapers, but these should be supplemented by Graeme H. Patterson, "Studies in Election and Public Opinion in Upper Canada," (Ph.D. thesis, University of Toronto, 1969), and by Ian MacPherson, *Matters of Loyalty: the Buells of Brockville, 1830-1850* (Belleville: 1981). The Andrew Norton Buell papers in the Archives of Ontario, Toronto, contain a good deal of information relating to the political maneuvering of Gowan.

On the cholera epidemic, see: Geoffrey Bilson, *A Darkened House: Cholera in Nineteenth-Century Canada* (Toronto: 1980) and

C.M. Godfrey, *The Cholera Epidemic in Upper Canada, 1832-1866* (Toronto: 1968).

For both family and political matters concerning Gowan during the 1830s, see the James and Ogle Gowan Papers, Archives of Ontario, Toronto.

The facts on Gowan's expulsion from the Irish order and his uneasy position with the English Grand Lodge were revealed in a series of investigations conducted by the United Kingdom Parliament in the mid-1830s. The evidence included in these commissions involved Ogle's expulsion and the correspondence in 1832 referred to in the text. The entire set of reports is crucial background, but see especially, *Second Report from the Select Committee appointed to Enquire into the Nature, Character, Extent and Tendency of Orange Lodges, Associations or Societies in Ireland* (6 August 1835), Appendix, pp. 13-14; *Third Report from Select Committee . . . Orange Lodges, Associations or Societies in Ireland* (6 August 1835), p. 250; *Report from the Select Committee appointed to inquire into the Origin, Nature, Extent and Tendency of Orange Institutions in Great Britain and the Colonies* (7 September 1835), p.137, and appendix pp. 22,27, and 218.

The Edinburgh Review took a considerable interest in these parliamentary investigations and provided a long discussion of them (January 1836, pp. 471-522), wherein the curious matter of Ogle Gowan was given a good deal of attention (pp. 503-505).

The letter Gowan sent to the Orangeman in England is reproduced in Ian E. Wilson, "Ogle R. Gowan — Orangeman," *Douglas Library Notes*, vol. 17 (summer 1969), pp. 18-20.

CHAPTER NINE

The "witch of Plum Hollow," Jane Elizabeth Martin Harrison Barnes, was a well-known local figure. Born in Northern Ireland, she emigrated to New York City in 1819, later to upstate New York, and thence to the Johnstown district of Upper Canada (See L.P. information file, Special Collections, Queens University). She was a major character in Thaddeus W.H. Leavitt's novel, *The Witch of Plum Hollow* (Toronto: 1892).

For the social context of the political action in this chapter, and for specific references to sources, see Donald Harman Akenson, *The Irish In Ontario: A Study in Rural History* (Kingston and Montreal, 1984), pp. 139-201. Besides the Patterson thesis and the

MacPherson book cited above, particularly valuable is Elva Mr. Richards, "The Joneses of Brockville and the Family Compact," *Ontario History*, vol. 60 (1968), pp. 169-184.

The Gray case and the falsely-charged rape against Jonas Jones were the subject of remarkably full court reportage in the local press. The nineteenth-century press's fascination with legal matters is fortunate, given Gowan's propensity for legal problems.

CHAPTER TEN

Gowan's actions in Parliament and the reports resulting in his expulsion therefrom, are found in the *Journals of the House of Assembly* (of Upper Canada).

For an indication of the nature of the salacious correspondence between James Gowan and Frances Gowan, see James and Ogle Gowan papers, Archives of Ontario, 21 May 1836.

In addition to the Brockville papers, in this period the Kingston *Chronicle and Gazette* is useful on Gowan's activities.

On the political pact with Bishop Macdonnell, see Wilfred Kerr, "When Orange and Green United, 1832-1839: the Alliance of Macdonnell and Gowan," *Ontario Historical Society, Papers and Records*, vol. 34 (1942), pp. 34-42.

CHAPTER ELEVEN

Walter Cavendish Crofton's comments on Gowan are found in "Erinensis," (pseud.), *Sketches of the Thirteenth Parliament of Upper Canada* (Toronto: 1840), pp. 17-18.

Perkins Bull's oath as to the authenticity of the *Interesting Trial* was sworn before two J.P.s in Brockville on 29 June 1833. Bull sent it with a covering letter dated 19 June, 1837 to *Mackenzie's British, Irish, and Canadian* Gazette where it was published. It was also published in the *Brockville Record* 13 June 1837.

There is a mass of local material on the alarums of 1837-1838. Ogle Gowan himself wrote a history of the rebellion which, if somewhat self-serving, is still fairly perceptive and quite accurate. This was set in type, presumably at the *Statesman* office, with the thought of turning it eventually into a book. It is found bound in a scrapbook in the PAC Ferguson papers.

"Col. Gowan's March," and many of Gowan's militia papers are found in the PAC, Ferguson papers, while James Gowan's letter concerning Lord Durham is in the James and Ogle Gowan Papers, AO. For a sidelight see "Sir James Gowan, Sir John A. Macdonald, and the Rebellion of 1837," by J.K. Johnson, *Ontario History*, vol. 60 (June 1968), pp. 61-64. For more background, see Hereward Senior, "A bid for Rural Ascendancy: The Upper Canadian Orangemen, 1836-1840," *Canadian Papers in Rural History*, vol. 5 (1986), pp. 224-234. For other local material see: The F.P. Smith Papers, in the Archives of Ontario; the Sir George Arthur Papers, Queen's University; George F.G. Stanley, "The Battle of the Windmill," *Historic Kingston*, no. 3 (November 1954), pp. 41-56; Ernest Green, "The Song of the Battle of the Windmill," *Ontario Historical Society*, Papers and Records, vol. 36 (1944), pp. 43-45. Information, not complimentary to Gowan or the Loyalists, is found in Donald McLeod, *A Brief Review of the Settlement of Upper Canada* (Cleveland, Ohio: 1972), pp. 59-259.

CHAPTER TWELVE

The No Surrender Inn existed. See Edna Chant, *Beautiful Charleston* (Belleville: 1975).

On the relationships of Gowan, the government, and the Orange question see: Senior, *Orangeism: The Canadian Phase*, pp. 31-39; PRO, London, CO 42/462, p. 459 ff; and *Despositions from Sir George Arthur relating to Orange Lodges in Canada*, H.C. 1839 (542), xxxiv, and the *Journals of the Upper Canadian House of Assembly*.

An Important Letter on Responsible Government from Lieutenant-Col. Gowan, M.P.P. for the County of Leeds in Upper Canada (Toronto: 1839) is fairly widely available. The copy used here was supplied by Special Collections, Queen's University.

The Durham report is found in the United Kingdom parliamentary papers but is more easily accessible in the three-volume edition by C.P. Lucas (Oxford: 1912). Still highly serviceable are three articles published in the *Canadian Historical Review* on the anniversary of Durham's report: Chester New, "Lord Durham and the British Background of his Report," vol. 20 (June 1939), pp. 119-135; George W. Brown, "The Durham Report and the Upper Canadian Scene," *ibid.*, pp. 130-160; Chester Martin, "Lord Durham's Report and its consequences," *ibid.*, pp. 178-194.

CHAPTER THIRTEEN

For details on Dr. Charles Buchanan, in addition to the Ferguson and Gowan papers, see William Canniff, *The Medical Profession in Upper Canada 1783-1850* (Toronto: 1894), pp. 263-267.

On local government, and Gowan's part in the Johnstown districts see, in addition to local newspapers, William Jelly, *A Summary of the Proceedings of the Johnstown District Council, 1842-1849* (Brockville: 1929).

Kingston is described in Charles Dickens's *American Notes* (London: 1842), vol. II, pp. 194-195.

On the 1841 election see Gowan papers, AO and see Irving Abella, "The 'Sydenham Election' of 1841," CHR, vol. 47 (Dec. 1966), pp. 328-343.

Historic Kingston, the publication of the Kingston Historical Society, has too many articles on the city in this period to permit individual listing here. See, especially, George F.G. Stanley, "Kingston, and the Choice of Canada's Capital," *Historic Kingston*, no. 24 (March 1976), pp. 18-37. For a framework, see Donald Swainson, "Chronicling Kingston: An Interpretation," *Ontario History*, vol. 74 (December 1982), pp. 303-333.

According to the records of the L.O.L. of British American (Toronto Archives), John A. Macdonald became an Orangeman in 1841. The Orange archives have several mezzotints of him in full regalia.

The Grimason House which served Macdonald and Gowan so well still serves, now as the Royal Tavern on Princess Street, Kingston.

CHAPTER FOURTEEN

For Gowan's parliamentary activities see *Debates of the Legislative Assembly of United Canada 1841-1867* (ed.) Elizabeth Gibbs. This as-yet-uncompleted project deserves special mention, for it is nothing less than an attempt to reconstruct, from myriad newspaper reports, the life of the United Canadas Parliament.

On James Gowan's promotion, see Colquhoun, and Ardagh, mentioned earlier.

The correspondence with William Morris is in PAC, Ferguson papers.

The standard biography of John A. Macdonald is Donald Creighton, *John A. Macdonald*, 2 vols. (Toronto: 1955). It avoids mentioning Macdonald's Orange connections and plays down his relationship with Gowan. That Gowan and Macdonald were close in these years, is shown by the letters from Macdonald to Gowan in the Ferguson papers, PAC. See, "The Macdonald-Gowan Letters, 1847," by Frederick H. Armstrong, *Ontario History*, vol. 73 (March 1971), pp. 2-14.

On the psycho-sexual nature of the problems of Macdonald's first wife, I am grateful to Dr. James McSherry, Director of the Student Health Service, Queen's University, for sharing the results of his research.

The internal politics of the Orange Lodges are found in the Grand Lodge minutes, Orange Archives, Toronto. Many of these items (which were well printed) are found in the Baldwin Room, Toronto Public Library.

CHAPTER FIFTEEN

Ireland's Great Famine colours the history of the entire English-speaking world in this era. The most comprehensive study remains R. Dudley Edwards and T. Desmond Williams (eds), *The Great Famine. Studies in Irish History 1845-1852* (Dublin: 1956).

The Black Flag matter is depicted in *One Man's Loyalty*, pp. 73-82, and in the local press.

The Toronto fire and its rebuilding are described in two articles by Frederick Armstrong, "The First Great Fire of Toronto, 1849," *Ontario History*, vol. 53 (September 1961), pp. 201-221, and "The Rebuilding of Toronto after the Great Fire of 1849," *Ibid.*, (December 1961), pp. 233-249.

On the British North American League see: Cephas A. Allin, "The British North American League, 1849," *Ontario Historical Society. Papers and Records*, vol. 13 (1915), pp. 74-115; C.D. Allin and G.M. Jones, *Annexation, Preferential Trade, and Reciprocity* (Toronto: 1911); Gerald A. Hallowell, "The Reaction of the Upper Canadian Tories to the Adversity of 1849: Annexation and the British American League," *Ontario History*, vol. 72 (1970), pp. 41-56.

On Ogle's fall from local influence, see the *Brockville Recorder* and William Jelly (ed.) *A Summary of the Proceedings of the Council of the District of Johnstown and the Council of the United Counties of Leeds and Grenville, 1842-1942* (Brockville: 1943).

Correspondence with John A. Macdonald is in the Ferguson Papers, PAC.

Eliza McCormick, as a transvestite, became the first female member of the Canadian Parliament. I am at present engaged in writing the story of her life.

The closing quotation from the *Brockville Recorder* is from 13 November 1851.

CHAPTER SIXTEEN

The Dun and Company reports are in the manuscript department, Baker Library, Harvard Business School.

For Toronto local politics and Gowan's place in them see: Toronto City Archives, City Council Minutes, and, for background, Jesse E. Middleton, *The Municipality of Toronto. A History* (Toronto: 1923); Barrie Drummond Dyster, "Toronto, 1840-1860; Making it a British Protestant Town," (PH.D. thesis, University of Toronto, 1970); and Paul Romney, " 'The Ten Thousand Pound Job': Political Corruption, Equitable Jurisdiction, and the Public Interest in Upper Canada 1852-1856," in David H. Flaherty (ed.) *Essays in the History of Canadian Law* (Toronto: 1983), vol. 2, pp. 143-199. The *Globe*, though partisan, is very helpful in its political reporting.

Information on Gowan's land sales comes from the registry office, Brockville.

Gowan's fight to regain control of the Order is documented in the printed reports found in the Orange Archives, Toronto, and in the Baldwin Room, Toronto Public Library. After the schism, each side published its own version of events, and in the Benjaminite publication was contained the material documenting Gowan's being in trouble with the Irish Order before he sailed for British North America. This material is corrorborated by several other sources mentioned above. For an interpretation of the Order's character in Toronto that is quite different from Hereward Senior's, see Gregory R. Kealey, *Toronto Workers Respond to Industrial Capitalism 1867-1892* (Toronto: 1980), pp. 98-123.

CHAPTER SEVENTEEN

Gowan's political life in the period is best documented by the clippings in the Ferguson papers, PAC, and the Mackenzie-Lindsey clipping collection in AO, Toronto. The correspondence with Macdonald is in the Ferguson papers.

The Nicolls trials are reported fully in the *Brockville Recorder* which had an unfriendly, but well-informed, continuing interest in Gowan.

The events in the Toronto police court are best understood against the background of Paul Craven's excellent article "Law and Ideology: The Toronto Police Court, 1850-1880," in Flaherty, vol. II, pp. 248-307. For his evaluation of the essential accuracy of the police columns of the two leading newspapers, the *Globe* and *The Leader*, see pp. 248-251. This is important, because the police court records are skeletal, and the nearest thing one has to a transcript is the police court columns in the newspapers, which, in the instances of important cases, were very detailed. I have reconstructed events as accurately as possible in the Gowan case from the newspaper reports and from Gowan's subsequent letters to the press.

On Gowan's declining years see: Toronto City Archives; Council Minutes for 1876; clippings and correspondence Ferguson papers, PAC; *One Man's Loyalty*, pp. 94-95; Martin Galvin, "The Jubilee Riots in Toronto, 1875," *Canadian Catholic Historical Association Report 1959*, pp. 93-107.